HOLT *Traditions*

Warriner's Handbook

Third Course

Grammar • Usage • Mechanics • Sentences

Instructional Framework by

John E. Warriner

HOLT, RINEHART AND WINSTON

A Harcourt Education Company

Orlando • **Austin** • New York • San Diego • London

CONTENTS IN BRIEF

Parts of Speech Overview
The Work That Words Do 1

The Parts of a Sentence
Subject, Predicate, Complement

The Phrase

Prepositional, Verbal, and Appositive Phrases **68**

The Clause

Independent and Subordinate Clauses **96**

Agreement

Using Verbs Correctly

6

Principal Parts, Tense, Voice, Mood **144**

DIAGNOSTIC PREVIEW 144
  Proofreading Sentences for Correct Verb Forms

THE PRINCIPAL PARTS OF VERBS. 145
  Regular Verbs 146
  Irregular Verbs 147

TENSE. 156
  Consistency of Tense 161

ACTIVE AND PASSIVE VOICE 163
  Using the Passive Voice 165

SIX TROUBLESOME VERBS 167
  Lie and *Lay* 167
  Sit and *Set*. 168
  Rise and *Raise* 169

MOOD 171

CHAPTER REVIEW. 173
  A. Identifying Correct Forms of Verbs
  B. Identifying Active and Passive Voice
  C. Proofreading a Paragraph for Correct Verb Forms
  D. Identifying the Correct Forms of Six Troublesome Verbs
  Writing Application: *Using Verbs in Instructions* 175

Using Pronouns Correctly

7

Nominative and Objective Uses; Clear Reference . . . **176**

DIAGNOSTIC PREVIEW 176
  A. Correcting Pronoun Forms
  B. Proofreading a Paragraph for Correct Pronoun Forms

CASE 177
  The Case Forms of Personal Pronouns. 178
  The Nominative Case 178
  The Objective Case 181
  The Possessive Case. 184

Using Modifiers Correctly
Comparison and Placement **198**

A Glossary of Usage
Common Usage Problems **222**

Capital Letters
The Rules for Capitalization **244**

Punctuation

The Granger Collection, New York.

Punctuation
Semicolons and Colons

Punctuation
Italics and Quotation Marks

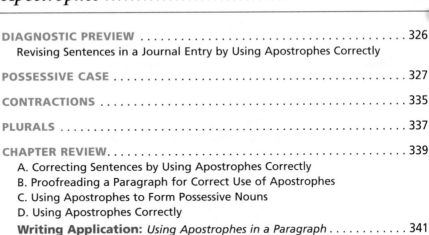

Punctuation

Punctuation

Spelling

Correcting Common Errors

CHAPTER

20 Sentence Diagramming 474

John Warriner:
In His Own Words

In the 1940s and '50s, John Warriner (1907–1987) published his first grammar and composition textbooks. Mr. Warriner's goal as a teacher and as a writer was to help students learn to use English effectively in order to be successful in school and in life. Throughout the years that followed, Mr. Warriner revised his original books and wrote others, creating the series on which this textbook is based. Included in Mr. Warriner's books were a number of short essays to his students. In these essays, Mr. Warriner explored the role of language in human life, the importance of studying English, and the value of mastering the conventions of standard English.

We could tell you what John Warriner thought about the study of English, but we'd rather let you read what he himself had to say.

Language Is Human

"Have you ever thought about how important language is? Can you imagine what living would be like without it?

"Of all creatures on earth, human beings alone have a fully developed language, which enables them to communicate their thoughts to others in words, and which they can record in writing for others to read. Other creatures, dogs, for example, have ways of communicating their feelings, but they are very simple ways and very simple feelings. Without words, they must resort to mere noises, like barking, and to physical actions, like tail wagging. The point is that one very important difference between human beings and other creatures is the way human beings can communicate with

Warriner's first grammar and composition textbooks, published in the 1940s and '50s.

one another by means of this remarkable thing called language. When you stop to think about it, you realize that language is involved to some extent in almost everything you do. "

(from *English Grammar and Composition: First Course*, 1986)

Warriner's English Grammar and Composition: Fourth Course, 1977

Why Study English?

" The reason English is a required subject in almost all schools is that nothing in your education is more important than learning how to express yourself well. You may know a vast amount about a subject, but if you are unable to communicate what you know, you are severely handicapped. No matter how valuable your ideas may be, they will not be very useful if you cannot express them clearly and convincingly. Language is the means by which people communicate. By learning how your language functions and by practicing language skills, you can acquire the competence necessary to express adequately what you know and what you think. "

(from *English Grammar and Composition: Fourth Course*, 1977)

Why Study Grammar?

" Grammar is a description of the way a language works. It explains many things. For example, grammar tells us the order in which sentence parts must be arranged. It explains the work done by the various kinds of words—the work done by a noun is different from the work done by a verb. It explains how words change their form according to the way they are used. Grammar is useful because it enables us to make statements about how to use our language. These statements we usually call rules.

"The grammar rule that the normal order of an English sentence is subject-verb-object may not seem very important to us, because English is our native tongue and we naturally use this order without thinking. But the rule would be very helpful to people who are learning English as a second language. However, the rule that subjects and verbs 'agree' (when the subject is plural, the verb is plural), and the rule that some pronouns (*I, he, she, we, they*) are used as subjects while others (*me, him, her, us,*

Warriner's English Grammar and Composition: Third Course, 1982

them) are used as objects—these are helpful rules even for native speakers of English.

"Such rules could not be understood—in fact, they could not be formed—without the vocabulary of grammar. Grammar, then, helps us to state how English is used and how we should use it. "

(from *English Grammar and Composition: Third Course,* 1982)

Why Is Punctuation Important?

"The sole purpose of punctuation is to make clear the meaning of what you write. When you speak, the actual sound of your voice, the rhythmic rise and fall of your inflections, your pauses and hesitations, your stops to take breath—all supply a kind of 'punctuation' that serves to group your words and to indicate to your listener precisely what you mean. Indeed, even the body takes part in this unwritten punctuation. A raised eyebrow may express interrogation more eloquently than any question mark, and a knuckle rapped on the table shows stronger feeling than an exclamation point.

"In written English, however, where there are none of these hints to meaning, simple courtesy requires the writer to make up for the lack by careful punctuation. "

(from *English Grammar and Composition: Fourth Course,* 1973)

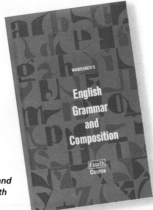

English Grammar and Composition: Fourth Course, 1973

John Warriner

Why Learn Standard English?

"Consider the following pair of sentences:

1. George don't know the answer.
2. George doesn't know the answer.

"Is one sentence clearer or more meaningful than the other? It's hard to see how. The speaker of sentence 1 and the speaker of sentence 2 both convey the same message about George and his lack of knowledge. If language only conveyed information about the people and events that a speaker is discussing, we would have to say that one sentence is just as good as the other. However, language often carries messages the speaker does not intend. The words he uses to tell us about events often tell us something about the speaker himself. The extra, unintended message conveyed by 'George don't know the answer' is that the speaker does not know or does not use one verb form that is universally preferred by educated users of English.

"Perhaps it is not fair to judge people by how they say things rather than by what they say, but to some extent everyone does it. It's hard to know what is in a person's head, but the language he uses is always open to inspection, and people draw conclusions from it. The people who give marks and recommendations, who hire employees or judge college applications, these and others who may be important in your life are speakers of educated English. You may not be able to impress them merely by speaking their language, but you are likely to impress them unfavorably if you don't. The language you use tells a lot about you. It is worth the trouble to make sure that it tells the story you want people to hear. "

(from *English Grammar and Composition: Fourth Course,* 1973)

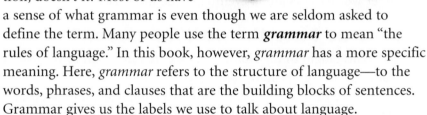

TO OUR STUDENTS

What is grammar?

That seems like a simple question, doesn't it? Most of us have a sense of what grammar is even though we are seldom asked to define the term. Many people use the term **grammar** to mean "the rules of language." In this book, however, *grammar* has a more specific meaning. Here, *grammar* refers to the structure of language—to the words, phrases, and clauses that are the building blocks of sentences. Grammar gives us the labels we use to talk about language.

What about the rules that govern how language is used in various social situations? In this book, these rules are called usage. Unlike grammar, **usage** determines what is considered standard ("isn't") or nonstandard ("ain't") and what is considered formal ("why") or informal ("how come"). Usage is a social convention, a behavior or rule customary among members of a group. As a result, what is considered acceptable usage can vary from group to group and from situation to situation.

To speak standard English requires a knowledge of grammar and of standard usage. To write standard English requires something more—a knowledge of mechanics. *Mechanics* refers to the rules for written, rather than spoken, language. Spelling, capitalization, and punctuation are concepts we don't even think about when we are speaking, but they are vital to effective written communication.

Why should I study grammar, usage, and mechanics?

Many people would say that you should study grammar to learn to root out errors in your speech and writing. Certainly, the *Holt Handbook* can help you learn to avoid making errors and to correct the errors you do make. More importantly, though, studying grammar, usage, and mechanics gives you the skills you need to take sentences and passages apart and to put them together, to learn which parts go together and which don't. Instead of writing sentences and passages that you hope sound good, you can craft your sentences to create just the meaning and style you want.

Knowing grammar, usage, and mechanics gives you the tools to understand and discuss your own language, to communicate clearly the things you want to communicate, and to develop your own communication style. Further, mastery of language skills can help you succeed in your other classes, in future classes, on standardized tests, and in the larger world—including, eventually, the workplace.

How do I use the *Holt Handbook*?

The skills taught in the *Holt Handbook* are important to your success in reading, writing, speaking, and listening.

Not only can you use this book as a complete grammar, usage, and mechanics textbook, but you can also use it as a reference guide when you work on any piece of writing. Whatever you are writing, you can use the *Holt Handbook* to answer your questions about grammar, usage, capitalization, punctuation, and spelling.

How is the *Holt Handbook* organized?

The *Holt Handbook* is divided into three main parts:

PART 1 The **Grammar, Usage, and Mechanics** chapters provide instruction on and practice using the building blocks of language— words, phrases, clauses, capitalization, punctuation, and spelling. Use these chapters to discover how to take sentences apart and analyze them. The last chapter, **Correcting Common Errors,** provides additional practice on key language skills as well as standardized test practice in grammar, usage, and mechanics.

PART 2 The **Sentences** chapters include Writing Complete Sentences, Writing Effective Sentences, and Sentence Diagramming. **Writing Complete Sentences** and **Writing Effective Sentences** provide instruction on and practice with writing correct, clear, and interesting sentences. **Sentence Diagramming** teaches you to analyze and diagram sentences so you can see how the parts of a sentence relate to each other.

PART 3 The **Resources** section includes **Manuscript Form,** a guide to presenting your ideas in the best form possible; **The History of English,** a concise history of the English language; **Test Smarts,** a handy guide to taking standardized tests in grammar, usage, and mechanics; and **Grammar at a Glance,** a glossary of grammatical terms.

How are the chapters organized?

Each chapter begins with a Diagnostic Preview, a short test that covers the whole chapter and alerts you to skills that need improvement, and ends with a Chapter Review, another short test that tells you how well you have mastered that chapter. In between, you'll see rules, which are basic statements of grammar, usage, and mechanics principles. The rules are illustrated with examples and followed by exercises and reviews that help you practice what you have learned.

What are some other features of this textbook?

- **Oral Practice**—spoken practice and reinforcement of rules and concepts
- **Writing Applications**—activities that let you apply grammar, usage, and mechanics concepts in your writing
- **Tips & Tricks**—easy-to-use hints about grammar, usage, and mechanics
- **Meeting the Challenge**—questions or short activities that ask you to approach a concept from a new angle
- **Style Tips**—information about formal and informal uses of language
- **Help**—pointers to help you understand either key rules and concepts or exercise directions

go.hrw.com

Holt Handbook on the Internet

As you move through the *Holt Handbook,* you will find the best online resources at **go.hrw.com.**

Grammar, Usage, and Mechanics

GO TO: go.hrw.com

Parts of Speech Overview

The Work That Words Do

┌HELP┐

Some items in
the Diagnostic Preview
have more than one itali-
cized word. These words
work together as a single
part of speech.

Diagnostic Preview

Identifying Parts of Speech

Write the part of speech (*noun, pronoun, adjective, verb, adverb, preposition, conjunction,* or *interjection*) of the italicized words in the paragraph below.

EXAMPLE   Pioneers [1] *learned* how to recognize danger.

1. *verb*

The [1] *first* pioneers on the Great Plains [2] *encountered* many kinds [3] *of* dangerous animals. Grizzly bears and [4] *huge* herds of bison were menaces to [5] *early* settlers. One of the [6] *most* ferocious beasts of the plains [7] *was* a [8] *grizzly* protecting her cubs. However, [9] *neither* the bison *nor* the grizzly was the most feared animal [10] *on* the frontier. Not even the deadly [11] *rattlesnake*—nor [12] *any* of the other prairie creatures—was dreaded as much as the skunk. You may think, [13] "*Oh,* that is [14] *ridiculous.*" However, it is true. Skunks were feared not because [15] *they* smelled bad [16] *but*, instead, because they [17] *so* often carried [18] *rabies.* Since there was no vaccine for rabies in [19] *those* days, the bite of a rabid skunk spelled certain [20] *doom* for the unlucky victim.

The Noun

1a. A *noun* is a word or word group that is used to name a person, a place, a thing, or an idea.

Persons	Sharon, Major Brown, hairstylist, joggers
Places	Iowa, districts, Mars, Antarctica, library
Things	okra, Great Pyramid, toothpicks, merry-go-round
Ideas	peace, truth, artistry, excellence, beauty

Common and Proper Nouns

A *proper noun* names a particular person, place, thing, or idea and is capitalized. A *common noun* names any one of a group of persons, places, things, or ideas and is generally not capitalized.

Common Nouns	Proper Nouns
scientist	Marie Curie, Charles Drew
woman	Coretta Scott King, Rita Moreno
city	Cairo, St. Louis, Paris
building	World Trade Center, Eiffel Tower
continent	North America, South America, Africa
day	Monday, Thursday, Labor Day

Reference Note

For more information on **capitalizing proper nouns,** see page 248.

Oral Practice **Classifying Nouns**

Read the following nouns aloud, and identify each one as a *common noun* or a *proper noun*. If the noun is proper, name a corresponding common noun.

EXAMPLE   **1.** Zora Neale Hurston

1. proper noun—writer

1. man
2. month
3. Vietnam
4. singer
5. Athena
6. city
7. gumbo

8. self-esteem
9. Virginia
10. ocean
11. Mount Hood
12. Australia
13. Detroit
14. street

15. Amelia Earhart
16. mercy
17. cousin
18. automobile
19. blues
20. Christopher Columbus

Concrete and Abstract Nouns

A *concrete noun* names a person, place, or thing that can be perceived by one or more of the senses (sight, hearing, taste, touch, and smell). An *abstract noun* names an idea, a feeling, a quality, or a characteristic.

Concrete Nouns	cloud, poison ivy, thunder, silk, yogurt, Sarah
Abstract Nouns	freedom, well-being, beauty, kindness, Buddhism

Exercise 1 Identifying and Classifying Nouns

Write all the nouns that you find in each sentence. Then, circle the proper nouns.

EXAMPLE   1. English grows daily with the addition of new words.
          1. (English,) addition, words

1. Some words come from other languages, such as Spanish and French.
2. Books, music, and movies often feature new words that are then added to everyday English.
3. Many useful and amusing words came into our language during World War II.
4. Now these words are familiar throughout the United States.
5. One of these words is *gremlin.*
6. Fliers were often troubled by mysterious mechanical problems.
7. Not knowing what caused these problems, they joked that gremlins—small, mischievous creatures—were in the aircraft.
8. According to Grandpa Leroy, these gremlins could be helpful as well as harmful.
9. Many fliers claimed that they had miraculously escaped danger only because the gremlins had come to their rescue.
10. Artists drew the imps as little men with beards and funny hats who played all over the planes.

Compound Nouns

A *compound noun* consists of two or more words used together as a single noun. The parts of a compound noun may be written as one word, as separate words, or as a hyphenated word.

One Word	firefighter, Iceland, newspaper
Separate Words	prime minister, Red River Dam, fire drill
Hyphenated Word	sister-in-law, Port-au-Prince, pull-up

NOTE If you are not sure how to write a compound noun, look in a dictionary. Some dictionaries may give more than one correct form for a word. For example, you may find the word *vice-president* written both with and without the hyphen. As a rule, use the form the dictionary lists first.

Exercise 2 **Identifying Compound Nouns**

Each of the sentences below contains at least one compound noun. Write the compound noun(s) in each sentence.

EXAMPLE **1.** My cousin John is a political scientist.

  1. political scientist

1. I use a word processor or a typewriter in class.
2. We went swimming in the Gulf of Mexico.
3. My sister and my brother-in-law live in Council Bluffs, Iowa.
4. My Old English sheepdog is still a puppy.
5. Some almanacs give exact times for sunrises and sunsets.
6. We used to play hide-and-seek in the old barn.
7. Sitting Bull was the war chief who masterminded the Sioux victory at the Battle of the Little Bighorn.
8. Meet me at the bowling alley near the post office.
9. The fountain pen is not as popular as the ballpoint.
10. Luís Valdez is a playwright, actor, and director.

Collective Nouns

A *collective noun* is a word that names a group.

People	audience, chorus, committee, crew
Animals	brood, flock, gaggle, herd
Things	assortment, batch, bundle, cluster

Reference Note

For more on **collective nouns,** see page 129.

Exercise 3 Identifying Nouns

Identify the twenty-five nouns in the sentences below.

EXAMPLE   1. To enter the wildlife park, we walked through the mouth of a huge fake alligator.

1. *park, mouth, alligator*

1. Businesses sometimes use gigantic objects to advertise their products.
2. A stand that sells fruit might look like an enormous orange, complete with doors and windows.
3. A restaurant in Austin, Texas, has a delivery van shaped like a dinosaur.
4. Huge dogs, windmills, and figures of Paul Bunyan are formed with cement or fiberglass to help sell chain saws, trucks, and souvenirs.
5. An old hotel in New Jersey was even built to look like an elephant!

The Pronoun

1b. A *pronoun* is a word that is used in place of one or more nouns or pronouns.

EXAMPLES   Stan bought a suit and an overcoat. **He** will wear **them** tomorrow. [The pronoun *He* stands for the noun *Stan*. The pronoun *them* stands for the nouns *suit* and *overcoat*.]

Several of the horses have gone into the stable because **they** are hungry. [The pronoun *Several* refers to the noun *horses*. The pronoun *they* stands for the pronoun *Several*.]

Reference Note

For more information about **antecedents,** see page 135.

The word that a pronoun stands for or refers to is called the ***antecedent*** of the pronoun. In the following examples, the arrows point from the pronouns to their antecedents.

EXAMPLES   The tour guide showed the **students** where **they** could see Mayan pottery.

Why did **Oscar** give **his** camera to the film school?

Darius scored a **field goal. It** was his first of the season.

Notice that a pronoun may appear in the same sentence as its antecedent or in a nearby sentence.

Personal Pronouns

A *personal pronoun* refers to the one speaking (first person), the one spoken to (second person), or the one spoken about (third person).

First Person	I, me, my, mine, we, us, our, ours
Second Person	you, your, yours
Third Person	he, him, his, she, her, hers, it, its, they, them, their, theirs

Reference Note

For information on **choosing pronouns that agree with their antecedents,** see page 135. For information on **clear pronoun reference,** see page 193.

EXAMPLES   **I** hope that **they** can find **your** apartment by following **our** directions.

She said that **we** could call **them** at home.

He asked **us** to help **him** clear away the fallen branches from **his** backyard.

Their dog obeyed **them** immediately and went to **its** bed.

NOTE   In this book, the words *my, your, his, her, its,* and *their* are called pronouns. Some authorities prefer to call these words adjectives. Follow your teacher's instructions on labeling these words.

Exercise 4   Identifying Antecedents

Give the antecedent for each italicized pronoun in the following paragraph.

EXAMPLE   In about A.D. 1150, a historian wrote down a strange tale English villagers had told [1] *him.*

1. *him*—historian

Since numerous people told the same story, the historian believed [1] *it.* Supposedly, a young boy and girl with bright green skin had been found wandering in the fields. [2] *They* spoke a foreign language and wore clothing made of an unknown material. At first, the two children would eat only green beans, but after [3] *they* learned to eat bread, [4] *their* skin gradually lost [5] *its* greenness. After learning English, the girl said [6] *she* and [7] *her* brother had come from a land called Saint Martin. The story sounds like science fiction, doesn't [8] *it* ? Perhaps the villagers invented [9] *it* to amuse [10] *their* friends and fool historians.

STYLE   TIP

To keep your readers from getting confused, place pronouns near their antecedents—generally within the same sentence or in the next sentence.

CONFUSING
Please hand me the scissors. I also need some strapping tape. They are in the top drawer on the left. [Does *They* refer to the scissors or to both the scissors and the strapping tape?]

CLEAR
Please hand me the **scissors. They** are in the top drawer on the left. I also need some strapping tape. [Only the scissors are in the top drawer on the left.]

TIPS & TRICKS

To find out if a pronoun is reflexive or intensive, leave it out of the sentence. If the meaning of the sentence stays the same without the pronoun, the pronoun is intensive.

EXAMPLES
Ron looked at himself in the mirror. [*Ron looked at in the mirror* doesn't mean the same thing. The pronoun is reflexive.]

Jenny painted the room herself. [*Jenny painted the room* means the same thing. The pronoun is intensive.]

Reflexive and Intensive Pronouns

A *reflexive pronoun* refers to the subject of a sentence and functions as a complement or as an object of a preposition. An *intensive pronoun* emphasizes its antecedent and has no grammatical function.

First Person	myself, ourselves
Second Person	yourself, yourselves
Third Person	himself, herself, itself, themselves

EXAMPLES   Elena treated **herself** to a snack. [reflexive]

Albert **himself** organized the fund-raiser. [intensive]

Demonstrative Pronouns

A *demonstrative pronoun* is used to point out a specific person, place, thing, or idea.

this	that	these	those

EXAMPLES   **That** is Soon-Hee's favorite restaurant in San Francisco.

The tacos I made taste better than **those.**

Interrogative Pronouns

An *interrogative pronoun* introduces a question.

who	whom	which	what	whose

EXAMPLES   **Which** of the songs is your favorite?

What is your parakeet's name?

Relative Pronouns

Reference Note
For more information on **relative pronouns,** see page 101. For information on **subordinate clauses,** see page 99.

A *relative pronoun* introduces a subordinate clause.

that	which	who	whom	whose

EXAMPLES   The ship **that** you saw is sailing to Greece.

Isabel is my friend **who** is training for the Boston marathon.

Indefinite Pronouns

An *indefinite pronoun* refers to one or more persons, places, ideas, or things that may or may not be specifically named.

all	each	most	one
another	either	much	other
any	everyone	neither	several
anybody	everything	nobody	some
anyone	few	none	somebody
anything	many	no one	something
both	more	nothing	such

EXAMPLES   Angelo has **everything** he will need to go rock climbing.

Is **anyone** at home?

Most of the birds had already flown south for the winter.

┌H E L P──

Many of the pronouns you have studied so far may also be used as adjectives.

EXAMPLES

this street
whose puppy
many acorns

Reference Note

For more about using **pronouns,** see Chapter 7.

GRAMMAR

Exercise 5   Identifying Pronouns

Identify all the pronouns in the sentences below.

EXAMPLE   **[1]** My friend Hideko invited me to a Japanese tea ceremony at her house.

1. *My, me, her*

[1] The tea ceremony at Hideko's house was more like some I have seen in movies than the traditional one shown in this picture. [2] "What happens during the tea ceremony, Hideko?" I asked as we entered the house. [3] According to Hideko, the purpose of the tea ceremony, a custom that dates back hundreds of years, is to create a peaceful mood. [4] In the ceremony, everyone sits quietly and watches the tea being made. [5] Before entering the room for the ceremony, I reminded myself to take off my shoes. [6] During the ceremony, each of us kneeled on a straw mat. [7] Hideko's mother was our tea hostess, the person who conducts the ceremony and prepares all of the tea. [8] She prepared the tea and served it in bowls that had been in the family for generations. [9] Then she served us sweet cakes called *kashi* (KAH-shee). [10] Afterward, Hideko herself gave me a box of tea leaves to take home with me.

The Adjective

1c. An *adjective* is a word that is used to modify a noun or a pronoun.

TIPS & **TRICKS**

The phrase *these five interesting books* can help you remember the questions an adjective can answer: Which books? These books. How many books? Five books. What kind of books? Interesting books.

To *modify* a word means to describe the word or to make its meaning more definite. An adjective modifies a noun or a pronoun by telling *what kind, which one,* or *how many.*

What Kind?	**gray** skies	**Irish** lace
	far-fetched tale	**lowest** price
Which One?	**either** way	**those** girls
	next day	**last** chance
How Many?	**five** fingers	**fewer** hours
	one river	**some** problems

Demonstrative Adjectives

Reference Note

For more information about **demonstrative pronouns,** see page 8.

This, that, these, and *those* can be used both as adjectives and as pronouns. When they modify nouns or pronouns, they are called **demonstrative adjectives.** When they take the place of nouns or pronouns, they are called **demonstrative pronouns.**

Demonstrative Adjectives	Did Jennifer draw **this** picture or **that** one?
	Let's take **these** sandwiches and **those** apples on our picnic.
Demonstrative Pronouns	**This** is mine and **that** is his.
	These are much more expensive than **those** are.

Pronoun or Adjective?

Some words may be used as either pronouns or adjectives. When used as pronouns, these words take the place of nouns or other pronouns. When used as adjectives, they modify nouns or pronouns.

Pronoun	Adjective
I like **that.**	I like **that** shirt.
Either will do.	**Either** car will do.
Which is yours?	**Which** one is yours?
Whose is it?	**Whose** hat is it?

NOTE In this book, demonstrative, interrogative, and indefinite terms, such as those in boldface in the preceding chart, are called pronouns when they function as pronouns and are called adjectives when they function as adjectives.

The words *my, your, his, her, its, our,* and *their* are called possessive pronouns throughout this book. Some authorities, however, prefer to call these words adjectives. Follow your teacher's instructions on labeling these words.

─HELP─

Possessive forms of nouns are also sometimes referred to as adjectives. Follow your teacher's instructions regarding these forms.

Noun or Adjective?

Many words that can stand alone as nouns can also be used as adjectives modifying nouns or pronouns.

Common Nouns	Adjectives
cheese	**cheese** sandwich
snow	**snow** sculpture
winter	**winter** sale
weather	**weather** report
steel	**steel** girder

Adjectives formed from proper nouns are called ***proper adjectives.**full

Proper Nouns	Proper Adjectives
Choctaw	**Choctaw** tradition
Texas	**Texas** coast
Picasso	**Picasso** painting
Dublin	**Dublin** streets
Roosevelt	**Roosevelt** administration

Reference Note

For information about **capitalizing proper adjectives,** see page 248. See page 4 for more on **compound nouns.**

GRAMMAR

NOTE Sometimes a proper adjective and a noun are used together so frequently that they become a compound noun: *Brazil nut, French bread, Christmas tree, Swiss cheese.*

Exercise 6 **Identifying Nouns and Adjectives**

Indicate whether each italicized word or word group in the paragraph below is used as a *noun* or an *adjective.*

EXAMPLE   Do you want to see my new **[1]** *baseball* card?

   1. *baseball—adjective*

I love anything that has to do with **[1]** *baseball.* I save the **[2]** *money* I make mowing the golf course, and then I go to the **[3]** *card* **[4]** *store.* The **[5]** *store* owner sold me a terrific **[6]** *Don Mattingly* **[7]** *card* today. It came in its own **[8]** *plastic* case. I'll display my new card with my other favorites in a special **[9]** *glass* **[10]** *case* on the wall in my room.

Articles

The most frequently used adjectives are *a, an,* and *the.* These words are usually called ***articles.***

A and *an* are called ***indefinite articles*** because they refer to any member of a general group. *A* is used before words beginning with a consonant sound. *An* is used before words beginning with a vowel sound.

EXAMPLES   **A** girl won.

   They are having **a** one-day sale. [Even though *o* is a vowel, the term *one-day* begins with a consonant sound.]

   An elephant escaped.

   This is **an** honor. [Even though *h* is a consonant, the word *honor* begins with a vowel sound. The *h* is not pronounced.]

The is called the ***definite article*** because it refers to someone or something in particular.

EXAMPLES   **The** girl won.

   The one-day sale is on Saturday.

   Where is **the** elephant?

   The honor goes to her.

Adjectives in Sentences

An adjective usually comes before the noun or pronoun it modifies.

EXAMPLES   Ms. Farrell tells **all** students that **good** workers will be given **special** privileges.

A **sweating, exhausted** runner crossed the line.

In some cases, adjectives follow the word they modify.

EXAMPLE   A dog, **old** and **overweight,** snored in the sun.

Other words may separate an adjective from the noun or pronoun it modifies.

EXAMPLES   Beverly was **worried.** She felt **nervous** about the play.

Cheered by the crowd, the band played an encore.

NOTE An adjective that is in the predicate and that modifies the subject of a clause or sentence is called a *predicate adjective*.

Reference Note

For more information about **predicate adjectives,** see page 201.

Exercise 7 Revising Sentences by Using Appropriate Adjectives

Add adjectives to make two entirely different sentences from each of the sentences below.

EXAMPLE   **1.** The waiter showed the woman to a table in the corner.

    1. The kindly waiter showed the shy woman to a pleasant table in the sunny corner.

    The haughty waiter showed the elegant woman to a private table in the shadowy corner.

1. The blossoms on the trees filled the air with a scent.
2. As the clouds gathered in the sky, the captain spoke to the crew.
3. At the end of the hall were stairs that led to a room.
4. The car has a stereo and an air conditioner.
5. The singers and comedians gave a performance for the audience.
6. The birds flew to the birdhouse near the barn.
7. Theresa's interest in science began when she attended the class.
8. The house in the valley was constructed by builders.
9. The curtains on the windows added to the look of the room.
10. As the waves washed onto the shore, the children ran away.

COMPUTER TIP

Using a software program's thesaurus can help you choose appropriate adjectives. To make sure that an adjective has exactly the connotation you intend, look up the word in a dictionary.

Review A **Identifying Nouns, Pronouns, and Adjectives**

Indicate whether each of the italicized words in the following paragraph is used as a *noun,* a *pronoun,* or an *adjective.*

EXAMPLE   **[1]** Most high school *students* read at least *one* play by William Shakespeare.

1. *students—noun; one—adjective*

[1] *This* article tells about Shakespeare's *life.* [2] *Shakespeare,* perhaps the most *famous* playwright of all time, was born in Stratford-on-Avon in 1564. [3] He was baptized in the *small* church at Stratford shortly after *his* birth. [4] In 1616, *he* was buried in the *same* church. [5] If you visit his grave, you can find an *inscription* placing a curse on *anyone* who moves his bones. [6] Out of *respect* for his wish or because of fear of his curse, *nobody* has disturbed the grave. [7] As a result, his remains have never been moved to Westminster Abbey, where many *other* famous *English* writers are buried. [8] Visitors to *Stratford* can also see the house in *which* Shakespeare was born. [9] At *one* time tourists could visit the large house that Shakespeare bought for *himself* and his family. [10] *This* was where they lived when he retired from the London *theater.*

The Verb

1d. A *verb* is a word that is used to express action or a state of being.

In this book verbs are classified in three ways—(1) as main or helping verbs, (2) as action or linking verbs, or (3) as transitive or intransitive verbs.

Main Verbs and Helping Verbs

A *verb phrase* consists of at least one *main verb* and one or more helping verbs. A *helping verb* (also called an *auxiliary verb*) helps the main verb express action or a state of being.

Besides all forms of the verb *be,* the following verbs can be used as helping verbs.

can	do	has	might	should
could	does	have	must	will
did	had	may	shall	would

Notice how helping verbs work together with main verbs to form complete verb phrases.

EXAMPLES   **is** leaving   **had** seemed   **might have** remained

Sometimes the parts of a verb phrase are interrupted by other parts of speech.

EXAMPLES   She **had** always **been thinking** of her future.

Has my sister **played** her new CD for you?

> NOTE   The word *not* is an adverb. It is never part of a verb phrase, even when it is joined to a verb as the contraction *–n't.*
>
> EXAMPLES   She **should** not **have borrowed** that necklace.
>
> She **should**n't **have borrowed** that necklace.

Reference Note

For information about **contractions,** see page 335.

Exercise 8   Identifying Main Verbs and Helping Verbs

Identify all the main verbs and helping verbs in each of the following sentences.

EXAMPLE   **1.** How well did your brother recover from his back injury?

1. *recover—main; did—helping*

1. Fortunately, he didn't need surgery.
2. His physical therapist has designed an exercise program for him.
3. Before exercise, he must spend at least five minutes warming up.
4. He will be using a back-extension machine.
5. Does he walk indoors on a treadmill or outdoors on a track?
6. At home, he will be exercising on a treadmill.
7. The doctor is always reminding my brother about proper techniques for lifting.
8. When lifting heavy objects, my brother must wear a back brace.
9. Should he try acupuncture or massage therapy?
10. Without physical therapy, he might not have healed as quickly.

Exercise 9   Identifying Verbs and Verb Phrases

Identify all the verbs and verb phrases in the sentences on the next page. Include all helping verbs, even if the parts of a verb phrase are separated by other words.

EXAMPLE   **1.** We will probably go to the movie if we can finish our assignment.

1. *will go, can finish*

1. Mr. Jensen always sweeps the floor first.
2. Then he washes the chalkboards.
3. He works slowly but steadily.
4. The weather forecaster had not predicted rain.
5. All morning the barometer was dropping rapidly.
6. The storm was slowly moving in.
7. Your dog will become fat if you feed it too much.
8. Dogs will usually eat everything you give them.
9. Generally, cats will stop when they have had enough.
10. After our team has had more practice, we will win.

Action Verbs and Linking Verbs

An **action verb** expresses either physical or mental action.

Physical Action	write	sit	arise
	describe	receive	go
Mental Action	remember	think	believe
	consider	understand	know

EXAMPLES   The audience **cheered** the lead actors.

The children **hoped** for sunshine.

Exercise 10 Writing Action Verbs

Write twenty action verbs, not including those previously listed. Include and underline at least five verbs that express mental action.

EXAMPLES   **1.** *soar*   **2.** *imagine*

A **linking verb** connects the subject to a word or word group that identifies or describes the subject. The most commonly used linking verbs are forms of the verb *be.*

be	shall be	should be
being	will be	would be
am	has been	can be
is	have been	could be

(continued)

(continued)

are	had been	should have been
was	shall have been	would have been
were	will have been	could have been

Here are some other frequently used linking verbs.

appear	grow	seem	stay
become	look	smell	taste
feel	remain	sound	turn

The noun, pronoun, or adjective that is connected to the subject by a linking verb completes the meaning of the verb and refers to the verb's subject.

EXAMPLES   The answer **is** "three." [The verb *is* links *answer* and "three."]

The answer **is** correct. [The verb *is* links *answer* and *correct.*]

The winners **are** they. [The verb links *winners* and *they.*]

The winners **are** happy. [The verb links *winners* and *happy.*]

Many linking verbs can be used as action verbs as well.

EXAMPLES   The wet dog **smelled** horrible. [The linking verb *smelled* links *dog* and *horrible.*]

The dog **smelled** the baked bread. [action verb]

The motor **sounded** harsh. [The linking verb *sounded* links *motor* and *harsh.*]

The engineer **sounded** the horn. [action verb]

The chef **tasted** the casserole. [action verb]

The casserole **tasted** strange. [The linking verb *tasted* links *casserole* and *strange.*]

Even *be* is not always a linking verb. Sometimes *be* expresses a state of being and is followed only by an adverb.

EXAMPLE   I **was** there. [*There* tells *where.* It does not identify or describe the subject *I.*]

To be a linking verb, the verb must be followed by a ***subject complement***—a noun or a pronoun that names the subject or an adjective that describes the subject.

Reference Note

For a discussion of **adverbs,** see page 21.

Reference Note

For more on **subject complements,** see page 57.

Identifying Linking Verbs and the Words They Link

Identify the linking verb in each of the sentences below. Then, give the words that are linked by the verb.

EXAMPLE   **1.** Dixie can be a very obedient dog.

       1. can be—Dixie, dog

1. He felt foolish when his car ran out of gas.
2. Suddenly, it turned very dark, and the wind began to blow fiercely.
3. We had waited so long for dinner that anything would have tasted wonderful.
4. The plot of that fantasy novel seems awfully childish to me now.
5. Kevin and I stayed best friends throughout middle school.
6. I am happy that you won the chess match.
7. If the coach had let me play, this game would have been my first one with the Tigers.
8. My father thinks that you should become a lawyer.
9. After practicing hard, Stef's band sounded great in the concert.
10. For a moment, Dr. Kostas thought the planet's rings appeared smaller.

Writing Appropriate Linking Verbs

Choose a linking verb for each blank. Try to use a different verb for each sentence.

EXAMPLE   **1.** The baby _____ sleepy after he was fed.

       1. The baby grew sleepy after he was fed.

1. That building _____ the new public library.
2. The car _____ funny.
3. The moose _____ huge.
4. I _____ very nervous about the driving test.
5. Her garden _____ dried and brown in the drought.
6. Let's hope the evening _____ cool.
7. We can eat the raspberries when they _____ red.
8. Burt _____ grouchy early in the morning.
9. The soup _____ too salty.
10. The puppy _____ healthy and playful.

Exercise 13 Writing Sentences with Action Verbs and Linking Verbs

Choose five nouns from the numbered items below. For each noun, write two sentences, using the noun as the subject of each sentence. Use an action verb in one sentence and a linking verb in the other. Indicate which sentence contains the action verb and which contains the linking verb.

EXAMPLE
1. fireworks

1. *The fireworks filled the night sky with bursts of color.—action verb*

   The fireworks grew more colorful toward the end of the program.—linking verb

1. pilot
2. locomotive
3. taco
4. skater
5. football
6. coins
7. foghorn
8. Mrs. Wu
9. movie
10. Lincoln

Transitive and Intransitive Verbs

A *transitive verb* is a verb that expresses an action directed toward a person, place, or thing. The action expressed by a transitive verb passes from the doer—the subject—to the receiver of the action. Words that receive the action of a transitive verb are called *objects.*

EXAMPLES
When **will** Neil **ring** the bell? [The action of the verb *will ring* is directed toward the object *bell.*]

Juanita **mailed** the package. [The action of the verb *mailed* is directed toward the object *package.*]

Tell the truth. [The action of the verb *Tell* is directed toward the object *truth.*]

An *intransitive verb* expresses action (or tells something about the subject) without the action passing to a receiver, or object.

EXAMPLES
Last Saturday we **stayed** inside. [The verb *stayed* does not pass the action to an object.]

After their long walk, the children **ate** quickly. [The verb *ate* does not pass the action to an object.]

When she told her story, my, how we **laughed**! [The verb *laughed* does not pass the action to an object.]

Reference Note

For more about **objects and their uses in sentences,** see page 59.

---HELP---

Because they do not have objects (words that tell who or what receives the action of the verb), linking verbs are considered intransitive.

A verb may be transitive in one sentence and intransitive in another.

EXAMPLES   Marcie **studied** her notes. [transitive]

Marcie **studied** very late. [intransitive]

The poet **wrote** a sonnet. [transitive]

The poet **wrote** carefully. [intransitive]

Exercise 14 **Using Transitive and Intransitive Verbs**

Choose a verb from the following list for each blank in the paragraph below. Then, identify each verb as *transitive* or *intransitive*.

drifted	landed	watched	experienced
floated	rode	met	admired
climbed	arrived	left	did
awaited	suggest	tried	drove

EXAMPLE   Can you **[1]** _____ an activity for this weekend?

1. *suggest—transitive*

Aunt Pam and I **[1]** _____ something really different last summer. We **[2]** _____ on inner tubes down a river in the wilderness. A guide **[3]** _____ our group with a truckful of giant tubes and picnic lunches and **[4]** _____ us about twenty miles upstream. Then everyone **[5]** _____ into a tube in the water. The guide **[6]** _____ in the truck for a picnic spot downstream, halfway back to the base. All morning, we **[7]** _____ lazily along in the sunshine and **[8]** _____ the wildlife along the shore. When we **[9]** _____ at the picnic spot, a delicious lunch **[10]** _____ us.

Exercise 15 **Revising Dialogue Using Verbs**

Using a variety of verbs can make dialogue more interesting. Rewrite the dialogue on the next page. In six of the ten items, replace *said* with one of the verbs from the following list. In the other four items, choose your own verbs.

wailed	bellowed	gloated	reported
responded	teased	soothed	confessed
exclaimed	replied	whined	accused
snapped	cried	muttered	called
howled	roared	pleaded	snapped

EXAMPLE   1. "Mom, I'm home!" said Tony, sprinting in the door.

1. "Mom, I'm home!" bellowed Tony, sprinting in the door.

2. "I've got great news!" he said.

2. "I've got great news!" he shouted.

1. "Guess what? I won the spelling bee," he said.
2. "Honey, that's wonderful," said his mother.
3. "I spelled 'expeditious' when no one else could, not even Stephanie Greenblatt," said Tony.
4. "I'm so proud of you," said his mother.
5. "Who cares?" said his sister Amy.
6. "You're just jealous," said Tony.
7. "I am not!" Amy said, running out of the kitchen.
8. "Don't let her bother you," said his mother. "You should enjoy your success."
9. "I am enjoying it," said Tony, "but I wish I could share my happiness with Amy."
10. "She'll come around," his mother said. "Meanwhile, sit down and tell me all about it."

The Adverb

1e. An *adverb* modifies a verb, an adjective, or another adverb.

An adverb tells *where, when, how,* or *to what extent* (*how long* or *how much*). Just as an adjective makes the meaning of a noun or a pronoun more definite, an adverb makes the meaning of a verb, an adjective, or another adverb more definite.

Adverbs Modifying Verbs

In the following examples, each boldface adverb modifies a verb.

Where?	When?
We lived **there**.	May we go **tomorrow**?
Please step **up**.	Water the plant **weekly**.
I have the ticket **here**.	We'll see you **later**.
Put that **down**.	He arrived **early**.

---HELP---

To identify a word as an adverb, ask yourself:

Does this word modify a verb, an adjective, or an adverb?

Does it tell *when, where, how,* or *to what extent*?

How?	To What Extent?
She **quickly** agreed.	Fill the tank **completely.**
The rain fell **softly.**	He **hardly** moved.
Drive **carefully.**	Did she hesitate **slightly**?
He sang **beautifully.**	They **partly** completed the form.

As you can see in the preceding examples, adverbs may come before or after the verbs they modify. Sometimes adverbs interrupt the parts of a verb phrase.

Adverbs may also introduce questions.

EXAMPLE   **Where** in the world did you ever find that pink-and-purple necktie? [The adverb *Where* introduces the question and modifies the verb phrase *did find.* The adverb *ever* interrupts the verb phrase and also modifies it.]

NOTE   Although many adverbs end in *–ly*, the *–ly* ending does not necessarily mean that a word is an adverb. Many adjectives also end in *–ly*: the *daily* newspaper, an *early* train, an *only* child, a *lonely* person. Also, some words, such as *now, then, far, already, somewhat, not*, and *right*, are often used as adverbs, yet they do not end in *–ly*.

Exercise 16 Completing Sentences by Supplying Appropriate Adverbs

Complete each of the following sentences by supplying an appropriate adverb. The word or phrase in parentheses tells you what information the adverb should give about the action.

EXAMPLE   **1.** He moved his hand (*how*).

     1. gracefully

1. The soldiers must travel (*how*).
2. You will probably sleep well (*when*).
3. They whispered (*how*) to Mr. Baldwin.
4. Tonya took a deep breath and dove (*where*).
5. Did you study (*to what extent*)?
6. Handle the ducklings (*how*).
7. My uncle Hans is (*when*) in a bad mood.
8. Your taxi should be (*where*) soon.
9. I could (*to what extent*) taste the tangy pizza.
10. (*When*), you should paste the pictures on the poster.

Adverbs Modifying Adjectives

EXAMPLES   Beth did an **exceptionally** fine job. [The adverb *exceptionally* modifies the adjective *fine*, telling *to what extent*.]

Slightly cooler temperatures are forecast. [The adverb *slightly* modifies the adjective *cooler*, telling *to what extent*.]

Mr. Lomazzi is an **especially** talented chef. [The adverb *especially* modifies the adjective *talented*, telling *to what extent*.]

STYLE   **TIP**

The most frequently used adverbs are *too, so, really,* and *very*. In fact, these words are often over-worked. To make your speaking and writing more interesting, replace these general adverbs with more specific ones, such as *completely, especially,* and *quite.*

Exercise 17   Identifying Adverbs That Modify Adjectives

Identify the adverbs that modify adjectives in the sentences below. For each adverb, give the adjective it modifies.

EXAMPLE   1. The compass I bought was incredibly cheap.

1. *incredibly—cheap*

HELP

In Exercise 17, a sentence may contain more than one adverb modifying an adjective.

1. If you are ever really lost in the woods at night, knowing how to find the North Star may be extremely important.
2. Here is one method that is quite useful.
3. First, find the Big Dipper, which is surprisingly easy to spot.
4. It consists of seven rather bright stars in the northern sky that are arranged in the shape of a large dipper.
5. Do not confuse it with the Little Dipper, which is somewhat smaller.
6. After you have found the Big Dipper, you must be very careful to sight along the two stars that form the front of the dipper bowl.
7. They are two points on an almost straight line to the North Star.
8. This method for getting your bearings is completely reliable—except when the clouds are so dense that you cannot see the stars.
9. It would be especially wise to check the weather forecast before going on a hike.
10. Remember to take a compass, water, and a fully stocked first-aid kit.

Exercise 18 Revising with Adverb Modifiers

Make each of the phrases and sentences below more descriptive by adding one adverb that modifies each of the italicized adjectives. Use a different adverb in each item.

EXAMPLE   1. a *confusing* sentence

1. an especially confusing sentence

1. a *sharp* turn
2. *playful* kittens
3. an *easy* question
4. a *swept* floor
5. Her little brother has a *bright* smile.
6. Terri felt *satisfied* that she had done her best.
7. The old mansion was *silent*.
8. Robert became *sick* and had to leave early.
9. Had Clara been *safe*?
10. Most of the questions on the test were *difficult*.

Adverbs Modifying Other Adverbs

EXAMPLES   Calvin was **almost** never there. [The adverb *almost* modifies the adverb *never,* telling *to what extent.*]

We'll meet **shortly** afterward. [The adverb *shortly* modifies the adverb *afterward,* telling *to what extent.*]

She slept **too** late. [The adverb *too* modifies the adverb *late,* telling *to what extent.*]

Reference Note

For information about **compound sentences,** see page 109. For information on **adverb clauses,** see page 104.

NOTE   One kind of adverb—the ***conjunctive adverb***—is an adverb used as a connecting word between independent clauses in a compound sentence.

EXAMPLE   We tried to be at the stadium by 6:30 P.M.; **however,** we arrived at the wrong time.

Another kind of adverb—the ***relative adverb***—is often used to introduce adjective clauses.

EXAMPLES   Uncle Lionel told us about the time **when** he drove across the country.

In 1815, Napoleon was sent into exile on the island of St. Helena, **where** he died in 1821.

Noun or Adverb?

Some words that can be used as nouns can also be used as adverbs.

EXAMPLES   **Tomorrow** never seems to arrive. [*noun*]

We will leave **tomorrow**. [*Tomorrow* is used as an adverb telling *when*.]

Think of this place as your **home**. [*noun*]

He was eager to come **home**. [*Home* is used as an adverb telling *where*.]

    When identifying parts of speech, remember: A word used to modify a verb, an adjective, or another adverb is called an adverb.

"I miss the good old days when all we had to worry about was nouns and verbs."

© 1984 by Sidney Harris–Punch.

Exercise 19 **Identifying Adverbs That Modify Other Adverbs**

Identify all the adverbs that modify other adverbs in the sentences below. After each adverb, give the adverb it modifies.

EXAMPLE   **1.** Brian is so terribly shy that he blushes when people speak to him.

    1. so, terribly

1. The cat leapt to the windowsill quite agilely.
2. The books were stacked rather haphazardly.
3. Corrie knew she'd have to get up incredibly early to watch the eclipse tomorrow.
4. The tornado almost completely destroyed the barn.
5. The famous diamond was more heavily guarded than any other exhibit at the museum.
6. My brother is nearly always finished with his paper route before I am finished with mine.
7. She registered too late to be eligible for the classes she wanted.
8. In the final four minutes of the game, Isiah Thomas shot extremely accurately.
9. Usually it seems that each month goes more rapidly than the month before.
10. They walked onto the stage most calmly, as if they felt completely relaxed.

Exercise 20 Identifying Adverbs and the Words They Modify

Identify the adverb or adverbs in each of the following sentences. Then, give the word or expression that each adverb modifies. If a sentence does not contain an adverb, write *none*.

EXAMPLE   1. Have you ever thought about writing a movie script?

           1. *ever—have thought*

1. Successful movie scripts, or screenplays, are written according to a very rigid formula.
2. The main character and the action of the story must grab an audience's interest quickly.
3. Almost exactly twenty-five minutes into the movie comes a "plot point."
4. A plot point is a surprising event that swings the story around in another direction.
5. Most of the action and conflict occurs in the next hour of the movie.
6. Then comes another plot point, about eighty-five minutes into the movie.
7. Finally, the audience learns what happens to the characters.
8. The last time I went to a movie I really liked, I checked my watch.
9. It was quite interesting to find that the movie's timing matched this formula.
10. Try this test yourself sometime.

Exercise 21 Revising Sentences by Using Appropriate Adverbs

Revise each of the sentences below by adding at least one appropriate adverb. Try not to use the adverbs *too, so, really,* and *very.*

EXAMPLE   1. Dana, bring me the fire extinguisher!

           1. *Dana, bring me the fire extinguisher now!*

1. Angelo promised me that he would try to meet the train.
2. My coat was torn during the long hike, so Barbara lent me her plastic poncho.
3. Engineering degrees are popular with students because job opportunities in engineering are good.
4. The Wallaces are settled into a new house, which they built by themselves.

5. When the baseball season begins, I will be attending games every day.
6. Ronald dribbled to his left and threw the ball into a crowd of defenders.
7. Visits to national monuments and parks remind us that our country has an exciting history.
8. We returned the book to Marcella, but she had planned her report without it.
9. Georgia O'Keeffe displayed her paintings and received the admiration of a large audience.
10. The recipe calls for two eggs, but I did not have time to buy any at the store.

Review B **Identifying Nouns, Pronouns, Adjectives, Verbs, and Adverbs**

Indicate whether the italicized words in the paragraph below are used as *nouns, pronouns, adjectives, verbs,* or *adverbs.*

EXAMPLE   **[1]** *You* may know that Brazil is the *largest* country in South America.

1. *You—pronoun; largest—adjective*

[1] My *best* friend's mother just *came* back from visiting her family in Brazil. [2] *She* showed us *some* pictures she took in Brasília, the capital, and told us about it. [3] It was amazing to learn that *this* area had been *jungle* until construction began in the 1950s. [4] At first, few people lived in Brasília because it was so *isolated.* [5] However, over the *years* hundreds of thousands of people *have* moved *there.* [6] Several other Brazilian cities *also* lie within one hundred *miles* of Brasília. [7] *A* number of *good* highways *connect* Brasília with other major cities. [8] Residents enjoy the wide streets and open spaces *that* are *shown* in this picture. [9] *One* of Brasília's *most* striking features is its bold architecture. [10] Aren't the government buildings at the *Plaza* of the Three Powers *fantastic*?

The Preposition

1f. A *preposition* is a word that shows the relationship of a noun or a pronoun to another word.

By changing the prepositions in the following examples, you can change the relationship of *Saint Bernard* to *bed* and *Everything* to *beach*.

The Saint Bernard slept **near** my bed.	Everything **about** the beach was wonderful.
The Saint Bernard slept **under** my bed.	Everything **except** the beach was wonderful.
The Saint Bernard slept **on** my bed.	Everything **from** the beach was wonderful.
The Saint Bernard slept **beside** by bed.	Everything **on** the beach was wonderful.

The noun or pronoun that a preposition relates another word to is called the *object of the preposition*. In the examples above, *bed* and *beach* are the objects of the prepositions.

MEETING THE CHALLENGE

Prepositional phrases are generally used as modifiers. You can use prepositional phrases to add specific details to your sentences and so make the sentences more interesting. To see the difference that well-chosen prepositional phrases make, write a paragraph or poem describing a friend of yours—but without using any prepositional phrases. Then, write a second version of your paragraph or poem, this time using five or more prepositional phrases. Underline each prepositional phrase in the second version.

Commonly Used Prepositions

aboard	below	from	since
about	beneath	in	through
above	beside	inside	throughout
across	besides	into	till
after	between	like	to
against	beyond	near	toward
along	but (meaning	of	under
amid	except)	off	underneath
among	by	on	until
around	concerning	onto	up
as	down	out	upon
at	during	outside	with
before	except	over	within
behind	for	past	without

NOTE Many words in the preceding list can also be used as adverbs. To be sure that a word is used as a preposition, ask whether the word relates a noun or a pronoun to another word. Compare the following sentences:

Welcome **aboard.** [adverb]
Welcome **aboard** our boat. [preposition]

The runner fell **behind.** [adverb]
The paper fell **behind** the cabinet. [preposition]

Prepositions that consist of two or more words are called *compound prepositions.*

Compound Prepositions	
according to	in place of
as of	in spite of
aside from	instead of
because of	next to
by means of	on account of
in addition to	out of
in front of	prior to

NOTE As a rule, the object of the preposition follows the preposition.

EXAMPLE Add a teaspoon of freshly ground **cinnamon.**
[*Cinnamon* is the object of the preposition *of.*]

Sometimes, however, the object of the preposition comes before the preposition.

EXAMPLE He is a singer **whom** I've never heard of before.
[*Whom* is the object of the preposition *of.*]

Objects of prepositions may be compound.

EXAMPLES Kyoko called to **Nancy** and **me.**
[Both *Nancy* and *me* are objects of the preposition *to.*]

The marbles were scattered under the **table** and **chairs.**
[Both *table* and *chairs* are objects of the preposition *under.*]

The preposition, its object, and any modifiers of the object together form a **prepositional phrase.** Notice in the following examples that modifiers of the object of the preposition can come before or after the object.

Reference Note
For more information about **prepositional phrases,** see page 70.

EXAMPLES   Joe went **to the nearest store.** [The noun *store* is the object of the preposition *to.* The adjectives *the* and *nearest* modify the noun *store.*]

Is she one **of those trailing behind**? [The pronoun *those* is the object of the preposition *of. Those* is modified by the participial phrase *trailing behind.*]

The kitten hopped **into the big paper bag that Anita brought.** [The noun *bag* is the object of the preposition *into. Bag* is modified by the adjectives *the, big,* and *paper* and by the subordinate clause *that Anita brought.*]

Reference Note
For more information about **infinitives,** see page 85.

NOTE   Be careful not to confuse a prepositional phrase that begins with *to* (*to town, to her club*) with an infinitive that begins with *to* (*to run, to be seen*). Remember: A prepositional phrase always has a noun or a pronoun as an object.

Exercise 22   **Identifying Prepositions and Their Objects**

Identify each preposition and its object in the following sentences.

EXAMPLE   1. I've been studying Spanish in school for three years.
       1. *in—school; for—years*

┌HELP─
Sentences in Exercise 22 may have a compound object of a preposition.

1. Last week, my Spanish class went on a field trip to Monterrey, 140 miles southwest of Laredo, where we live.
2. Señora Ayala, our teacher, wanted us to practice speaking and reading Spanish outside the classroom.
3. Everyone was supposed to speak only Spanish during the trip.
4. We first went to the *Museo de la Historia Mexicana* and saw colorful displays of art and crafts and many other cultural exhibits.
5. J. D., Leo, Yolanda, and I looked around the museum and read the information about each exhibit.
6. Besides the museum, we visited the *Barrio Antiguo,* a beautiful district that dates from the seventeenth century.
7. Later, we decided to go to a restaurant near the *Gran Plaza,* the big square.
8. As Señora Ayala walked among our tables, she listened to us order our tacos, enchiladas, and frijoles in Spanish.

9. We walked around the *Gran Plaza* and then went into the cathedral, which was completed in the eighteenth century.

10. As we got ready to leave, we chatted in Spanish about all of the interesting things we had seen.

Exercise 23 Using Appropriate Prepositions

Use appropriate prepositions to fill the blanks in the following sentences.

EXAMPLE   1. Tasty, fresh lobster is a treat, _____ many diners.
            1. *Tasty, fresh lobster is a treat, according to many diners.*

1. Lobsters are large, green or gray, bottom-dwelling shellfish that live _____ the sea.
2. The people who fish _____ these creatures are hardy and very determined folk.
3. Using small, specially built boats and a number _____ cratelike traps made _____ wood, they go to work.
4. Lobster fishing _____ the United States has been practiced only _____ the last century; before that time people thought lobster was not good to eat.
5. For centuries, farmers used the plentiful lobsters as fertilizer _____ their gardens.
6. To catch lobsters, the fishers first lower traps _____ chunks _____ bait _____ the sea.
7. Then the fishers mark the location _____ colorful floats that identify the owners.
8. If the fishers are lucky, the lobster enters the trap _____ the part called the *kitchen,* tries to escape _____ another opening called the *shark's mouth,* and then is trapped _____ the section called the *parlor.*
9. Fishers call a lobster _____ only one claw a *cull;* one _____ any claws is called a *pistol* or a *buffalo.*
10. By law, undersized lobsters must be returned _____ the sea.

The Conjunction

1g. A *conjunction* is a word that joins words or word groups.

A *coordinating conjunction* joins words or word groups that are used in the same way.

TIPS & TRICKS

You can remember the
coordinating conjunctions
as FANBOYS:

For
And
Nor
But
Or
Yet
So

Coordinating Conjunctions

and	but	or	nor
for	yet	so	

EXAMPLES   streets **and** sidewalks [two nouns]

on land **or** at sea [two prepositional phrases]

Judy wrote down the number, **but** she lost it.
[two independent clauses]

Correlative conjunctions are pairs of conjunctions that join
words or word groups that are used in the same way.

Correlative Conjunctions

both . . . and	not only . . . but also
either . . . or	neither . . . nor
whether . . . or	

Reference Note

A third kind of conjunc-
tion—the **subordinating
conjunction**—is discussed
on page 105.

EXAMPLES   **Both** Jim Thorpe **and** Roberto Clemente were outstanding
athletes. [two proper nouns]

We want to go **not only** to Ontario **but also** to Quebec.
[two prepositional phrases]

Either we will buy it now, **or** we will wait for the next sale.
[two independent clauses]

Neither Mark Twain **nor** James Joyce won the Nobel Prize
in literature. [two proper nouns]

We should decide **whether** to stay **or** to go.
[two infinitives]

HELP

In the first
example for Exercise 24,
and is a coordinating conjunction, and *both . . . and*
is a correlative conjunction.
In the second example,
Neither . . . nor is a correlative conjunction.

Exercise 24   Identifying and Classifying Conjunctions

Identify all the coordinating and correlative conjunctions in the sentences
below. Be prepared to tell which ones are *coordinating conjunctions* and
which ones are *correlative conjunctions*.

EXAMPLES   **1.** For my family and me, moving is both an exciting
and a dangerous experience.

1. and, both . . . and

2. Neither my father nor I have a sense of our limitations.

2. Neither . . . nor

1. When we bought our new house, my mother wanted to hire movers, but my father and I said we could do the moving more efficiently by ourselves.
2. We said that doing the job ourselves would be not only much faster and easier but also far less expensive than having movers do it for us.
3. Neither my mom nor my brother was enthusiastic, but at last Dad and I convinced them.
4. Luckily, Uncle Waldo and my cousin Fred volunteered to help, for they thought it was a great idea.
5. Both Uncle Waldo and Fred lift weights, and they love to show off their muscles.
6. The rental truck we had reserved wasn't large enough, so we had to make several trips.
7. At the new house, we could get the sofa through neither the back door nor the front door, and Uncle Waldo strained his back trying to loosen the sofa from the door frame.
8. On the second load, either Fred or my father lost his grip, and the refrigerator fell on Dad's foot.
9. By the end of the day, all of us were tired and sore, but we had moved everything ourselves.
10. Whether we saved money or not after paying both Uncle Waldo's and Dad's medical bills and having the doorway widened is something we still joke about in our family.

The Interjection

1h. An *interjection* is a word that expresses emotion. An interjection has no grammatical relation to the rest of the sentence.

ah	hurrah	uh-oh	wow
aha	oh	well	yahoo
boy-oh-boy	oops	whew	yikes
hey	ouch	whoa	yippee

Since an interjection is not grammatically related to other words in the sentence, it is set off from the rest of the sentence by an exclamation point or by a comma or commas.

STYLE TIP

Interjections are common in casual conversation. In writing, however, they are usually used only in informal notes and letters, in advertisements, and in dialogue. When you use an interjection, make sure the punctuation after it reflects the intensity of emotion you intend. Use an exclamation point to indicate strong emotion and a comma to indicate mild emotion.

GRAMMAR

EXAMPLES   **Hey!** Be careful of that wire!

There's a skunk somewhere**, ugh!**

Well, I guess that's that.

I like that outfit, but**, wow,** it's really expensive.

Oops! The stoop is slippery.

Our team won the playoff! **Yippee!**

Exercise 25 Using Interjections

In the following dialogue, Jason is telling his friend Michelle about a concert he attended. Use appropriate interjections to fill in the numbered blanks. Be sure you punctuate each interjection that you use.

EXAMPLES   **[1]** "_____ You mean you actually got to go?" Michelle gasped.

1. *"Wow! You mean you actually got to go?" Michelle gasped.*

[2] "_____ I wish I could have gone!"

2. *"Boy-oh-boy! I wish I could have gone!"*

[1] "_____ how was the concert?" asked Michelle. "Tell me all about what happened."

Jason shook his head. "The opening act was terrible. [2] _____ It seemed as if they played forever!"

"How was the rest of the show, though? [3] _____ Give me some details, Jason!"

"The drummer was fantastic. [4] _____ He acted like a wild man. He was all over the drums! But the best part was Stevie's twenty-minute guitar solo. [5] _____ he really let loose. The crowd went crazy!"

Determining Parts of Speech

1i. **The way a word is used in a sentence determines what part of speech the word is.**

The same word may be used as different parts of speech. To figure out what part of speech *well* is in each of the sentences on the next page, read the entire sentence. What you are doing is studying the word's *context*—the way the word is used in the sentence.

EXAMPLES At the bottom of the old **well** were more than five thousand pennies. [noun]

Whenever the reunion was mentioned, tears of joy would **well** in her eyes. [verb]

Well, you may be right. [interjection]

Do you really speak four languages **well**? [adverb]

Fortunately, the baby is quite **well** now. [adjective]

Exercise 26 **Identifying Words as Different Parts of Speech**

Read each of the sentences below. Then, identify the part of speech of the italicized word. Be ready to justify your answer by telling how the word is used in the sentence.

EXAMPLE **1.** Aunt Shirley got a *raise*.

       1. noun

1. Did Gander Pond *ice* over last year?
2. An *ice* storm struck.
3. *Many* of these items are on sale.
4. The light flashed *on* and we entered the garage.
5. We rode *on* the subway.
6. The radio is *on*.
7. They went to the *park*.
8. We can *park* the car here.
9. We waited, *oh*, about five minutes.
10. We are all here *but* Natalya.
11. I slipped, *but* I didn't fall, thank goodness.
12. *Off* the road they could see a light.
13. The shop was *off* the main street.
14. The deal was *off*.
15. "Can you climb *up* that tree?" asked Yolanda.
16. The sun was already *up* when they left for work.
17. Ernesto lives a few miles *up* the coast.
18. We had a long wait before the show started, but, *wow*, it was worth it!
19. *Most* cats dislike taking baths.
20. Did they go all the way *through* the town?

┌HELP┐

Each missing
word in Exercise 27 is a
different part of speech.

Exercise 27 Determining Parts of Speech

A soldier in the American Revolution brings his general this spy message he found in a hollow tree. Unfortunately, termites have eaten holes in the paper. For each hole, supply one word that makes sense, and give its part of speech.

EXAMPLE   Please _____ this message to General Baxter immediately.
            deliver—verb

> ! The Redcoats are chasing me,   I expect them
> to   me soon. They are camped   the river and
> they are well rested. They will attack your   at
> dawn's   light tomorrow. General,   must
> prepare your troops to leave   .
>   Yours in haste, John Cadrain

Review C Writing Sentences Using the Same Words as Different Parts of Speech

Write forty sentences, using each of the words in the list below as two different parts of speech. Underline the word, and give its part of speech in parentheses after each sentence.

┌HELP┐

Some words
may be used as more
than two parts of speech.
You need to give only
two uses for each word
in Review C.

EXAMPLE   **1.** up
            1. *We looked up. (adverb)*
                We ran up the stairs. (preposition)

1. light	**6.** ride	**11.** help	**16.** that
2. run	**7.** in	**12.** drive	**17.** right
3. over	**8.** love	**13.** plant	**18.** signal
4. line	**9.** below	**14.** well	**19.** home
5. cook	**10.** picture	**15.** for	**20.** one

Chapter Review

A. Identifying Parts of Speech

In each of the following sentences, identify the italicized word or word group as a *noun, pronoun, adjective, verb, adverb, conjunction, preposition,* or *interjection.*

1. Kofi Annan, who *became* secretary-general of the United Nations in 1997, is from Ghana.
2. *All* of the episodes of that show have been interesting.
3. I made *myself* a pimento cheese sandwich to take along.
4. This copy of the magazine is *hers.*
5. I wondered *whose* sculptures were on exhibit at the Dallas Museum of Art.
6. *That* is the third time Luisa has called me today.
7. "*Wow,* that was the fastest fly ball I've ever seen!" exclaimed Ernesto.
8. Rajiv *himself* was planning to show them around Kashmir.
9. Which of the liquids in the *smaller* beakers is clear?
10. Are those the bonsai trees *Mr. Yamamoto* told you about?
11. One of the oldest poems in the collection deals with the concept of *honor.*
12. The *cast* of the film includes many genuine descendants of Napoleon.
13. Erika and Mike *wrote* the screenplay together.
14. *Should* the alarm clock *have been set* to go off at 6:00 A.M.?
15. Those Italian clothes are well-made and *extremely* stylish.
16. *We* had been warned not to be late, yet by the time we arrived the show had already begun.
17. Warn Selena and him *about* the fire ants in the backyard before it's too late!
18. Marcel was coming down with a cold, *but* he felt obliged to keep his appointments.
19. Nancy enjoys reading about current affairs because it helps to broaden her general *knowledge.*
20. The gorilla admired *itself* in the mirror.

B. Identifying Parts of Speech

In each of the following sentences, identify the italicized word or word group as a *noun, pronoun, adjective, verb, adverb, conjunction, preposition,* or *interjection.*

21. Football's most important contest *is* the annual Super Bowl game.
22. Thousands attend the game at the stadium, *and* millions watch it on television.
23. Professional football began with no system for *fairly* choosing a championship team.
24. Later, the *National Football League* was formed.
25. The two NFL teams *with* the best records play a championship game.
26. In the late 1950s, the American Football League was formed, and *it* also held a championship game every year.
27. *Eventually,* the AFL and NFL championship teams played each other at the end of the season.
28. Ever since the *first* Super Bowl was played in Los Angeles in 1967, the competition has continued to improve.
29. Do *you* know any amazing records set by NFL players?
30. *Amazing!* Fran Tarkenton threw over three hundred touchdown passes in his professional football career.

C. Identifying Parts of Speech

Identify the part of speech of each italicized word or word group in the following paragraph.

For [**31**] *me,* no [**32**] *spot* is [**33**] *better* than the beach. On [**34**] *hot,* sunny days, when the sand [**35**] *burns* my feet, I am always [**36**] *careful* [**37**] *about* putting on [**38**] *sunscreen.* I like to run [**39**] *through* the foaming surf and later relax under a beach umbrella. Most of the time, I [**40**] *enjoy* [**41**] *both* being with friends *and* being by [**42**] *myself.* With only [**43**] *strangers* around me, I [**44**] *feel* free to think my [**45**] *own* thoughts. I wander [**46**] *slowly* along the waterline, looking at all the interesting things that the sea [**47**] *has* washed up. Once I accidentally stepped on a [**48**] *jellyfish* and couldn't help but yell [**49**] "*ouch!*" when it stung my foot. Since then, I've learned to be [**50**] *more* careful about where I step.

Writing Application
Writing a Descriptive Paragraph

Using Specific Adjectives   Your class visited a wildlife park, but one of your friends was sick and could not go. Write a paragraph telling your friend about the field trip. Use specific adjectives to help your friend picture what he or she missed.

Prewriting   Make a list of the animals and the scenes that will interest your friend. Beside each item on your list, write one or two specific adjectives.

Writing   You may want to look at pictures of wildlife in magazines or books to help you think of exact descriptions as you write your first draft. Use a thesaurus to find adjectives that will help your reader visualize the animals you are describing.

Revising   Have a friend or classmate read your paragraph to see if you have created clear images. Revise your paragraph by adding specific adjectives if any descriptions are unclear or too general.

Publishing   Check your paragraph for errors in spelling and punctuation. Be sure that you have capitalized any proper adjectives. You and your classmates may want to create a wildlife-park bulletin board or multimedia presentation.

Reference Note
For more about **proper adjectives,** see page 248.

The Parts of a Sentence

Subject, Predicate, Complement

Diagnostic Preview

A. Identifying the Parts of a Sentence

In the following paragraphs, identify each of the numbered italicized words, using these abbreviations:

s.	subject	**p.a.**	predicate adjective
v.	verb	**d.o.**	direct object
p.n.	predicate nominative	**i.o.**	indirect object

EXAMPLE   Are you a mystery [1] *fan*?
            1. p.n.

   Sir Arthur Conan Doyle certainly gave [1] *readers* a wonderful [2] *gift* when he [3] *created* the character of Sherlock Holmes. [4] *Holmes* is a [5] *master* of the science of deduction. He [6] *observes* seemingly insignificant [7] *clues*, applies logical reasoning, and reaches simple yet astounding conclusions. The Hound of the Baskervilles is an excellent [8] *example* of how Holmes solves a baffling [9] *mystery*. The [10] *residents* of a rural area are afraid of a supernatural dog that [11] *kills* people at night. Helpless against this beast, they seek the [12] *services* of Sherlock Holmes. Using logic, he solves the mystery and relieves the people's [13] *fear*. This story is [14] *one* of Conan Doyle's best because it is both [15] *eerie* and mystifying.

B. Identifying and Punctuating the Kinds of Sentences

Copy the last word of each of the following sentences. Then, punctuate each with the correct end mark. Classify each sentence as *imperative, declarative, interrogative,* or *exclamatory.*

EXAMPLE   1. Sherlock Holmes has many dedicated fans
            1. *fans. —declarative*

16. How clever Sherlock Holmes is
17. Sir Arthur Conan Doyle wrote four novels and fifty-six short stories about Holmes
18. Have you read any of these stories
19. I particularly like the stories in which Holmes confronts the evil Professor Moriarty
20. Read just one of these stories, and see why millions of mystery fans love Sherlock Holmes

The Sentence

In casual conversation, people often leave out parts of sentences. In writing, however, it is better to use complete sentences most of the time. They help to make meaning clear to the reader.

2a. A *sentence* is a word or word group that contains a subject and a verb and that expresses a complete thought.

A *sentence fragment* is a word or word group that is capitalized and punctuated as a sentence but that does not contain both a subject and a verb or does not express a complete thought.

FRAGMENT   Was waiting by the door. [no subject]
SENTENCE   The clerk was waiting by the door.

FRAGMENT   The room with the high ceiling. [no verb]
SENTENCE   The room with the high ceiling glowed in the sunset.

FRAGMENT   After you have finished the test. [not a complete thought]
SENTENCE   Exit quietly after you have finished the test.

Some sentences contain an understood subject (*you*).

EXAMPLES   [You] **Stop!**
             [You] **Pass the asparagus, please.**

Reference Note

For information on **how to correct sentence fragments,** see Chapter 18. For information on **punctuating sentences,** see page 265.

COMPUTER TIP

Many style-checking software programs can help you identify sentence fragments. If you have access to such a program, use it to help you evaluate your writing.

Reference Note

For more about **understood subjects,** see page 51.

Identifying Sentences and Revising Fragments

Decide whether each of the following word groups is a sentence or a sentence fragment. If the word group is a sentence, correct its capitalization and punctuation. If the word group is a sentence fragment, revise it to make a complete sentence. Be sure to use correct capitalization and punctuation.

EXAMPLES   1. here are your glasses
            1. *Here are your glasses.*

            2. before going out
            2. *Before going out, I always turn off the lights.*

1. on Monday or later this week
2. patiently waiting for the mail carrier
3. will you be there tomorrow
4. four people in a small car
5. just yesterday I discovered
6. two strikes and no one on base
7. it runs smoothly
8. leaning far over the railing
9. give me a hand
10. while waiting in line at the theater
11. on the way to the science fair
12. stand up
13. learning English
14. when is the marathon
15. it is time
16. to the left of the spiral staircase
17. romping along the shore this morning
18. it is theirs
19. you surprised me, Ellen
20. how you are

Subject and Predicate

Sentences consist of two basic parts: *subjects* and *predicates*.

2b. The *subject* tells whom or what the sentence is about, and the *predicate* says something about the subject.

In the following examples, the subjects are separated from the predicates by blue vertical lines. Notice that the subject and the predicate may be only one word each, or they may be more than one word.

> Coyotes | were howling in the distance.

> The telephone in the lobby | rang.

> The woman wearing the red blouse | is my aunt.

In these three examples, the words that appear to the left of the vertical line make up the *complete subject*. The words to the right of the vertical line make up the *complete predicate*.

The subject may appear anywhere in the sentence—at the beginning, in the middle, or at the end.

EXAMPLES   In the dim light, **the eager scientist** examined the cave.

Does **Brian's car** have a CD player?

On the table stood **a silver vase.**

┌─HELP─
The order and
relationship of the
parts of sentences is
known as *syntax.*

Exercise 2   Identifying the Complete Subject

Identify the complete subject of each of the following sentences.

EXAMPLE   **1.** The art of quilting has been popular in the United States for a long time.
   1. The art of quilting

1. Ever since colonial times, Americans have made quilts.
2. Traditional designs, with names like Honeycomb, Tumbling Blocks, and Double Diamond, have been handed down from generation to generation.
3. The designs on this page are quilt blocks from a modern quilt.
4. They certainly don't look like Great-grandmother's quilts!
5. However, quilting techniques have stayed basically the same for well over a hundred years.
6. Small scraps of bright cloth are still painstakingly stitched together to create each block.
7. As in many antique quilts, each quilt block shown here was designed and sewn by a different person.
8. Some of the designs are simple.
9. In others, colorful details bring circus scenes to life.
10. A dark background is sometimes chosen to set off the brilliant colors of a quilt.

Rewrite each of the following items, adding a complete predicate to make a complete sentence. Be sure to use correct capitalization and punctuation.

EXAMPLE   1. that famous painting

          1. *That famous painting sold for three million dollars.*

1. justice

2. some commercials

3. the store on the corner

4. the woman next door

5. one way to study

6. these guitars

7. the bicycle on the porch

8. the family reunion

9. a band

10. the best route

The Subject

2c. The main word or word group that tells whom or what the sentence is about is called the *simple subject.*

The *complete subject* consists of the simple subject and any words, phrases, or clauses that modify the simple subject.

Reference Note

A compound noun, such as *Gloria Estefan,* is considered one noun. For more about **compound nouns,** see page 4.

EXAMPLES   The supportive and enthusiastic crowd cheered for the marathon runners.

complete subject	The supportive and enthusiastic crowd
simple subject	crowd

Out of the beaker rose a foul-smelling foam.

complete subject	a foul-smelling foam
simple subject	foam

Did you make the grits, Travis?

complete subject	you
simple subject	you

NOTE   In this book, the term *subject* generally refers to the simple subject unless otherwise indicated.

Make each of the following fragments a sentence by adding a complete subject. Underline each simple subject.

EXAMPLE   1. Did _____ watch the Super Bowl?

          1. *Did your little <u>brother</u> watch the Super Bowl?*

1. _____ was baying at the moon.
2. _____ can make the pizza.
3. _____ is needed for this recipe.
4. Was _____ the person who won the match?
5. _____ rose and soared out over the sea.
6. _____ stood on the stage singing.
7. _____ were late for their classes.
8. Over in the next town is _____.
9. Buzzing around the room was _____.
10. In the middle of the yard grew _____.

The Predicate

2d. The *simple predicate,* or *verb,* is the main word or word group that tells something about the subject.

The *complete predicate* consists of a verb and all the words that describe the verb and complete its meaning.

EXAMPLES   The ambulance raced out of the hospital driveway and down the street.

complete predicate	raced out of the hospital driveway and down the street
simple predicate	raced

Diego may have borrowed my book.

complete predicate	may have borrowed my book
simple predicate	may have borrowed

Are you following Mr. Fayed's advice?

complete predicate	Are following Mr. Fayed's advice
simple predicate	Are following

Notice that the simple predicate may be a single verb or a *verb phrase* (a verb with one or more helping verbs).

Commonly Used Helping Verbs

am	did	has	might	was
are	do	have	must	were
can	does	is	shall	will
could	had	may	should	would

TIPS & TRICKS

When you are identifying the simple predicate in a sentence, be sure to include all parts of a verb phrase.

EXAMPLE
Should Marshal Ney **have used** the infantry at Waterloo? [The simple predicate is the verb phrase *Should have used.* The complete predicate is *Should have used the infantry at Waterloo.*]

NOTE In this book, the word *verb* refers to the simple predicate unless otherwise indicated.

Exercise 5 Identifying the Complete Predicate and Verb

For each of the following sentences, write the complete predicate. Then, underline the verb or verb phrase in each complete predicate.

EXAMPLE 1. Surfing and snow skiing are different in many ways.
1. <u>are</u> *different in many ways*

1. The warm-weather sport of surfing uses the force of incoming waves.
2. The wintertime activity of snow skiing relies on gravity.
3. Surfers can pursue their sport with only a surfboard, a flotation vest, a swimsuit, and a safety line.
4. A skier's equipment includes ski boots, skis with bindings, safety cables, ski poles, warm clothing, and goggles.
5. Under their own power, surfers paddle out to their starting places, far from shore.
6. Must a skier buy a ticket for a ski-lift ride to the top of the mountain?
7. Oddly enough, some important similarities exist between surfing and skiing.
8. Both depend on the cooperation of nature for pleasant weather and good waves or good snow.
9. Do both surfing and snow skiing require coordination and balance more than strength?
10. In fact, each of these sports would probably make an excellent cross-training activity during the other's off-season.

Exercise 6 Writing Complete Sentences

Make each of the following sentence fragments a complete sentence by adding a subject, a predicate, or both. Be sure to add correct capitalization and punctuation.

EXAMPLE 1. the barking dog
1. *We were kept awake by the barking dog.*

1. the trouble with my class schedule
2. the legs of the table
3. appeared deserted
4. my billionaire aunt from Detroit
5. thousands of screaming fans

6. my grandparents in Oaxaca
7. thought quickly
8. after the intermission
9. until sunset
10. the science fair

MEETING THE CHALLENGE

Write a passage of ten or more sentences about something that interests you. In five sentences, underline the complete subject and circle the simple subject. In the other sentences, underline the complete predicate and circle the simple predicate.

Review A **Distinguishing Between Sentence Fragments and Sentences; Identifying Subjects and Predicates**

Identify each word group as a sentence (*S*) or a sentence fragment (*F*). Then, for each sentence, write the simple subject, underlining it once, and the simple predicate (verb), underlining it twice.

EXAMPLE   1. The talented musicians played well together.

　　　　　1. S—<u>musicians</u>—<u>played</u>

1. Jazz music filled the room.
2. Supporting the other instruments, the piano carried the melody.
3. The saxophonist, with lazy, lingering notes.
4. Beside him, the bass player added depth to the band.
5. A female vocalist with a deep, rich voice.
6. Charmed the audience with her delivery.
7. The band's star performer was the drummer.
8. For most of the evening, she stayed in the background.
9. Until the last half-hour.
10. Then she dazzled everyone with her brilliant, high-speed technique.

Finding the Subject

To find the subject of a sentence, find the verb first. Then, ask "Who?" or "What?" before the verb.

EXAMPLES   Here you can swim year-round. [The verb is *can swim*. Who can swim? *You* can swim. *You* is the subject.]

There is Aunt Ivory's new truck. [What is there? *Truck* is. *Truck* is the subject.]

Into the pond jumped the frog. [What jumped? *Frog* jumped. *Frog* is the subject.]

Please close the window. [Who is to close the window? *You* are—that is, the person spoken to. *You* is the understood subject.]

Reference Note

For information on the **understood subject,** see page 51.

Exercise 7 **Identifying Subjects and Verbs**

Identify the verb and its subject in each of the following sentences. Be sure to include all parts of a verb phrase.

EXAMPLE
1. Long before the equal rights movement of the 1960s, U.S. women were excelling in their professions.

1. *were excelling—verb; women—subject*

1. Anne Bissell ran a carpet sweeper business in the late 1800s.
2. For a time, she served as corporation president.
3. Under her direction, the company sold millions of sweepers.
4. In the late nineteenth century, a journalist named Nellie Bly reported on social injustice.
5. On assignments, she would often wear disguises.
6. Ida Wells-Barnett became editor and part owner of the *Memphis Free Speech* in 1892.
7. By the early 1930s, she had been crusading for forty years against racial injustice and for suffrage.
8. At the end of her fourth term as general of the Salvation Army, Evangeline Booth retired in 1939.
9. Booth's efforts helped to make the Salvation Army financially stable.
10. She also improved many Salvation Army services.

Prepositional Phrases

2e. The subject of a verb is never in a prepositional phrase.

EXAMPLES
Most of the women voted. [Who voted? *Most* voted. *Women* is the object in the prepositional phrase *of the women.*]

One of the parakeets in the pet shop looks like ours. [What looks? *One* looks. *Parakeets* and *pet shop* are each part of a prepositional phrase.]

Are **two** of the books missing? [What are missing? *Two* are missing. *Books* is the object in the prepositional phrase *of the books.*]

Reference Note

For more information about **prepositional phrases,** see page 70.

A *prepositional phrase* includes a preposition, the object of the preposition, and any modifiers of that object.

EXAMPLES

next to Jorge	by the open door	on the floor
of a good book	at intermission	after class
in the photograph	for all of them	instead of this

Prepositional phrases can be especially misleading when the subject follows the verb.

EXAMPLE   Around the corner from our house is a **store.** [What is? *Store* is. Neither *corner* nor *house* can be the subject because each is part of a prepositional phrase.]

Exercise 8   **Identifying Verbs and Subjects**

Identify the verb and the subject in each of the following sentences.

EXAMPLE   1. Most of the students in our class have enjoyed discussing our town's folklore.

       1. *have enjoyed—verb; Most—subject*

1. Many regions of the United States have local legends.
2. One pine-forested area in New Jersey is supposedly inhabited by the Jersey Devil.
3. This fearsome monster reportedly chases campers and wayward travelers through the woods.
4. In contrast, Oregon is haunted by numerous legends of the less aggressive Bigfoot.
5. This humanlike creature supposedly hides in heavily forested areas.
6. Its shaggy coat of hair looks like a bear's fur.
7. According to legend, Bigfoot is gentle and shy by nature, avoiding contact with strangers.
8. Stories from the Lake Champlain area tell about a monster resembling a sea serpent in the depths of the lake.
9. Many sightings of this beast have been reported to authorities.
10. No one, however, has ever taken a convincing photograph of the monster.

Sentences That Ask Questions

Questions often begin with a verb, a helping verb, or a word such as *what, when, where, how,* or *why.* The subject of a question usually follows the verb or helping verb.

EXAMPLES   How is the **movie** different from the book?

             Where is the **CD** I gave you?

             Does **she** have a ride home?

In questions that begin with a helping verb, like the third example above, the subject comes between the helping verb and the main verb.

You can find the subject by turning the question into a statement and then finding the verb and asking "Who?" or "What?" before it.

EXAMPLES   Was the train late? becomes The train was late. [What was late? The *train* was.]

Has she answered the letter? becomes She has answered the letter. [Who has answered? *She* has.]

Sentences Beginning with *There* or *Here*

The word *there* or *here* is almost never the subject of a sentence. Both *there* and *here* may be used as adverbs telling *where*. To find the subject in a sentence beginning with *there* or *here*, ask "Who?" or "What?" before the verb and the adverb.

EXAMPLES   There are my cousins. [Who are there? *Cousins* are.]

Here is your backpack. [What is here? *Backpack* is.]

NOTE   Sometimes *there* starts a sentence but does not tell where. In this use, *there* is not an adverb but an expletive. An **expletive** is a word that fills out a sentence's structure but does not add to its meaning.

                          V   S
EXAMPLES   There is a drawbridge over the river. [*There* adds no information to the sentence, which could be rewritten as *A drawbridge is over the river*.]

                          V   S
There are insects in our garden. [The sentence could be rewritten as *Insects are in our garden*.]

To find the subject in such a sentence, omit *there* and ask "Who?" or "What?" before the verb.

EXAMPLE   There was a clerk at the counter. [Who was? A *clerk* was.]

Exercise 9 Identifying Subjects and Verbs

Identify the subjects and the verbs in the following sentences.

EXAMPLE   **1.** Will you help me study for my history test?

             1. you—subject; will help—verb

1. There are many questions on American history in my book.
2. Naturally, there are answers, too.
3. Under whose flag did Columbus sail?
4. Here is Plymouth Rock, Anita.
5. How much do you know about the Lost Colony?

6. What does *squatter's rights* mean?

7. In what area did most of the early Dutch colonists settle?

8. Was there disagreement among settlers in Massachusetts?

9. What kinds of schools did the colonists' children attend?

10. How did people travel in colonial America?

The Understood Subject

In a request or a command, the subject of a sentence is usually not stated. In such sentences, *you* is the **understood subject.**

REQUEST   **Please answer the phone.** [Who is to answer? *You* are—that is, the person spoken to.]

COMMAND   **Listen carefully to his question.** [Who is to listen? *You*—the person spoken to—are.]

Sometimes a request or a command includes a name.

EXAMPLES   **Amber, please send us your new address.**

             Line up, class.

Amber and *class* are not subjects in the sentences above. These words are called **nouns of direct address.** They identify the person spoken to or addressed. *You* is the understood subject of each sentence.

EXAMPLES   **Amber,** [you] **please send us your new address.**

             [You] **line up, class.**

Exercise 10   Writing Requests or Commands

Using the following five situations, write sentences that are requests or commands. In two of your sentences, use a noun of direct address.

EXAMPLES

	Setting	Person Speaking	Person Addressed
1.	castle	queen	wizard
2.	kitchen	parent	teenager

     1. Wizard, make this straw into gold.

     2. Please don't drink out of the carton.

Setting	Person Speaking	Person Addressed
1. desert oasis	Aladdin	genie
2. courtroom	judge	defense attorney
3. child's room	child	baby sitter
4. spaceship	alien invader	crew member
5. forest	Big Bad Wolf	Little Red Riding Hood

Compound Subjects

Reference Note

For more information about **conjunctions,** see page 31. For more about using **commas between words in a series,** see page 272.

2f. A *compound subject* consists of two or more subjects that are joined by a conjunction and that have the same verb.

The conjunctions most commonly used to connect the words of a compound subject are *and* and *or*.

EXAMPLE   **Antony** and **Mae** baked the bread. [Who baked the bread? Antony baked it. Mae baked it. *Antony* and *Mae* form the compound subject.]

When more than two words are included in the compound subject, the conjunction is generally used only between the last two words. Also, the words are separated by commas.

EXAMPLE   Antony, Mae, **and** Pamela baked the bread. [compound subject: *Antony, Mae, Pamela*]

Correlative conjunctions, such as *neither . . . nor* and *not only . . . but also*, may be used with compound subjects.

EXAMPLE   **Either** Antony **or** Mae baked the bread. [compound subject: *Antony, Mae*]

Exercise 11 Identifying Compound Subjects and Their Verbs

Identify the compound subjects and their verbs in the following sentences.

EXAMPLE   1. Roast turkey and cranberry sauce are often served at Thanksgiving.

1. *turkey, sauce—compound subject; are served—verb*

1. Gerbils and goldfish make good, low-maintenance pets.
2. April, May, and June provide the best opportunity for studying wildflowers in Texas and Oklahoma.
3. Kettles of soup and trays of sandwiches sat on the counter.
4. Both you and I should go downtown or to the movies.
5. Either *Macbeth* or *Othello* features witches in its plot.
6. In that drawer lay her scissors, ruler, and markers.
7. Star-nosed moles and eastern moles live in the United States.
8. There are many good jokes and riddles in that book.
9. Where will you and your family go on vacation this year?
10. There were eggs and milk in the refrigerator.

Compound Verbs

2g. A *compound verb* consists of two or more verbs that are joined by a conjunction and that have the same subject.

EXAMPLES Jim Thorpe **entered** and **won** several events in the 1912 Olympics.

     The committee **met, voted** on the issue, and **adjourned.**

     My sister **will buy** or **lease** a car.

Both the subject and the verb may be compound.

EXAMPLES The **students** and **teachers wrote** the play and **produced** it.

     Either **Jan** or **Beverly will write** the story and **send** it to the newspaper.

> NOTE There are other cases in which a sentence may contain more than one subject and verb.

EXAMPLES The **defeat** of the Germans at Verdun in 1916 **was** a victory for France, but the **battle cost** each side nearly half a million casualties. [This kind of sentence is called a *compound sentence.*]

     Because **crocodiles are** descended from dinosaurs, **they are** the nearest living relatives of birds. [This kind of sentence is called a *complex sentence.*]

     Before the **movie started, Siva offered** to buy popcorn; **Melissa said** that **she would save** his seat. [This kind of sentence is called a *compound-complex sentence.*]

| STYLE | TIP |

The helping verb may or may not be repeated before the second part of a compound verb if the helping verb is the same for both parts of the verb.

EXAMPLES
My sister **will buy** or **will lease** a car.

My sister **will buy** or **lease** a car.

Reference Note

For more about **compound, complex, and compound-complex sentences,** see page 109.

For more about **compound, complex, and compound-complex sentences,** see page 109.

GRAMMAR

Exercise 12 Identifying Subjects and Compound Verbs

Identify the compound verbs and the subjects in the following sentences. Be sure to include helping verbs. If a sentence contains an understood subject, write *(You).*

EXAMPLE **1.** Should I buy this pair of jeans now or wait for a sale?

     1. compound verb—should buy, wait; subject—I

1. Tony rewound the cassette and then pressed the playback button.
2. Toshiro sings, acts, and dances in the show.
3. At the fair, Dan ran faster than the other boys and won the prize of twenty-five dollars.

4. Will you walk home or wait for the four o'clock bus?

5. This kitchen appliance will slice, dice, and chop.

6. Velma will not only bring the salad but also bake bread for the party.

7. Please pick your socks up and put them either in the hamper or downstairs by the washing machine.

8. The marching band practiced hard and won the state competition.

9. Visit, rest, and relax.

10. The newborn calf rose to its feet with a wobble and stood.

Exercise 13 Identifying Subjects and Predicates

Write each of the following sentences, underlining the complete subject once and the complete predicate twice. Be sure to include all parts of compound subjects and compound verbs.

EXAMPLE 1. Gary Soto and Amy Tan are my favorite authors.

1. *Gary Soto and Amy Tan* <u>are my favorite authors.</u>

1. Soto's poetry and short stories often are about his life.

2. Will he read from his works and sign books here tonight?

3. Carlos, Ted, and I will find front-row seats.

4. Where is your copy of *Too Many Tamales*?

5. Here is Gary Soto's latest collection of poetry.

6. His realistic way of presenting life appeals to me.

7. This particular poem brings back childhood memories.

8. Something similar happened to me in the first grade.

9. There are Sandra Cisneros and Rudolfo Anaya, other successful Hispanic American authors.

10. Their stories reflect a rich cultural heritage.

Review B Finding Subjects and Verbs

Copy each of the sentences in the following paragraph. Then, complete steps A through D to find the subject and the verb in each sentence.

┌HELP──

Not all steps apply to every sentence in Review B.

A. Cross out all prepositional phrases to help you isolate the verb and the subject.

B. Cross out *Here* or *There* at the beginning of a sentence to eliminate these words as possible subjects.

C. Underline all verbs twice, including all helping verbs and all parts of any compound verbs.

D. Underline all subjects once, including all parts of any compound subjects. If a sentence contains an understood subject, write and underline *you*.

EXAMPLE   [1] Quicksand can be dangerous to a hiker.

1.   <u>Quicksand</u> <u>can be</u> dangerous ~~to a hiker~~.

[**1**] In quicksand, you must remain calm. [**2**] Violent movement, such as kicking your legs, will only worsen the situation. [**3**] There are several steps to escaping from quicksand. [**4**] First, discard your backpack or any other burden. [**5**] Next, gently fall onto your back and spread your arms. [**6**] In this position, you will be able to float. [**7**] Only then should you slowly bring your feet to the surface. [**8**] Perhaps a companion or someone else nearby can reach you with a pole or a rope. [**9**] Are you alone? [**10**] Then you should look for the shortest distance to solid ground and paddle slowly toward safety.

Complements

2h. A *complement* is a word or word group that completes the meaning of a verb.

Some groups of words need more than a subject and a verb to express a complete thought. Notice how the following sentences need the boldface words to complete their meaning. These boldface words are called *complements*.

EXAMPLES   It is a good **car** even though it is **old**.

Who gave **Mr. Garcia** the **present**?

A complement may be compound.

EXAMPLES   Aunt Edna looks **happy** and **relaxed** today.

My cats enjoy **eating** and **napping**.

A complement may be a noun, a pronoun, or an adjective.

                          S   V   C
EXAMPLES   Marcella might become a **chemist**.

                          S   V   C
The raccoon watched **us** gardening in the backyard.

                          S   V   C
The clerks at that store are **helpful**.

Reference Note

For information on **adverbs,** see page 21.

Reference Note

For information on **prepositional phrases,** see page 70.

Reference Note

For information on **independent and sub-ordinate clauses,** see Chapter 4.

An adverb is not a complement.

EXAMPLES   **Where did we go wrong?** [*Wrong* is used as an adverb, not a complement.]

               That answer is not **wrong.** [*Wrong,* an adjective, is a complement in this sentence.]

Sentence complements are never in prepositional phrases.

EXAMPLES   She watched the **cardinals.** [*Cardinals* is the complement.]

               She watched **all** of the cardinals. [*Cardinals* is part of the prepositional phrase *of the cardinals.*]

NOTE   Both independent and subordinate clauses contain subjects and verbs and may contain complements.

                  S   V   C   S   V   C
EXAMPLES   This **kitten is** the **one that climbed** the **curtains.**

                  S   V   C   S   V   C
                 Before **Eli rides** his **bicycle, he checks** his **tires.**

Exercise 14   Identifying Subjects, Verbs, and Complements

Identify the subject, verb, and complement in each of the following sentences.

EXAMPLE   1. Many modern slang expressions used to sound okay to my great-grandfather.

                1. *expressions—subject; sound—verb; okay—complement*

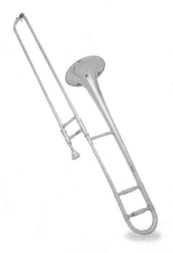

1. Like every generation, my great-grandfather's generation had its own slang.
2. He used it all the time, particularly in stories about his youth.
3. Great-grandpa played the trombone in a jazz band in the 1930s.
4. He and other musicians developed many slang expressions.
5. Their language became *jive talk.*
6. Many of Great-grandpa's expressions were sayings of the entertainer Cab Calloway.
7. Great-grandpa used phrases such as Calloway's *beat to my socks* (tired) and *out of this world* (perfect).
8. Great-grandpa's speech was full of words like *hepcat* (a lover of jazz music) and *hip* (wise) and *groovy* (wonderful).
9. Such language became popular all over the United States.
10. My great-grandfather, at least, used it.

Writing Sentence Complements

Write ten sentences by adding a complement to each of the following word groups. Be sure to punctuate each sentence correctly.

EXAMPLE   **1.** The puppy is

            1. The puppy is playful.

1. Jesse usually seems
2. Tomorrow the class will hear
3. That broiled fish looks
4. Last week our class visited
5. Do you have
6. Coretta finished the
7. The winners felt
8. Saturday the museum will sell
9. Fruits and vegetables filled the
10. How do you like

The Subject Complement

2i. A *subject complement* is a word or word group in the predicate that identifies or describes the subject.

EXAMPLES   Mark Twain's real name was **Samuel Clemens.**
           [*Samuel Clemens* identifies *name*.]

           The surface felt **sticky.** [*Sticky* describes *surface*.]

Subject complements may be compound.

EXAMPLES   The prizewinners are **Jennifer, Marcus,** and **Raul.**

           That winter seemed especially **mild** and **sunny.**

Subject complements sometimes precede the subject of a sentence or a clause.

EXAMPLES   I know what a **treat** this is for her. [*Treat* is a predicate nominative identifying *this*.]

           How **kind** he is! [*Kind* is a predicate adjective describing *he*.]

NOTE Subject complements always complete the meaning of linking verbs. A word that completes the meaning of an action verb is not a subject complement.

―HELP―

To find the subject complement in an interrogative sentence, rearrange the sentence to make a statement.

EXAMPLE
Is Darnell the treasurer?
Darnell is the **treasurer.**

    To find the subject complement in an imperative sentence, insert the understood subject *you.*

EXAMPLE
Be good.
(You) Be **good.**

Reference Note

For more about **action and linking verbs,** see page 16.

(1) A *predicate nominative* is a word or word group that is in the predicate and that identifies the subject or refers to it.

EXAMPLES   Has she become a **dentist**?

Friendship is **what I value most.**

The new teacher is **he**—the man in the blazer.

(2) A *predicate adjective* is an adjective that is in the predicate and that modifies the subject.

EXAMPLES   The soup is **hot.** [hot soup]

That soil seems **dry** and **crumbly.** [dry and crumbly soil]

How **expensive** are those shoes? [expensive shoes]

STYLE **TIP**

The use of the nominative-case pronoun, as in the last example of the predicate nominative, is uncommon in everyday speech. You will often hear *It is him,* rather than *It is he.* Remember that in formal English you should use the nominative-case pronoun.

Reference Note

For more about the **nominative case,** see page 178.

Exercise 16 **Identifying Subject Complements**

Each of the following sentences has at least one subject complement. For each sentence, give the complement or complements and tell whether each is a *predicate nominative* or a *predicate adjective.*

EXAMPLE   1. Gloria is my favorite character on the show.

    1. *character—predicate nominative*

1. Does the lemonade taste too sour?
2. The chirping of the birds became more and more shrill as the cat approached.
3. The window washers on the fifteenth floor appeared tiny.
4. Why does he always look so serious?
5. Our candidate for the city council was the winner in the primaries.
6. You should feel proud of yourself.
7. Will the hall monitors for Wednesday be Charlene and LaReina?
8. Soft and cool was the grass under the catalpa tree.
9. Be a friend to animals.
10. The crowd grew quiet when Governor Markham spoke.

Exercise 17 **Writing Subject Complements**

Make complete sentences of the following word groups by adding nouns, pronouns, or adjectives as subject complements. Use five compound complements. Identify each subject complement as a *predicate nominative* or a *predicate adjective.*

EXAMPLE   1. The sky turned

    1. *The sky turned cloudy and dark. —predicate adjectives*

1. The artist frequently was
2. Those are
3. Sara Brown became
4. It could be
5. The house looked

6. Are you
7. The weather remained
8. The test seemed
9. Manuel had always felt
10. That recording sounds

Objects

Objects are complements that do not refer to the subject. Objects follow transitive verbs—verbs that express an action directed toward a person, place, or thing.

EXAMPLE   **Lee Trevino sank the putt.** [The object *putt* does not explain or describe the subject *Lee Trevino*. *Sank* is a transitive verb, not an intransitive verb.]

NOTE   Transitive verbs may express mental action (for example, *believe, trust, imagine*) as well as physical action (for example, *give, hit, draw*).

EXAMPLE   **Now I remember your name.** [Remember *what*? Name.]

Reference Note

For more about **transitive and intransitive verbs,** see page 19.

2j. A *direct object* is a noun, pronoun, or word group that tells who or what receives the action of a verb or shows the result of the action.

A direct object answers the question "Whom?" or "What?" after a transitive verb.

        S   V   DO

EXAMPLES   **Germs cause illness.** [Germs cause *what*? Germs cause illness. *Illness* shows the result of the action of the verb.]

        S   V   DO

Peter said Gesundheit. [Peter said *what*? Peter said *Gesundheit*. *Gesundheit* receives the action of the verb.]

        S   V DO

Lucy visited me. [Lucy visited *whom*? Lucy visited me. *Me* receives the action of the verb.]

          DO   S V

What a scary movie we saw! [We saw *what*? We saw a movie. *Movie* receives the action of the verb.]

        S   V   DO

They were taking whatever was left. [They were taking *what*? They were taking whatever was left. *Whatever was left* receives the action of the verb.]

Direct objects are generally not found in prepositional phrases.

EXAMPLES   Josh was riding on his bicycle. [*Bicycle* is part of the prepositional phrase *on his bicycle.* The sentence has no direct object.]

Josh was riding his **bicycle.** [*Bicycle* is the direct object.]

Exercise 18 Identifying Direct Objects

Identify the direct object in each of the following sentences.

EXAMPLE   **1.** I enjoy this magazine very much.

1. *magazine*

1. This article gives interesting facts about libraries.
2. The city of Alexandria, in Egypt, had the most famous library of ancient times.
3. This library contained the largest collection of plays and works of philosophy in the ancient world.
4. The Roman emperor Augustus founded two public libraries.
5. Fire destroyed all of these libraries.
6. Readers could not borrow books from either the library in Alexandria or the Roman libraries.
7. During the Middle Ages, the monastery libraries introduced a circulating library.
8. By the sixth century, Benedictine monks were borrowing books from their libraries for daily reading.
9. In the United States, we now have thousands of libraries.
10. Readers borrow millions of books from them every year.

┌**HELP**──
Indirect objects generally precede direct objects.

2k. An *indirect object* is a noun, pronoun, or word group that often appears in sentences containing direct objects. An indirect object tells *to whom* or *to what* (or *for whom* or *for what*) the action of a transitive verb is done.

| | S | V | IO | DO |

EXAMPLES   Natalie knitted her **friend** a sweater. [Natalie knitted a sweater for whom? For her *friend*.]

S V IO DO
My little sister sang **me** a song. [My little sister sang a song to whom? To *me*.]

S   V   IO   DO
Uncle Gene sends **whoever requests it** a pamphlet on earthworms. [Uncle Gene sends a pamphlet to whom? To *whoever requests it*.]

Reference Note
┌ For information on **transitive verbs,** see page 19.

If the word *to* or *for* is used, the noun or pronoun following it is part of a prepositional phrase and not an indirect object.

OBJECTS OF PREPOSITIONS	My teacher showed the bird's nest to the **class.**
	I left some dessert for **you.**
INDIRECT OBJECTS	The teacher showed the **class** the bird's nest.
	I left **you** some dessert.

Both direct and indirect objects may be compound.

EXAMPLES   Lydia sold **cookies** and **lemonade.** [compound direct object]

Lydia sold **Geraldo, Freddy,** and **me** lemonade. [compound indirect object]

Reference Note

For information on **prepositional phrases and objects of prepositions,** see page 70.

NOTE Do not mistake an adverb in the predicate for a complement.

ADVERB	Go **inside,** Skippy. [*Inside* is an adverb telling *where.*]
COMPLEMENT	Tamisha sanded the **inside** of the wooden chest. [*Inside* is a noun used as a direct object.]

Reference Note

For information on **adverbs,** see page 21.

Oral Practice **Identifying Direct Objects and Indirect Objects**

Read the following sentences aloud, and identify the direct and indirect objects. Make sure that you give all parts of compound direct and indirect objects.

EXAMPLE   1. Sometimes I read my little brother stories from Greek mythology.

          1. *indirect object—brother; direct object—stories*

1. In one myth, the famous artist and inventor Daedalus built the king of Crete a mysterious building known as the Labyrinth.
2. The complicated passageways of this building give us the word *labyrinth* ("a maze or confusing structure").
3. After the completion of the Labyrinth, the king imprisoned Daedalus and his son, whose name was Icarus.
4. To escape, Daedalus made Icarus and himself wings out of feathers and beeswax.
5. He gave Icarus careful instructions not to fly too near the sun.
6. However, Icarus soon forgot his father's advice.
7. He flew too high, and when the sun melted the wax in the wings, he plunged to his death in the ocean.

┌HELP─

Not every sentence in the Oral Practice contains an indirect object.

8. Though saddened by the death of his son, Daedalus flew on and reached Sicily in safety.

9. Mythology tells us other stories of his fabulous inventions.

10. Even today, the name Daedalus suggests genius and inventiveness.

Review C Identifying Complements

Identify the complements in the following sentences. Then, tell whether each complement is a *predicate nominative*, a *predicate adjective*, a *direct object*, or an *indirect object*. If a sentence does not contain a complement, write *no complement*.

EXAMPLE   [1] My brother Bill gave Mom a birthday surprise.

1. *Mom—indirect object; surprise—direct object*

[1] My brother made Mom a birthday cake. [2] However, the project soon became a fiasco. [3] First, Bill cracked three eggs into a bowl. [4] Unfortunately, bits of the shells went in, too. [5] Then he added the flour and other dry ingredients. [6] The electric mixer whirled the batter right onto the ceiling. [7] The batter was so sticky that it stayed there and didn't fall off. [8] Bill did not clean the ceiling immediately, and the sticky substance hardened overnight. [9] Mom was not angry, but she did give Bill a suggestion for a gift. [10] "A clean kitchen would be a great birthday present."

Review D Identifying the Parts of a Sentence

Identify the italicized words in the following passage. Use these abbreviations.

s.	subject	*p.a.*	predicate adjective
v.	verb	*d.o.*	direct object
p.n.	predicate nominative	*i.o.*	indirect object

EXAMPLE   When you draw faces, do they look [1] *realistic*?

1. *p.a.*

Before this winter, I couldn't draw a human [1] *face* well. However, our [2] *neighbor*, Mr. Teng, is a portrait [3] *painter*, and he has been giving [4] *me* some instructive [5] *tips*. He says that the most important

┌HELP┐

Not every sentence in Review C contains a complement; some sentences contain more than one.

┌HELP┐

Remember that subordinate clauses contain subjects and verbs and may also contain complements.

[6] *thing* is the correct [7] *placement* of the eyes. Apparently, most [8] *people* draw the [9] *eyes* too high. In fact, [10] *they* should be placed halfway down the head. Many people also [11] *make* the ears too small. The [12] *top* of each ear [13] *should align* with the eyebrow, and the [14] *bottom* should align with the tip of the nose. Getting the width of the face right is also [15] *important.* Mr. Teng says, "Use one eye's [16] *width* as a unit of measure and make the head five eye-widths wide." There are many other [17] *guidelines,* but these tips from Mr. Teng are the most [18] *basic.* By following them, I can now draw a human [19] *face* that [20] *looks* realistic.

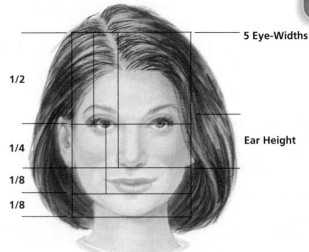

5 Eye-Widths

1/2

1/4

1/8

1/8

Ear Height

Classifying Sentences by Purpose

2I. A sentence may be classified, depending on its purpose, as *declarative, imperative, interrogative,* or *exclamatory.*

(1) A *declarative sentence* makes a statement and ends with a period.

EXAMPLES   Jody Williams won the Nobel Peace Prize in 1997.

That one-celled organism is an amoeba.

(2) An *imperative sentence* gives a command or makes a request. Most imperative sentences end with a period. A strong command ends with an exclamation point.

EXAMPLES   Please keep to the right. [request]

Take care of your little brother, Rick. [command]

Stop! [strong command]

Notice in these examples that a command or a request has the understood subject *you.*

Reference Note

For more information about **understood subjects,** see page 51.

(3) An *interrogative sentence* asks a question and ends with a question mark.

EXAMPLES   Can they finish in time**?**

How did she find Yoshi and Sarah**?**

(4) An *exclamatory sentence* shows excitement or expresses strong feeling and ends with an exclamation point.

EXAMPLES   What a good friend you are**!**

The battery is dead**!**

I can't believe this is happening**!**

NOTE In conversation, any sentence may be spoken so that it becomes exclamatory or interrogative. When you are writing dialogue, use periods, exclamation points, and question marks to show how you intend a sentence to be read.

EXAMPLES   They won**.** [declarative]

They won**!** [exclamatory]

They won**?** [interrogative]

Exercise 19 **Identifying the Four Kinds of Sentences**

Punctuate each of the following sentences with an appropriate end mark. Classify each sentence as *imperative, declarative, interrogative,* or *exclamatory.*

EXAMPLE   **1.** There are many delicious foods from India

    1. period—declarative

1. Do you like spicy food

2. Some Indian food is hot, and some isn't

3. *Sambar* is a soup made with lentils and vegetables

4. Save me some of those curried shrimp

5. What is that wonderful bread called

6. *Palek alu* is a spicy dish of potatoes

7. Watch out for the hot chilies

8. Isn't this yogurt drink called *lassi* good

9. Be sure to add the curry and other spices to the onions

10. How tasty this rice-and-banana pudding is

Chapter Review

A. Identifying Types of Sentences and Sentence Fragments

Identify each of the following word groups as a *declarative sentence,* an *interrogative sentence,* an *imperative sentence,* an *exclamatory sentence,* or a *sentence fragment.* Supply the appropriate end mark after the last word of each item that is *not* a sentence fragment.

1. Why don't we go to the wildlife park tomorrow
2. What a good time we'll have
3. The big cats especially at feeding time
4. Actually, I enjoy the entire park
5. Meet me at the front gate at ten o' clock
6. We'll first go see the elephants
7. Don't forget the camera
8. My favorite animal is Bonzo the baboon
9. His amazing stunts and antics
10. How graceful the gazelles are

B. Identifying the Complete Subject and the Simple Subject

Identify the complete subject in each of the following sentences. Then, underline the simple subject.

11. One of the first advocates of medical hygiene and the use of anti-septics was Ignaz Semmelweis.
12. This German-Hungarian physician was born in 1818.
13. In 1844, he earned a degree from Vienna University.
14. His first position was as an assistant at the obstetric clinic in Vienna.
15. Semmelweis was appalled by the high mortality rate among his patients.
16. He taught medical staff members always to wash their hands in a chlorine solution and by doing so soon reduced the mortality rate.
17. Semmelweis, who was a true pioneer, lobbied the medical establishment to make antiseptic operating conditions a top priority.

18. The medical establishment in many countries remained hostile to Semmelweis for many years.
19. In 1865, the year of Semmelweis's death, a famous British surgeon named Joseph Lister performed his first antiseptic operation.
20. The method introduced by Semmelweis made medicine safer and more humane.

┌ H E L P ─
In Part C of
the Chapter Review,
the simple predicate may
be compound.

C. Identifying Complete Predicates and Simple Predicates (Verbs)

Identify the complete predicate in each of the following sentences. Then, underline the simple predicate (or verb).

21. Have you met my brother Lewis?
22. Then listen to this.
23. My brother often dawdles.
24. He chooses odd times for some activities.
25. One day last week, Lewis gathered all of the pencils in the house and sharpened them.
26. Today he woke early and completely rearranged his room.
27. Then my poor little brother was almost late for the school bus.
28. I reminded him, however, of his first-period test.
29. Somehow, Lewis finishes all his chores and assignments.
30. I might buy him a book about time management, though.

D. Identifying Sentence Parts

Identify each italicized word in the following paragraphs as a *subject,* a *verb,* a *predicate nominative,* a *predicate adjective,* a *direct object,* or an *indirect object.*

A [**31**] *carwash* can be a good [**32**] *fund-raiser.* The freshman class [**33**] *planned* a carwash for last Saturday. On Saturday morning, the [**34**] *sky* did not look [**35**] *good.* In fact, the weather forecast [**36**] *predicted* thunderstorms. Did [**37**] *any* of this send [**38**] *us* a message? Yes, but we had our **[39]** *carwash* anyway. Our first **[40]** *customer,* at 9:00 A.M., was a **[41]** *woman* in a pickup truck. Glancing at the sky, she paid **[42]** *us* a compliment. "You're really **[43]** *brave,*" she said. The rain **[44]** *began* as she was speaking, and our disappointment must have been **[45]** *obvious.* "Don't worry," she added. "There is **[46]** *nothing* like a rainwater rinse." We **[47]** *charged* her only one **[48]** *dollar* because she had cheered us up so much. The morning was intermittently **[49]** *rainy.* Later, however, the clouds parted and the weather was **[50]** *perfect.*

Writing Application
Using Verbs in a Summary

Fresh, Lively Verbs Your little sister likes you to tell her exciting stories. You have told her so many stories that you have run out of new ones. To get ideas for new stories, you think about events you have read about or seen. Write a summary of an exciting incident from a book, a movie, or a television show. Use action verbs that are fresh and lively. Underline these verbs.

Prewriting Think about books that you have read recently or movies and television shows that you have seen. Choose an exciting incident from one of these works. Freewrite what you remember about that incident.

Writing As you write your first draft, think about how you are presenting the information. When telling a story, you usually should use chronological order (the order in which events occurred). This method would be easiest for your young listener to follow, too. Try to use fresh, lively action verbs.

Revising Imagine that you are a young child hearing the story for the first time. Look over your summary and ask yourself if you could follow this account of the story.

Publishing Read over your summary again, looking for any errors in grammar, usage, and mechanics. You may want to share your story with a younger sibling or with children at a local preschool or kindergarten.

The Phrase

Prepositional, Verbal, and Appositive Phrases

Diagnostic Preview

A. Identifying and Classifying Prepositional Phrases

Identify each prepositional phrase in the following sentences. After each phrase, write the word(s) it modifies and the type of phrase it is (*adj.* for adjective phrase, *adv.* for adverb phrase).

—HELP—

Some sentences in Part A have more than one prepositional phrase.

EXAMPLE   **1.** The museums of different cities are fascinating to tourists.

     1. of different cities—museums—adj.
     to tourists—fascinating—adv.

1. New York City offers tourists a number of museums.
2. Perhaps the best-known museum is the American Museum of Natural History.
3. This huge museum has exhibits on human history and culture and also shows animals, even dinosaurs, in natural-looking displays, called dioramas.
4. The museum houses the Hayden Planetarium, which teaches visitors about the heavens.
5. Exhibits about earth and space interest young and old alike.
6. The entire complex of exhibits is popular because it offers something for everyone.

7. The city's other museums, which are also fascinating, attract visitors who are interested in specific topics.
8. New York is home to the Museum of Broadcasting, which is filled with old films and radio broadcasts.
9. One of the city's newest museums, Ellis Island Immigration Museum, opened during 1990 and displays many artifacts that had been owned by immigrants who entered the United States through Ellis Island.
10. People who enjoy art can visit museums like the Metropolitan Museum of Art and the Museum of Modern Art.

B. Identifying Verbals and Appositives

In the following sentences, identify each italicized word or word group as a *participle*, a *gerund*, an *infinitive*, or an *appositive*.

EXAMPLES   **1.** For some reason, *cleaning* a room, that *dreaded project,* always seems *to create* new projects.

      1. cleaning—gerund; dreaded—participle; project—appositive; to create—infinitive

11. John began with every intention of *cleaning* his entire room, the official disaster *area* of his home.
12. He first tackled the pile of CDs *lying* near his *unused* sound system.
13. *Sorting* through them, he found them mostly *outdated.*
14. John decided that his *broken* stereo system, a *gift* from his parents, was the reason.
15. By *repairing* the stereo, he could give himself a reason *to update* his music collection.
16. *Trained* in electronics, John soon saw the problem and began *to work* on it.
17. Some hours later, John had a *working* stereo system but an *uncleaned* room.
18. He had just started *playing* a CD when his sister announced, "Mom's coming *to see* how your room looks!"
19. A tough *taskmaster,* Mom wanted him *to have* it spotless.
20. She applauded his success in *fixing* his stereo but insisted that he clean the room before *doing* anything else.

What Is a Phrase?

3a. A *phrase* is a group of related words that is used as a single part of speech and that does not contain both a verb and its subject.

EXAMPLES   could have been [no subject]

instead of Debra and him [no subject or verb]

A group of words that has *both* a verb and its subject is not a phrase.

EXAMPLES   **We found** your pen. [*We* is the subject of *found*.]

if **she will go** [*She* is the subject of *will go*.]

Reference Note

For more about **clauses,** see Chapter 4.

N O T E   If a group of words contains both a verb and its subject, it is called a *clause.*

Oral Practice   **Identifying Phrases**

Read each of the following groups of words aloud, and identify it as a *phrase* or *not a phrase.*

EXAMPLES   **1.** with a hammer   **2.** because we agree

1. phrase   *2. not a phrase*

1. was hoping
2. if she really knows
3. with Abdullah and me
4. will be writing
5. inside the house
6. since Mallory wrote
7. after they leave
8. has been cleaned
9. on Miriam's desk
10. as the plane lands

Prepositional Phrases

Reference Note

For a list of **commonly used prepositions,** see page 28.

3b. A *prepositional phrase* includes a preposition, the object of the preposition, and any modifiers of that object.

EXAMPLES   **to** the pool   **at** the Jacksons' house   **instead of** them

Notice that one or more modifiers may appear in a prepositional phrase. The first example contains *the*; the second contains *the Jacksons'*.

3c. The noun or pronoun in a prepositional phrase is called the *object of the preposition.*

EXAMPLE   Clarice went to the **ballet.** [The noun *ballet* is the object of the preposition *to*.]

NOTE Do not be misled by a modifier coming after the noun or pronoun in a prepositional phrase. The noun or pronoun is still the object.

EXAMPLE   Heidi and Mrs. Braun worked **at the polls** today. [*Polls* is the object of the preposition *at*. The adverb *today* tells when and modifies the verb *worked*.]

Objects of prepositions may be compound.

EXAMPLES   On the plaza, a guitarist sang for **Victor** and **me**. [The preposition *for* has a compound object: *Victor* and *me*.]

In A.D. 79, the city of Pompeii was buried beneath **lava, rocks,** and **ashes**. [The preposition *beneath* has a compound object: *lava, rocks,* and *ashes*.]

A prepositional phrase can modify the object of another prepositional phrase.

EXAMPLE   Next to the door **of the old barn** stood two horses. [The prepositional phrase *of the old barn* modifies *door,* which is the object of the compound preposition *Next to*.]

A prepositional phrase can contain another prepositional phrase.

EXAMPLE   Meet us **at the Museum of Science and Industry.** [The prepositional phrase *at the Museum of Science and Industry* contains the prepositional phrase *of Science and Industry*.]

NOTE Sometimes a prepositional phrase is combined with a noun to form a compound noun.

EXAMPLES   Strait of Hormuz   hole in one

Stratford-on-Avon   University of Pittsburgh

TIPS & TRICKS

Be careful not to confuse the preposition *to* with the *to* that is the sign of the verb's infinitive form: *to swim, to know, to see*.

Reference Note
For more about **infinitives,** see page 85.

Reference Note
For more about **compound nouns,** see page 4.

The Adjective Phrase

3d. A prepositional phrase that modifies a noun or pronoun is called an *adjective phrase.*

EXAMPLE   The members **of the club** want sweatshirts **with the club emblem.** [The prepositional phrase *of the club* is used as an adjective to modify the noun *members. With the club emblem* is used as an adjective to modify the noun *sweatshirts*.]

Unlike a one-word adjective, which usually precedes the word it modifies, an adjective phrase almost always follows the noun or pronoun it modifies.

ADJECTIVE   Amy closed the **cellar** door.
ADJECTIVE PHRASE Amy closed the door **to the cellar.**

More than one adjective phrase may modify the same word.

EXAMPLE   Here's a letter **for you from Aunt Martha.** [The prepositional phrases *for you* and *from Aunt Martha* both modify the noun *letter.*]

An adjective phrase may also modify the object of another prepositional phrase.

EXAMPLE   The horse **in the trailer with the rusted latch** broke **loose.** [The phrase *in the trailer* modifies the noun *horse. Trailer* is the object of the preposition *in.* The phrase *with the rusted latch* modifies *trailer.*]

Often you can convert the objects of adjective phrases into adjectives. Doing so makes your writing less wordy.

Adjective Phrases	Nouns Used as Adjectives
The light **in the kitchen** is on.	The **kitchen** light is on.
The airports **in Chicago and New York** are crowded.	The **Chicago** and **New York** airports are crowded.

However, not all adjective phrases can be changed into one-word modifiers that make sense. Sometimes, changing an adjective phrase makes a sentence awkward and ungrammatical.

CLEAR   Please hand me the book on the table.
AWKWARD   Please hand me the table book.

Exercise 1   Identifying Adjective Phrases

Identify the adjective phrases in the following paragraph, and give the word that each modifies.

EXAMPLE   [1] A few years ago our family visited South Dakota and saw a famous monument to great American leaders.

1. *to great American leaders—monument*

[1] My mom took the pictures on the next page when we were visiting this scenic spot at Mount Rushmore National Memorial. [2] As

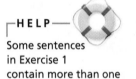

┌─HELP─
Some sentences in Exercise 1 contain more than one adjective phrase.

you can see, the mountainside behind us is a lasting tribute to George Washington, Thomas Jefferson, Theodore Roosevelt, and Abraham Lincoln. **[3]** The figures on the granite cliff were carved under the direction of Gutzon Borglum, an American sculptor. **[4]** Looking at the sculpture, I can certainly believe that this is one of the world's largest. **[5]** The faces are sixty feet high and show a great deal of detail and expression. **[6]** Each president symbolizes a part of United States history. **[7]** Washington represents the founding of the country, and Jefferson signifies the Declaration of Independence. **[8]** Lincoln symbolizes an end to slavery, and Roosevelt stands for expansion and resource conservation. **[9]** Tourists on the viewing terrace must gaze up nearly five hundred feet to see this art. **[10]** As both symbols for the nation and works of art, these massive faces are an inspiration to all who visit Mount Rushmore.

The Adverb Phrase

3e. A prepositional phrase that modifies a verb, an adjective, or an adverb is called an **adverb phrase**.

An adverb phrase tells *how, when, where, why,* or *to what extent.*

EXAMPLES   Britney answered **with a smile.** [The adverb phrase *with a smile* tells *how* Britney answered.]

They sailed **across the lake** yesterday. [The adverb phrase *across the lake* tells *where* they sailed.]

By Wednesday Christopher will be finished. [The adverb phrase *By Wednesday* tells *when* Christopher will be finished.]

The calculations erred **by more than two inches.** [*By more than two inches* is an adverb phrase telling *to what extent* the calculations erred.]

In the examples above, the adverb phrases all modify verbs.

An adverb phrase may modify an adjective or an adverb.

EXAMPLES   Melissa is good **at tennis** but better **at volleyball.** [The adverb phrase *at tennis* modifies the adjective *good.* The adverb phrase *at volleyball* modifies the adjective *better.*]

Is the water warm enough **for swimming**? [The adverb phrase *for swimming* modifies the adverb *enough.*]

| STYLE | TIP |

Be sure to place phrases carefully so that they express the meaning you intend.

EXAMPLES
The conductor compli-mented Lia's performance after the concert. [Did Lia perform after the concert was over?]

After the concert, the conductor complimented Lia's performance. [The compliment was made after the concert.]

Adjective phrases almost always follow the words they modify, but an adverb phrase may appear at various places in a sentence.

EXAMPLES   **Before noon** the race started.

The race started **before noon.**

Like adjective phrases, more than one adverb phrase may modify the same word.

EXAMPLE   **During summers,** my older sister works **at the museum.** [The adverb phrases *During summers* and *at the museum* both modify the verb *works.* The first phrase tells *when* my sister works; the second phrase tells *where* she works.]

┌HELP─

Some sentences in Exercise 2 contain more than one phrase.

Exercise 2 Identifying Adverb Phrases

Identify the adverb phrases in the following sentences, and give the word or words each phrase modifies.

EXAMPLE   1. The concept of time has inspired many figures of speech over the years.

     1. *over the years—has inspired*

1. We use time expressions in everyday speech.
2. In conversation, you may have heard the expression "time out of mind," which means "long ago."
3. When you fall in love, you may feel that "time stands still."
4. Is twenty minutes too long for a "time-out"?
5. If something happens "in no time," it happens very fast.
6. Have you ever noticed that "time flies" when you are chatting with your friends?
7. However, if you are sitting in a waiting room, "time drags."
8. Are you keeping someone's secret "until the end of time"?
9. Do people stop you on the street to ask if you "have the time"?
10. In the meantime, "time marches on" under the steady gaze of "Father Time."

Review A ▸ Writing Sentences Using Adjective and Adverb Phrases

You are a reporter for your school newspaper. The Young Business Leaders Club has given you an announcement for its upcoming banquet. Write an article about this event, using the information from the announcement below. Use five adjective phrases and five adverb phrases to help you include the necessary information in your article.

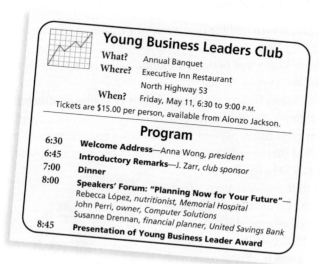

Young Business Leaders Club

What?   Annual Banquet
Where?   Executive Inn Restaurant
        North Highway 53
When?   Friday, May 11, 6:30 to 9:00 P.M.
Tickets are $15.00 per person, available from Alonzo Jackson.

Program

6:30   **Welcome Address**—Anna Wong, *president*
6:45   **Introductory Remarks**—J. Zarr, *club sponsor*
7:00   **Dinner**
8:00   **Speakers' Forum: "Planning Now for Your Future"**—
        Rebecca López, *nutritionist, Memorial Hospital*
        John Perri, *owner, Computer Solutions*
        Susanne Drennan, *financial planner, United Savings Bank*
8:45   **Presentation of Young Business Leader Award**

Review B ▸ Identifying Adjective and Adverb Phrases

Identify each italicized prepositional phrase in the following paragraph as an *adjective phrase* or as an *adverb phrase*. Then, identify the word or words each phrase modifies.

EXAMPLE   I enjoy reading all sorts **[1]** *of myths and legends.*

        1. *adjective phrase—sorts*

    Have you heard the Greek myth **[1]** *about Narcissus and Echo?* It is a story rich **[2]** *in irony.* Narcissus was a handsome young man **[3]** *with many admirers.* However, he rejected everyone who loved him, including the nymph Echo. As punishment **[4]** *for his arrogant behavior,* the gods sentenced Narcissus to stare forever **[5]** *at his own reflection* **[6]** *in a pond.* **[7]** *For days,* Narcissus gazed adoringly **[8]** *at himself.* Echo the nymph stayed **[9]** *with him* until she wasted away. Finally Narcissus, too, wasted away, and when he died he turned **[10]** *into the narcissus flower.*

Review C Identifying and Classifying Prepositional Phrases

List all the prepositional phrases in each of the following sentences. Write *adj.* if the phrase is used as an adjective; write *adv.* if the phrase is used as an adverb. Be prepared to identify the word each phrase modifies.

EXAMPLE 1. Theories about the universe have changed over the years.
1. *about the universe—adj.; over the years—adv.*

1. In 1929, Edwin Hubble discovered the existence of galaxies outside the Milky Way.
2. Now we know that perhaps a million galaxies exist inside the bowl of the Big Dipper alone.
3. Astronomers believe that our galaxy is only one among billions throughout the universe.
4. Knowledge has expanded since 500 years ago, when most people believed that the earth was the center of the entire universe.
5. By the 1500s, the Polish astronomer Copernicus suggested that the earth and other planets revolved around the sun.
6. In 1633, the Italian scientist Galileo was tried and convicted for the crime of teaching that the sun is the center of the universe.

7. The Catholic Church condemned Galileo because in his teachings earth and humans were not the center of all things.
8. In Galileo's time, people knew of only five planets besides our own—Mercury, Venus, Mars, Jupiter, and Saturn.
9. Since then we have identified the planets Uranus, Neptune, and Pluto, and we have sent probes into our solar system.
10. Galileo, Copernicus, and other early astronomers would be amazed at the extent of our knowledge of space today.

Verbals and Verbal Phrases

Verbals are formed from verbs. Like verbs, they may have modifiers and complements. However, verbals are used as nouns, adjectives, or adverbs, not as verbs. The three kinds of verbals are *participles,* *gerunds,* and *infinitives.*

The Participle

3f. A *participle* is a verb form that can be used as an adjective.

EXAMPLES   We saw the raccoon **escaping** through the back door. [The participle *escaping,* formed from the verb *escape,* modifies the noun *raccoon.*]

Waxed floors can be dangerously slippery. [The participle *Waxed,* formed from the verb *wax,* modifies the noun *floors.*]

Two kinds of participles are *present participles* and *past participles.*

(1) Present participles end in *–ing.*

EXAMPLES   We ran inside to get out of the **pouring** rain. [The present participle *pouring* modifies the noun *rain.*]

Watching the clock, the coach became worried. [The present participle *watching* modifies the noun *coach.*]

Although participles are forms of verbs, they cannot stand alone as verbs. Participles need to be joined to a helping verb to form a verb phrase. When a participle is used in a verb phrase, it is part of the verb and is not an adjective.

VERB PHRASES   The rain **was pouring.**

The coach **had been watching** the clock.

(2) Past participles usually end in *–d* or *–ed.* Other past participles are formed irregularly.

EXAMPLES   A **peeled** and **sliced** cucumber can be added to a garden salad. [The past participles *peeled* and *sliced* modify the noun *cucumber.*]

The speaker, **known** for her strong support of recycling, was loudly applauded. [The irregular past participle *known* modifies the noun *speaker.*]

Reference Note

For a discussion of **irregular verbs,** see page 147.

Like a present participle, a past participle can also be part of a verb phrase. When a past participle is used in a verb phrase, it is part of the verb and is not an adjective.

VERB PHRASES   I **have peeled** and **sliced** the cucumber.

The speaker **was known** for her strong support of recycling.

Reference Note
For more about the **passive voice,** see page 163.

NOTE   Notice in the second example above that a past participle used with a form of the verb *be* creates a *passive-voice* verb. A verb in the passive voice expresses an action done to its subject.

EXAMPLE   The goal **was made** by Josh. [The action of the verb *was made* is done to the subject *goal.*]

Exercise 3   **Identifying Participles and the Words They Modify**

Identify the participles used as adjectives in each of the following sentences. After each participle, write the noun or pronoun it modifies.

EXAMPLES   1.   We searched the island for buried treasure.
     1.   *buried—treasure*

     2.   The speeding train raced past the platform.
     2.   *speeding—train*

─HELP─

Some sentences in Exercise 3 contain more than one participle used as an adjective.

1. The prancing horses were loudly applauded by the audience.
2. Colorful flags, waving in the breeze, brightened the gloomy day.
3. Swaggering and boasting, the new varsity quarterback made us extremely angry.
4. The game scheduled for tonight was postponed because of rain.
5. Leaving the field, the happy player rushed to her parents sitting in the bleachers.
6. Branches tapping on the roof and leaves rustling in the wind made an eerie sound.
7. We thought the banging shutter upstairs was someone walking in the attic.
8. Painfully sunburned, I vowed always to use sunscreen and never to be so careless again.
9. Terrified by our dog, the burglar turned and fled across the yard.
10. The platoon of soldiers, marching in step, crossed the field to the stirring music of the military band.

Using Appropriate Participles

For each blank in the following sentences, provide a participle that fits the meaning of the sentence.

EXAMPLE   **1.** The _____ tide washed over the beach.

     1. rising

1. Mr. Ortiz explained the effects of pollution and drought on plants _____ in a rain forest.

2. _____ from the point of view of a firefighter, the story is full of accurate details.

3. The tiger, _____ from the hunters, swam across the river to safety.

4. _____ at the traffic light, the driver put on his sunglasses.

5. The tourists _____ in the hotel were given a free meal.

6. _____ as an excellent place to camp, the park lived up to its reputation.

7. _____ by a bee, Steven hurried to the infirmary.

8. The poem describes a spider _____ on a thread.

9. We stumbled off the racecourse, _____.

10. _____, I quickly phoned the hospital.

The Participial Phrase

3g. A *participial phrase* is used as an adjective and consists of a participle and any complements or modifiers the participle has.

EXAMPLES   **Seeing the cat,** the dog barked loudly.

     The cat hissed at the dog **barking in the yard next door.**

     The dog **noisily barking at the cat** had to be brought in.

In each of the following sentences, an arrow points from the participial phrase to the noun or pronoun that the phrase modifies.

EXAMPLES   **Switching its tail,** the mountain lion paced back and forth. [participle with object *tail*]

     She heard me **sighing loudly.** [participle with the adverb *loudly*]

     Living within his budget, Adam never needs to borrow money. [participle with adverb phrase *within his budget*]

     Quickly grabbing the keys, I dashed for the front door. [participle with preceding adverb *Quickly* and object *keys*]

Reference Note

For information on **punctuating participial phrases,** see page 281. The participle as a **dangling modifier** is discussed on page 213. For information on **using participles to combine sentences,** see page 453.

┌─**HELP**─

A participial phrase should be placed very close to the word it modifies. Otherwise, the phrase may appear to modify another word, and the sentence may not make sense.

MISPLACED
He saw a moose riding his motorcycle through the woods. [The placement of the modifier *riding his motorcycle* calls up a silly picture. He, not the moose, is riding the motorcycle.]

IMPROVED
Riding his motorcycle through the woods, he saw a moose.

Exercise 5 **Identifying Participial Phrases**

Identify the participial phrases in the following sentences, and give the word each phrase modifies.

EXAMPLE   **1.** The sight of skyscrapers towering against the sky always impresses me.

   1. towering against the sky—skyscrapers

1. How are skyscrapers created, and what keeps them standing tall?
2. As the drawing shows, columns of steel or of concrete reinforced with steel are sunk into bedrock beneath the building.
3. If a layer of rock isn't present, these columns are sunk into a thick concrete pad spread across the bottom of a deep basement.
4. From this foundation rises a steel skeleton, supporting the walls and floors.
5. This cutaway drawing shows how this skeleton, covered with a "skin" of glass and metal, becomes a safe working and living space for people.
6. This method of building, first developed in the United States, is used now in many other places in the world.
7. Chicago, nearly destroyed by fire in 1871, was later rebuilt with innovative designs.
8. The first skyscraper constructed on a metal frame was built there during this period.
9. Architects, using the latest materials, were glad to design in new ways.
10. Chicago, known as the site of the original 10-story skyscraper, now is home to the 110-story Sears Tower.

Review D **Identifying Participles and Participial Phrases**

Identify the participial phrases and participles that are used as adjectives in the following sentences. Then, give the words they modify.

EXAMPLE   **1.** Cats, known for their pride and independence, are supposedly hard to train.

   1. known for their pride and independence—Cats

1. One day I was giving Chops, my spoiled cat, treats.
2. Standing on her hind legs, she reached up with her paw.
3. Chops, grabbing for my fingers, tried to bring the tasty morsel closer.

—HELP—

Some sentences in Review D contain more than one participle or participial phrase.

4. Pulling my hand back a little, I tugged gently on her curved paw, and she stepped forward.

5. Praising my clever cat, I immediately gave her two treats.

6. The next time I held a treat up high, Chops, puzzled but eager, repeated the grab-and-step movement.

7. Soon Chops was taking steps toward treats held out of her reach.

8. I now have an educated cat who can walk on two legs.

9. Grabbing the treats and gobbling them down, she has learned that certain moves always get her a snack.

10. Sometimes after Chops has had her treat, she just sits and looks at me, no doubt thinking that humans are truly a strange bunch!

The Gerund

3h. A *gerund* is a verb form ending in *–ing* that is used as a noun.

Like other nouns, gerunds are used as subjects, predicate nominatives, direct objects, indirect objects, and objects of prepositions.

EXAMPLES   The **dancing** was fun. [subject]

My favorite part of the show was his **juggling.** [predicate nominative]

Shauna tried **climbing** faster. [direct object]

Give **winning** the game your best. [indirect object]

We worked better after **resting.** [object of a preposition]

Like other nouns, gerunds may be modified by adjectives and adjective phrases.

EXAMPLES   We listened to **the beautiful** singing **of the famous soprano.** [The article *the,* the adjective *beautiful,* and the adjective phrase *of the famous soprano* modify the gerund *singing. Singing* is used as the object of the preposition *to.*]

The Mallorys enjoy talking **about their vacation.** [The adjective phrase *about their vacation* modifies the gerund *talking,* which is the direct object of the verb *enjoy.*]

The harsh clacking **of the tappets** alerted us to a serious problem in the car's engine. [The article *The,* the adjective *harsh,* and the adjective phrase *of the tappets* modify the gerund *clacking.*]

Like verbs, gerunds may also be modified by adverbs and adverb phrases.

EXAMPLES   Reading **widely** is one way to acquire judgment, maturity, and a good education. [The gerund *Reading* is the subject of the verb *is*. The adverb *widely* modifies the gerund *Reading*.]

Floating **lazily in the pool** is my favorite summer pastime. [The gerund *Floating* is used as the subject of the sentence. It is modified by the adverb *lazily* (telling *how*) and also by the adverb phrase *in the pool* (telling *where*).]

Brandywine likes galloping **briskly on a cold morning.** [The gerund *galloping* is the direct object of the verb *likes*. The adverb *briskly* (telling *how*) and the adverb phrase *on a cold morning* (telling *when*) both modify *galloping*.]

Gerunds, like present participles, end in *–ing*. To be a gerund, a verbal must be used as a noun. In the following sentence, three words end in *–ing*, but only one of them is a gerund.

EXAMPLE   **Circling** the runway, the pilot was **preparing** for **landing.** [*Circling* is a present participle modifying *pilot*. *Preparing* is part of the verb phrase *was preparing*. Only *landing*, used as the object of the preposition *for*, is a gerund.]

Exercise 6   Identifying and Classifying Gerunds

Identify each gerund in the following sentences. Then, write how each is used: as a *subject*, a *predicate nominative*, a *direct object*, or an *object of a preposition*.

EXAMPLE   1. Instead of driving, let's walk.
    1. *driving—object of a preposition*

1. Her laughing attracted my attention.
2. By studying, you can improve your grades.
3. Why did the birds stop chirping?
4. Writing in my journal has helped me understand myself better.
5. Smiling, Dad said that we would all go to a movie when we had finished the cleaning.
6. What Joseph liked best was hiking to the peak.
7. Before leaving the beach, we sat and watched the fading light.
8. Yesterday, Mrs. Jacobs was discussing having a garage sale.
9. One of Alvin's bad habits is boasting.
10. Without knocking, the crying child threw open the door.

The Gerund Phrase

3i. A *gerund phrase* consists of a gerund and any modifiers or complements the gerund has. The entire phrase is used as a noun.

EXAMPLES   **The gentle pattering of the rain** was a welcome sound. [The gerund phrase is the subject of the sentence. The gerund *pattering* is modified by the article *The,* the adjective *gentle,* and the prepositional phrase *of the rain.* Notice that the modifiers preceding the gerund are included in the gerund phrase.]

I feared **skiing down the mountain alone.** [The gerund phrase is used as the object of the verb *feared.* The gerund *skiing* is modified by the prepositional phrase *down the mountain* and by the adverb *alone.*]

My dog's favorite game is **bringing me the newspaper.** [The gerund phrase is used as a predicate nominative. The gerund *bringing* has a direct object, *newspaper,* and an indirect object, *me.*]

Evelyn Ashford won a gold medal for **running the 100-meter dash.** [The gerund phrase is the object of the preposition *for.* The gerund *running* has a direct object, *dash.*]

> **STYLE   TIP**
>
> A noun or a pronoun that comes before a gerund should be in the possessive form.
>
> EXAMPLES
> **My** playing the radio loudly is a bad habit.
>
> **Ed's** constant TV watching interferes with **our** studying.

Exercise 7 Identifying and Classifying Gerund Phrases

Find the gerund phrases in the following sentences. Then, tell how each phrase is used: as a *subject,* a *predicate nominative,* a *direct object,* or an *object of a preposition.*

EXAMPLE   **1.** My favorite hunting trophies are the ones I get by photographing wild animals.

1. *photographing wild animals—object of a preposition*

> **HELP—**
>
> Sentences in Exercise 7 may contain more than one gerund phrase.

1. Exciting and challenging, wildlife photography is surprisingly similar to pursuing prey on a hunt.
2. In both activities, knowing the animals' habits and habitats is vital to success.
3. Scouting out locations is important to both the hunter and the nature photographer.
4. This preparation gives you time for figuring out the best natural light for photography.

5. Other important skills are being quiet and keeping your aim very steady.

6. In photography, you must also consider choosing the correct film.

7. Photographers often like taking pictures of animals feeding near ponds and rivers.

8. Setting up a tripod and camera in underbrush nearby is a way to be ready when the animals come.

9. Advance preparation often makes the difference between getting good pictures and getting great ones.

10. Your patience and skill are rewarded when you "capture" a wild creature without scaring it.

Review E **Identifying and Classifying Gerunds and Gerund Phrases**

Identify the gerunds or gerund phrases in the following sentences. Then, tell how each is used: as a *subject*, a *predicate nominative*, a *direct object*, or an *object of a preposition*.

EXAMPLE   1. Drawing a good caricature is hard to do.

1. *Drawing a good caricature—subject*

1. A caricature is a picture, usually of a person, that draws attention to key features by emphasizing them.

2. Usually, caricature artists enjoy poking fun at famous people.

3. Looking at caricatures is an entertaining way to capture the "feel" of a historical period.

4. No one looking at this sketch of Teddy Roosevelt can help smiling.

5. The artist began by simplifying the shape of his subject's head.

6. Then he started outlining the temples and round cheeks with bold strokes of his pen.

7. As you probably realize, magnifying reality is very important to good caricature.

8. By enlarging Roosevelt's engaging grin and bristly mustache, the artist emphasizes these features and suggests Roosevelt's energetic, outgoing personality.

9. The artist also uses his subject's narrowed eyes and oval glasses for comic effect by drawing them closer together than they really were.

10. Exaggerating Roosevelt's features has resulted in an amusing but unmistakable likeness.

The Infinitive

3j. An *infinitive* is a verb form that can be used as a noun, an adjective, or an adverb. Most infinitives begin with *to.*

Infinitives can be used as nouns.

EXAMPLES   **To fly** is glorious. [*To fly* is the subject of the sentence.]

             Brandon wanted **to work** on the play. [*To work* is the object of the verb *wanted.*]

Infinitives can be used as adjectives.

EXAMPLES   The place **to visit** is Williamsburg. [*To visit* modifies the noun *place.*]

             That record was the one **to beat.** [*To beat* modifies the pronoun *one.*]

Infinitives also can be used as adverbs.

EXAMPLES   Sabina jumped **to look.** [*To look* modifies the verb *jumped.*]

             Ready **to go,** we soon loaded the car. [*To go* modifies the adjective *Ready.*]

NOTE   *To* plus a noun or a pronoun (*to school, to him, to the beach*) is a prepositional phrase, not an infinitive.

Exercise 8   Identifying and Classifying Infinitives

Identify the infinitives in the following sentences. Then, tell how each infinitive is used: as a *noun,* an *adjective,* or an *adverb.*

EXAMPLE   **1.** I would like to help you.

         1. to help—noun

1. Tamisha's ambition is to teach.
2. To persist can sometimes be a sign of stubbornness.
3. Chen has learned to tap dance.
4. I am happy to oblige.
5. An easy way to win at tennis does not exist.
6. We need to weed the garden soon.
7. The hockey team went to Coach Norton's house to study last night.
8. We met at the lake to swim.
9. That is not the correct amount of paper to order for this project.
10. According to the map, the road to take is the one to the left.

STYLE   TIP

A *split infinitive* occurs when a word is placed between the sign of the infinitive, *to,* and the base form of a verb. Although split infinitives are common in informal speaking and writing, you should avoid using them in formal situations.

SPLIT
   The bear seemed to suddenly appear from the shadows.

REVISED
   The bear seemed **to appear** suddenly from the shadows.

Reference Note

For more about **prepositional phrases,** see page 70.

COMPUTER TIP

Some software programs can identify and highlight split infinitives in a document. Using such a feature will help you eliminate split infinitives from your formal writing.

To find out if an infinitive phrase is being used as a noun, replace the phrase with *what.*

EXAMPLES

To fix an air conditioner is my next project. [What is my next project? *To fix an air conditioner is my next project.* The infinitive is a noun.]

In New York, we went to see Gramercy Park. [We went what? This question makes no sense. The infinitive is not a noun. It is used as an adverb modifying the verb *went.*]

The Infinitive with *to* Omitted

Sometimes the sign of the infinitive, *to,* is omitted in a sentence.

EXAMPLES   She's done all her chores except [to] **feed** the cat.

I'll help you [to] **pack.**

The dogs like **to roam** in the field and [to] **chase** rabbits.

Fuel injection helps cars [to] **run** better and [to] **last** longer.

The Infinitive Phrase

3k. An *infinitive phrase* consists of an infinitive and any modifiers or complements the infinitive has. The entire phrase can be used as a noun, an adjective, or an adverb.

EXAMPLES   **To make tamales quickly** was hard. [The infinitive phrase is used as a noun, as the subject of the sentence. The infinitive has a direct object, *tamales,* and is modified by the adverb *quickly* and by the predicate adjective *hard.*]

Chris is the player **to watch in the next game.** [The infinitive phrase is used as an adjective modifying the predicate nominative *player.* The infinitive is modified by the adverb phrase *in the next game.*]

We are eager **to finish this project.** [The infinitive phrase is used as an adverb modifying the predicate adjective *eager.* The infinitive has a direct object, *project.*]

NOTE   An infinitive may have a subject. An *infinitive clause* consists of an infinitive with a subject and any modifiers and complements of the infinitive. The entire infinitive clause functions as a noun.

EXAMPLES   I wanted **him to help me with my algebra.** [The entire infinitive clause is the direct object of the verb *wanted. Him* is the subject of the infinitive *to help.* The infinitive *to help* has a direct object, *me,* and is modified by the adverb phrase *with my algebra.*]

Would Uncle Jim like **us to clear the brush in the backyard**? [The entire infinitive clause is the direct object of the verb *Would like. Us* is the subject of the infinitive *to clear.* The infinitive *to clear* has a direct object, *brush,* which is modified by the adjective phrase *in the backyard.*]

Notice that a pronoun that functions as the subject of an infinitive clause is in the objective case.

Exercise 9 · Identifying and Classifying Infinitives and Infinitive Phrases

Identify the infinitives and infinitive phrases in the following sentences. After each, tell whether it is used as a *noun*, an *adjective*, or an *adverb*.

EXAMPLE **1.** Scott is the person to elect.

    1. to elect—adjective

1. To dance gracefully requires coordination.
2. Raymond wanted to join the team.
3. Sandy needs to study.
4. I'm going to the pond to fish.
5. A good way to stay healthy is to exercise often.
6. After our long vacation, we needed to get back in training.
7. The best way to get there is to take the bus.
8. Don't you dare open that present before your birthday.
9. Juanita and Matt tried to find the perfect gift.
10. He lives to swim and water-ski.

Exercise 10 · Identifying and Classifying Infinitive Phrases

Identify the infinitive phrases in the following sentences. Then, tell how each phrase is used: as a *noun*, an *adjective*, or an *adverb*.

EXAMPLE **1.** To create a miracle fabric was the aim of the chemist Joe Shivers.

    1. To create a miracle fabric—noun

1. He succeeded with spandex, and athletes of all shapes and sizes have learned to appreciate the qualities of his "power cloth."
2. This material has the ability to stretch and snap back into shape.
3. Its sleek fit lessens friction to give the wearer faster movement through air or water.
4. Its slick surface makes an athlete such as a wrestler hard to hold.
5. To say that spandex has athletes covered is not stretching the truth.
6. Spandex is just one of many synthetic fibers to meet today's fashion needs.
7. Nylon was the first synthetic; it originally was made to take the place of silk in women's garments.
8. To replace silk was also the purpose of rayon, another early, low-priced synthetic.

9. Polyester, developed later, often is combined with natural fibers to reduce wrinkling.

10. To distinguish synthetic fibers (most made from plastic) from natural fibers is not easy.

Review F Identifying Infinitives and Infinitive Phrases

Identify the infinitives and infinitive phrases in the following paragraph.

EXAMPLE   **[1]** Laurel and Hardy are a comic team to remember.

    1. to remember

┌HELP─
In Review F, the sign of the infinitive, *to*, is sometimes omitted.

GRAMMAR

[1] Together, Stan Laurel and Oliver Hardy have made millions of moviegoers laugh. [2] In their day, to be funny in the movies required the use of body language. [3] Both of them were geniuses in their ability to keep audiences laughing. [4] For his famous head scratch, Stan grew his hair long so that he could scratch and pull it to make a comic mess. [5] Stan also developed a hilarious cry that he used to show his character's childish nature. [6] He would shut his eyes tightly, pinch up his face, and begin to wail. [7] Ollie, too, had an uncanny ability to create his own distinctive mannerisms. [8] For example, he was known for the long-suffering look he used to express frustration. [9] He would also waggle his tie at a person he and Stan had managed to offend and then start giggling nervously. [10] Ollie's intent was to make the person less angry, but his gesture usually had the opposite effect.

Review G Identifying and Classifying Verbals and Verbal Phrases

Identify each verbal or verbal phrase in the following paragraph as a *participle, participial phrase, gerund, gerund phrase, infinitive, infinitive phrase,* or as a part of an *infinitive clause.*

EXAMPLE   **[1]** Building the railroad across the United States in the late 1800s required thousands of workers.

    1. Building the railroad across the United States in the late 1800s—gerund phrase

[1] The government commissioned two companies to build railway tracks between Omaha, Nebraska, and Sacramento, California. [2] Building eastward from Sacramento, the Central Pacific Railroad relied on Chinese workers. [3] One fourth of the Chinese immigrants

in the United States in 1868 helped with laying the track. [4] The terrain was difficult to cover, but the laborers rose to the challenge. [5] Known for their dependability, the Chinese were strong workers. [6] Complaining was a problem with some workers, but seldom with Chinese laborers. [7] It was often necessary to blow up parts of mountains, and the Chinese workers became experts at this task. [8] Chinese and Irish workers set a record on April 28, 1869, by spiking ten miles and fifty-six feet of track in twelve hours. [9] The railroad company divided the Chinese immigrants into working groups, or gangs, each with twelve to twenty men. [10] Keeping many of their traditional ways, Chinese workers ate food that was shipped to them from San Francisco's Chinatown.

Appositives and Appositive Phrases

3l. An *appositive* is a noun or a pronoun placed beside another noun or pronoun to identify or describe it.

EXAMPLES   The sculptor **Isamu Noguchi** has designed sculpture gardens. [The appositive *Isamu Noguchi* identifies the noun *sculptor.*]

Eric, a talented **musician,** plans to study in Europe. [The appositive *musician* describes the noun *Eric.*]

Those, the **ones** on the right, are on sale. [The appositive *ones* identifies the pronoun *Those.*]

3m. An *appositive phrase* consists of an appositive and any modifiers it has.

EXAMPLES   Lucy Sánchez, **my longtime friend from my old neighborhood,** has a new Scottish terrier.

Dr. Jackson has a degree in entomology, **the scientific study of insects.**

NOTE   Sometimes, an appositive phrase precedes the noun or pronoun to which it refers.

EXAMPLE   **The terror of our block,** little Anthony was on the rampage.

GRAMMAR

Reference Note

For more about **essential and nonessential phrases,** see page 276.

Appositives and appositive phrases that are not essential to the meaning of the sentence are set off by commas. If the appositive is essential to the meaning, it is generally not set off by commas.

EXAMPLES   My teacher, **Mr. Byrd,** trains parrots. [The writer has only one teacher. The appositive is not necessary to identify the teacher. Because the information is nonessential, it is set off by commas.]

My teacher **Mr. Byrd** trains parrots. [The writer has more than one teacher. The appositive is necessary to tell which teacher is meant. Because this information is essential to the meaning of the sentence, it is not set off by commas.]

NOTE Commas are generally used with appositives that refer to proper nouns.

EXAMPLE   Linda, **the editor,** assigned the story.

However, a word or phrase that is commonly accepted as part of a person's name or title is not set off by a comma.

EXAMPLE   The Roman Army defeated Attila **the Hun** in A.D. 451.

Exercise 11 **Identifying Appositives and Appositive Phrases**

Identify the appositives and appositive phrases in the following sentences. Then, give the noun or pronoun that each appositive or appositive phrase identifies or describes.

EXAMPLE   1. I usually write haiku, poems in a traditional Japanese form.

     1. *poems in a traditional Japanese form—haiku*

┌H E L P┐

A sentence in Exercise 11 may contain more than one appositive or appositive phrase.

1. Our community has a new organization, a writers' club called Writers, Inc.
2. Marquita Wiley, a college instructor, started the group at the request of former students.
3. A published author, she conducts the meetings as workshops.
4. The writers meet to read their works in progress, fiction or poetry, and to discuss suggestions for improvement.
5. The members, people from all walks of life, have varied interests.
6. A mechanic by trade, J. D. Ellis writes funny poems about his hobby, bird-watching.
7. My friend Lusita just had a short story about her people, the Zuni, published in a national magazine.

8. Next week, we'll meet at our regular time, 3:30 P.M.
9. Our guest speaker is Pat Mora, a Mexican American poet whose work emphasizes harmony between cultures.
10. Have you read her poem "Bribe"?

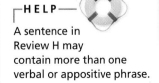

Review H **Identifying Verbal Phrases and Appositive Phrases**

Find the verbal phrases and appositive phrases in the following sentences. Identify each phrase as a *participial phrase,* a *gerund phrase,* an *infinitive phrase,* or an *appositive phrase.*

┌HELP┐

A sentence in Review H may contain more than one verbal or appositive phrase.

EXAMPLE 1. Automobiles have been partly responsible for drastically changing life in the twentieth century.

1. drastically changing life in the twentieth century—gerund phrase

1. Developing the automobile was actually the creative work of many people, but Henry Ford deservedly receives much credit.
2. Ford's company, using an assembly line and interchangeable parts, first produced the Model T in 1909.
3. Many people in the early 1900s wanted to buy cars because of their low prices and novelty.
4. By giving people an alternative to mass transit, automobiles did much to change the social and business scene of the United States.
5. No longer dependent on streetcars and trains, the first motorists used automobiles for going on recreational and family trips.
6. Clearly overjoyed with their vehicles, many Americans regarded automobiles as necessities by the 1920s.
7. One writer, a famous historian, noted that the automobile industry led to such new businesses as gas stations, repair garages, tire companies, and motels.

8. To get a clear idea of changes in automobile designs over the years, look at the picture to the right.
9. The photo shows Henry Ford, looking contented and proud, in his first car.
10. What are some of the main differences between Ford's car, one of the most advanced vehicles of its day, and modern cars?

┌─HELP─┐

Although several possible answers are given in the example in Review I, you need to write only one sentence for each item.

(Review I) **Writing Appropriate Phrases**

Rewrite each of the following sentences, supplying an appropriate prepositional, verbal, or appositive phrase to fill in the blank. Use each type of phrase at least twice. Identify each phrase you use as *prepositional, participial, infinitive, gerund,* or *appositive.*

EXAMPLE   1. We have room for only a single passenger _____.

1. *We have room for only a single passenger weighing less than one hundred fifty pounds. — participial*

or

We have room for only a single passenger in the boat. — prepositional

or

We have room for only a single passenger, a small one! — appositive

or

We have room for only a single passenger to come aboard. — infinitive

1. Only one _____ was left on the plate.
2. Joyfully, she danced _____.
3. Richard, _____, is moving back to the town!
4. During the whole trip to Mexico, her goal was _____.
5. _____, the new computer still sat in boxes on the floor.
6. At the bottom of the river, a huge old catfish lay _____.
7. _____ made them strong enough for the race.
8. Navajo dancers _____ stepped lightly into the open circle.
9. _____ became their goal for the rest of the year.
10. All the clothes _____ had been made in the United States.
11. The lace curtains _____ were not for sale.
12. Are these puppies _____ all yours?
13. What a marvelous aroma is rising _____!
14. _____, the engine finally started.
15. With a glance at the other runners _____, Gretchen pulled ahead.
16. Bill Briggs, _____, greeted the enthusiastic fans.
17. Everyone _____ should move down one seat.
18. _____ was the thought of each student in the class.
19. The children _____ made mud pies.
20. _____ gave them the endurance they needed.

Chapter Review

A. Identifying Phrases

In each of the following sentences, identify each italicized phrase as *prepositional, participial, gerund, infinitive,* or *appositive.*

1. Now I would like *to tell you about my sister Alexandra.*

2. She likes *arriving at school early.*

3. By *doing so,* she can spend extra time preparing for her day.

4. She will resort to anything to get *to school* early, including waking me up, too.

5. For example, when *the beeping of my alarm* woke me yesterday, the sky was as dark as night.

6. I soon realized that Alexandra, *a volunteer crossing guard at school,* had adjusted the alarm.

7. It was, I could see, an occasion for *applying my special technique.*

8. *Called my slow-motion technique,* it always achieves the result I want.

9. I moved *around the house* as if I were underwater; Alexandra watched until she could stand it no longer.

10. Then, I moved faster; I certainly did not want *to be late for school.*

B. Identifying and Classifying Prepositional Phrases

Identify the prepositional phrases in the following sentences. Identify the word or words modified by each phrase. Then, state whether the prepositional phrase is an *adjective phrase* or an *adverb phrase.*

11. A daily newspaper has something for almost everyone.

12. In addition to news, the paper offers entertainment, classified ads, and much more.

13. Our entire family reads the newspaper in the morning.

14. Dad always begins with the sports pages; Mom prefers the general news.

15. My sister's favorite part of the newspaper is the lifestyle section.

16. She enjoys features like "How-to Hints."

17. I find the editorial and opinion pages interesting, especially when a debate between two sides develops.

18. Sometimes I see the logic behind an argument.

19. Other times I wonder why grown people argue about a trivial issue.

20. I also like to read news about local events.

C. Identifying Verbals

Identify each italicized verbal in the following sentences as a *participle,* a *gerund,* or an *infinitive.*

21. Many amateur athletes want *to earn* medals for their abilities.

22. *Enjoyed* by people throughout history, amateur athletic competitions can be very beneficial.

23. *Winning* an event is only part of the reason athletes compete.

24. When talented amateurs compete *to test* their skills, they learn a great deal about their sport.

25. In addition, the love of a sport, the best reason for *entering* into competition, usually grows as an athlete's performance improves.

26. Furthermore, *sharing* hard work with teammates leads a person to appreciate cooperative efforts.

27. Competitions *organized* on many levels give amateur athletes a motive for increased practice.

28. *Participating* in state, national, and international competitions is important to many amateur athletes.

29. *Wanting* to be recognized for their talent, the athletes compete against their peers in such events.

30. These competitions also provide athletes with opportunities *to put* their abilities to the test.

D. Identifying Verbal Phrases

In each of the following sentences, identify the italicized verbal phrase as a *participial phrase,* an *infinitive phrase,* or a *gerund phrase.*

31. Maxine gets her exercise by *dancing for at least three hours a week.*

32. Eddie likes *to make pizza for his friends.*

33. The mother baboon watched her infant *eating a berry.*

34. Yolanda went *to get her book.*

35. Is the man *pushing the grocery cart* an employee or a customer?

36. *Winning the contest* was a thrill for our cheerleaders.
37. I made a tote bag *to hold my gym clothes.*
38. Richard's summer job is *delivering groceries to the hospital.*
39. Enzo Ferrari became famous by *building fast and stylish cars.*
40. *Preparing for that play* took quite a long time.
41. Samantha overheard Tina and Sue *talking about their vacation plans.*
42. Prepare *to run your fastest.*
43. *Excited by the thought of the trip,* we finished packing early.
44. Koalas get most of their nutrition by *eating eucalyptus leaves.*
45. *Tired of the noise outside,* we closed the window.

Writing Application
Using Prepositional Phrases in a Game

Adjective and Adverb Phrases You are planning a treasure hunt for a group of neighborhood children. The treasure hunt will include six stops for clues. For each clue, write a sentence containing at least one prepositional phrase. Use a combination of adjective and adverb phrases.

Prewriting First, think about your neighborhood and pick a good place to hide a treasure. Then, think of six places to hide clues.

Writing Write a sentence giving a clue about each location. The final sentence should lead the children directly to the hidden treasure.

Revising Ask someone who is familiar with the area of the treasure hunt to look over your clues. Revise any clues that are not clear. Be sure that each clue contains at least one prepositional phrase and that you have used both adjective and adverb phrases in your clues.

Publishing Check to be sure that your prepositional phrases are properly placed. An adverb phrase may occur at various places in a sentence. Proofread your sentences for correct capitalization and punctuation. You may want to organize a treasure hunt for younger children in your family or for children that you baby-sit.

The Clause
Independent and Subordinate Clauses

Diagnostic Preview

A. Identifying and Classifying Subordinate Clauses

Identify the subordinate clause in each of the following sentences. Then, classify each subordinate clause as an adjective clause (*adj.*), an adverb clause (*adv.*), or a noun clause (*n.*). If the clause is used as an adjective or adverb, write the word or phrase it modifies. If the clause is used as a noun, indicate whether it is used as a subject (*subj.*), a direct object (*d.o.*), an indirect object (*i.o.*), a predicate nominative (*p.n.*), or an object of a preposition (*o.p.*).

EXAMPLES   1. After our last class, Elena, Frieda, and I agreed that we would go bicycling in the park.
    1. *that we would go bicycling in the park—n.—d.o.*

    2. As we set out for the park, we had no idea of the difficulties ahead.
    2. *As we set out for the park—adv.—had*

1. Since none of us own bicycles, we decided to rent them there.
2. The man who rented us the bikes was helpful.
3. After we had bicycled six miles, Frieda's bike got a flat tire.
4. What we found was a nail in the tire.
5. We decided to take the bike to whatever bike shop was the nearest.
6. The woman at the bike shop told us that she could fix the tire.
7. After we had paid for the repair and gotten a receipt, we rode back to the park and bicycled for an hour.

8. Our only worry was that the man at the rental shop might not pay us back for the repair.

9. When we returned our bikes, we showed the man the receipt.

10. He refunded the money we had spent to fix the tire.

B. Classifying Sentences According to Structure

Classify each of the following sentences as *simple, compound, complex,* or *compound-complex.* Be sure that you can identify all subordinate and independent clauses.

EXAMPLES
1. Amanda now plays the violin because of a winter concert that she heard when she was in the third grade.

1. complex

2. The concert featured a talented, young violinist from Russia and a famous local pianist.

2. simple

11. Amanda loved the sound of the orchestra at her school's winter concert, and she decided then to study the violin.

12. Amanda's first violin was not the standard size, for she was still quite small.

13. When she started the sixth grade, however, Amanda was playing a full-sized violin.

14. She did not always enjoy the many hours of practice, but they were necessary because playing the instrument is complicated.

15. Amanda knew that playing the proper notes could be especially difficult on a violin.

16. On a keyboard instrument, you simply press a key and hear the note for that key.

17. On a violin, however, the placement of a finger on a string can affect the pitch of a note.

18. If the pitch of each note is not exact, even a common tune can be difficult to recognize.

19. Once a student has mastered finger placement to some extent, he or she still has a great deal to think about; posture, hand position, and bowing technique all require great concentration.

20. When students can actually create music with this stubborn instrument, they have reason to be proud.

What Is a Clause?

4a. A *clause* is a word group that contains a verb and its subject and that is used as a sentence or as part of a sentence.

┌HELP───

A subordinate
clause that is capitalized
and punctuated as a
sentence is a **sentence
fragment.**

Reference Note

For information about
**correcting sentence
fragments,** see page 434.

Although every clause contains a subject and a verb, not every clause expresses a complete thought. Clauses that do are called **independent clauses.** Clauses that do not express a complete thought are called **subordinate clauses.**

INDEPENDENT CLAUSE	The people left the building
SUBORDINATE CLAUSE	when the fire alarm sounded
SENTENCE	When the fire alarm sounded, the people left the building.

The Independent Clause

4b. An *independent* (or *main*) *clause* expresses a complete thought and can stand by itself as a sentence.

In the following examples, each boldface clause has its own subject and verb and expresses a complete thought.

EXAMPLES   **Ms. Santana works in a law office in downtown Concord.**

Ms. Santana works in a law office that has a view of downtown Concord.

Ms. Santana works in a law office in downtown Concord, and **she has a successful practice.**

Reference Note

For a list of **coordinating
conjunctions,** see page
32. For more about using
semicolons and **con-
junctive adverbs** to join
independent clauses, see
page 298.

In the last example, the independent clauses are joined by a comma and the coordinating conjunction *and.* The clauses also could be written with a semicolon between them:

> Ms. Santana works in a law office in downtown Concord; she has a successful practice.

or with a semicolon, a conjunctive adverb, and a comma:

> Ms. Santana works in a law office in downtown Concord; **indeed,** she has a successful practice.

or as separate sentences:

> Ms. Santana works in a law office in downtown Concord. She has a successful practice.

The Subordinate Clause

4c. A *subordinate* (or *dependent*) *clause* does not express a complete thought and cannot stand by itself as a sentence.

Words such as *when, whom, because, which, that, if,* and *until* signal that the clauses following them are likely to be subordinate. *Subordinate* means "lesser in rank or importance." To make a complete sentence, a subordinate clause must be joined to an independent clause. Like phrases, subordinate clauses can be used as adjectives, adverbs, or nouns.

SUBORDINATE   when you arrive at the airport in Dallas
CLAUSES   which grow only locally
    that he had granted us an interview

SENTENCES   **When you arrive at the airport in Dallas,** call us.
    These wildflowers, **which grow only locally,** are of interest to scientists.
    Did you know **that he had granted us an interview**?

As the preceding examples show, subordinate clauses may appear at the beginning, in the middle, or at the end of a sentence. The placement of a subordinate clause depends on how the clause is used in the sentence.

NOTE Many subordinate clauses contain complements (such as predicate nominatives, predicate adjectives, direct objects, or indirect objects), modifiers, or both.

EXAMPLES   **what** it is . . . [*What* is a predicate nominative: It is *what*?]

because you look **tired** . . . [*Tired* is a predicate adjective modifying *you.*]

that you chose . . . [*That* is the direct object of *chose.*]

before he gave **us** the **quiz** . . . [*Us* is the indirect object of *gave; quiz* is the direct object of *gave.*]

that I bought **yesterday** . . . [*Yesterday* is an adverb modifying *bought.*]

when the coach was calling **to her** . . . [*To her* is an adverb phrase modifying *was calling.*]

Reference Note

For more about **sentence complements,** see page 55. For more information on **modifiers,** see Chapter 8.

┌HELP─

Although short, simple sentences can be effective, a variety of sentence structures is usually more effective. To make choppy sentences into smoother writing, combine shorter sentences by changing some into subordinate clauses. Also, avoid unnecessary repetition of subjects, verbs, and pronouns.

CHOPPY
I enjoy feta cheese. It comes from Greece. It is traditionally made from sheep's or goat's milk.

SMOOTH
I enjoy feta cheese, which comes from Greece and is traditionally made from sheep's or goat's milk.

In the example above, two of the short sentences are combined into a single subordinate clause.

Exercise 1 Identifying Independent and Subordinate Clauses

For each of the following sentences, identify the clause in italics as *independent* or *subordinate*.

EXAMPLE 1. *When you think of baseball,* you may think of lightning-fast pitches, bat-splitting home runs, or secret hand signals from coaches and catchers.

1. subordinate

1. *Baseball is a game* that generally depends on good eyesight as well as athletic skill.
2. For this reason, until recently, playing the great American game has been something *that people with visual impairments found virtually impossible.*
3. Only sighted players could participate *until an engineer named Charley Fairbanks invented beep baseball.*
4. *In this version of baseball, the ball beeps and the bases buzz* so that players like the one pictured here can tell when to swing and where to run.
5. Each team has a sighted pitcher and a sighted catcher, *who never get a turn at bat,* and six fielders who wear blindfolds so that they don't have a visual advantage.
6. The pitcher shouts "Ready!" *before the ball is pitched* and "Pitch!" when the ball is released.

7. When the bat strikes the ball, the umpire activates the buzzer in first base, *to which the batter must then run.*
8. When a team is on defense, the pitcher and catcher cannot field the batted ball themselves; *they can only shout directions to the fielders.*
9. *Beep baseball is fun to play,* and its challenges create a bond between sighted players and players with visual impairments.
10. Sighted players *who put on blindfolds and join in* come away from a game with a new respect for the abilities of their visually impaired teammates.

The Adjective Clause

4d. An *adjective clause* is a subordinate clause that modifies a noun or a pronoun.

An adjective clause usually follows the word or words it modifies and tells *what kind* or *which one*. An *essential* (or *restrictive*) clause is necessary to the basic meaning of the sentence; it is not set off by commas. A *nonessential* (or *nonrestrictive*) clause gives only additional information and is not necessary to the meaning of a sentence; it is set off by commas.

EXAMPLES This is the new music video **that I like best.** [The clause *that I like best* is necessary to tell which video is being mentioned. Because this information is essential to the meaning of the sentence, it is not set off by commas.]

     Griffins, **which are mythological beasts,** are included on many coats of arms. [The clause *which are mythological beasts* is not necessary to identify *Griffins*. Because this information is nonessential to the meaning of the sentence, it is set off by commas.]

Relative Pronouns

Adjective clauses are often introduced by relative pronouns.

Common Relative Pronouns	who, whom, whose, which, that

  These words are called *relative pronouns* because they *relate* an adjective clause to the word that the clause modifies. Besides introducing an adjective clause and relating it to another word in the sentence, the relative pronoun has a grammatical function within the adjective clause.

EXAMPLES Luís, **who enjoys running,** has decided to enter the marathon. [The relative pronoun *who* relates the adjective clause to *Luís*. *Who* also functions as the subject of the adjective clause.]

     The students questioned the data **on which the theory was based.** [The relative pronoun *which* relates the adjective clause to *data* and functions as the object of the preposition *on*.]

     We met the singer **whose new CD was released this week.** [The relative pronoun *whose* relates the adjective clause to *singer*. *Whose* functions as a possessive pronoun in the adjective clause.]

Reference Note

For help in deciding whether a clause is **essential or nonessential,** see page 276.

Reference Note

For more information on **using *who* and *whom*** correctly, see page 187. For more about **using *that* and *which*** correctly, see page 235.

GRAMMAR

4
d

Janice, **whom I have known for years,** is my lab partner this semester. [The relative pronoun *whom* relates the adjective clause to *Janice. Whom* functions as the direct object of the verb phrase *have known* in the adjective clause.]

In many cases, the relative pronoun in the clause may be omitted. The pronoun is understood and still has a function in the clause.

EXAMPLES   Here is the salad **you ordered.** [The relative pronoun *that* is understood. The pronoun relates the adjective clause to *salad* and functions as the direct object of the verb *ordered* in the adjective clause.]

He is the one **I met yesterday.** [The relative pronoun *whom* or *that* is understood. The pronoun relates the adjective clause to *one* and functions as the direct object of the verb *met* in the adjective clause.]

Occasionally an adjective clause is introduced by the word *where* or *when.* When used in such a way, these words are called ***relative adverbs.***

EXAMPLES   They showed us the stadium **where the game would be held.**

Saturday is the day **when I mow the lawn.**

Exercise 2 Identifying Adjective Clauses

Each of the following sentences contains an adjective clause. Write the adjective clause, and underline the relative pronoun or relative adverb that introduces it. If the relative pronoun has been omitted, write it in parentheses and then underline it.

EXAMPLE   **1.** Do you know anyone who is familiar with briffits, swalloops, and waftaroms?

    1. <u>who</u> is familiar with briffits, swalloops, and waftaroms

1. Cartoonists use a variety of unusual names for the symbols that commonly appear in comic strips.
2. For example, a *briffit* is the little puff of dust hanging in the spot where a swiftly departing character was previously standing.
3. For times when cartoonists want to make something appear hot or smelly, they use wavy, rising lines called *waftaroms.*
4. *Agitrons* are the wiggly lines around an object that is supposed to be shaking.

5. The limbs of a character who is moving are usually preceded or trailed by a set of curved lines called *blurgits* or *swalloops.*

6. *Plewds,* which look like flying droplets of sweat, are drawn around the head of a worried character.

7. In fact, there are very few motions or emotions for which cartoonists have not invented a clever, expressive symbol.

8. Almost everyone who likes to doodle and draw has used some of these symbols, probably without knowing the names for them.

9. Look at the example cartoon, where you will find the names of other common symbols from the world of cartooning.

10. Now you know a "language" almost nobody outside the cartooning profession knows!

Exercise 3 **Revising Sentences by Supplying Adjective Clauses**

Revise the following sentences by substituting an adjective clause for each italicized adjective. Add specific details to make your sentences interesting. Underline the adjective clauses in your sentences.

EXAMPLE   1. The *angry* citizens gathered in front of City Hall.

1. The citizens, <u>who were furious over the recent tax increase</u>, gathered in front of City Hall.

1. As I entered the building, a *colorful* painting caught my eye.
2. The *patient* photographer sat on a small ledge all day.
3. The two attorneys argued all week over the *important* contract.
4. The team of mountain climbers decided to try to reach the top of the *tallest* peak.
5. At the assembly, Ms. León made two *surprising* announcements.
6. Saburo and his friends cautiously entered the *dark* cave.
7. Edna Jackson easily won her *first* political campaign.

8. The trainer spoke harshly to the *disobedient* dog.
9. Dodging to his left and then to his right, Manuel scored the *winning* goal.
10. The veterinarian told Pamela that he was taking good care of her *lame* horse.

The Adverb Clause

4e. An *adverb clause* is a subordinate clause that modifies a verb, an adjective, or an adverb.

An adverb clause generally tells *how, when, where, why, how much, to what extent,* or *under what condition* the action of a verb takes place.

EXAMPLES **After I had proofread my paper,** I input the corrections. [The adverb clause *After I had proofread my paper* tells *when* I input the corrections.]

Because crêpes are delicious, Joy makes them on special occasions. [*Because crêpes are delicious* tells *why* Joy makes them on special occasions.]

You and your brother may come with us **if you want to.** [*If you want to* tells *under what condition* you and your brother may come with us.]

NOTE As you can see in the first two examples above, introductory adverb clauses are usually set off by commas.

Reference Note

For more about using **commas** to set off introductory elements, see page 280.

Like adverbs, adverb clauses may also modify adjectives or adverbs.

EXAMPLES Have computers made office work easier **than it was before**? [The adverb clause *than it was before* modifies the adjective *easier,* telling *to what extent* work is easier.]

My cousin Adele reads faster **than I do.** [The adverb clause *than I do* modifies the adverb *faster,* telling *how much* faster my cousin Adele reads.]

NOTE When using adverb clauses to make comparisons, be sure your comparisons are complete.

Reference Note

For more about **complete comparisons,** see page 211.

INCOMPLETE I like dancing better than you. [Do I like dancing better than I like you? Do I like dancing better than you like dancing?]

COMPLETE I like dancing better **than you do.**

Subordinating Conjunctions

Adverb clauses are introduced by **subordinating conjunctions**—words that show the relationship between the adverb clause and the word or words that the clause modifies.

Common Subordinating Conjunctions			
after	because	since	when
although	before	so that	whenever
as	even though	than	where
as if	if	though	wherever
as long as	in order that	unless	whether
as soon as	once	until	while

Some subordinating conjunctions, such as *after*, *before*, *since*, and *until*, may also be used as prepositions.

EXAMPLES   Be sure to hand in your report **before the end** of class today. [prepositional phrase]

Be sure to hand in your report **before class ends today.** [adverb clause]

Exercise 4 Identifying and Classifying Adverb Clauses

Identify each adverb clause in the following sentences. Then, write what the clause tells: *when, where, how, why, to what extent,* or *under what condition.* A sentence may have more than one adverb clause.

EXAMPLE   1. When you see the humble man on the next page, can you believe that he is considered one of the twentieth century's greatest leaders?

1. *When you see the humble man on the next page—when*

1. If you look through newspapers from the first half of the twentieth century, you will see many pictures of Mohandas K. Gandhi.
2. This man led India to independence from Britain, and he took his spinning wheel wherever he went.
3. He did so because he viewed spinning as a symbol of the peaceful, traditional Indian lifestyle.
4. He also hoped to encourage the Indian people to make their own clothes so that they would not have to depend on British industry.
5. As a form of protest, he led marches or fasted until the government met his requests.

STYLE   TIP

Because an adverb clause does not have a fixed location in a sentence, you must choose where to put the clause. Write different versions of a sentence containing an adverb clause. Then, read aloud each version to see how the placement of the clause affects flow, rhythm, and overall meaning.

EXAMPLES
After we leave for school, Mom works on her novel.

Mom works on her novel after we leave for school.

COMPUTER TIP

If you use a computer to write compositions, you can easily experiment with the placement of adverb clauses in sentences.

6. Gandhi's nonviolent methods were more powerful than anyone could have predicted.
7. As India's Congress and people increasingly supported Gandhi's nonviolent program, the British government was forced to listen.
8. Gandhi was well qualified to represent India as a diplomat since he had studied law in London before he became involved in India's freedom movement.
9. After independence was assured, Gandhi turned his attention to helping India's many poor people.
10. Because he was loved throughout India and the world, Gandhi was called *Mahatma,* meaning "Great Soul."

The Noun Clause

4f. A *noun clause* is a subordinate clause that is used as a noun.

A noun clause may be used as a subject, as a complement (such as a predicate nominative, direct object, or indirect object), or as the object of a preposition.

Reference Note

For more information on **subjects, predicate nominatives, direct objects,** and **indirect objects,** see Chapter 2. For more about **objects of prepositions,** see page 70.

SUBJECT	**What Mary Anne did to rescue the injured bird** was brave.
PREDICATE NOMINATIVE	The winner of the race will be **whoever runs fastest in the final stretch.**
DIRECT OBJECT	She finally discovered **what the answer to her question was.**
INDIRECT OBJECT	Give **whatever parts need cleaning** a rinse in detergent.
OBJECT OF PREPOSITION	He checks the ID cards of **whoever visits.**

Noun clauses are usually introduced by the following words.

that	when	whether	whom
what	whenever	who	whomever
whatever	where	whoever	why

Sometimes these words have a grammatical function in the noun clause. Other times they just introduce the clause and have no other function in it.

EXAMPLES   They did not know **who it could be.** [The introductory word *who* is the predicate nominative of the noun clause—*it could be who.* The entire clause is the direct object of the verb *did know.*]

Show us **what you bought.** [The introductory word *what* is the direct object in the noun clause—*you bought what.* The entire clause is the direct object of the verb *show.*]

What you learn is your decision. [The introductory word *what* is the direct object in the noun clause—*you learn what.* The entire clause is the subject of the verb *is.*]

She wished **that she were older.** [The introductory word *that* simply introduces the noun clause and has no function within the noun clause. The entire clause is the direct object of the verb *wished.*]

Sometimes the word that introduces a noun clause is omitted. In such cases, the introductory word is understood.

EXAMPLE   Didn't you know **the party was canceled?** [The introductory word *that* is understood.]

Exercise 5   Identifying and Classifying Noun Clauses

Most of the following sentences contain noun clauses. If a sentence contains a noun clause, identify that clause. Then, tell how the clause is used: as a *subject,* a *predicate nominative,* a *direct object,* an *indirect object,* or an *object of a preposition.* If a sentence does not contain a noun clause, write *no noun clause.*

EXAMPLE   **1.** We moved to Massachusetts and did not know what we would find there.

    1.   *what we would find there—direct object*

1. What surprised me first was the yellowish green fire engine.
2. I had thought fire engines were always red.
3. Our neighbors explained that this color keeps the fire engines from being confused with other large red trucks.
4. My sister Michelle made another discovery at the bowling alley.
5. The small grapefruit-sized bowling balls with no holes were not what she was used to!
6. We learned that this sport is called candlepin bowling.

7. Whoever can knock down the pins with one of those bowling balls must be an expert.
8. Later, I was surprised by how delicious the baked beans were.
9. Someone should give whoever invented Boston baked beans an award for this marvelous creation.
10. Now, after we have lived in New England for a year, both Michelle and I are happy in our new home.

Review A   Identifying Subordinate Clauses

For most of the sentences in the following paragraph, identify the subordinate clause or clauses. Then, tell whether each clause is an *adjective clause,* an *adverb clause,* or a *noun clause.* If a sentence has no subordinate clauses, write *none.*

EXAMPLE **[1]** In paintings created before 1880, horses are usually shown in poses that now look quaint and unnatural.

1. *that now look quaint and unnatural—adjective clause*

[1] If you stop to think about it, you can see why painters had a problem. [2] Stop-action photography had not yet been invented, and when painters looked at rapidly moving horses, they could not possibly see where the legs and hooves were at any one instant. [3] Whenever painters wanted to portray a galloping horse, they made up a position they thought suggested speed. [4] The horses in some paintings had both front legs extended far to the front and both hind legs stretched far behind. [5] Today, we know that this is an impossible position for a horse. [6] Stop-action photography was first used in the 1870s by a Californian named Eadweard Muybridge, who took this series of photographs of a galloping horse. [7] Along a racetrack, he set up many cameras whose shutters were controlled by threads stretched across the track. [8] As the horse ran by, it broke the threads and tripped the cameras' shutters one after the other. [9] Painters of the time thought this new technology was truly amazing! [10] They were the first artists in history to know what a horse really looked like at each point in its stride.

Sentences Classified According to Structure

Sentences may be classified according to purpose as declarative, imperative, interrogative, or exclamatory. Sentences may also be classified according to structure. The term *structure* refers to the number and types of clauses in a sentence.

4g. Depending on its structure, a sentence can be classified as simple, compound, complex, or compound-complex.

In the following examples, independent clauses are underlined once. Subordinate clauses are underlined twice.

(1) A *simple sentence* contains one independent clause and no subordinate clauses. It may have a compound subject, a compound verb, and any number of phrases.

EXAMPLES

        S   V

The boys wanted to take a vacation last summer.

      S   S   V   V

Ray and Joe worked and saved enough for a trip to Ohio.

(2) A *compound sentence* contains two or more independent clauses and no subordinate clauses.

The independent clauses in a compound sentence may be joined by a comma and a coordinating conjunction; by a semicolon; or by a semicolon, a conjunctive adverb, and a comma.

EXAMPLES

           S   V

Originally, they wanted to ride bikes all the way**, but**

  S   V

they decided to take the train instead.

  S   V   S   V

Ray looked forward to seeing his cousins; Joe was eager to play with his uncle's band.

      S   V

Uncle James played in a country-music band; **however,**

  S   V

Joe preferred rock music.

Reference Note

For more on **classifying sentences by purpose,** see page 63.

STYLE   **TIP**

Paragraphs in which all the sentences have the same structure can be monotonous to read. To keep your readers interested in your ideas, evaluate your writing to see whether you've used a variety of sentence structures. Then, use revising techniques—adding, cutting, replacing, and reordering—to enliven your writing by varying the structure of your sentences.

NOTE Don't confuse a simple sentence that contains a compound predicate with a compound sentence. Compound sentences always have two or more complete clauses.

                          S   V   V

COMPOUND   **Joe considered** country music corny and **said** so.
  PREDICATE

                          S   V   S V

COMPOUND   **Joe considered** country music corny, and **he said** so.
  SENTENCE

COMPUTER TIP

A word processor can help you check for varied sentence structure in your writing. Make a copy of your document to work on. By inserting a return or a page break after every period, you can view the sentences in a vertical list and compare the structures of all the sentences in a particular paragraph. Make any revisions on the properly formatted copy of your document.

(3) A *complex sentence* contains one independent clause and at least one subordinate clause.

                                S V

EXAMPLES   Because Joe wanted to keep his guitar with him,

                     S   V

                     they decided against taking a plane.

                     S   V   S   V

                     If they took a train, they could see all the sights, too.

(4) A *compound-complex sentence* contains two or more independent clauses and at least one subordinate clause.

                     S   V   S   V

EXAMPLES   The band played at a dance, and Ray was pulled into a line

                     S   V

                     dance that was starting.

                                S   V

                     To his surprise, he was good at line dancing; afterward,

                   S   V   S   V

                     he joined in whenever he got the chance.

Exercise 6 **Classifying Sentences According to Structure**

Classify each of the following sentences as *simple*, *compound*, *complex*, or *compound-complex*. Be sure that you can identify all subordinate and independent clauses.

EXAMPLE   1. The Iroquois are American Indian peoples originally
              from New York State.

    1. *simple*

1. Members of the Iroquois—which include the Mohawk, Oneida, Onondaga, Cayuga, Tuscarora, and Seneca—have an ancient history of storytelling.
2. In the early days, professional storytellers went from house to house, and they were paid for their storytelling with small gifts.
3. Most of what is known today about Iroquois folk tales comes from the Senecas, whose stories have been written down by historians.
4. Some of the most popular stories are about a creature who is hairless except for one strip of fur down his back.
5. He is so huge that his back can be seen above the trees.
6. He eats people; because he cannot be killed in any ordinary way, he is especially frightening.
7. The tales about this creature are even more frightening than are the ones about Stone Coat, who has skin like stone.
8. Fortunately, Stone Coat is not very smart, and many of the folk tales tell of ways that the Iroquois outsmart him.
9. There are also tales about the Whirlwinds, who usually appear as bodiless heads with fiery eyes; in some stories, the Whirlwinds eat sticks and rocks when they cannot catch people.
10. Other Iroquois stories tell about the adventures of Elk, Partridge, Skunk, and Rattlesnake.

Oral Practice   **Classifying Sentences According to Structure**

Read each of the following sentences aloud, and classify it as *simple, compound, complex,* or *compound-complex.*

EXAMPLE   1. In Norway, there is an art museum for
              children's art.

    1. *complex*

1. This museum is the International Museum of Children's Art, which occupies a big, old house in Oslo.
2. The walls are covered from top to bottom with brilliantly colored creations by young artists up to age seventeen.

3. Many of the 100,000 works, which come from 150 countries, deal with objects from nature, but a few, like the bicycle sculpture on the previous page, focus on manufactured objects.
4. Of course, a few of the paintings depict troubles or problems, but most of the works express happiness and energy.
5. Rafael Goldin, the museum's director, says a child's first meeting with exhibited art is very important.
6. Children visit the museum, and they "see that a museum can mean joy and color."
7. "If their first visit is to a boring, dusty museum, children will always associate museums with *dusty* and *boring*."
8. Mr. Goldin has even hung some of the paintings at toddlers' eye level to encourage each young visitor's own personal relationship with art.
9. Young visitors are very excited when they learn that all the artwork was created by children, and they are often inspired to start painting.
10. Wouldn't it be great if there were a museum like that here?

Review B Identifying and Classifying Subordinate Clauses

Identify the subordinate clause or clauses in each of the following sentences. Tell whether each clause is used as an *adjective*, an *adverb*, or a *noun*. If a clause is used as an adjective or an adverb, write the word or words the clause modifies. If a clause is used as a noun, write *subj.* for subject, *d.o.* for direct object, *i.o.* for indirect object, *p.n.* for predicate nominative, or *o.p.* for object of a preposition.

EXAMPLES
1. When our science teacher described insect-eating plants, we listened with amazement.
1. *When our science teacher described insect-eating plants—adverb—listened*

2. What we heard sounded like science fiction.
2. *What we heard—noun—subj.*

1. Plants that eat insects usually live in swampy areas.
2. Because the soil in these regions lacks nutrients, these plants do not get enough nitrogen through their roots.
3. The nitrogen that these plants need comes from the protein in the bodies of insects.
4. How these plants catch their food is interesting.
5. A pitcher plant's sweet scent appeals to whatever insect is nearby.

6. The insect thinks that it will find food inside the plant.
7. What happens instead is that the insect drowns in the plant's digestive juices.
8. The Venus' flytrap shown on the preceding page has what looks like small bear traps at the ends of its stalks.
9. When a trap is open, an insect can wander in and spring the trap.
10. The insect is then digested by the plant in a process that can take several days.

Review C Classifying Subordinate Clauses

Classify each of the following italicized clauses as an *adjective*, an *adverb*, or a *noun clause*. Be prepared to explain your answers.

EXAMPLES [1] *Until our class visited the county courthouse,* we had imagined [2] *that most court cases were like the ones on TV.*

1. *adverb*
2. *noun*

[1] *As we left the courtroom,* we thought about the men [2] *who had been on trial.* [3] *Although they had not committed a serious crime,* they had broken the law. The law says [4] *that removing sand from our local beach is illegal.* A police officer caught the men [5] *when they could not move their truck,* [6] *which had become stuck in the sand.* [7] *After the judge had read the law to them,* the men claimed [8] *that they had never heard of that law.* The judge, who reminded them [9] *that ignorance of the law is no excuse,* fined each man one hundred dollars. The men promised [10] *that they would not take any more beach sand.*

HELP

In the examples in Review C, the first italicized clause is an adverb clause that modifies the verb phrase *had imagined.* The second italicized clause is a noun clause that acts as a direct object of the verb phrase *had imagined.*

Review D Rewriting a Paragraph to Include a Variety of Sentence Structures

You and a partner are working together on an essay about life in the 1800s. While researching the topic, the two of you discover a diary written by a young woman named Barbara Sneyd. You and your partner have made copies of Sneyd's paintings and have recorded information about her life. Your job is to rewrite the paragraph on the next page to improve its style. You will need to vary the sentence structure, and you may want to add or delete details to improve the organization. Write at least one sentence with each kind of structure: *simple, compound, complex,* and *compound-complex.* Be prepared to identify the structure of each sentence you write.

Barbara Sneyd lived more than one hundred years ago. Her home was in the English countryside. She came from a wealthy family. Her family loved to ride and hunt. Barbara had a governess. The governess kept Barbara very busy studying. Barbara did have time to pursue her greatest passion. Her greatest passion was riding. Her mother encouraged her to keep a diary. The diary would be about Barbara's life. Barbara started the diary. She was fourteen. It took the form of a sketchbook. In it she recorded her family's life. She painted many small pictures of her family's activities. They went fishing, visiting, and picnicking. Barbara was also a keen observer of nature. She drew and painted her family's horses and pets and the flowers from the garden. She painted many small landscapes. The landscapes showed the countryside around her home. Above all, her diary is full of paintings of horses. She loved horses. You may want to see what her paintings look like. Some pictures from her diary are shown on this page.

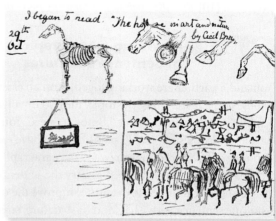

Chapter Review

A. Identifying Clauses

Identify each italicized clause in the following sentences as *independent* or *subordinate.*

1. The fire started *because someone did not smother a campfire.*
2. The family *that bought our house* is moving in next week.
3. Did you know *that Dr. Joel is the new ambassador to Lebanon?*
4. Mr. Kim will buy the store *if the bank lends him the money.*
5. According to Ms. Garza, our math teacher, *the binary system is important to know.*
6. *Wherever Maggie goes,* her poodle Jack follows.
7. *She won the golf match* because she had practiced diligently.
8. *Whatever you decide* is fine with me.
9. *I saw the job advertised in the school paper* and decided to apply for it.
10. We were proud *that you conceded defeat so graciously.*

B. Identifying and Classifying Subordinate Clauses

Identify the subordinate clause in each of the following sentences. Tell whether each clause is used as an *adjective,* an *adverb,* or a *noun.*

11. Emily Dickinson, who was born in 1830 in Amherst, Massachusetts, was a great American poet.
12. She appeared to lead a fairly normal life until she became a recluse in her family's home.
13. There she wrote poems that literary critics now call "great American poetry."
14. Unfortunately, only a few of Dickinson's poems were published while she was alive.
15. After she died in 1886, her other poems were published.
16. I think everyone should read at least some of Dickinson's poetry.
17. Dickinson is a poet whose work I now read often.
18. The poems I have just finished reading are "A Narrow Fellow in the Grass" and "Apparently with No Surprise."

19. The rhythms of Dickinson's poems are best appreciated when you read the poems aloud.

20. Whatever I read by Emily Dickinson surprises and inspires me.

C. Classifying Sentences According to Structure and Identifying Independent and Subordinate Clauses

Classify each of the following sentences as *simple, compound, complex,* or *compound-complex.* Identify all subordinate and independent clauses.

21. After eating and drinking, the elephants galloped through the wheat field.

22. Mr. Chisholm wanted to go bowling, but Mrs. Chisholm preferred the dinner theater.

23. Ten steps up the dark staircase, the twins lost their nerve; dinner at home suddenly seemed much more appealing.

24. Kenzuo insisted that the bullet train was the best way to get to Osaka after midnight.

25. When the travelers arrived at the inn, the innkeeper greeted them.

26. Dr. Bourgeois knew that singing loudly would only irritate others, so he decided to keep his high spirits to himself.

27. Preparing to eat, the dog spotted itself in the mirror.

28. Mom always wanted to live in New Mexico, but Dad was too used to living in North Carolina to move.

29. Before the concert began, the first violinist leaned forward to tie his shoe; this innocent action set off a whole chain of unlikely events.

30. Tom Bell is Angela's favorite actor, but Sally likes Ricky Blake.

31. Washing the car, Benito paused to admire the vintage biplane flying overhead.

32. Joseph had worked hard for straight A's on his exams, and when the results came in, he discovered that his hard work had paid off.

33. When the crocodile approached, the heron flew away.

34. Arnie carefully lined up the pieces on the chessboard; however, Dario's foot caught the edge of the board, and both board and pieces flew into the air.

35. We had hoped that being subtle would be enough, and, indeed, for a while this tactic seemed to be working; but as the day wore on, we slowly realized that a bolder approach was needed.

36. President Kennedy was assassinated in Dallas on November 22, 1963.

37. Charles argued that a picnic lunch was the best idea.

38. Professor Chan showed his class his slides of the Great Wall of China, and he used the slides later as the basis for a lecture on Genghis Khan.

39. After the cyclists rounded the bend, the Swiss champion Michel Neibergall took the lead.

40. When the crows descended on the barren field, the field mice scurried for shelter.

Writing Application

Using Sentence Variety in Postcards

Sentence Structures   You are writing postcards about your summer activities, such as baseball or soccer camp, computer camp, or cheerleading camp. Write a brief note telling your six-year-old cousin about a few experiences that you think he or she would find interesting. Write another note to an adult friend or relative about your experiences. Use sentence structure and language that are appropriate to each reader.

Prewriting   If you have been to a summer camp, make a list of experiences that you could describe. If you haven't been to camp, list activities that you enjoy during the summer.

Writing   As you write your first draft, make sure to include details that would interest your different audiences. Show the relationships between your details by using a variety of subordinate adjective, adverb, and noun clauses.

Revising   Read your notes to a classmate, without telling which note is to your cousin and which is to your adult friend or relative. If your classmate can't tell which note is to which person, you should revise your language, information, and sentence structures.

Publishing   Check to be sure that all your sentences are complete sentences. Pay special attention to the use of commas to separate clauses. You may want to post your notes on a class bulletin board or create a Web page for them.

Reference Note
For more about using **commas,** see page 271.

Agreement
Subject and Verb, Pronoun and Antecedent

Diagnostic Preview

A. Proofreading Sentences for Subject-Verb and Pronoun-Antecedent Agreement

Each of the following sentences contains an error in agreement. Identify each incorrect verb or pronoun, and supply the correct form.

EXAMPLE　**1.** Rochelle Richardson, one of our city's former mayors, live next door to me.

　　　1. live—lives

1. When the truck overturned, a herd of cattle were set free on the expressway.
2. The teacher reminded everyone to sharpen their pencil.
3. Not one of our tomato plants are producing any fruit, but the green beans seem to be thriving.
4. Has each of the girls memorized their part?
5. Everybody have been talking about the class picnic ever since you thought of the idea.
6. Both of the finalists played his or her best.
7. Many of their experiments have failed, but neither Dr. Jenkins nor his assistants ever gives up hope.
8. There is a brush, a comb, and a mirror on the dresser top.
9. Many a sailor have perished when his or her ship ran aground on that reef.
10. Read *Little Women* and write a plot summary about them.

B. Proofreading Sentences for Subject-Verb and Pronoun-Antecedent Agreement

Most of the following sentences contain at least one agreement error. For each error, identify the incorrect verb or pronoun and supply the correct form. If the sentence is already correct, write *C*.

EXAMPLE 1. Filming an animal in its natural surroundings present many problems.

1. *present—presents*

11. One problem is that the filmmaker, in most cases, have to get quite close to the animal.
12. Ten yards often make the difference between a good scene and no scene at all.
13. A zoom lens or a telephoto lens are generally used, but even then, getting good photographs can be very difficult.
14. Before filming, the crew usually take turns watching the animal for weeks to learn its habits and find good vantage points for taking pictures.
15. In addition, the filmmaker and the crew uses every trick of the trade in filming wild animals.
16. For example, *Foxes at Night* were almost certainly not filmed at night!
17. "Nighttime" films are generally made during daylight hours, when there is plenty of natural light.
18. Later, all of the daytime footage are darkened through the use of filters.
19. Also, many of the animals used in a nature film has been trained or partially tamed.
20. For example, if a filmmaker or a member of the crew take care of a bird from the moment it hatches, it will instinctively follow them.
21. The photographer can then easily take close-up pictures of the bird after it matures.
22. In many films, scenes of animals giving birth and raising its young are filmed in a studio, not in the wild.
23. Photographers get good footage by building a den where he or she can film the baby animals through a window beside the nest.
24. This film, along with footage taken in the natural habitat, are then skillfully edited.
25. As a result, few of the viewers ever suspect that the film shown to him or her has been shot indoors.

Number

Number is the form a word takes to indicate whether the word is singular or plural.

5a. A word that refers to one person, place, thing, or idea is *singular* in number. A word that refers to more than one is *plural* in number.

Singular	Plural
student	students
princess	princesses
child	children
tooth	teeth
it	they
himself	themselves
berry	berries
deer	deer

Exercise 1 Classifying Nouns and Pronouns by Number

Identify each italicized word as either *singular* or *plural*.

EXAMPLE   As a child, the girl in the [1] *photograph* was sure she was not very good at anything.

1. singular

She was overshadowed by the other [1] *children* in her family, especially by her older sister Madge, who wrote [2] *stories* and plays. Lonely and full of self-doubt, the girl surrounded herself with imaginary [3] *companions*. [4] *Everything* changed, though, when she caught influenza and became restless during her recovery. Her mother brought her a [5] *notebook* and suggested that, like Madge, she might write a story. After practicing on short stories, she decided to tackle a detective [6] *novel*. [7] *"They* are very difficult to do," said Madge. "I don't think you could write one." Madge was wrong: The young author was Agatha Christie, who became the most successful mystery [8] *writer* in history. Her mystery novels and story collections have sold many millions of copies in [9] *English* and in at least sixty other [10] *languages*.

Agreement of Subject and Verb

5b. A verb should agree in number with its subject.

(1) Singular subjects take singular verbs.

EXAMPLES   **He washes** the dishes. [The singular verb *washes* agrees with the singular subject *He.*]

A **girl** in my neighborhood **plays** in the band. [The singular subject *girl* takes the singular verb *plays.*]

(2) Plural subjects take plural verbs.

EXAMPLES   **They wash** the dishes.

Several **girls** in my neighborhood **play** in the band.

   In the examples above, the verbs agree in number with their subjects. Like the single-word verbs above, verb phrases also agree with their subjects. However, in a verb phrase, only the first helping (auxiliary) verb changes its form to agree with a singular or plural subject.

EXAMPLES   **He has been washing** the dishes.

They have been washing the dishes.

A **girl** in my neighborhood **was playing** in the band.

Several **girls** in my neighborhood **were playing** in the band.

> NOTE   Generally, nouns ending in *–s* are plural (*friends, girls*), but verbs ending in *–s* are generally singular (*sees, hears*).

5c. The number of the subject usually is not determined by a word in a phrase or clause following the subject.

EXAMPLES   The apartments **across the street** do not have balconies. [*Do have* agrees with *apartments*, not *street*.]

The planes **pulling up to the gate** were purchased by a movie company. [*Were purchased* agrees with *planes*, not *gate*.]

Eli, **one of my friends**, was late. [*Was* agrees with *Eli*, not *friends*.]

The movie **that I saw two weeks ago** was reviewed in today's paper. [*Was reviewed* agrees with *movie*, not *weeks*.]

USAGE

Reference Note

For more about **helping verbs,** see page 14.

Reference Note

For guidelines on **forming plurals of nouns,** see page 367.

Reference Note

For more about **phrases,** see Chapter 3. For more about **clauses,** see Chapter 4. For examples of **subjects whose number is determined by a phrase following the subject,** see page 124.

NOTE   *As well as, along with, together with,* and *in addition to* are compound prepositions. Words in phrases beginning with compound prepositions do not affect the number of the subject or verb.

EXAMPLE   **Anne,** together with her cousins, **is** backpacking in Nevada.

Exercise 2   Identifying Verbs That Agree in Number with Their Subjects

For each of the following sentences, choose the verb in parentheses that agrees with the subject.

EXAMPLE   **1.** Did you know that people in Japan frequently (*eat, eats*) noodles?

1. *eat*

1. These pictures (*show, shows*) how noodles are prepared.
2. First, the noodle maker (*roll, rolls*) out the dough as thin as possible.
  3. Then, the cook (*slice, slices*) the folded layers.
  4. Next, the strands of noodles (*is, are*) separated and dusted with flour to prevent sticking.
  5. After the noodles have dried a little, they (*go, goes*) into boiling water or broth to cook.
  6. The Japanese (*enjoy, enjoys*) noodles made from either wheat flour, called *udon,* or buckwheat flour, called *soba.*
  7. A dish of cooked noodles mixed with sauce, broth, fish, or vegetables (*makes, make*) a popular lunch.
  8. Noodle shops all over Japan (*serves, serve*) a variety of noodle dishes.
  9. These shops often (*resemble, resembles*) fast-food restaurants in the United States.
  10. For lunch or a snack, customers at a noodle shop (*order, orders*) noodles with their favorite toppings.

USAGE

Exercise 3 Identifying Subjects and Verbs
That Agree in Number

Identify the subject of each verb in parentheses in the following paragraph. Then, choose the form of the verb that agrees with the subject.

EXAMPLE   Units of measure sometimes **[1]** (*causes, cause*) confusion.

     1. *Units—cause*

Confusion among shoppers **[1]** (*is, are*) understandable because
the traditional system for indicating quantities **[2]** (*makes, make*)
shopping a guessing game. For example, the quantity printed on
yogurt containers **[3]** (*is, are*) the number of ounces in a container. A
shopper on the lookout for bargains **[4]** (*does, do*) not know whether
liquid or solid measure is indicated. In addition, different brands of
juice **[5]** (*shows, show*) the same quantity in different ways. A can
labeled "twenty-four ounces" **[6]** (*contains, contain*) the same quantity
as a can labeled "one pint eight ounces." Shoppers' confusion over such
labeling, along with rising prices, **[7]** (*is, are*) a matter of concern to
consumer groups. These groups believe that the metric system, in use
in European countries, **[8]** (*clears, clear*) up most of the confusion. The
units in the metric system **[9]** (*has, have*) fixed relationships to one
another. As a result, consumer groups in this country **[10]** (*continues,
continue*) to advocate our adopting this system of measurement.

Exercise 4 Choosing Verbs with the Correct Number

Each of the following sentences contains an italicized pair of verbs in
parentheses. From each pair, choose the form of the verb that agrees
with its subject.

EXAMPLE   **1.** Of all numbers, the number 12 (*is, are*) one of the most
          versatile.

     1. *is*

 1. The even division of 12 by 1, 2, 3, 4, and 6 (*is, are*) possible.
 2. Curiously, the sum of these five divisors (*is, are*) a square, 16; and
     their product is 144, which is the square of 12 itself.
 3. When the Greek philosopher Plato devised his ideal state, the sys-
     tem of weights and measures (*were, was*) based on the number 12
     because it could be evenly divided in so many ways.
 4. To this day, many quantities in our lives (*involve, involves*) the
     number 12.

5. The number of months in a year, inches in a foot, and items in a dozen (*is, are*) 12.
6. In our courts of law, 12 members of a jury (*decides, decide*) a defendant's guilt or innocence.
7. Each player in a game of checkers (*begin, begins*) with 12 pieces.
8. In bowling, 12 consecutive strikes (*give, gives*) you a perfect game.
9. The number of black pentagons on a soccer ball (*equal, equals*) the number of buttons on a push-button telephone—12.
10. Samuel Clemens even used this number as his pen name—the riverboat slang for 2 fathoms, or 12 feet, (*are, is*) *mark twain*!

5d. The following indefinite pronouns are singular: *anybody, anyone, anything, each, either, everybody, everyone, everything, neither, nobody, no one, nothing, one, somebody, someone,* and *something.*

EXAMPLES   **Each** of the athletes **runs** effortlessly.

        Neither of the women **is** ready to start.

        Someone was waving a large flag.

        Does everyone who signed up **enjoy** playing tennis?

5e. The following indefinite pronouns are plural: *both, few, many,* and *several.*

EXAMPLES   **Were both** of the games **postponed**?

        Few that I know of **have qualified.**

        Several of the runners **are exercising.**

5f. The indefinite pronouns *all, any, more, most, none,* and *some* may be singular or plural, depending on their meaning in a sentence.

These pronouns are singular when they refer to a singular word and plural when they refer to a plural word.

EXAMPLES   **Some** of the test **is** hard. [*Some* refers to the singular noun *test.*]

        Some of the questions **are** easy. [*Some* refers to the plural noun *questions.*]

        All of the exhibit **is** open to the public.

        All of the paintings **are** on display.

TIPS & TRICKS

The words *one, thing,* and *body* are singular, and so are the indefinite pronouns that contain these words.

EXAMPLES
Is [any]**one** late?

[Every]**body was** welcome.

[No]**thing has** been lost.

MEETING THE CHALLENGE

Authors must write clear and informative descriptions to truly immerse a reader into the world of the book. Imagine that you are writing a description of a place or person you love. Write a brief paragraph of ten sentences describing this person or place. Be precise in your description, and use at least one indefinite pronoun in each sentence. Be sure to check for proper subject-verb agreement.

Most of his routine **sounds** familiar.
Most of his jokes **sound** familiar.

Was any of the feedback positive?
Were any of the reviews positive?

The rice was eaten. **None is** left.
The potatoes were eaten. **None are** left.

More of the class **is** going to the archaeological dig.
More of the students **are** going to the archaeological dig.

5
d–f

| TIPS & TRICKS |

Some of the words listed in **Rule 5d** can also be used as adjectives or as parts of correlative conjunctions: *each, either, neither, one.* Used as these parts of speech, such words cannot function as subjects.

USAGE

Exercise 5 **Identifying Subjects and Verbs That Agree in Number**

Identify the subject of each verb in parentheses. Then, choose the form of the verb that agrees with that subject.

EXAMPLE   1. Several of the kittens (*has, have*) been adopted.
            1. *Several—have*

1. Each of the comedians (*tries, try*) to outdo the other.
2. Somebody on the bus (*was, were*) whistling.
3. (*Is, Are*) all of the apples spoiled?
4. Neither of these books (*has, have*) an index.
5. (*Do, Does*) everybody in the class have a pencil?
6. Few of these jobs (*sounds, sound*) challenging.
7. (*Is, Are*) more of the vendors in the market?
8. She said that no one in the office (*leaves, leave*) early.
9. Both of her parents (*has, have*) offered us a ride.
10. (*Do, Does*) most of those CDs belong to her?

Reference Note

For more information about **adjectives,** see page 10. For more about **correlative conjunctions,** see page 32.

Reference Note

For more information about **indefinite pronouns,** see page 9. For information on distinguishing **indefinite pronouns from adjectives,** see page 11.

Review A **Proofreading a Paragraph for Subject-Verb Agreement**

Identify the agreement errors in the following paragraph. Then, supply the correct form of each incorrect verb.

EXAMPLE   [1] On weekends, I often goes with my mother to antique shops.
            1. *goes—go*

[1] Until recently, this hunt for old things were very boring.
[2] Then one day I noticed that a dusty shoe box full of antique postcards were sitting near me on a counter. [3] Soon I was flipping through the cards, and before you knows it, I had decided to start a

postcard collection! [4] The cards in my collection is very precious to me. [5] Because I am interested in American history, I has chosen to specialize in cards showing American Indians. [6] On one of my cards, the flames of a campfire glows in front of several Plains Indian tepees under a colorful sunset. [7] Most of the postcards in my collection shows pictures of Native American leaders and warriors. [8] On my favorite card, a Navajo mother wrapped in beautiful blankets are posing with her baby on her back. [9] Collecting postcards are not an expensive hobby either. [10] Many of my cards was priced at a dollar or less.

The Compound Subject

A **compound subject** consists of two or more subjects that are joined by a conjunction and that have the same verb.

5g. Subjects joined by *and* generally take a plural verb.

The following compound subjects joined by *and* name more than one person, place, thing, or idea and take plural verbs.

EXAMPLES   **George Lucas** and **Steven Spielberg make** movies. [Two persons make movies.]

           Rhyme, rhythm, and **imagery help** poets express their feelings. [Three things help.]

Compound subjects that name only one person, thing, place, or idea take a singular verb.

EXAMPLES   My **pen pal and best friend is** my cousin. [One person is my best friend and pen pal.]

           Broccoli and melted cheese makes a tasty dish. [The one combination makes a dish.]

5h. Singular subjects joined by *or* or *nor* take a singular verb. Plural subjects joined by *or* or *nor* take a plural verb.

EXAMPLES   After dinner, either **Anne** or **Tony loads** the dishwasher. [Anne loads the dishwasher *or* Tony loads the dishwasher.]

           Neither the **coach** nor the **principal is** happy with the team's performance. [Neither *one* is happy.]

           Either the **boys** or their **sisters take** the garbage out.

           Neither the **dogs** nor the **cats come** when we call them.

Reference Note

For more information about **compound subjects,** see page 52.

5i. When a singular subject and a plural subject are joined by *or* or *nor,* the verb agrees with the subject nearer the verb.

ACCEPTABLE   Neither the children nor their **mother was** ready for the trip.

ACCEPTABLE   Neither the mother nor her **children were** ready for the trip.

Oral Practice 1 **Using Verbs That Agree in Number with Their Subjects**

Read the following sentences aloud, stressing the italicized words.

1. The *books* on that shelf *need* dusting.
2. A *carton* of duck eggs *is* in the refrigerator.
3. *Tina and Betty are* first cousins once removed.
4. *Playing* games *or listening* to old records *is* an enjoyable way to spend a rainy Saturday.
5. *Several* of these insects *eat* through wood.
6. Every *one* of you *has* met my friend Phil.
7. Neither the *twins nor Greg enjoys* listening to that kind of music.
8. Both *Mr. and Mrs. Chen agree* to be chaperons for our spring dance.

Exercise 6 **Choosing Verbs That Agree in Number with Their Subjects**

Choose the correct form of the verb in parentheses in each of the following sentences.

EXAMPLE   1. In August, eager players and their fans (*looks, look*) forward to the start of football season.

   1. *look*

1. The coach and the player (*was, were*) surprised by the referee's call.
2. (*Is, Are*) Drew or Virgil going out for the pass?
3. Neither the quarterback nor the wide receiver (*hear, hears*) the referee's whistle.
4. The marching band or the pep squad (*has, have*) already performed.
5. (*Do, Does*) Christopher and Alexander enjoy football as much as Rachel does?
6. Either Albert or Selena (*leads, lead*) the student fight song.
7. The drum major and student council president (*is, are*) my older sister Janet.
8. The principal, the band director, and the gymnastics coach (*was, were*) proud of the half-time show.

STYLE TIP

Constructions like those shown with Rule 5i can sound awkward. Try rephrasing sentences to avoid such awkward constructions.

EXAMPLES
The **children were** not ready for the trip, and neither **was** their **mother.**

or

The **mother was** not ready for the trip, and neither **were** her **children.**

USAGE

9. Neither the coach nor the players (*has, have*) ever won a state championship game.

10. (*Was, Were*) the announcer or the referees prepared for the triumphant fans to rush the field?

Review B **Revising Sentences for Subject-Verb Agreement**

Revise each of the following sentences according to the directions given in parentheses. Change the verb in the sentence to agree with the subject as necessary.

EXAMPLE
1. The teachers have finished grading the tests. (Change *The teachers* to *Each of the teachers.*)

1. *Each of the teachers has finished grading the tests.*

1. My aunt is planning a trip to Nairobi National Park in Kenya. (Change *aunt* to *aunts.*)

2. Have Yoko and Juan already seen that movie? (Change *and* to *or.*)

3. Nobody on the team plans to attend the award ceremonies. (Change *Nobody* to *Many.*)

4. My grandmother, as well as my mother and aunts, raises tropical fish to earn extra money. (Change *grandmother* to *grandparents.*)

5. Most of the food for the party is in the refrigerator. (Change *food* to *salads.*)

6. Neither the librarian nor the aides have found the missing book. (Change *Neither the librarian nor the aides* to *Neither the aides nor the librarian.*)

7. Black bean soup and a tossed salad make an inexpensive meal. (Change *Black bean soup and a tossed salad* to *Macaroni and cheese.*)

8. Some of my friends take the bus to school. (Change *Some* to *One.*)

9. Few of the reporter's questions were answered in detail. (Change *Few* to *Neither.*)

10. The puppy playing with my sisters is two months old. (Change *puppy* to *puppies* and *sisters* to *sister.*)

Other Problems in Agreement

5j. The contractions *don't* and *doesn't* should agree with their subjects.

The word *don't* is the contraction of *do not.* Use *don't* with all plural subjects and with the pronouns *I* and *you.*

EXAMPLES

I **don't** know.	They **don't** give up.
You **don't** say.	**Don't** these shrink?
We **don't** want to.	Apathetic people **don't** care.

The word *doesn't* is the contraction of *does not*. Use *doesn't* with all singular subjects except the pronouns *I* and *you*.

EXAMPLES

He **doesn't** know.	One **doesn't** give up.
She **doesn't** say.	This **doesn't** shrink.
It **doesn't** want to.	**Doesn't** Donna care?

5
j, k

STYLE ✏ TIP

Many people consider contractions informal. Therefore, it is generally best not to use contractions in formal speaking and writing.

Exercise 7 Using *Doesn't* and *Don't* Correctly

Write the correct form (*doesn't* or *don't*) for each of the following sentences.

EXAMPLE
1. _____ that bouquet of roses look great?
1. *Doesn't*

1. This apple _____ taste sweet.
2. _____ he want to see the game?
3. These _____ impress me.
4. One of the players _____ plan to go.
5. _____ Jason and Tanya like the new band uniforms?
6. You and she _____ have time to play computer games now.
7. The engine in that old pickup _____ start in winter.
8. Tonio asked why we _____ want to go mountain biking.
9. _____ several of those in the front window cost more than these in the fruit cart?
10. The international children's chorus is so marvelous that their new fans _____ want to leave the theater.

5k. A collective noun may be either singular or plural, depending on its meaning in a sentence.

The singular form of a *collective noun* names a group of persons or things.

Reference Note

For more information about **collective nouns,** see page 5.

USAGE

Collective Nouns				
army	class	family	group	public
assembly	club	fleet	herd	swarm
audience	committee	flock	jury	team

Use a plural verb with a collective noun when the noun refers to the individual parts or members of the group. Use a singular verb when the noun refers to the group as a unit.

EXAMPLES   The class **have completed** their projects. [*Class* is thought of as individuals.]

The class **has elected** its officers. [*Class* is thought of as a unit.]

Notice in the examples above that any pronoun referring to a collective noun has the same number as the noun. In the first example, *their* refers to *class*. In the second example, *its* refers to *class*.

See page 139 for more

See page 139 for

Reference Note

See page 139 for more about **pronoun-antecedent agreement** with **collective nouns.**

Exercise 8   **Writing Sentences with Collective Nouns**

Select five collective nouns, and write five pairs of sentences that show clearly how the nouns you choose may be singular or plural.

EXAMPLE   1.   *The jury is ready.*

The jury are still arguing among themselves.

5l. A verb agrees with its subject, but not necessarily with a predicate nominative.

EXAMPLES
              S   PN
The marching **bands are** the main attraction.

             S   PN
The main **attraction is** the marching bands.

5m. When the subject follows the verb, find the subject and make sure that the verb agrees with it.

The subject generally follows the verb in questions and in sentences that begin with *here* and *there*.

EXAMPLES   Here **is** a **list** of addresses.

Here **are** two **lists** of addresses.

There **is** my **notebook.**

There **are** my **notebooks.**

Where **is Heather**? Where **is Chris**?

Where **are Heather** and **Chris**?

TIPS & TRICKS

To find the subject in a sentence in which the subject follows the verb, rearrange the sentence.

EXAMPLES

A **list** of addresses **is** here.

My **notebooks are** there.

Heather and **Chris are** where?

Contractions such as *here's, where's, how's,* and *what's* include the singular verb *is.* Use these contractions only with singular subjects.

NONSTANDARD   There's some facts on that topic in a chart.
STANDARD   There **are** some **facts** on that topic in a chart.
STANDARD   There**'s** a **chart** with some facts on that topic.

5n. An expression of an amount (a measurement, a percentage, or a fraction, for example) may be singular or plural, depending on how it is used.

A word or phrase stating an amount is singular when the amount is thought of as a unit.

EXAMPLES   **Thirty dollars is** too much for a concert ticket.

           Two hours is a long time to wait.

Sometimes, however, the amount is thought of as individual pieces or parts. If so, a plural verb is used.

EXAMPLES   **Five dollars were scattered** on the desk.

           Two hours—one before school and one after—**are** all I have for practice.

A fraction or a percentage is singular when it refers to a singular word and plural when it refers to a plural word.

EXAMPLES   **Three fourths** of the pizza **is** gone.

           Of these songs, **three fourths are** new.

5o. Some nouns that are plural in form take singular verbs.

EXAMPLES   **Politics is** a controversial topic.

           The **news** of the nominee **was** a surprise.

           Rickets is a serious health problem in some countries.

NOTE   Some nouns that end in *–s* take a plural verb even when they refer to a single item.

EXAMPLES   The **scissors need** to be sharpened.

           Were these **pants** on sale?

           The **Olympics are** on television.

l–o

Reference Note

For more on **contractions,** see page 335.

Reference Note

For a discussion of **standard and nonstandard English,** see page 223.

USAGE

─HELP─

If you do not know whether a noun that is plural in form is singular or plural in meaning, look up the word in a dictionary.

Agreement of Subject and Verb   **131**

5p. Even when plural in form, the title of a creative work (such as a book, song, film, or painting), the name of an organization, or the name of a country or city generally takes a singular verb.

EXAMPLES   ***The Souls of Black Folk* is** often **cited** as a classic of African American literature. [one book]

"Greensleeves" is an old English folk song. [one piece of music]

The United Nations was founded in 1945. [one organization]

White Plains is home to several colleges. [one city]

Review C   Using Titles That Agree with Verbs in Number

Terence and Janeese are at the video rental store deciding what movies they will rent for the weekend. In the following sentences, wherever *TITLE* appears, supply the name of a movie of your choice. Then, choose the correct form of the verb to complete each sentence.

EXAMPLE   1. Look, Terence. TITLE (*is, are*) supposed to be very funny.

1. *Horse Feathers—is*

1. Terence: According to LaShonda, TITLE and TITLE (*is, are*) very exciting.
2. Janeese: Well, TITLE or TITLE (*sounds, sound*) more interesting to me. Let's ask the clerk.
3. Terence: Sir, (*is, are*) TITLE in stock?
4. Clerk: I'm afraid not, but TITLE (*entertain, entertains*) almost everyone, and you might enjoy it.
5. Terence: Janeese, TITLE (*is, are*) a fairly recent movie, but TITLE (*are, is*) an old-timer.
6. Janeese: Well, I like animated films, and TITLE (*fit, fits*) that category.
7. Clerk: If you ask me, TITLE (*beat, beats*) every other film we have, but someone just rented my last copy.
8. Janeese: Both TITLE and TITLE (*are, is*) good, but I've seen each of them twice.
9. Terence: (*Isn't, Aren't*) TITLE any good? I'm surprised.
10. Janeese: All right, here's my vote. TITLE (*is, are*) tonight's movie, and either TITLE or TITLE (*is, are*) the movie for Saturday night's party.

5q. Subjects preceded by *every* or *many a* take singular verbs.

EXAMPLES   **Every** homeowner and storekeeper **has joined** the cleanup drive sponsored by the town council.

             Many a litterbug **was surprised** by the stiff fines.

5r. When the relative pronoun *that, which,* or *who* is the subject of an adjective clause, the verb in the adjective clause agrees with the word to which the relative pronoun refers.

Reference Note

For more about **relative pronouns,** see page 8. For more about **adjective clauses,** see page 101.

EXAMPLES   This is the store **that has** the discount sale. [*That* refers to the singular noun *store.*]

             London, **which is** the capital of England, is the largest city in Europe. [*Which* refers to the singular noun *London.*]

             The Garcias, **who live** next door, are going with us to the lake. [*Who* refers to the plural noun *Garcias.*]

Oral Practice 2   Using Subject-Verb Agreement

Read each of the following sentences aloud, stressing the italicized words.

1. Of the inhabitants, *two thirds are* registered to vote.
2. *Many a* writer and scholar *has* puzzled over that problem.
3. *Is economics* taught at your high school?
4. *Are* there any green *apples* in that basket?
5. *Romeo and Juliet has* been made into a ballet, a Broadway musical, and several movies.
6. *Two weeks is* more than enough time to write a report.
7. My *family is* planning to hold its reunion in October.
8. My *family are* planning their schedules now.

Exercise 9   Identifying Subjects and Verbs That Agree in Number

Identify the subject of each verb in parentheses. Then, choose the form of the verb that agrees with the subject.

EXAMPLE   **1.** (*Do, Does*) Meals on Wheels deliver in your neighborhood?

           1. Meals on Wheels—Does

1. The class (*has, have*) chosen titles for their original plays.
2. First prize (*was, were*) two tickets to Hawaii.

3. Three quarters of the movie (*was, were*) over when we arrived at the theater.
4. Rattlesnakes (*was, were*) the topic of last week's meeting of the hiking club.
5. (*Has, Have*) every student in the class memorized a poem to present for the oral interpretation contest?
6. *Crime and Punishment* (*is, are*) a world-famous novel.
7. Two thirds of the missing books (*was, were*) returned to the downtown branch of the library.
8. Mathematics (*is, are*) an important part of many everyday activities.
9. Where (*is, are*) the paragraphs you wrote?
10. Four weeks (*is, are*) enough time to rehearse the play.

Review D Identifying Verbs That Have the Correct Number

Choose the correct form of the verb in parentheses in each of the following sentences.

EXAMPLE **1.** Fifty pesos (*was, were*) a great price for that carving.

     1. *was*

1. Mumps (*is, are*) a common childhood disease that causes swelling in glands in the neck.
2. Politics (*is, are*) always a popular subject both to debate and to study at college.
3. Not one of the ushers (*know, knows*) where the lounge is.
4. The team (*is, are*) on a winning streak.
5. Carol, as well as Inés, (*write, writes*) a weekly column for the *East High Record*.
6. "Beauty and the Beast" (*is, are*) a folk tale that exists in many different cultures.
7. Ten pounds (*is, are*) too much weight for a young child to carry in a backpack.
8. It is difficult to concentrate when there (*is, are*) radios and stereos blasting away.
9. (*Has, Have*) either of you read the book or seen the movie version of *To Kill a Mockingbird*?
10. In most situation comedies, there (*is, are*) a very wise character, a very foolish character, and a very lovable character.

Agreement of Pronoun and Antecedent

A pronoun usually refers to a noun or another pronoun that comes before it. The word that a pronoun refers to is called its *antecedent.*

5s. A pronoun should agree in number and gender with its antecedent.

(1) A pronoun that refers to a singular antecedent is singular in number.

EXAMPLES   **Daniel Defoe** wrote **his** first book at the age of fifty-nine.

               The **elephant** is a long-lived animal. **It** grows **its** tusks at maturity.

(2) A pronoun that refers to a plural antecedent is plural in number.

EXAMPLES   Reliable **cars** make **their** owners happy.

               We walk **our** dogs daily.

Reference Note

For a further discussion of **antecedents,** see page 6.

A few singular pronouns have forms that indicate the gender of the antecedent. Masculine pronouns refer to males; feminine pronouns refer to females. Neuter pronouns refer to places, things, ideas, and, often, to animals.

Masculine	Feminine	Neuter
he	she	it
him	her	it
his	hers	its
himself	herself	itself

Often, when the antecedent of a personal pronoun is another kind of pronoun, a word in a phrase following the antecedent will help to determine gender.

EXAMPLES   **One** of the **women** designs **her** own costumes.

               Each of the **boys** rode **his** bicycle to school.

               Neither of the **kittens** has opened **its** eyes yet.

USAGE

HELP

In many cases you can avoid the awkward *his or her* construction by rephrasing the sentence and using the plural form of the pronoun or by substituting an article (*a, an,* or *the*).

EXAMPLES
The **passengers** will be shown where **they** can check in.

A **person** should choose **a** college carefully.

STYLE TIP

In informal conversation, plural personal pronouns are often used to refer to singular antecedents that can be either masculine or feminine. Such usage is becoming increasingly common in writing. However, you should avoid such usage in formal writing and speaking.

INFORMAL
Everybody has packed their lunch in an insulated cooler.

FORMAL
Everybody has packed **his or her** lunch in an insulated cooler.

When a singular antecedent may be either masculine or feminine, use both the masculine and the feminine forms, connected by *or*.

EXAMPLES **Each passenger** will be shown where **he or she** can check in.

A **person** should choose **his or her** college carefully.

If you talk on the phone with **someone** you don't know well, speak clearly to **him or her.**

5t. Some indefinite pronouns are singular, and some are plural. Other indefinite pronouns can be either singular or plural, depending on their meaning in a sentence.

(1) Use a singular pronoun to refer to *anybody, anyone, anything, each, either, everybody, everyone, everything, neither, nobody, no one, nothing, one, somebody, someone,* or *something.*

EXAMPLES **Either** of the girls can bring **her** CD player.

Neither of the workmen forgot **his** tool belt.

Did **each** of the mares recognize **her** own foal?

Someone left **his or her** hat on the field.

One of the parakeets escaped from **its** cage.

NOTE Sometimes the meaning of *everyone* or *everybody* is clearly plural. In informal situations, the plural pronoun should be used.

CONFUSING Everyone laughed when he or she saw the clowns.
INFORMAL **Everyone** laughed when **they** saw the clowns.

In formal situations, it is best to revise the sentence so that it is both clear and grammatically correct.

FORMAL The **audience** laughed when **they** saw the clowns.

(2) Use a plural pronoun to refer to *both, few, many,* and *several.*

EXAMPLES **Both** of the sisters recited **their** lines.

Few of the animals willingly leave **their** natural habitat.

Many of the volunteers shared **their** coats with the flood victims.

Several of the audience were late getting to **their** seats.

(3) The indefinite pronouns *all, any, more, most, none,* and *some* may be singular or plural, depending on their meaning in a sentence.

EXAMPLES **All** of the water has melted; **it** is pooling in the valley.
All of the streams are full; **they** are rushing torrents.

Most of her cooking tastes good. In fact, **it** is delicious.
Most of the dishes she cooks taste good. **They** contain unusual spices.

5u. Use a singular pronoun to refer to two or more singular antecedents joined by *or* or *nor.*

EXAMPLES Neither **Richard nor Bob** distinguished **himself** in the finals.

Paula or Janet will present **her** views on the subject.

5v. Use a plural pronoun to refer to two or more antecedents joined by *and.*

EXAMPLES **Mona and Janet** left early because **they** had to be home before ten o'clock.

Mom and Dad celebrated **their** twentieth wedding anniversary yesterday.

5w. The number of a relative pronoun (such as *who, which,* or *that*) is determined by its antecedent.

EXAMPLES Aretha is one **friend who** always keeps **her** word. [*Who* refers to the singular noun *friend*. Therefore, the singular form *her* is used to agree with *who*.]

Many who volunteer **their** time find the experience rewarding. [*Who* refers to the plural pronoun *Many*. Therefore, the plural form *their* is used to agree with *who*.]

STYLE TIP

Sentences like those shown under **Rule 5u** can sound awkward if the antecedents are of different genders. If a sentence sounds awkward, revise it to avoid the problem.

AWKWARD
Ben or Maya will read his or her report.

REVISED
Ben will read **his** report, or **Maya** will read **hers.**

Reference Note

For more information on **relative pronouns in adjective clauses,** see page 101.

Review E **Identifying Antecedents and Writing Pronouns**

Each of the sentences on the following page contains a blank where a pronoun should be. Complete each sentence by inserting at least one pronoun that agrees with its antecedent. Identify the antecedent.

EXAMPLE **1.** Carmen and Tina said that _____ thought my idea was sensible.

1. *they—Carmen and Tina*

1. Please give me Ronald's address so that I can send _____ a letter.
2. The uniform company finally sent Jerome and Ken the shirts that _____ had ordered.
3. Claire or Ida will go to the nursing home early so that _____ can help the residents into the lounge.
4. Several of the volunteers contributed _____ own money to buy the shelter a new van.
5. Did each of the contestants answer _____ questions correctly?
6. Both of the girls packed _____ suitcases carefully for the trip to Canada and Alaska.
7. Every car at the service center had _____ oil changed.
8. Neither of the women withdrew _____ job application.
9. Anyone can belong to the International Students Association if _____ is interested.
10. Neither the coaches nor the players blamed _____ for the loss.

Review F Proofreading Sentences for Pronoun-Antecedent Agreement

Many of the following sentences contain errors in agreement between pronouns and their antecedents. Identify each of these errors, and give the form of the pronoun that agrees with its antecedent. If a sentence is already correct, write *C*.

EXAMPLE   1. All of us need to choose a topic for his or her reports.
          1. *his or her—our*

┌HELP┐
Some sentences in Review F may contain more than one error in agreement.

1. George has chosen Walt Disney as the subject of his report.
2. Several others in our class have also submitted his or her topics.
3. Dominic, one of the Perrone twins, has chosen Alfred Hitchcock as their subject.
4. Neither George nor Dominic will have difficulty finding material for their report.
5. Each of these moviemakers has left their mark on the world.
6. Either Minnie or Sue offered their help with proofreading.
7. Each of the boys refused politely, saying that they would proofread the report on their own.
8. Does everyone, including George and Dominic, know that they must assemble facts, not opinions?
9. Neither George nor Dominic should forget to include amusing anecdotes about their subject.
10. Nobody likes to discover that they just read a dull report about an interesting subject.

5x. A collective noun is singular when it refers to the group as a unit and plural when it refers to the individual members of the group.

EXAMPLES   The **pride** of lions is hunting **its** prey on the savanna. [*Pride* is thought of as a unit.]

The **pride** of lions are licking **their** chops in anticipation. [*Pride* is thought of as separate individuals.]

NOTE   Sometimes the number of a collective noun depends on the meaning the writer intends.

EXAMPLES   The swim **team** proudly displayed **their** trophies. [The members of the team displayed individual trophies.]

The swim **team** proudly displayed **its** trophy. [The team as a whole displayed a shared trophy.]

Reference Note

For information on **subject-verb agreement** with **collective nouns,** see page 129. For a list of **collective nouns,** see page 5.

5y. An expression of an amount (a measurement, a percentage, or a fraction, for example) may be singular or plural, depending on how it is used.

A word or phrase stating an amount is singular when the amount is thought of as a unit.

EXAMPLES   **Ten minutes** isn't long; **it** will go by quickly.

Here is **five dollars.** Is **it** enough?

Sometimes, however, the amount is thought of as individual pieces or parts. If so, a plural pronoun is used.

EXAMPLES   **Ten** of the twenty minutes were wasted; we spent **them** arguing.

Five dollars were counterfeit, weren't **they**?

A fraction or a percentage is singular when it refers to a singular word and plural when it refers to a plural word.

EXAMPLES   **One third** of the total is yours. Would you like **it** in ones?

One third of the birds have left. Are **they** migrating?

5z. Singular pronouns are used to refer to some nouns that are plural in form.

EXAMPLES   Aunt Jean rarely watches the **news** because she finds **it** depressing.

The **United States** celebrated **its** bicentennial in 1976.

After Chad finished reading ***Mules and Men,*** he wrote a report on **it.**

Future Farmers of America meets tomorrow to plan **its** convention.

Marble Falls is in Texas; **it** is north of San Antonio and Blanco.

NOTE Plural pronouns are used to refer to some nouns that end in *–s* but that refer to a single item.

EXAMPLES I'll buy these **pants** because **they** fit better and are a better value than **those.**

If you're looking for the **scissors,** you'll find **them** in the third drawer on the left.

Review G **Agreement of Pronoun and Antecedent**

Some of the following sentences contain errors in pronoun-antecedent agreement. Identify each incorrect pronoun, and give the pronoun that agrees with its antecedent. If a sentence is already correct, write *C.*

EXAMPLE 1. Several people in the neighborhood have expressed his or her views.

1. *his or her—their*

1. The school finally sent Michael and Kathryn the results of the tests he or she had taken.
2. On the Serengeti Plain, a cheetah enjoys its freedom.
3. After World War II, the United States gave most of their foreign aid to help Europe rebuild.
4. Five percent of the profit will be donated, won't they?
5. The U.S. Olympic team won their third gold medal.
6. A person with a health problem should always select the best doctor for their needs.
7. During *ferragosto,* or August holiday, the Italian Parliament takes its recess.
8. Each of the mimes gave their impression of a chimney sweep.
9. I like the way the pants look; also, at that price, it's a great bargain.
10. *War and Peace* are the most famous of Leo Tolstoy's works.

Chapter Review

A. Identifying Verbs that Agree in Number with Their Subjects

For each of the following sentences, choose the correct form of the verb in parentheses.

1. (*Doesn't, Don't*) she know when she'll be back?
2. Most of my jewelry (*was, were*) lost in the fire.
3. For better or for worse, politics (*play, plays*) an important part in all our lives.
4. Many ideas in her book (*requires, require*) a great deal of thought.
5. (*Has, Have*) Lisa and Haruo been paid for their work?
6. (*Is, Are*) everybody finished with the project?
7. Neither the president nor the vice-president (*goes, go*) to every meeting.
8. There (*has, have*) been many accidents at that intersection.
9. Three fourths of the apartments (*was, were*) rented before the building was completed.
10. Our class president, with the help of several others, usually (*sets, set*) the agenda for the meeting.
11. Nobody here (*has, have*) the correct time.
12. A herd of cattle (*is, are*) by the river.
13. Some of Pat's nacho recipes (*contains, contain*) very hot spices.
14. One of the owners (*work, works*) at the store on weekends.
15. Physics (*is, are*) a challenging and fascinating subject.
16. Where (*do, does*) the scissors go?
17. The main attraction in the parade (*is, are*) the student floats.
18. Van Gogh's *The Potato Eaters* (*show, shows*) a Dutch farm family at dinner.
19. If two thirds of the people (*vote, votes*) for the measure, it will become law.
20. Here (*is, are*) a new football and a helmet for your birthday.

B. Proofreading Sentences for Subject-Verb Agreement

Each of the following sentences contains an error in agreement. Identify each incorrect verb, and supply the correct form.

21. Every man and woman were questioned by the police.

USAGE

22. The pile of papers were scattered by the wind.
23. Each of the girls have her own tennis balls.
24. Some of the sheep from that flock is lost.
25. Your explanation don't really help that much.
26. Most of the poetry are in English.
27. Each of the students were happy the exam was over.
28. Many a student have been grateful for being in Ms. Makowski's history class.
29. Someone have my umbrella.
30. Either Bill or his uncles is waiting downstairs.

C. Identifying Antecedents and Writing Pronouns

Each of the following sentences contains a blank where a pronoun should be. Complete each sentence by writing a pronoun that agrees with its antecedent. Identify the antecedent.

31. Uncle Harry and Aunt Nell said that _____ would be happy to contribute to the silent auction.
32. Can I have Trevor's phone number, so that I can tell _____ about the ceremony?
33. Every horse in the stable had _____ own bucket of oats.
34. Louis Pasteur, the great French scientist, made _____ first scientific discovery at the age of twenty-six.
35. Teresa or Sandra will go to the airport early so that _____ will be sure to meet Jorge's plane.
36. Patsy and Debbie will be late because _____ forgot the appointment.
37. Neither of the men changed _____ mind on the issue.
38. Because of the strike, several of the drivers had to change _____ own oil.
39. Both Henry James and his brother William became famous through _____ writings.
40. Neither Marie nor Delilah blamed _____ for the mistake.

D. Proofreading a Paragraph for Subject-Verb and Pronoun-Antecedent Agreement

For each error in the following paragraph, identify the incorrect verb or pronoun and supply the correct form.

[41] Karate are a great sport to learn. [42] The instructors, Mr. Ward and Ms. Chan, is very motivating. [43] Each class begin with sit-ups and stretches. [44] They also teaches us that learning karate is for self-defense, not for picking fights. [45] Several of the students are new to the class, and he or she don't know the form. [46] Each student can work to their own ability. [47] Karate teach character development, too. [48] Our student motto are "We are on a quest to be our best." [49] The values of karate is a positive attitude and working hard to achieve goals. [50] Many students can benefit from karate in both his or her body and mind.

Writing Application
Using Agreement in a Paragraph

Subject-Verb Agreement During Career Day, the school counselor asks you to write a paragraph beginning with this statement: "People I know work at a variety of jobs." Using subjects and verbs that agree, describe the jobs of three people you know.

Prewriting Start by listing at least three people you know who have different kinds of jobs. Think of action verbs that describe what these people do. For example, instead of saying "Mrs. Ruíz is a chemistry teacher," say "Mrs. Ruíz teaches chemistry."

Writing As you write your first draft, be sure to include some details that clearly show how the jobs differ from one another.

Revising Check your rough draft to be sure that the examples you have chosen show a variety of jobs. If not, you may want to replace some examples or add new ones. Make sure each job is described vividly.

Publishing Identify the subjects and verbs in each sentence, and be sure that they agree. Read your paragraph aloud to help you recognize any errors in usage, spelling, and punctuation. Be sure that you have capitalized all proper names. Your class might photocopy and display their paragraphs during Career Day. With the permission of the people you wrote about, your class could also prepare a job information directory.

6

Using Verbs Correctly

Principal Parts, Tense, Voice, Mood

Diagnostic Preview

┌─HELP─┐

Some sentences
in the Diagnostic Preview
have more than one
incorrect verb.

Proofreading Sentences for Correct Verb Forms

Read the following sentences. If a sentence contains an incorrect or awkward verb form, write the correct form or revise the sentence. If a sentence is already correct, write *C*.

EXAMPLES   **1.** I have always wanted a pet.

    1. C

    2. As a child, I use to dream about having a dog or cat.

    2. *used*

1. Every time I ask my parents, they said, "No, not in an apartment."
2. One day last year, I was setting on the front steps reading the newspaper when I spot an ad for a female ferret.
3. Deciding to investigate, I fold the paper, hop on my bike, and rode to the pet shop that had placed the ad.
4. When I walked into the store, I seen the ferret right away.
5. She was laying in a cardboard box on top of the counter.
6. I told the owner I wanted to hold her, and he reaches into the box.
7. When he withdrew his hand, the ferret was holding on to his finger with what looked like very sharp teeth.
8. I cautiously reached out and taked the ferret's hindquarters in my cupped hands.

9. The rest of her long body poured slowly into my hands until she was sitting on her haunches.
10. She looked up at me and suddenly clamps her teeth onto my thumb.
11. The ferret done it to show me who was boss.
12. I should have knowed then that my troubles had just began.
13. I ran all the way home and persuaded my parents to let me keep the ferret on a trial basis.
14. I had already give her a name—Ferris the Ferret—and I lose no time rushing back to the pet shop.
15. When I come home with Ferris, I sit a dish of cat food in front of her.
16. She stuck her snout into the dish and ate greedily.
17. After she had went into each room in the apartment, she choosed the top of the TV as her special place.
18. When my parents objected, I made a cardboard house with two entry holes and set it in a corner of my bedroom.
19. Ferris sniffed around her new home; then she goes in and laid down for a nap.
20. For the next few days, Ferris spent her time either napping or nipping.
21. She always attackted me when I least expected it.
22. Once, as she lies on my desk while I am studying, she suddenly locked her teeth onto my earlobe.
23. I was so startled that I jump up quickly, and Ferris wound up laying on the floor with a look that makes me feel guilty.
24. The next day the bad news was gave to me by my parents: Ferris had to go back to the pet shop.
25. I no longer want a pet ferret, but I have wrote to the local zookeeper to ask about snakes.

The Principal Parts of Verbs

The four basic forms of a verb are called the *principal parts* of the verb.

6a. The four principal parts of a verb are the *base form,* the *present participle,* the *past,* and the *past participle.*

The principal parts of the verb *ring,* for example, are *ring* (base form), *ringing* (present participle), *rang* (past), and *rung* (past participle). These principal parts are used to form all of the different verb tenses.

HELP
Some teachers refer to the base form as the *infinitive.* Follow your teacher's directions when labeling this form.

EXAMPLES   The bells **ring** every day.   The bells **rang** at noon.
            The bells **are ringing** now.   The bells **have rung** already.

Notice that the tenses made from the present participle and past participle contain helping verbs, such as *am, is, are, has,* and *have.*

Regular Verbs

6b. A *regular verb* forms its past and past participle by adding *–d* or *–ed* to the base form.

Base Form	Present Participle	Past	Past Participle
ask	[is] asking	asked	[have] asked
use	[is] using	used	[have] used
suppose	[is] supposing	supposed	[have] supposed
risk	[is] risking	risked	[have] risked

The words *is* and *have* are included in the preceding chart because helping verbs are used with the present participle and past participle to form some tenses.

> **NOTE** The present participle of most regular verbs ending in *–e* drops the *–e* before adding *–ing.*
>
> EXAMPLE   smile + ing = smil**ing**

One common error in the use of the past and the past participle forms is to leave off the *–d* or *–ed* ending.

NONSTANDARD   We use to play soccer.
   STANDARD   We **used** to play soccer.

NONSTANDARD   She was suppose to come home early.
   STANDARD   She was **supposed** to come home early.

Another common error is to misspell or mispronounce verbs.

NONSTANDARD   We were attackted by mosquitoes.
   STANDARD   We were **attacked** by mosquitoes.

Reference Note
For more about how **participles and helping verbs** work together, see page 77.

Reference Note
See page 363 for more on **spelling words when adding suffixes.**

STYLE   TIP
A few regular verbs have an alternate past form ending in *–t*. For example, the past form of *burn* is *burned* or *burnt*. Both forms are correct.

USAGE

Oral Practice 1 **Pronouncing the Past and Past Participle Forms of Regular Verbs Correctly**

Read each sentence aloud, stressing the italicized verb.

1. Aunt Rosie *used* to do needlepoint.
2. What has *happened* to your bicycle?
3. Several people were *drowned* in the flood.
4. The agents *risked* their lives.
5. Aren't you *supposed* to sing?
6. The game was well *advertised*.
7. The critics *praised* Amy Tan's new book.
8. He *carried* the suitcases to the car.

Irregular Verbs

6c. An ***irregular verb*** forms its past and past participle in some other way than by adding *–d* or *–ed.*

An irregular verb forms its past and past participle in one of these ways:

- changing consonants
- changing vowels
- changing vowels *and* consonants
- making no change at all

	Base Form	Past	Past Participle
Consonant Change	bend	bent	[have] bent
	send	sent	[have] sent
Vowel Change	sing	sang	[have] sung
	begin	began	[have] begun
Vowel and Consonant Change	catch	caught	[have] caught
	go	went	[have] gone
	fly	flew	[have] flown
No Change	set	set	[have] set
	burst	burst	[have] burst

"When I say 'runned,' you know I mean 'ran.' Let's not quibble."

© 1998 by Sidney Harris.

┌─HELP─

If you are not sure about the principal parts of a verb, look in a dictionary, which lists the principal parts of irregular verbs. If no principal parts are listed, the verb is regular.

Reference Note

For more about **standard and nonstandard English,** see page 223.

NOTE Since most English verbs are regular, people sometimes try to make irregular verbs follow the regular pattern. However, such words as *throwed, knowed, shrinked,* and *choosed* are considered nonstandard.

Principal Parts of Common Irregular Verbs			
Base Form	**Present Participle**	**Past**	**Past Participle**
become	[is] becoming	became	[have] become
begin	[is] beginning	began	[have] begun
blow	[is] blowing	blew	[have] blown
break	[is] breaking	broke	[have] broken
bring	[is] bringing	brought	[have] brought
build	[is] building	built	[have] built
burst	[is] bursting	burst	[have] burst
buy	[is] buying	bought	[have] bought
choose	[is] choosing	chose	[have] chosen
come	[is] coming	came	[have] come
cost	[is] costing	cost	[have] cost
cut	[is] cutting	cut	[have] cut
do	[is] doing	did	[have] done
draw	[is] drawing	drew	[have] drawn
drink	[is] drinking	drank	[have] drunk
drive	[is] driving	drove	[have] driven
eat	[is] eating	ate	[have] eaten
fall	[is] falling	fell	[have] fallen
feel	[is] feeling	felt	[have] felt
fight	[is] fighting	fought	[have] fought
find	[is] finding	found	[have] found
fly	[is] flying	flew	[have] flown
freeze	[is] freezing	froze	[have] frozen
get	[is] getting	got	[have] gotten *or* got
give	[is] giving	gave	[have] given
go	[is] going	went	[have] gone
grow	[is] growing	grew	[have] grown

USAGE

Principal Parts of Common Irregular Verbs			
Base Form	Present Participle	Past	Past Participle
have	[is] having	had	[have] had
hear	[is] hearing	heard	[have] heard
hide	[is] hiding	hid	[have] hidden *or* hid
hit	[is] hitting	hit	[have] hit
hold	[is] holding	held	[have] held
keep	[is] keeping	kept	[have] kept
know	[is] knowing	knew	[have] known
lead	[is] leading	led	[have] led
leave	[is] leaving	left	[have] left
let	[is] letting	let	[have] let
light	[is] lighting	lighted *or* lit	[have] lighted *or* lit
lose	[is] losing	lost	[have] lost
make	[is] making	made	[have] made
put	[is] putting	put	[have] put
read	[is] reading	read	[have] read
ride	[is] riding	rode	[have] ridden
ring	[is] ringing	rang	[have] rung
run	[is] running	ran	[have] run
say	[is] saying	said	[have] said
see	[is] seeing	saw	[have] seen
seek	[is] seeking	sought	[have] sought
shake	[is] shaking	shook	[have] shaken
sing	[is] singing	sang	[have] sung
sink	[is] sinking	sank *or* sunk	[have] sunk
slide	[is] sliding	slid	[have] slid
speak	[is] speaking	spoke	[have] spoken
spend	[is] spending	spent	[have] spent
stand	[is] standing	stood	[have] stood
steal	[is] stealing	stole	[have] stolen
sting	[is] stinging	stung	[have] stung
strike	[is] striking	struck	[have] struck *or* stricken

(continued)

STYLE TIP

Some verbs have two correct past or past participle forms. However, these forms are not always interchangeable.

EXAMPLES
I **shone** the flashlight into the woods. [*Shined* would also be correct.]

I **shined** my shoes. [*Shone* would be incorrect in this usage.]

If you are unsure about which past participle form to use, check an up-to-date dictionary.

(continued)

Principal Parts of Common Irregular Verbs			
Base Form	**Present Participle**	**Past**	**Past Participle**
swim	[is] swimming	swam	[have] swum
take	[is] taking	took	[have] taken
teach	[is] teaching	taught	[have] taught
tear	[is] tearing	tore	[have] torn
tell	[is] telling	told	[have] told
think	[is] thinking	thought	[have] thought
throw	[is] throwing	threw	[have] thrown
wear	[is] wearing	wore	[have] worn
win	[is] winning	won	[have] won
write	[is] writing	wrote	[have] written

When the present participle and past participle forms are used as verbs in sentences, they require helping verbs.

Helping Verb	+	Present Participle	=	Verb Phrase
forms of ***be***	+	taking walking going	=	am taking was walking have been going

Helping Verb	+	Past Participle	=	Verb Phrase
forms of ***have***	+	taken walked gone	=	have taken has walked had gone

┌─ **HELP** ─

To avoid non-standard usage, include a form of *be* with the present participle and a form of *have* with the past participle. Say *do, is doing, did, have done,* for example, or *see, is seeing, saw, have seen.*

NONSTANDARD
  We already seen that program.

STANDARD
  We **have** already **seen** that program.

Reference Note

┌ For more about **passive voice,** see page 163.

NOTE Sometimes a past participle is used with a form of *be: was chosen, are known, is seen.* This use of the verb is called the ***passive voice.***

USAGE

Oral Practice 2 **Using the Past and Past Participle Forms of Irregular Verbs Correctly**

Read each of the following sentences aloud, stressing the italicized verbs.

1. *Have* you *begun* the research for your report?
2. Last week we *saw* a video about Alexander the Great.
3. The bell *rang*, and the door *burst* open.
4. I *have known* her since the first grade.
5. He *brought* his rock collection to school.
6. They *fought* to rescue the survivors.
7. Elizabeth *has written* a short article for the school newspaper.
8. She *has given* us her permission.

Exercise 1 **Writing the Past and Past Participle Forms of Irregular Verbs**

Change each of the following verb forms. If the base form is given, change it to the past form. If the past form is given, change it to the past participle. Use *have* before the past participle form.

EXAMPLES
    1. eat   **2.** took
    1. ate   *2. have taken*

1. do	**5.** went	**9.** blew	**13.** drink	**17.** ran
2. began	**6.** know	**10.** bring	**14.** froze	**18.** ring
3. see	**7.** spoke	**11.** choose	**15.** drove	**19.** fell
4. rode	**8.** stole	**12.** broke	**16.** sang	**20.** swim

Exercise 2 **Identifying Correct Forms of Irregular Verbs**

Choose the correct form of the verb in parentheses in each of the following sentences.

EXAMPLE
    1. Mai's grandparents (*telled, told*) her about their journey in a boat from South Vietnam to Malaysia.
    1. told

1. They (*rode, rid*) in a crowded boat like the one you see in the picture on the next page.
2. Along with many other people, Mai's grandparents (*chose, choosed*) to make such a journey rather than stay in South Vietnam after the Vietnam War ended.

3. These refugees (*came, come*) to be called boat people.

4. Mai's grandparents abandoned their home after the South Vietnamese capital, Saigon, had (*fell, fallen*) to North Vietnamese forces.

5. The people on the boat (*brang, brought*) few possessions or supplies.

6. After they had (*drank, drunk*) what little water was on board, they went thirsty.

7. Mai's grandfather said the people had (*ate, eaten*) all the food in a few days.

8. When another boat of refugees had (*sank, sunk*), its passengers crowded onto Mai's grandparents' boat.

9. They spent many days and nights on the ocean before they (*saw, seen*) land again.

10. Then it (*took, taked*) months for Mai's grandparents to be moved from Malaysian refugee camps to the United States.

Exercise 3 Identifying Correct Forms of Irregular Verbs

For each sentence in the following paragraph, choose the correct form of the verb in parentheses.

EXAMPLE   I just **[1]** (*wrote, written*) to my Russian pen pal!

     1. wrote

Joining the Russian-American pen-pal club Druzhba is one of the most interesting things I have ever **[1]** (*did, done*). The founder of the club **[2]** (*chose, chosen*) the name *Druzhba* because it means "friendship" in Russian. This club has **[3]** (*given, gave*) American and Russian students the chance to become friends. I **[4]** (*began, begun*) to write to my pen pal Vanya last September. His reply to my first letter **[5]** (*took, taken*) weeks to get to me. I wish it could have **[6]** (*flew, flown*) here faster from the other side of the globe. In his letters, Vanya has often **[7]** (*written, wrote*) about his daily life, his family, and his thoughts and feelings. We have **[8]** (*become, became*) good friends through our letters even though we have never **[9]** (*spoke, spoken*) to each other. Reading each other's essays in the club newsletter has also **[10]** (*brung, brought*) us closer together.

Review A) Writing the Past and Past Participle Forms of Verbs

For each of the following sentences, write the correct past or past participle form of the verb given.

EXAMPLE   **1.** run   Yesterday we _____ around the track twice.

    1. ran

1. *sing*   Boyz II Men _____ last night.
2. *burst*   The car suddenly _____ into flames.
3. *drink*   Yesterday they _____ juice with their tossed salads and turkey sandwiches.
4. *use*   He _____ to camp out every summer.
5. *do*   They _____ their best to repair the damage caused by the very large hail.
6. *give*   Grandma has _____ us some old photos.
7. *risk*   The detective _____ her life.
8. *ring*   My alarm _____ at six o'clock.
9. *speak*   Toni has not _____ to me since our argument.
10. *fall*   A tree has _____ across the highway.

Review B) Writing the Past and Past Participle Forms of Verbs

Write the correct past or past participle form of each italicized verb in the following paragraph.

EXAMPLE   All my life I have **[1]** (*know*) that I must make my own choices.

    1. known

I have never **[1]** (*choose*) to be on a sports team because I am not a very athletic person. Some people are surprised because my brother and sister have **[2]** (*drive*) themselves very hard and have **[3]** (*become*) excellent athletes. For example, my brother, Emilio, **[4]** (*break*) three swimming records this year alone. He has **[5]** (*swim*) better than anyone else in our school. He also **[6]** (*go*) out for tennis and track this year. My sister, Elena, is only a junior, but she has already **[7]** (*run*) the 100-meter dash faster than any senior girl. I **[8]** (*use*) to think I wanted to follow in my brother's and sister's footsteps, but now I have **[9]** (*take*) a different path in life. My English teacher just **[10]** (*give*) me a chance to lead the debating team, and I am going to grab it!

BORN LOSER reprinted by permission of Newspaper Enterprise Association, Inc.

Review C **Writing the Past and Past Participle Forms of Verbs**

Write the correct past or past participle form of the verb given for each of the following sentences.

EXAMPLES **1.** *go*   We _____ to the Ozark Mountains.

1. *went*

2. *swim*   I have never _____ in an ocean.

2. *swum*

1. *throw*   Kerry should have _____ the ball to Lee, who could have tagged the runner out.

2. *freeze*   Has the water _____ yet?

3. *write*   Theo has _____ me a long letter.

4. *see*   Have you _____ that actor in person?

5. *sing*   The tenors have _____ in Rome, Paris, and New York.

6. *throw*   I finally _____ my old running shoes away and bought a new pair at the mall.

7. *drown*   No one has ever _____ in this lake.

8. *give*   Taro _____ me a bowl of miso soup.

9. *blow*   The strong wind this afternoon _____ down our treehouse in the backyard.

10. *take*   I have already _____ a picture of you, Molly.

Review D **Writing the Past and Past Participle Forms of Verbs**

Write the correct past or past participle form of each of the ten italicized verbs in the following paragraph.

EXAMPLE   Have you ever **[1]** (*take*) a trip to the country?

1. *taken*

We have always **[1]** (*spend*) summer vacations at Uncle Dan's farm in Vermont. We **[2]** (*do*) the most relaxing things there last year! We **[3]** (*swim*) in the millpond and **[4]** (*eat*) watermelon on the back porch. A few times, we **[5]** (*ride*) our bikes into town to get groceries. We also **[6]** (*take*) turns riding Horace, the mule. I have **[7]** (*fall*) off Horace twice, but I have never **[8]** (*break*) any bones. Both times, I **[9]** (*come*) down in a pile of soft hay. Then I dusted myself off and **[10]** (*climb*) on again.

Proofreading Sentences for Correct Verb Forms

Some of the following sentences contain an incorrect verb form. If a verb form is wrong, write the correct form. If the sentence is already correct, write *C*.

EXAMPLE   **1.** Marian Anderson sung her way out of poverty.

　　　　　　　1. sang

1. She went on to earn fame and the Medal of Freedom.
2. Can you tell from this picture that she use to sing classical music?
3. In 1955, Marian Anderson become the first African American singer to perform with the Metropolitan Opera in New York City.
4. She performed in concerts and operas all over the world, but she begun her career as a child singing hymns in church.
5. Anderson, who was from a poor Philadelphia family, was awarded a scholarship to study music in Europe.
6. European audiences soon taked notice of her.
7. Audiences admired her determination and courage.
8. In 1939, Anderson was not permitted to sing at a hall in Washington, D.C., so she give a free concert, attended by 75,000 people, at the Lincoln Memorial.
9. In the 1950s, the U.S. government choosed her to go on a goodwill tour of Asia and to be a United Nations delegate.
10. Anderson writed of her experiences in her autobiography, *My Lord, What a Morning.*

Review F **Proofreading a Paragraph for Correct Verb Forms**

The following paragraph contains ten incorrect verb forms. If a verb form is wrong, write the correct form. If a sentence is already correct, write *C*.

EXAMPLE   **[1]** A Confederate search party had went out to get boots for their soldiers and saddles for their horses.

　　　　　　　1. had gone

　　[1] By chance, the search party runned into the Union cavalry.
[2] It is not clear who attackted first, but a battle begun near

Gettysburg, Pennsylvania, on July 1, 1863. [3] The fighting goed on for three days. [4] First one side and then the other got the upper hand. [5] Shells bursted in the air, and cannonballs whistled in all directions. [6] At one point, some Confederate soldiers clumb to the top of Cemetery Ridge, and their flag flown there a brief time. [7] However, the Union army drived them back. [8] By the time the battle had came to an end, 20,000 Union soldiers and 25,000 Confederate soldiers had fell.

Tense

6d. The *tense* of a verb indicates the time of the action or of the state of being expressed by the verb.

The tenses are formed from the verb's principal parts. Verbs in English have the six tenses shown on the following time line:

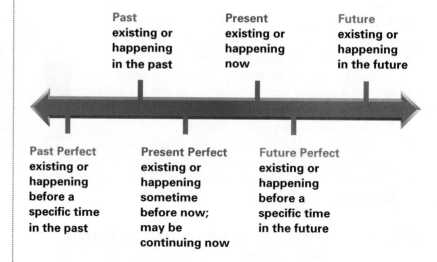

Past
existing or happening in the past

Present
existing or happening now

Future
existing or happening in the future

Past Perfect
existing or happening before a specific time in the past

Present Perfect
existing or happening sometime before now; may be continuing now

Future Perfect
existing or happening before a specific time in the future

EXAMPLES   Max **has worked** [present perfect] all summer, and now he **has** [present] enough money to buy a bicycle.

The chorus **had practiced** [past perfect] for weeks before they **sang** [past] in public last night.

The surgeon **will have reviewed** [future perfect] the test results by next Friday, and she **will decide** [future] whether or not to operate then.

Conjugation of the Verb *Give* in the Active Voice

Present Tense

Singular	Plural
I give	we give
you give	you give
he, she, *or* it gives	they give

Past Tense

Singular	Plural
I gave	we gave
you gave	you gave
he, she, *or* it gave	they gave

Future Tense

Singular	Plural
I will (shall) give	we will (shall) give
you will (shall) give	you will (shall) give
he, she, *or* it will (shall) give	they will (shall) give

Present Perfect Tense

Singular	Plural
I have given	we have given
you have given	you have given
he, she, *or* it has given	they have given

Past Perfect Tense

Singular	Plural
I had given	we had given
you had given	you had given
he, she, *or* it had given	they had given

Future Perfect Tense

Singular	Plural
I will (shall) have given	we will (shall) have given
you will (shall) have given	you will (shall) have given
he, she, *or* it will (shall) have given	they will (shall) have given

Reference Note

See page 164 for a **conjugation of *give* in the passive voice.**

USAGE

STYLE TIP

Traditionally, the helping verbs *shall* and *will* were used differently. Now, however, *shall* can be used almost interchangeably with *will*.

The Progressive Form

Each of the six tenses has an additional form called the *progressive form,* which expresses continuing action. It consists of a form of the verb *be* plus the present participle of a verb. The progressive is not a separate tense but an additional form of each of the six tenses.

PRESENT PROGRESSIVE	am, are, is giving
PAST PROGRESSIVE	was, were giving
FUTURE PROGRESSIVE	will (shall) be giving
PRESENT PERFECT PROGRESSIVE	has, have been giving
PAST PERFECT PROGRESSIVE	had been giving
FUTURE PERFECT PROGRESSIVE	will (shall) have been giving

NOTE   The *emphatic form* of a verb is used to show emphasis. The emphatic form consists of the present or past tense of *do* with the base form of the main verb.

PRESENT EMPHATIC	Although the grass is green, the lawn **does need** watering.
PAST EMPHATIC	The writer endured many setbacks in his career, yet he **did** finally **become** famous.

6e. Each of the six tenses has its own special uses.

(1) The *present tense* is used mainly to express an action or a state of being that is occurring now.

EXAMPLES   The new jet **has** two engines.

Leotie **belongs** to the Latin Club.

They **are decorating** the gym. [progressive form]

The present tense is also used

- to show a customary or habitual action or state of being
- to express a general truth—something that is always true
- to make historical events seem current (such use is called the *historical present*)
- to discuss a literary work (such use is called the *literary present*)
- to express future time

STYLE	TIP

The emphatic form is also used in questions and negative statements. These uses do not place special emphasis on the verb.

QUESTION
  Why **do** bears hibernate?

NEGATIVE STATEMENT
  If the car **does**n't [does not] start, check the battery.

EXAMPLES   We **recycle** newspapers, glass, and aluminum cans.
[customary actions]

The sun **sets** in the west. [general truth]

In 1905, Albert Einstein **makes** history when he **proposes** his theory of relativity. [historical present]

In *David Copperfield,* Dickens **shows** us the extremes of Victorian life. [literary present]

Finals **begin** next week. [future time]

(2) The *past tense* is used to express an action or state of being that occurred in the past but that is not occurring now.

EXAMPLES   They **looked** for seashells.

The manatees **were swimming** in the canal.
[progressive form]

NOTE A past action or state of being may also be shown with the past form *used*, plus *to,* plus the base form of the main verb.

EXAMPLE   Chicago **used to be** the second-largest U.S. city.

(3) The *future tense* is used to express an action or a state of being that will occur. It is formed with *will* or *shall* and the main verb's base form.

EXAMPLES   **Shall** we **set** the table?

The new model cars **will arrive** soon.

They **will be selling** them soon. [progressive form]

NOTE A future action or state of being may also be shown in other ways.

EXAMPLES   We **are going to make** our own Mardi Gras costumes.

The president **holds** a press conference **next Monday.**

(4) The *present perfect tense* is used to express an action or a state of being that occurred at some indefinite time in the past. It is formed with the helping verb *have* or *has.*

EXAMPLES   The Mendozas **have invited** us over for a cookout.

The Red Cross **has been delivering** medical supplies.
[progressive form]

NOTE Do not use the present perfect tense to express a specific time in the past. Instead, use the past tense.

NONSTANDARD	We have seen that movie last Saturday. [*Last Saturday* indicates a specific time in the past.]
STANDARD	We **saw** that movie last Saturday.

The present perfect tense is also used to express an action or a state of being that began in the past and continues into the present.

EXAMPLES   Li Hua **has taken** violin lessons for eight years.

We **have been living** in Amarillo since early 1998. [progressive form]

(5) The **past perfect tense** is used to express an action or a state of being that was completed in the past before some other past action or event. It is formed with the helping verb *had.*

EXAMPLES   Once the judges **had viewed** the paintings, they announced the winners. [The viewing occurred before the announcing.]

By the time that the Spanish conquistadors arrived, that redwood **had been growing** for three centuries. [progressive form]

(6) The **future perfect tense** is used to express an action or a state of being that will be completed in the future before some other future occurrence. It is formed with the helping verbs *will have* or *shall have.*

EXAMPLES   By the time Mom returns, I **will have done** my chores. [The doing will be completed before the returning.]

In August, Aaron **will have been taking** Hebrew lessons for two years. [progressive form]

Exercise 4 Explaining the Uses of Tenses in Sentences

Each item on the next page contains two correct sentences. Identify the tense or tenses used in each sentence. Be prepared to explain the meanings of the two sentences in each pair.

EXAMPLE   **1. a.** For breakfast she eats a bagel and some cereal.
        b. For breakfast she is eating a bagel and some cereal.

    1. a. present
       b. present progressive

─HELP─
In the examples for Exercise 4, the first sentence expresses customary action and the second sentence expresses action that is happening right now.

1. **a.** You will put down your pencils when the bell rings.
   b. You will have put down your pencils when the bell rings.
2. **a.** He worked at the gas station in the summertime.
   b. He has worked at the gas station in the summertime.
3. **a.** What caused the computer to crash?
   b. What has been causing the computer to crash?
4. **a.** When I arrived, Morton left.
   b. When I arrived, Morton had left.
5. **a.** Shelley was working on her bicycle.
   b. Shelley had been working on her bicycle when we arrived.

> **Exercise 5** **Using the Different Tenses of Verbs in Sentences**

Change the tense of the verb in each of the following sentences to the tense indicated in parentheses.

EXAMPLE   **1.** Maria always goes home at five o'clock. (*past*)

   1. went

1. The quick, graceful otter swam to the edge of the pool. (*present perfect*)
2. Our class will read Shakespeare's *Much Ado About Nothing*. (*future progressive*)
3. Before the concert, the orchestra practices the new pieces. (*past perfect*)
4. The guests will be arriving at the train station. (*present perfect progressive*)
5. By then, I will solve the riddle. (*future perfect*)
6. The three sisters regularly meet for lunch. (*past*)
7. The new computers have been working fine for three weeks. (*past perfect progressive*)
8. Wasps were entering the house through the torn screen. (*present*)
9. The lawn mower has started after all! (*past emphatic*)
10. We reset the clocks for daylight saving time. (*future*)

Consistency of Tense

6f. Do not change needlessly from one tense to another.

When describing events that occur at the same time, use verbs in the same tense. When describing events that occur at different times, use different tenses to show the order of events clearly.

NONSTANDARD	Cara fielded the ball and throws the runner out. [*Fielded* is past tense; *throws* is present tense.]
STANDARD	Cara **fielded** the ball and **threw** the runner out. [*Fielded* and *threw* are both past tense.]
STANDARD	Cara **fields** the ball and **throws** the runner out. [*Fields* and *throws* are both present tense.]
NONSTANDARD	She stands on the mound and will stare at the batter. [*Stands* is present tense; *will stare* is future tense.]
STANDARD	She **stands** on the mound and **stares** at the batter. [*Stands* and *stares* are both present tense.]
STANDARD	She **will stand** on the mound and **stare** at the batter. [*Will stand* and *stare* are both future tense.]
NONSTANDARD	The batter wished that he practiced more before the game. [Because the action of practicing was completed before the action of wishing, the verb should be *had practiced*, not *practiced*.]
STANDARD	The batter **wished** that he **had practiced** more before the game.

Exercise 6 Proofreading a Paragraph to Make the Tenses of the Verbs Consistent

Proofread the following paragraph, looking for needless changes of verb tense. Choose whether to rewrite the paragraph in the present or past tense. Then, change the verbs to make the tenses consistent.

EXAMPLE **[1]** It all started as soon as I come home from school.

1. *It all started as soon as I came home from school.*

or

It all starts as soon as I come home from school.

[1] I am in my room, and I have planned to study for two hours. [2] It was about five o'clock in the afternoon. [3] To my surprise, Nancy Meng dropped by. [4] She dashes into the house, runs up the stairs, and calls my name. [5] What she wanted is a fishing companion. [6] All week she has been thinking about going fishing. [7] Getting my fishing gear together, I become excited and can almost see the fish fighting over which one is to be my first catch of the day. [8] On our way out to the lake, we see clouds beginning to form, and we knew we are in for trouble. [9] It rains all right—for the whole weekend. [10] The fish were safe for another week.

┌─H E L P ─
For the paragraph in Exercise 6, either the present tense or the past tense can be used correctly.

Active and Passive Voice

6g. A verb in the *active voice* expresses an action done by its subject. A verb in the *passive voice* expresses an action done to its subject.

ACTIVE VOICE   The coach **instructed** us. [The subject, *coach*, performs the action.]

PASSIVE VOICE   We **were instructed** by the coach. [The subject, *We*, receives the action.]

ACTIVE VOICE   **Did** Brandon **score** the winning touchdown? [The subject, *Brandon*, performs the action.]

PASSIVE VOICE   **Was** the winning touchdown **scored** by Brandon? [The subject, *touchdown*, receives the action.]

Compare the following related sentences:

               S   O

ACTIVE   The author **provides** helpful diagrams.

               S

PASSIVE   Helpful diagrams **are provided** by the author.

In these two sentences, the object of the active sentence is the subject of the passive one. The subject of the active sentence is expressed in a prepositional phrase in the passive sentence. Note that this phrase can be omitted.

PASSIVE   Helpful diagrams **are provided.**

In a passive sentence, the verb phrase includes a form of *be* and the past participle of the main verb. Other helping verbs may also be included.

           S   O

ACTIVE   The tutor **is helping** Sharon.

           S

PASSIVE   Sharon **is being helped** by the tutor.

           S   O

ACTIVE   Someone **has erased** the tapes.

           S

PASSIVE   The tapes **have been erased.**

The chart on the following page shows the conjugation of the verb *give* in the passive voice.

Reference Note

For more information on **helping verbs,** see page 14.

Reference Note

For the **conjugation of the verb** *give* **in the active voice,** see page 157.

USAGE

Conjugation of the Verb *Give* in the Passive Voice

Present Tense

Singular	Plural
I am given	we are given
you are given	you are given
he, she, *or* it is given	they are given

Past Tense

Singular	Plural
I was given	we were given
you were given	you were given
he, she, *or* it was given	they were given

Future Tense

Singular	Plural
I will (shall) be given	we will (shall) be given
you will (shall) be given	you will (shall) be given
he, she, *or* it will (shall) be given	they will (shall) be given

Present Perfect Tense

Singular	Plural
I have been given	we have been given
you have been given	you have been given
he, she, *or* it has been given	they have been given

Past Perfect Tense

Singular	Plural
I had been given	we had been given
you had been given	you had been given
he, she, *or* it had been given	they had been given

Future Perfect Tense

Singular	Plural
I will (shall) have been given	we will (shall) have been given
you will (shall) have been given	you will (shall) have been given
he, she, *or* it will (shall) have been given	they will (shall) have been given

The progressive forms of the passive voice exist for all six tenses. However, the use of *be* or *been* with *being* is extremely awkward—*give*, for example, in the passive future perfect is *will (shall) have been being given*. Consequently, the progressive form of the passive voice is generally used only in the present and past tenses.

Using the Passive Voice

Although the passive voice is not any less correct than the active voice, it is less direct, less forceful, and less concise. In general, you should avoid using the passive voice. First, it generally requires more words to express a thought than the active voice does. Consequently, the passive voice can result in awkward writing. Second, the performer of the action in a passive voice construction is revealed indirectly or not at all. As a result, a sentence written in the passive voice can sound weak. Compare the following pairs of sentences.

| PASSIVE | The ball **was hit** over the outfield fence by Jody. |
| ACTIVE | Jody **hit** the ball over the outfield fence. |

| PASSIVE | The totals for the new budget **were** carefully **checked.** |
| ACTIVE | The club treasurer carefully **checked** the totals for the new budget. |

The passive voice is useful, however, in situations such as the following ones:

(1) when you do not know the performer of the action

EXAMPLES   Over three thousand roses **were planted.**

Are the peaches **being harvested** on schedule?

(2) when you do not want to reveal the performer of the action

EXAMPLES   Charges **were brought** against the vandals.

Many large donations to the building fund **have been made.**

(3) when you want to emphasize the receiver of the action

EXAMPLES   Jacques Chirac **was elected** president of France in 1995.

These remarkable fossils **were found** nearby.

MEETING THE CHALLENGE

Mystery writers sometimes use the passive voice to relate information about a crime without revealing who performed the action. Write a one-page "mini-mystery" of your own in which you make use of the passive voice to describe an event while keeping the doer a secret. Try to include some clues in your story, and then see whether your classmates can solve the mystery.

COMPUTER TIP

Some software programs can identify and highlight verbs in the passive voice. If you use such a program, keep in mind that it can't tell why you used the passive voice. If you did so for a particular reason, you may want to leave the verb in the passive voice.

Exercise 7 Identifying Active and Passive Voice

For each of the following sentences, tell whether the verb is in the *active* or *passive* voice.

EXAMPLE   **1.** In the morning, I am awakened by the alarm clock.

1. passive

1. The newest CD by my favorite group was not reviewed by most music critics.
2. The student body elects the council president.
3. Angelo's courageous act of putting out the fire in the basement prevented a tragedy.
4. W. C. Handy composed the famous jazz classic "St. Louis Blues."
5. Your generous contribution to help the homeless is greatly appreciated.
6. The half-time show at the state championship was performed by the band from Millersville.
7. This afternoon the baby stood up by himself.
8. Was Mr. Yañez awarded the trophy?
9. I don't understand this math problem.
10. Brian has been appointed captain of the basketball team.

Exercise 8 Using Verbs in the Active Voice and the Passive Voice

Identify the verb in each of the following sentences as either *active* or *passive*. Then, revise each sentence that is in the passive voice so that it is in active voice.

EXAMPLE   **1.** My 4-H project was just completed.

1. passive; I just completed my 4-H project.

1. For my project I grew vegetables in containers.
2. Initially, 4-H clubs were joined only by farm children.
3. Their projects focused on crops and livestock.
4. Later projects, such as personal safety and career studies, interested young people in the city.
5. Projects are often exhibited by members at county fairs.
6. The 4-H club members also learn about good citizenship.
7. Summer camps are attended by many 4-H members.
8. Community projects are planned by our club yearly.
9. The city appreciated our tree-planting project.
10. Many young people are helped by participation in 4-H.

Six Troublesome Verbs

Lie and *Lay*

6h. The verb *lie* means "to rest," "to recline," or "to remain in a lying position." *Lie* does not take an object. The verb *lay* means "to put" or "to place (something somewhere)." *Lay* generally takes an object.

Reference Note

For more about **objects of verbs,** see page 59.

Principal Parts of *Lie* and *Lay*			
Base Form	**Present Participle**	**Past**	**Past Participle**
lie	[is] lying	lay	[have] lain
lay	[is] laying	laid	[have] laid

┌HELP─

The verb *lie* can also mean "to tell an untruth." Used in this way, *lie* still does not take an object. The past and past participle forms of this meaning of *lie* are *lied* and *[have] lied*.

USAGE

EXAMPLES   **Lie** down if you don't feel well.
Lay those books down.

Lambert **lay** on the lounge chair.
Lambert **laid** the towel on the lounge chair.

He **had lain** on the couch too long.
He **had laid** the newspaper on the couch.

Exercise 9   Choosing the Correct Forms of *Lie* and *Lay*

Write the correct form of *lie* or *lay* for the blank in each of the following sentences.

EXAMPLE   **1.** Jennifer _____ the flowers on the table and looked for a vase.

       1. laid

1. He _____ the report aside and called for order.
2. Alma will _____ down for a siesta.
3. She has _____ on the couch all morning, watching those silly cartoons and eating cereal.
4. The baby was _____ quietly in the nurse's arms.
5. Is that today's paper _____ in the mud?
6. I have _____ the shoes near the fire to dry, and I hung my wet clothes in the garage.
7. _____ down, Spot.
8. The lace had _____ in the trunk for years before we explored Grandmother's attic.

9. Our cat _____ in the sun whenever it can.

10. After reading for almost three hours, I _____ back and rested my head on the cushions.

Sit and *Set*

6i. The verb *sit* means "to rest in an upright, seated position." *Sit* seldom takes an object. The verb *set* means "to put" or "to place (something somewhere)." *Set* generally takes an object.

┌HELP──

You may know that the word *set* has more meanings than the two given here. Check in a dictionary to see if the meaning you intend requires an object.

EXAMPLE
We watched silently as the sun **set**. [Here, *set* does not take an object.]

Principal Parts of *Sit* and *Set*			
Base Form	**Present Participle**	**Past**	**Past Participle**
sit	[is] sitting	sat	[have] sat
set	[is] setting	set	[have] set

EXAMPLES   **Sit** down.
Set it down.

The cups **sat** on the tray.
I **set** the cups there.

How long **has** it **sat** on the bench?
She **had set** the picnic basket on the bench.

Exercise 10 **Writing the Forms of *Sit* and *Set***

Write the correct form of *sit* or *set* for the blank in each of the following sentences.

EXAMPLE   **1.** Will you _____ with me, Josh?
    1. sit

1. Please _____ here, Mrs. Brown.

2. Have you _____ the seedlings in the sun?

3. We were _____ in the park during the Fourth of July fireworks display.

4. Someone has already _____ the kettle on the stove.

5. Grandpa is busily _____ several varieties of tomato plants in the vegetable garden.

6. At the concert, Keith _____ near Isabelle.

7. Mrs. Levine _____ the menorah on the mantel and asked Rachel to light the first candle.

8. They were _____ on the rocks, watching the surfers who were riding the large waves.
9. We had _____ still for almost an hour.
10. Have you ever _____ on the beach at sundown and waited for the stars to come out?

Rise and *Raise*

6j. The verb *rise* means "to go in an upward direction." *Rise* does not take an object. The verb *raise* means "to move (something) in an upward direction." *Raise* generally takes an object.

Principal Parts of *Rise* and *Raise*			
Base Form	**Present Participle**	**Past**	**Past Participle**
rise	[is] rising	rose	[have] risen
raise	[is] raising	raised	[have] raised

EXAMPLES   She **rises** early.
She **raises** that question.

The price of cereal **rose**.
The store **raised** prices.

The lakes **have risen** since the spring rains.
The rains **have raised** the water level.

Exercise 11 **Writing the Forms of *Rise* and *Raise***

Write the correct form of *rise* or *raise* for the blank in each of the following sentences.

EXAMPLE   **1.** The river has been _____ rapidly since noon.
1. rising

1. Please _____ and face the audience; then, begin your oral interpretation of the poem.
2. After the speech, the reporters _____ several questions that the senator refused to answer.
3. Will the governor _____ sales tax again this year, or will he wait until after the election?
4. The price of fuel has _____ steadily.
5. Let's get there before the curtain _____.

6. Jerry and Alexander, two of the stagehands, will _____ the curtain for each act.

7. The bread has _____ beautifully.

8. The moon _____ and slipped behind a cloud, but there was still plenty of light for us to find our way home.

9. The candidate _____ to address her supporters.

10. The children _____ their flag for Cinco de Mayo.

Review G **Identifying the Correct Forms of *Lie* and *Lay*, *Sit* and *Set*, and *Rise* and *Raise***

Choose the correct verb in parentheses in each of the following sentences.

EXAMPLE **1.** The number of immigrants coming to the United States (*rose, raised*) steadily during the late 1800s and early 1900s.

1. *rose*

1. The Hungarian mother shown below (*sat, set*) with her children for this picture around 1910.

2. They were among thousands of immigrant families who (*sat, set*) their baggage on American soil for the first time at the immigration station on Ellis Island in New York Harbor.

3. (*Lying, Laying*) down was often impossible on the crowded ships that brought these immigrants to the United States.

4. Most immigrants were thankful to be able to (*lie, lay*) their few belongings on the deck and think of the future.

The Granger Collection, New York

5. Their hopes for new lives must have (*risen, raised*) as they drew closer to the United States.

6. The history book (*lying, laying*) on my desk states that eleven million immigrants came to the United States between 1870 and 1899.

7. (*Sit, Set*) down and read more about the immigrants who came from Germany, Ireland, Great Britain, Scandinavia, and the Netherlands in the early 1800s.

8. After 1890, the number of immigrants from Austria-Hungary, Italy, Russia, Poland, and Greece (*rose, raised*).

9. Many United States citizens were (*rising, raising*) concerns that there would not be enough jobs for everyone in the country.

10. However, we know now that immigrant workers helped the country to (*rise, raise*) to new industrial heights.

Mood

6k. *Mood* is the form a verb takes to indicate the attitude of the person using the verb.

(1) The *indicative mood* is used to express a fact, an opinion, or a question.

EXAMPLES   Seamus Heaney **is** the Irish poet who **won** the Nobel Prize in literature in 1995.

I **think** he **is** the best of the poets featured in this book.

Have you **read** the poem, Anita?

(2) The *imperative mood* is used to express a direct command or request.

EXAMPLES   **Halt!** [command]

Please **write** your answers on a separate sheet of paper. [request]

(3) The *subjunctive mood* is used to express a suggestion, a necessity, a condition contrary to fact, or a wish.

EXAMPLES   Gerald suggested that we **be** ready to board the train. [suggestion]

It is essential that all of the delegates **be** available for questions. [necessity]

If I **were** you, I would call them immediately. [condition contrary to fact]

Leilani wishes she **were** scuba diving off the Yucatán peninsula. [wish]

PEANUTS reprinted by permission of United Feature Syndicate, Inc.

> **Review H**   **Identifying the Mood of Verbs**

For each of the sentences on the following page, identify the mood of the italicized verb as *indicative, imperative,* or *subjunctive.*

EXAMPLE   **1.** Ferryboats *sail* frequently between Calais, France, and Dover, England.

    1. indicative

1. Please *hold* your applause until after all of the presentations.
2. La Paz, in Bolivia, *is* the world's highest capital city.
3. Female marsupials *carry* their young in pouches.
4. Is it necessary that he *rehearse* tonight?
5. *Take* out the trash immediately, Paul!
6. If I *were* you, I would not swim in that lake.
7. How much interest *does* State Bank *pay* on savings accounts and checking accounts?
8. Angela *intends* to continue her work at the humane society after school.
9. Mr. Guzman, please *consider* postponing the practice until next week.
10. For rust to form, it is essential that four atoms of solid iron and three molecules of oxygen *be* present.

Review I Identifying Correct Uses of Verbs

From each pair of words in parentheses, choose the correct item.

EXAMPLE   **[1]** Look at this great old photograph that Grandma has just (*gave, given*) me.

1. *given*

Grandma told me that the Pop Corn King **[1]** (*been, was*) her great-grandfather. This warmhearted man **[2]** (*took, taken*) Grandma's mother and aunt into his home after their parents had **[3]** (*drowned, drownded*) in a flood. He would sometimes let the girls **[4]** (*sit, set*) in the driver's seat with him. The photograph was **[5]** (*maked, made*) in 1914 in the resort town of Petoskey, Michigan. During the summer, the

Pop Corn King **[6]** (*use, used*) to drive through the streets in the late afternoon. He **[7]** (*rang, rung*) a bell, and children **[8]** (*run, ran*) out to buy treats just as kids do today. Look—the popcorn **[9]** (*cost, costed*) only five cents! The last time I **[10]** (*buyed, bought*) popcorn at the movies, I paid $3.75!

Chapter Review

A. Identifying Correct Forms of Verbs

If a sentence contains an incorrect verb form, write the correct form. If a sentence is already correct, write *C*.

1. That car breaked the land speed record.
2. Grandfather walks around the park every morning when he lived in Madrid.
3. The crocodile ran across the marsh and slips into the water.
4. Are the bells of Sant' Angelo rung every day at sunset?
5. After Lourdes had drove two hours, she stopped for a break.
6. Grandpa has swam across Santa Rosa Sound.
7. Our dog Pippa likes to set in the doorway and watch the traffic.
8. Will the bread raise faster in the oven or on the table?
9. Uncle Ben brung us a giant jigsaw puzzle of the Mojave Desert.
10. I could have sworn that the Green Bay Packers won the Super Bowl that year.
11. Carmilla's blouse was stained, but she knowed how to get the stain out.
12. Lilly has drunk two glasses of milk and still wants more.
13. Toucans fly by the window, and a cool breeze blew from the gulf.
14. Last night, Dr. Madison talks about the new laser operation.
15. The dogs are laying under the porch.
16. The curtains raised at the beginning of the first act.
17. She has apparently choosed the color blue.
18. The heron waits for the fish before it caught it.
19. We laid the tools down and had lunch.
20. It's a good thing that truck hasn't broke down—it was certainly an expensive investment.

B. Identifying Active and Passive Voice

For each of the following sentences, tell whether the verb is in the *active* or *passive* voice.

21. The United States president is elected every four years by a majority of electoral votes.

USAGE

22. Yesterday the fawn ate its first full meal.
23. Was Oscar told the news beforehand?
24. The Veterans of Foreign Wars banquet was well attended.
25. Jenny speaks French and Arabic as well as English.
26. Was Ruth Lopez appointed goodwill ambassador by the secretary-general?
27. Most early British racing cars had superchargers.
28. The best songs in the show were performed by a husband-and-wife duet from San Marcos, Texas.
29. Our club sponsors a variety of community projects.
30. Large numbers of elephants are herded into different areas of the park in order to preserve the foliage.

C. Proofreading a Paragraph for Correct Verb Forms

The following paragraph contains errors in verb usage. If a verb form is wrong, write the correct form. If a sentence is already correct, write *C*.

[31] Last night the wind blowed for hours during the snowstorm. [32] When Libby and I looked outside in the morning, at least a foot of snow had fell. [33] Instead of a brown, lifeless yard, we saw a glittering fantasy world. [34] Never in our lives had we ate our cereal as fast as we did that morning! [35] We quickly put on our parkas and ran out the door to build a snow fort. [36] Mom, smiling, come outside, too. [37] We should have knowed she would start a snowball fight! [38] Before we could get our revenge, Mom goes back into the house to warm up. [39] Soon afterward, our feet felt as if they had freezed solid. [40] When we were finally back inside, Mom brung us hot apple cider as a peace offering.

D. Identifying the Correct Forms of Six Troublesome Verbs

Choose the correct verb in parentheses for each of the following sentences.

41. Their hopes (*raised, rose*) when the sun broke through and shone on the city below.

42. Please (*set, sit*) the orchid next to the rhododendron in the greenhouse.

43. Tim (*sat, set*) in the old armchair and recalled long summer evenings from his childhood.

44. Was that you I saw (*laying, lying*) in the hammock a minute ago?

45. (*Lay, Lie*) that magazine down, and listen to what I have to say!

46. The cadets stood at attention as the color sergeant (*rose, raised*) the flag.

47. The mythical phoenix is a bird that (*rises, raises*) from its own ashes.

48. He has a cold, so he has (*laid, lain*) on the couch most of the afternoon.

49. The seals were (*laying, lying*) on the beach.

50. He has (*sat, set*) his tools on the workbench.

Writing Application

Using Verbs in Instructions

Verb Tense   You have been asked to teach your eight-year-old brother to make his own after-school snack. Write instructions for making a nutritious treat. Use correct verb tense so that your directions are easy to follow.

Prewriting   You will need to choose a snack that a child would be able to make and would enjoy. You may want to list all of the steps first and then go back and number them in order.

Writing   As you write your first draft, think about how to define or clarify words that an eight-year-old might not know. Make sure that your verb tenses show the sequence of the steps.

Revising   Ask a friend or young child you know to act out your instructions. Revise any steps that confuse your assistant. Add words that indicate chronological order (such as *first, second, then,* and *next*).

Publishing   Check to be sure your verb tenses are correct. Use your textbook or a dictionary to check the spelling of the verbs in your instructions. Pay special attention to irregular verbs. Your class may decide to make its own snack cookbook to share with elementary school students or your local parent-teacher organization.

Using Pronouns Correctly
Nominative and Objective Uses; Clear Reference

Diagnostic Preview

A. Correcting Pronoun Forms

Identify each incorrectly used pronoun in the following sentences. Then, write the correct form of that pronoun. If a sentence is already correct, write *C*.

EXAMPLE **1.** Excuse me, Rhonda, but this arrangement is strictly between Carl and I.

　　 1. I—me

1. The author spoke to we history students about Slavic culture in Eastern Europe.
2. During the Olympic trials every diver except she received a low score from the judges.
3. The instructor, who seemed nervous during the show, was proud of Lani's performance.
4. It couldn't have been her.
5. Van is more energetic than me.
6. Rick couldn't spot Maura and I in the huge crowd at the state fairgrounds.
7. Tyrone and he are playing backgammon at Regina's house this afternoon.

8. Laura gave he and Edwin a beautiful poem that she had written about friendship.
9. Angie's neighbors, Mrs. Brandt and he, helped plant the trees for Arbor Day.
10. Whomever can possibly take her place?

B. Proofreading a Paragraph for Correct Pronoun Forms

Some of the sentences in the following paragraph contain pronouns that have been used incorrectly. Identify each incorrectly used pronoun. Then, write the correct form of that pronoun. If a sentence is already correct, write *C*.

EXAMPLE   **[1]** To Velma and I, Dizzy Dean is one of the greatest baseball players of all time.

    1. I—me

[11] We think there never has been another baseball player like him. [12] Fans still talk about he and his teammates. [13] Dean pitched for the St. Louis Cardinals, to who his fastball was a great help, especially in the 1934 World Series. [14] Dean was such a character that his fans never knew what crazy notion might come to he during games. [15] He had a real confidence about him, too. [16] According to one famous story about Dean, whom was also known for his quips, he once said, "Tain't braggin' if you kin really do it!" [17] When Dean became a sportscaster, him and his informal speech appealed to fans. [18] He liked his fans, and they liked him. [19] A big honor for he was being elected to baseball's Hall of Fame. [20] Us fans can go to the Dizzy Dean Museum in Jackson, Mississippi, to find out more about Dean's career.

Case

7a. *Case* is the form that a noun or pronoun takes to show its relationship to other words in a sentence.

In English, there are three cases: *nominative*, *objective*, and *possessive*. Choosing the correct case form for a noun is usually simple because the form remains the same in the nominative and objective cases.

NOMINATIVE   My **dentist** has opened a new practice in the office building next to the mall.

OBJECTIVE   The receptionist who works for my **dentist** recently graduated from junior college.

Only in the possessive case does a noun change its form, usually by adding an apostrophe and an *s*.

POSSESSIVE   My **dentist's** business is thriving.

Personal pronouns, however, have distinct case forms. In the following example, the pronouns in boldface type all refer to the same person. They have different forms because of their different uses.

EXAMPLE   **I** [nominative] **forgot to bring my** [possessive] **notebook with me** [objective].

The Case Forms of Personal Pronouns

DIRTY EDDIE AND ME HAVE A LOT IN COMMON, BOY...

SON, DIDN'T THEY TEACH YOU IN SCHOOL WHEN TO USE "I"?

WELL, SURE...BEFORE "E," EXCEPT AFTER "C."

2-24

BORN LOSER reprinted by permission of Newspaper Enterprise Association, Inc.

Personal Pronouns			
	Nominative Case	**Objective Case**	**Possessive Case**
Singular			
First Person	I	me	my, mine
Second Person	you	you	your, yours
Third Person	he, she, it	him, her, it	his, her, hers, its
Plural			
First Person	we	us	our, ours
Second Person	you	you	your, yours
Third Person	they	them	their, theirs

Notice that *you* and *it* have the same form in the nominative and the objective cases. All other personal pronouns have different nominative and objective forms.

The Nominative Case

Nominative case pronouns—*I, you, he, she, it, we,* and *they*—are used as subjects of verbs and as predicate nominatives.

7b. The subject of a verb should be in the nominative case.

EXAMPLES   **I** told Phillip that **we** would win. [*I* is the subject of *told; we* is the subject of *would win.*]

Were **Renata** and **he** on time? [*Renata* and *he* are the compound subject of *were.*]

Reference Note

For more about the **subjects of verbs,** see page 44.

USAGE

Oral Practice 1 **Using Pronouns as Subjects**

Read the following sentences aloud, stressing the italicized pronouns.

1. *He* and *I* agree that lacrosse is the most exciting game *we*'ve ever played.
2. *They* and their friends enjoyed the field trip.
3. Will Sue Ann and *she* enter the art contest?
4. Our teacher and *we* are glad that *he* and *she* are returning from their vacation soon.
5. *He* and *she* said that *we* were responsible for counting the ballots and posting the results.
6. Where are *they* and my parents?
7. Will *you* and *he* help us with the book sale?
8. When are *you* and *I* going to Arizona?

┌─HELP─

To choose the correct pronoun forms in a compound subject, try each pronoun separately with the verb.

EXAMPLE
(*She, Her*) and (*they, them*) answered the ad.
[*She answered* or *Her answered*? *They answered* or *Them answered*?]

She and **they** answered the ad.

Exercise 1 **Identifying Pronouns Used as Subjects**

The following paragraph contains ten pairs of pronouns in parentheses. For each pair, choose the correct pronoun to use as a subject.

EXAMPLE   [1] (*They, Them*) may be the most famous husband and wife scientist team ever.

1. *They*

Although Marie and Pierre Curie were both brilliant physicists, [1] (*she, her*) is better known than her husband is today. In fact, [2] (*I, me*) was genuinely surprised to learn that [3] (*them, they*), along with another scientist, shared the Nobel Prize in physics in 1903. [4] (*We, Us*) tend to remember only Marie primarily because [5] (*her, she*) was the first woman to win a Nobel Prize. During their life together, Marie Curie always felt that [6] (*her, she*) and Pierre were a team. Working in a small laboratory in Paris, [7] (*they, them*) didn't have room for independent research. Before his death in 1906, [8] (*them, they*) collaborated on almost every project. In 1911, [9] (*she, her*) was again honored by the Nobel committee when [10] (*she, her*) was awarded the prize in chemistry.

Reference Note

For more information about **predicate nominatives,** see page 58.

STYLE TIP

Widespread usage has made such expressions as *It's me, That's him,* or *Could it have been her?* acceptable in informal conversation and writing. Avoid using them in formal speaking and in your written work unless you are writing notes, informal dialogue, or friendly letters.

STYLE TIP

Sometimes pronouns such as *I, he, she, we,* and *they* sound awkward when used as parts of a compound subject or a compound predicate nominative. In such cases, it is a good idea to revise the sentence.

AWKWARD
She and we are going to the concert.

BETTER
We are going to the concert with **her.**

7c. A predicate nominative should be in the nominative case.

A *predicate nominative* is a word or word group in the predicate that identifies the subject or refers to it. A predicate nominative is connected to its subject by a linking verb. A pronoun used as a predicate nominative generally follows a form of the verb *be* or a phrase ending in *be* or *been.*

EXAMPLES   This is **he.**

            Did you know that the pitcher was **she**?

Oral Practice 2 Using Pronouns as Predicate Nominatives

Read the following sentences aloud, stressing the italicized pronouns.

1. Do you know whether it was *he*?
2. I thought it was *they.*
3. The winner of the marathon is *she.*
4. The ones you saw dancing were not *we.*
5. Can the valedictorian be *she*?
6. The first ones to arrive were *he* and *she.*
7. Do you think it may have been *they*?
8. The best speakers are *she* and I.

Exercise 2 Identifying Pronouns Used as Subjects and Predicate Nominatives

Identify the correct pronoun in parentheses for each of the following sentences. Then, give its use in the sentence—as a *subject* or *predicate nominative.*

EXAMPLE   1. If the phone rings, it will probably be (*she, her*).

          1. *she—predicate nominative*

1. How did you know the guest speakers were (*they, them*)?
2. (*She, Her*) and (*he, him*) will move to San Miguel.
3. Open the door! It is (*I, me*)!
4. You and (*me, I*) are the only candidates left.
5. It was wonderful to hear that the winner was (*he, him*).
6. (*Us, We*) and (*them, they*) will meet at five o'clock.
7. That man looked a little like Harry, but it was not (*he, him*) after all.
8. Believe it or not, (*she, her*) was on the radio this morning.
9. Yes, the one in costume was really (*she, her*)!
10. You and (*we, us*) were the first visitors.

The Objective Case

Objective case pronouns—*me, you, him, her, it, us,* and *them*—are used as direct objects, indirect objects, and objects of prepositions.

7d. A direct object should be in the objective case.

A **direct object** is a noun, pronoun, or word group that tells who or what receives the action of the verb or shows the result of the action.

EXAMPLES   Phil called **her** last night. [*Her* tells *whom* Phil called.]

We still don't know what caused **them**. [*Them* shows the results of the action caused.]

> **Oral Practice 3** **Using Pronouns as Direct Objects**

Read the following sentences aloud, stressing the italicized pronouns.

1. They saw Liang and *me* at the fair.
2. Julia said that she recognized *him* and *me* at once.
3. Has anyone called *her* or *him* lately?
4. They took *us* to the reggae concert.
5. Alicia often visits Charlene and *her*.
6. A dog chased *her* and *me* out of the yard.
7. Within a few hours, the search party found Duane and *him*.
8. Did you ask *them* or *us*?

> **Exercise 3** **Choosing Pronouns Used as Direct Objects**

For each item below, write an appropriate pronoun in the objective case. Use a variety of pronouns. Do not use *you* or *it*.

EXAMPLE   **1.** Have you told _____ yet?

        1. him

1. I found Nina and _____ in the library.
2. Will you help _____ or _____ with their homework?
3. Sylvia Chu drove Candy and _____ to the movies.
4. We all watched Aaron and _____ as they ran the marathon.
5. These gloves fit both Carl and _____.
6. Did you tell _____ about the picnic?
7. If you don't call _____, I will.
8. The realtor showed _____ and _____ the apartment.
9. That solution suits _____.
10. The doctor cured _____.

Reference Note

For more about the different types of **objects,** see page 59.

STYLE   **TIP**

When the object is compound, try each pronoun separately with the verb. All parts of the compound must be correct for the sentence to be correct.

EXAMPLE

Phil's call surprised (*she, her*) and (*I, me*). [*Phil's call surprised she* or *Phil's call surprised her*? *It surprised I* or *It surprised me*?]

Phil's call surprised **her** and **me.**

MEETING THE CHALLENGE

To keep from confusing their readers, news reporters need to keep their pronouns straight when writing a story. Write a short news report in which you relate the details of an interesting event or crime. Use personal pronouns in the appropriate cases, and try to use at least four different pronoun forms.

USAGE

7e. An indirect object should be in the objective case.

An *indirect object* is a noun, pronoun, or word group that appears in sentences containing direct objects. An indirect object tells *to whom* or *to what* or *for whom* or *for what* the action of the verb is done.

EXAMPLES   Molly made **me** a tape. [*Me* tells *for whom* the tape was made.]

                The puppies were muddy, so we gave **them** a bath. [*Them* tells *to what* we gave a bath.]

NOTE   Indirect objects do not follow prepositions. If a preposition such as *to* or *for* precedes an object, the object is an object of a preposition.

TIPS & TRICKS

Generally, the indirect object comes between the verb and the direct object.

EXAMPLES
Grandma knitted **us** sweaters.

We gave **climbing the cliff** our full attention.

Oral Practice 4   **Using Pronouns as Indirect Objects**

Read the following sentences aloud, stressing the italicized pronouns.

1. Mrs. Petratos offered *them* delicious moussaka.
2. Show Yolanda and *her* your snapshots of Chicago.
3. Sara made Dad and *me* mittens and matching scarves.
4. Send Tom and *him* your new address.
5. My parents told *her* and *me* the news.
6. Mrs. Morita gave *him* and *her* applications.
7. Tell Willie and *them* the story that you told Erin and *me*.
8. The judges awarded *us* the trophy.

Exercise 4   **Writing Pronouns Used as Indirect Objects**

For each item below, write an appropriate pronoun in the objective case. Use a variety of pronouns. Do not use *you* or *it*.

EXAMPLE   1. The teacher gave _____ their homework assignments.

          1. *them*

1. Hassan asked _____ the most difficult question.
2. Alex baked _____ a loaf of banana bread.
3. The teacher handed _____ and _____ the homework assignments.
4. Linda threw _____ the ball.
5. Mr. Young has never told _____ and _____ the real story.
6. Writing stories gives _____ great pleasure.
7. We brought _____ T-shirts from California.
8. Mr. Cruz sent _____ a pen as a graduation gift.
9. My little sister gave _____ an animal carved out of soap.
10. Lee's cousin knitted _____ a sweater.

Review A **Identifying Correct Forms of Pronouns**

Identify the correct pronoun in parentheses for each of the following sentences. Then, give its use in the sentence—as a *subject, predicate nominative, direct object,* or *indirect object*.

EXAMPLE 1. Brian and (*I, me*) visited the computer fair.

1. *I—subject*

1. A guide showed (*we, us*) the latest in technology.
2. She told Brian and (*I, me*) some interesting facts about software.
3. In a short time, we had surprised (*she, her*) and several bystanders with our new computer game.
4. The new computer aces were (*we, us*)!
5. Another guide showed Brian and (*I, me*) all kinds of robotic machines.
6. The guide said that (*he, him*) and his twin sister were going to dance with two robots.
7. The crowd and (*they, them*) seemed to enjoy the performance.
8. One robot reached out and touched (*us, we*) with a metal hand.
9. Brian and (*I, me*) asked our guides how the machines worked.
10. (*They, Them*) patiently explained the control panels.

7f. An object of a preposition should be in the objective case.

A noun or pronoun that follows a preposition is called the ***object of a preposition.*** Together, a preposition, its object, and any modifiers of that object make up a prepositional phrase.

EXAMPLES   with **me**   before **her**   next to **them**

for **us**   behind **him**   instead of **me**

NOTE   Many people use incorrect pronoun forms with prepositions. You may have heard phrases like *between he and they* and *for you and I.* These phrases are incorrect. The pronouns are objects of a preposition and should be in the objective case: *between him and them, for you and me.*

EXAMPLES   The coaches rode in a bus in front of **us.**

She is always very polite to **him** and **me.**

May I play soccer with **you** and **them**?

Between **you** and **me**, I am worried about **them.**

Reference Note

For a **list of common prepositions,** see page 28.

TIPS & TRICKS

To determine the correct pronoun form when the object of a preposition is compound, try each pronoun separately in the prepositional phrase.

EXAMPLE

The company sent a letter to (*she, her*) and (*I, me*). [*To she* or *to her*? *To I* or *to me*?]

The company sent a letter to **her** and **me.**

Review B **Proofreading a Paragraph for Correct Pronoun Forms**

Identify the ten personal pronouns in the following paragraph. If a pronoun is incorrect, write the correct form. If a pronoun is already correct, write *C*.

EXAMPLE **[1]** She thinks all of we should have the experience of working at a store checkout counter.

1. *She—C; we—us*

[1] Mrs. Jenkins, the home economics teacher that Tricia and me admire, told us all about the Universal Product Code (UPC) yesterday. [2] You and us have seen the black-striped UPC symbols on nearly everything that is for sale. [3] Mrs. Jenkins patiently showed the other classes and we how to interpret the numerals on the UPC. [4] Her explained to we that the first digit identifies the product, the next several digits stand for the manufacturer, the next few digits tell things about the product (such as color and size), and the last digit is a check number that tells the computer if another digit is incorrect. [5] Tricia said that Gregory and her found the lesson especially interesting. [6] The two of they had used the code when they worked as clerks in a store last summer.

The Possessive Case

7g. The personal pronouns in the possessive case—*my, mine, your, yours, his, her, hers, its, our, ours, their, theirs*—are used to show ownership or possession.

(1) The possessive pronouns *mine, yours, his, hers, its, ours,* and *theirs* are used as parts of a sentence in the same ways in which the pronouns in the nominative and the objective cases are used.

SUBJECT	Your car and **mine** need tune-ups.
PREDICATE NOMINATIVE	This backpack is **hers.**
DIRECT OBJECT	We finished **ours** yesterday.
INDIRECT OBJECT	Ms. Kwan gave **theirs** a quick review.
OBJECT OF PREPOSITION	Next to **yours,** my Siamese cat looks puny.

(2) The possessive pronouns *my, your, his, her, its, our,* **and** *their* **are used as adjectives before nouns.**

EXAMPLES   **My** alarm clock is broken.

             Do you know **their** address?

NOTE Some authorities prefer to call these possessive forms adjectives. Follow your teacher's instructions regarding these words.

Generally, a noun or pronoun preceding a gerund should be in the possessive case.

Reference Note
For more about **gerunds,** see page 81.

EXAMPLES   We were all thrilled by **Ken's** scoring in the top 5 percent. [*Ken's* modifies the gerund *scoring.* Whose scoring? *Ken's* scoring.]

             We were all thrilled by **his** scoring in the top 5 percent. [Whose scoring? *His* scoring.]

Review C   **Identifying Correct Forms of Pronouns**

Choose the correct pronoun from each pair given in parentheses in the following paragraph.

EXAMPLE   My cousin Felicia showed **[1]** (*I, me*) some photographs of buildings designed by I. M. Pei.

          1. *me*

Felicia, who is studying architecture, told **[1]** (*I, me*) a little about Pei. **[2]** (*He, Him*) is a famous American architect who was born in China. In 1935, **[3]** (*him, he*) came to the United States to study, and in 1954, **[4]** the government granted (*he, him*) citizenship. Pei's reputation grew quickly, and by the 1960s many people easily recognized the structures **[5]** (*he, him*) designed. His buildings, such as the East

USAGE

DRABBLE reprinted by permission of United Feature Syndicate, Inc.

Building of the National Gallery of Art in Washington, D.C., are quite distinctive; consequently, many people greatly admire [6] (*they, them*). [7] (*Him, His*) being in charge of numerous projects in the United States, Europe, and Canada earned Pei an international reputation. Did you know that the architect of the glass pyramids at the Louvre is [8] (*him, he*)? Felicia doesn't like the pyramids because [9] (*they, them*) look so different from the buildings that surround them. However, I think that design of [10] (*him, his*) is a work of art.

Review D Identifying Correct Pronoun Forms

For each of the following sentences, choose the correct pronoun in parentheses. Then, give its use in the sentence—as a *subject, predicate nominative, direct object, indirect object,* or *object of the preposition.*

EXAMPLE 1. Did Alva or (*she, her*) leave a message?

        1. *she—subject*

1. The pranksters were (*they, them*).
2. (*He, Him*) and (*I, me*) are working on a special science project.
3. Is that package for Mom or (*I, me*)?
4. No one saw Otis or (*I, me*) behind the door.
5. I hope that you and (*she, her*) will be on time.
6. The teacher gave Rosa and (*I, me*) extra math homework.
7. That's (*he, him*) on the red bicycle.
8. Between you and (*I, me*), I like your plan better.
9. When are your parents and (*they, them*) coming home?
10. Everyone in the class except (*she, her*) and (*I, me*) had read the selection from the *Mahabharata.*

Review E Identifying Correct Pronoun Forms

For each sentence in the following paragraph, choose the correct pronoun in parentheses. Then, give its use in the sentence—as a *subject, predicate nominative, direct object, indirect object,* or *object of the preposition.*

EXAMPLE You may not know [1] (*they, them*) by name, but you may remember the actors Ossie Davis and Ruby Dee from movies or television shows.

        1. *them—direct object*

For many years, the actors Ossie Davis and Ruby Dee entertained [1] (*we, us*) with their talented performances. My friend Elvin and [2] (*me, I*) really admire both of [3] (*they, them*). Did you know that [4] (*they, them*) married in 1948? When Davis worked on Broadway, [5] (*he, him*) wrote and starred in *Purlie Victorious,* and critics gave [6] (*he, him*) great reviews. In addition, [7] (*him, he*) appeared on the TV show *Evening Shade.* One of the stars of the movie *The Jackie Robinson Story* was [8] (*she, her*). What Elvin and [9] (*me, I*) admire most about Davis and Dee is that [10] (*them, they*) actively supported civil rights and other humanitarian causes.

Special Pronoun Problems

Who and *Whom*

Nominative Case	Objective Case
who whoever	whom whomever

7h. Th   nds on how the pronoun functions in the clause.

When you are choosing between *who* and *whom* in a subordinate clause, follow these steps:

STEP 1 Find the subordinate clause.

STEP 2 Decide how the pronoun is used in the clause—as a subject, a predicate nominative, a direct or indirect object, or an object of a preposition.

STEP 3 Determine the case of the pronoun according to the rules of formal standard English.

STEP 4 Select the correct form of the pronoun.

EXAMPLE Do you know (*who, whom*) she is?

STEP 1 The subordinate clause is (*who, whom*) *she is.*

STEP 2 The pronoun (*who, whom*) is the predicate nominative: *she is* (*who, whom*).

STEP 3 As a predicate nominative, the pronoun is in the nominative case.

STEP 4 The nominative form is *who.*

ANSWER Do you know **who** she is?

7
h

STYLE   TIP

In informal English, the use of *whom* is becoming less common. In fact, when you are in informal situations, you may correctly begin any question with *who* regardless of the grammar of the sentence. In formal English, however, you should distinguish between *who* and *whom.*

Reference Note

For information on **subordinate clauses,** see page 99.

STYLE   TIP

Frequently, *whom* in subordinate clauses is omitted, but its use is understood.

EXAMPLE
The people (*whom*) you imitate are your role models.

Leaving out *whom* tends to make writing sound informal. In formal situations, it is generally better to include *whom.*

USAGE

If you are not sure whether to use *who* or *whom* in a sentence, try the following test. Omit everything but the subordinate clause; then, substitute a nominative case pronoun such as *he, she,* or *they* for *who* or substitute an objective case pronoun such as *him, her,* or *them* for *whom.* If the nominative case pronoun is correct, use *who.* If the objective case pronoun is correct, use *whom.*

EXAMPLE
The coach will help anyone (*who, whom*) tries hard. [*He tries hard* or *Him tries hard? He tries hard* is correct.]

The coach will help anyone **who** tries hard.

In the example on the previous page, the entire clause *who she is* is used as a direct object of the verb *do know.* However, the way the pronoun is used within the clause—as a predicate nominative—is what determines the correct case form.

EXAMPLE   Susan B. Anthony, about (*who, whom*) Sam reported, championed women's right to vote.

STEP 1   The subordinate clause is *about* (*who, whom*) *Sam reported.*

STEP 2   The subject is *Sam,* and the verb is *reported.* The pronoun is the object of the preposition *about: Sam reported about* (*who, whom*).

STEP 3   The object of a preposition is in the objective case.

STEP 4   The objective form is *whom.*

ANSWER   Susan B. Anthony, about **whom** Sam reported, championed women's right to vote.

Oral Practice 5 Using the Pronouns *Who* and *Whom* in Subordinate Clauses

Read each of the following sentences aloud, stressing the italicized pronouns.

1. Take this book to Eric, *whom* you met yesterday.
2. Mr. Cohen is the man *who* lives next door to us.
3. Can you tell me *who* they are?
4. Toni Morrison is an author *whom* many readers admire.
5. *Whom* Mona finally voted for is a secret.
6. The coach will penalize anyone *who* misses the bus.
7. *Whoever* wins the race will get a prize.
8. The woman to *whom* I was speaking is conducting a survey of people who ride the bus.

Exercise 5 Classifying Pronouns Used in Subordinate Clauses and Identifying Correct Forms

For each of the following sentences, choose the correct pronoun in parentheses. Then, give its use in the subordinate clause—as a *subject, predicate nominative, direct object, indirect object,* or *object of a preposition.*

EXAMPLE   **1.** I know (*who, whom*) you are.

    1. who—predicate nominative

1. Mrs. James, (*who, whom*) I work for, owns a pet shop in the mall and a feed store in our town.

2. Is there anyone here (*who, whom*) needs a bus pass?
3. She is the only one (*who, whom*) everybody trusts.
4. Both of the women (*who, whom*) ran for seats on the city council were elected.
5. I helped Mr. Thompson, (*who, whom*) was painting his garage and shingling his porch roof.
6. Eileen couldn't guess (*who, whom*) the secret agent was.
7. It was Octavio Paz (*who, whom*) won the Nobel Prize in literature in 1990.
8. Her grandmother, to (*who, whom*) she sent the flowers, won the over-fifty division of the marathon.
9. The person (*who, whom*) you gave the daisies is none other than my long-lost twin!
10. Shirley Chisholm, (*who, whom*) we are studying in history class, was the first African American woman elected to Congress.

Appositives

7i. A pronoun used as an appositive is in the same case as the word to which it refers.

An *appositive* is a noun or pronoun placed next to another noun or pronoun to identify or describe it.

EXAMPLES   The winners—**he, she,** and **I**—thanked the committee. [The pronouns are in the nominative case because they are used as appositives of the subject, *winners.*]

The teacher introduced the speakers, Laura and **me.** [The pronoun is in the objective case because it is used as an appositive of the direct object, *speakers.*]

NOTE   Sometimes a pronoun is followed by an appositive that indentifies or describes the pronoun. The case of the pronoun is not affected by the appositive.

EXAMPLES   **We** soloists will rehearse next week. [The pronoun is in the nominative case because it is the subject of the sentence. The appositive *soloists* identifies *We.*]

Give **us** girls a turn to bat. [The pronoun is in the objective case because it is the indirect object of the verb *Give.* The appositive *girls* identifies *us.*]

Reference Note

For more about **appositives,** see page 89.

TIPS & TRICKS

To determine the correct form for a pronoun used with an appositive or as an appositive, read the sentence with only the pronoun.

EXAMPLE
(*We, Us*) scouts offered to help. [*We offered to help* or *Us offered to help*? *We offered to help* is correct.]

We scouts offered to help.

Exercise 6 **Identifying Correct Pronoun Forms as Appositives and with Appositives**

For each of the following sentences, give the correct form of the pronoun in parentheses.

EXAMPLE　　**1.** The principal named the winners, Julia and (*I, me*).

　　　　　　1. me

1. The coach showed (*we, us*) girls the new uniforms.
2. Our friends, (*she, her*) and Lucas, made the refreshments.
3. All of the class saw it except three people—Floyd, Ada, and (*I, me*).
4. Mrs. López hired (*we, us*) boys for the summer.
5. (*We, Us*) girls are excellent chess players.
6. Kiole listed her three favorite actors: Leonardo DiCaprio, Cuba Gooding, Jr., and (*he, him*).
7. Come to the game with (*we, us*) hometown fans, and you'll have a better time.
8. The best singers in school may be the quartet, Ellen and (*they, them*).
9. I want to go to the concert with two friends, Iola and (*he, him*).
10. The librarian gave the best readers, Craig and (*I, me*), two books by our favorite authors.

Review F **Identifying Correct Pronoun Forms**

For each of the following sentences, choose the correct pronoun in parentheses. Then, give its use in the sentence—as a *subject, predicate nominative, direct object, indirect object, object of a preposition* or an *appositive*.

EXAMPLE　　**1.** The cyclist gave (*we, us*) a smile as she rode past.

　　　　　　1. us—indirect object

1. Students (*who, whom*) want to help organize the Kamehameha Day celebration should speak to Kai or me.
2. Give these magazines to (*whoever, whomever*) wants them.
3. Don't (*they, them*) know that (*we, us*) students do our best?
4. The candidates, Ralph and (*he, him*), will speak at the rally tomorrow.
5. The Earth Day planners from our community are (*they, them*).
6. Len and (*I, me*) had planned to watch the laser light show together.
7. Will you pass (*I, me*) the dictionary, please?
8. Celine Dion, (*who, whom*) I saw in concert, sings many songs that (*I, me*) like.

9. It would be a great help to (*we, us*) beginners if (*they, them*) would give us more time.

10. Visiting Australia is an exciting opportunity for Clay and (*she, her*).

Review G **Identifying Correct Pronoun Forms**

Choose the correct pronoun from each pair in parentheses in the following paragraph.

EXAMPLE **[1]** My sister Angela is one of many women in our society (*who, whom*) use makeup.

    1. who

The use of makeup to enhance beauty has a longer history than most of **[1]** (*we, us*) might imagine. In fact, **[2]** (*we, us*) cosmetic historians must look back to ancient times for the origins of makeup. For example, heavy, black eye makeup was worn by the ancient Egyptians, **[3]** (*who, whom*) originally used it as protection from reflected sunlight. It was they **[4]** (*who, whom*) first lined their eyes with a dark liquid called *kohl*, which **[5]** (*they, them*) applied with a small wooden or ivory stick. During the reign of Queen Nefertiti, **[6]** (*she, her*) and her noblewomen used not only *kohl* but other cosmetics as well. To **[7]** (*they, them*), dark, heavily made-up eyes and red lips were the marks of beauty. European nobles in the Middle Ages and the Renaissance wanted to emphasize their pale skin, so **[8]** (*them, they*) dusted their faces with chalk-white powder. It was Queen Elizabeth I, an English monarch, **[9]** (*who, whom*) set this style in her court. Although we might think that **[10]** (*them, they*) look strange today, both Nefertiti and Queen Elizabeth I were fashion-able in their times.

The Pronoun in an Incomplete Construction

7j. After *than* and *as* introducing an incomplete construction, use the form of the pronoun that would be correct if the construction were completed.

Notice how pronouns change the meaning of sentences with incomplete constructions.

EXAMPLES Everyone knows that you like Jolene much better than **I** [like Jolene].

Everyone knows that you like Jolene much better than [you like] **me.**

Did you help Ira as well as **they** [helped Ira]?

Did you help Ira as well as [you helped] **them**?

Exercise 7 Completing Incomplete Constructions and Classifying Pronoun Forms

┌HELP┐

Some items in Exercise 7 may have more than one correct answer, but you need to give only one.

Beginning with *than* or *as,* write the understood clause for each sentence, using the correct form of the pronoun. Then, tell whether the pronoun in the completed clause is a *subject* or an *object*.

EXAMPLE 1. Did the noise bother you as much as (*she, her*).

1. *as the noise bothered her—object*

or

as she bothered you—subject

1. Justin throws a football better than (*I, me*).
2. The story mystified him as much as (*we, us*).
3. Is your sister older than (*he, him*)?
4. Have they studied as long as (*we, us*)?
5. We have known him longer than (*she, her*).
6. Are you more creative than (*he, him*)?
7. Did you read as much as (*I, me*)?
8. I like René better than (*they, them*).
9. Many people are less fortunate than (*we, us*).
10. Are you as optimistic as (*she, her*)?
11. After winning the city championship, there were no girls happier than (*they, them*).
12. When did you become taller than (*I, me*)?
13. Mary has collected more coins than (*he, him*).

14. Do you like cantaloupe as much as (*she, her*)?
15. This label says the toy is not safe for a child as young as (*he, him*).
16. When you serve dessert, don't serve yourself more than (*he, him*).
17. Can he really play saxophone as well as (*I, me*)?
18. To win the contest, you must do as many sit-ups as (*she, her*).
19. I'm shocked that you gave her a nicer card than (*I, me*)!
20. Daniel doesn't visit his relatives as often as (*she, her*).

Clear Pronoun Reference

7k. A pronoun should refer clearly to its antecedent.

(1) An *ambiguous reference* occurs when any one of two or more words can be a pronoun's antecedent.

AMBIGUOUS   My uncle called my brother after he won the marathon.
                        [Who won the marathon, my uncle or my brother?]
        CLEAR   After my brother won the marathon, my uncle called him.
        CLEAR   After my uncle won the marathon, he called my brother.

(2) A *general reference* is the use of a pronoun that refers to a general idea rather than to a specific antecedent.

The pronouns commonly found in general-reference errors are *it, that, this, such,* and *which.*

GENERAL   The ski jumper faces tough competition and a grueling
                    schedule, but she says that doesn't worry her.
    CLEAR   The ski jumper faces tough competition and a grueling
                    schedule, but she says these problems don't worry her.

(3) A *weak reference* occurs when a pronoun refers to an antecedent that has been suggested but not expressed.

WEAK   Paul likes many of the photographs I have taken; he thinks
                I should choose this as my profession.
CLEAR   Paul likes many of the photographs I have taken; he thinks
                I should choose photography as my profession.

(4) An *indefinite reference* is the use of a pronoun that refers to no particular person or thing and that is unnecessary to the meaning of the sentence.

INDEFINITE   In the book it explains how cells divide.
    CLEAR   The book explains how cells divide.

USAGE

Familiar expressions such as *it is raining, it seems as though . . .,* and *it's early* are correct even though they contain inexact pronoun references.

Exercise 8　Correcting Inexact Pronoun References

Revise each of the following sentences, correcting each inexact pronoun reference.

EXAMPLE　**1.** Have you ever been physically unable to prepare a meal for yourself? That can be a serious problem.

1. Being physically unable to prepare a meal for yourself can be a serious problem.

1. Older persons, people with disabilities, and people who are ill sometimes cannot prepare meals for themselves, which is when Meals on Wheels can help.
2. Meals on Wheels is an organization in which they arrange to have meals delivered to people's homes.
3. Because it is a nonprofit organization, Meals on Wheels has a limited budget, which is why it relies on volunteers.
4. Many businesses, churches, clubs, and organizations supply volunteers, and they contribute money.
5. People who receive services provided by Meals on Wheels usually help to pay for these services, but it's voluntary and based on a person's ability to pay.
6. In some Meals on Wheels organizations, they offer clients a variety of other services in addition to delivering meals.
7. Grocery shopping is a service provided to clients by volunteers who purchase and then deliver them.
8. Some clients depend on volunteers for rides when they have appointments and errands to run.
9. To lift their spirits, some volunteers regularly call clients on the phone; other volunteers help clients by performing minor home safety repairs.
10. Volunteers not only provide needed services but also often form personal bonds with their clients; that is why you may want to volunteer at a local Meals on Wheels.

Chapter Review

A. Identifying Correct Forms of Pronouns

For each of the following sentences, choose the correct form of the pronoun or pronouns in parentheses.

1. Janell and (*I, me*) painted the room together.
2. Alan, for (*who, whom*) I did the typing, said that he would pay me on Friday.
3. The young Amish couple drove us and (*they, them*) into town in a horse-drawn buggy.
4. Carolyn has been playing the guitar longer than (*she, her*).
5. The last two people to arrive, Tranh and (*me, I*), had trouble finding the skating rink.
6. Hector wrote this song for you and (*I, me*).
7. The winner is (*whoever, whomever*) finishes first.
8. Ellis was worried about his project, but Ms. Atkinson gave (*he, him*) an A.
9. Was the winner of the race (*he, him*) or Aaron?
10. The pictures of the Grand Canyon made a greater impression on the Rileys than on (*we, us*).
11. To (*who, whom*) did you speak?
12. Schuyler and (*she, her*) will lead the group singalong.
13. Imagine my surprise when I saw Todd Franklin sitting behind Kenan and (*I, me*) in the theater.
14. The most productive employees at the plant were (*they, them*).
15. He was going to have dinner with (*her and me, she and I*), but fog delayed his departure from New York.
16. The prince knew precisely (*who, whom*) to appoint as his chamberlain.
17. Stanislas and Tina were at a Pulaski Day parade in Chicago, and I saw (*they, them*) there on the television news.
18. The ferret, annoyed at being woken up, bit (*she, her*) on the arm.
19. Why don't you come to the play with Carrie and (*I, me*)?
20. The first one to arrive was (*she, her*).

USAGE

B. Proofreading a Paragraph for Correct Pronoun Forms

Some of the sentences in the following paragraph contain a pronoun that has been used incorrectly. If a pronoun is incorrect, write the correct form. If the sentence is already correct, write *C*.

[21] Do you grow as many plants as me? [22] Nowadays, scientists are hard at work trying to develop blue roses for us plant enthusiasts. [23] My science teacher, Ms. Phillips, and me wonder whether they can do so. [24] She doubts even more than me that breeding a blue rose is possible. [25] Us modern rose-lovers have never seen a blue rose. [26] However, Ms. Phillips and me learned that an Arab agriculturist in the thirteenth century once grew one. [27] For centuries, rose breeders whom have tried to produce the legendary blue rose have failed. [28] Some genetic engineers that I read about are working on this project now. [29] Scientists aren't sure whom would buy a blue rose. [30] Still, like you and I, they can't resist a challenge.

C. Identifying Pronouns Used as Subjects and Objects

For each of the following sentences, give the correct form of the pronoun or pronouns in parentheses. Then, tell whether each pronoun is in *nominative* case or *objective* case.

31. Dr. Schultz sang to the birthday brothers, Otto and (*I, me*).

32. Ms. Vlatkin showed (*we, us*) how to dance a *pas de deux.*

33. (*Him and her, He and she*), the brother-and-sister team, were the first archaeologists present at the opening of the royal tomb.

34. They went on the trip with their cousins, Jin-Hua and (*he, him*).

35. The last remaining contestants—(*she and they, her and them*)—walked in silence to the podium.

36. (*We, Us*) students at King High are very proud of our football team.

37. The teacher gave the best students, (*her and him, she and he*), a commendation.

38. I thought they should give (*we, us*) junior actors a chance to shine.

39. Rosa mentioned her favorite Tejano musicians, Emilio, David Lee Garza, and (*he, him*).

40. With regard to the Garcia twins, Blair said the best way to tell (*they, them*) apart was to make them laugh.

D. Correcting Unclear Pronoun Reference

Revise each of the following sentences, correcting each unclear pronoun reference.

41. Sally called Carla while she was doing her homework.
42. The ship's captain explained to the passenger the meaning of the announcement he had just made.
43. Police Sergeant Molloy's daily assignments involve hard work and a certain amount of risk, but he claims that it doesn't bother him.
44. Jill is impressed by Jeff's track-and-field records. She thinks he should do it professionally.
45. On the radio it said that afternoon thunderstorms were likely.

Writing Application
Using Pronouns in a Magazine Article

Using Correct Case Forms You and three of your friends are planetary explorers. Write a magazine article about your exploration of Mars. Use a variety of pronouns as subjects, predicate nominatives, direct objects, indirect objects, and objects of prepositions.

Prewriting   To get started, jot down what you know about space travel and astronomy. You could get additional ideas from books and magazine articles about Mars. Think of things that a person might see or do while exploring that planet.

Writing   As you write your first draft, be sure to include details that draw your reader into the story.

Revising   Ask a classmate to read your story. Should you add or delete any details? Using your classmate's suggestions, revise your story to make it clearer and more entertaining.

Publishing   Do your pronouns clearly show who did what? As you check over the grammar, spelling, and punctuation of your story, make sure that all of your pronouns are in the correct case. With your teacher's permission, you may want to post the story on your class bulletin board or create a Web page for it on the Internet.

Using Modifiers Correctly
Comparison and Placement

Diagnostic Preview

A. Correcting Modifiers

The following sentences contain dangling modifiers, misplaced modifiers, and mistakes in comparisons. Revise each sentence so that it is clear and correct.

EXAMPLE   1. When traveling through Scotland, I discovered that stories about monsters were more popular than any kind of story.

          1. *When traveling through Scotland, I discovered that stories about monsters were more popular than any other kind of story.*

1. Having received a great deal of publicity, I had already read several articles about the so-called Loch Ness monster.
2. One article described how a young veterinary student spotted the monster who was named Arthur Grant.
3. While cycling on a road near the shore of Loch Ness one day, Grant came upon the most strangest creature he had ever seen.
4. Cycling closer, the monster took a leap and plunged into the lake.
5. Numerous theories have been discussed about the origin and identity of the monster in the local newspapers.

6. Of all the proposed theories, the better and more fascinating one was that the monster must be a freshwater species of sea serpent.

7. Having found a huge, dead creature on the shore of the lake in 1942, the mystery of the monster was thought to be solved finally.

8. One famous photograph of the monster has recently been revealed to be a hoax that seemed to confirm the creature's existence.

9. Skeptical, stories about the Loch Ness monster have always struck some people as unbelievable.

10. However, reported sightings of the monster have continued, perhaps more than of any mysterious creature.

B. Using Modifiers Correctly in Sentences

Most of the following sentences have mistakes in the use of modifiers. Revise each incorrect sentence to correct these errors. If a sentence is already correct, write *C*.

EXAMPLE
    1. In the United States, is the use of solar energy more commoner than the use of geothermal energy?

    1. *In the United States, is the use of solar energy more common than the use of geothermal energy?*

─HELP─

Although some sentences in Part B of the Diagnostic Preview can be correctly revised in more than one way, you need to give only one revision.

11. Kay has a better understanding of both solar and geothermal energy than anyone I know.

12. Yoko isn't sure she agrees with me, but I have talked with Kay more than Yoko.

13. Kay thinks that, of the two, solar energy is the best method for generating power.

14. She claims that the energy from the sun will soon be easier to harness than geothermal energy.

15. Arguing that the sun's energy could also be less expensive to use, Kay says that more research into solar energy is needed.

16. Yoko disagrees and thinks that geothermal energy would provide more cheaper power than solar energy.

17. She told me that for centuries people in other countries have been using geothermal energy, such as Iceland and Japan.

18. However, she added that geothermal energy is less well known than any source of power in our country.

19. Although infrequently used in the United States, Yoko feels that geothermal energy has already proven itself to be safe and efficient.

20. Unconvinced, both points of view seem to me to offer promising new sources of energy.

USAGE

What Is a Modifier?

A *modifier* is a word or word group that makes the meaning of another word or word group more specific. The two kinds of modifiers are *adjectives* and *adverbs*.

One-Word Modifiers

Adjectives

Reference Note

For more about **adjectives,** see page 10. For more about **adverbs,** see page 21.

8a. An adjective makes the meaning of a noun or pronoun more specific.

EXAMPLES   Samia gave a **broad** smile. [The adjective *broad* makes the meaning of the noun *smile* more specific.]

Only she knows the answer. [The adjective *only* makes the meaning of the pronoun *she* more specific.]

The sweater is **soft** and **warm.** [The adjectives *soft* and *warm* make the meaning of the noun *sweater* more specific.]

Isn't he a **well-mannered** boy? [The compound adjective *well-mannered* makes the meaning of the noun *boy* more specific.]

Adverbs

8b. An adverb makes the meaning of a verb, an adjective, or another adverb more specific.

EXAMPLES   Samia grinned **broadly.** [The adverb *broadly* makes the meaning of the verb *grinned* more specific.]

Sometimes I wonder about the future. [The adverb *sometimes* makes the meaning of the verb *wonder* more specific.]

The dog is **very** hungry. [The adverb *very* makes the meaning of the adjective *hungry* more specific.]

The alarm rang **surprisingly** loudly. [The adverb *surprisingly* makes the meaning of the adverb *loudly* more specific.]

Adjective or Adverb?

While many adverbs end in *–ly*, others do not. Furthermore, not all words with the *–ly* ending are adverbs. Some adjectives also end in *–ly*.

USAGE

Therefore, you can't tell whether a word is an adjective or an adverb simply by looking for the *–ly* ending. To decide whether a word is an adjective or an adverb, determine how the word is used in the sentence.

Adverbs Not Ending in *–ly*		
broadcast **soon**	return **home**	run **loose**
not sleepy	stand **here**	**very** happy

Adjectives Ending in *–ly*		
elderly people	**only** child	**silly** behavior
curly hair	**holy** building	**lonely** person

Some words can be used as either adjectives or adverbs.

Adjectives	Adverbs
She is an **only** child.	She has **only** one brother.
Tina has a **fast** car.	The car goes **fast.**
We caught the **last** train.	We left **last.**

8c. If a word in the predicate modifies the subject of the verb, use the adjective form. If it modifies the verb, use the adverb form.

ADJECTIVE	The gazelles were **graceful.** [*Graceful* modifies *gazelles.*]
ADVERB	The gazelles moved **gracefully.** [*Gracefully* modifies *moved.*]

ADJECTIVE	The boy grew **tall.** [*Tall* modifies *boy.*]
ADVERB	The boy grew **quickly.** [*Quickly* modifies *grew.*]

Reference Note

For more about **subjects** and **predicates,** see page 42.

Phrases Used as Modifiers

Like one-word modifiers, phrases can also be used as adjectives and adverbs.

EXAMPLES	It was time **for celebration.** [The prepositional phrase *for celebration* acts as an adjective that modifies the noun *time.*]
	Uprooting trees and bushes, the tornado swept across the Panhandle. [The participial phrase *Uprooting trees and bushes* acts as an adjective that modifies the noun *tornado.*]

Reference Note

For more about different **kinds of phrases,** see page 70.

USAGE

Professor Martinez is the one **to ask.** [The infinitive phrase *to ask* acts as an adjective that modifies the pronoun *one*.]

Ray is becoming quite good **at soccer.** [The prepositional phrase *at soccer* acts as an adverb that modifies the adjective *good*.]

Walk **with care on icy pavements.** [The prepositional phrases *with care* and *on icy pavements* act as adverbs that modify the verb *Walk*.]

The guide spoke slowly enough **to be understood.** [The infinitive phrase *to be understood* acts as an adverb that modifies the adverb *enough*.]

Clauses Used as Modifiers

Reference Note

For more about **clauses,** see Chapter 4.

Like words and phrases, clauses can also be used as adjectives and adverbs.

EXAMPLES   Vermeer is the painter **that I like best.** [The adjective clause *that I like best* modifies the noun *painter*.]

Before Toni left for work, she took the dog for a walk. [The adverb clause *Before Toni left for work* modifies the verb *took*.]

Exercise 1 **Identifying Modifiers**

Identify the italicized word or word group in each of the following sentences as a *modifier* or *not a modifier*.

EXAMPLES   **1.** Rudyard Kipling, *who was born in India,* wrote a wonderful story about a brave mongoose.

1. *modifier*

2. The mongoose's *name* was Rikki-tikki-tavi.

2. *not a modifier*

1. Rikki-tikki was adopted by a *very* kind family.
2. The family fed him meat and bananas and *boiled* eggs.
3. *Like all mongooses,* Rikki-tikki was always curious.
4. While exploring the garden, he *heard* Darzee and his wife, the tailorbirds, crying in their nest.
5. One of their babies had fallen out *of the nest* and been eaten by a cobra.
6. Rikki-tikki had to protect his family and friends *against the snakes.*

USAGE

7. Mongooses and snakes are *natural* enemies.
8. Rikki-tikki overheard *two* cobras planning to kill the family.
9. He attacked the first cobra *while it was waiting for the father to come into the room.*
10. The second *cobra* dragged Rikki-tikki down a hole in the ground, but Rikki-tikki killed the snake and came out alive.

Eight Troublesome Modifiers

Bad and *Badly*

Bad is an adjective. In most uses, *badly* is an adverb.

ADJECTIVE   The dog was **bad.**
ADVERB   The dog behaved **badly.**

Remember that a word that modifies the subject of a verb should be in adjective form.

NONSTANDARD   The stew tasted badly.
STANDARD   The stew tasted **bad.**

> **NOTE** In informal situations, *bad* or *badly* is acceptable after *feel.*
>
> INFORMAL   He feels **badly** about the incident.
> FORMAL   He feels **bad** about the incident.

Good and *Well*

Good is an adjective. It should not be used to modify a verb.

NONSTANDARD   He speaks Italian good.
STANDARD   He speaks Italian **well.**
STANDARD   His Italian sounds **good.** [*Good* is an adjective that modifies the noun *Italian.*]

Well may be used either as an adjective or as an adverb. As an adjective, *well* has two meanings: "in good health" and "satisfactory."

EXAMPLES   John is **well.** [John is in good health.]

All is **well.** [All is satisfactory.]

As an adverb, *well* means "capably."

EXAMPLE   They did **well** in the tryouts.

Slow and *Slowly*

Slow is used as both an adjective and an adverb.

EXAMPLES   We took a **slow** drive through the countryside. [*Slow* is an adjective modifying the noun *drive*.]

Go **slow.** [*Slow* is an adverb modifying the verb *Go.*]

Slowly is an adverb. In most adverb uses, it is better to use *slowly* than to use *slow.*

EXAMPLES   The train **slowly** came to a stop.

Drive **slowly** on slippery roads.

Real and *Really*

Real is an adjective meaning "actual" or "genuine." *Really* is an adverb meaning "actually" or "truly." Although *real* is commonly used as an adverb meaning "very" in everyday situations, avoid using it as an adverb in formal speaking and writing.

INFORMAL   He batted real well in the game.

FORMAL   He batted **really** well in the game.

Exercise 2 Revising Sentences with Modifier Errors

Most of the following sentences contain at least one error in modifier usage. If a sentence contains an error, revise the sentence with the correct modifier. If a sentence is already correct, write *C.*

EXAMPLE   1. The ball was thrown so bad it went over the fence.

1. *The ball was thrown so badly it went over the fence.*

1. You have done very good today, Marcia.
2. The nurse shark was moving very slow over the seabed.
3. The fireworks exploded with a real loud bang.
4. The team did not play badly, but they lost anyway.
5. James thinks that Jakob Dylan is a well singer.
6. The box was not damaged too bad when it fell.
7. The turtle is very slowly on land, but it is much faster underwater.
8. Is that really Sammy Sosa's autograph?
9. Even if your day is going bad, getting angry at me will not help.
10. Slowly but surely, the fawn improved until it could run real good.

HELP

A sentence in Exercise 2 may contain more than one error.

Comparison of Modifiers

8d. Modifiers change form to show comparison.

There are three degrees of comparison: *positive, comparative,* and *superlative.*

Positive	Comparative	Superlative
young	younger	youngest
fearful	more fearful	most fearful
rapidly	more rapidly	most rapidly
good	better	best

Regular Comparison

(1) Most one-syllable modifiers form the comparative degree by adding *–er* and the superlative degree by adding *–est.*

Positive	Comparative	Superlative
large	larger	largest
deep	deeper	deepest

(2) Two-syllable modifiers may form the comparative degree by adding *–er* or by using *more.* They may form the superlative degree by adding *–est* or by using *most.*

Positive	Comparative	Superlative
wealthy	wealthier	wealthiest
lovely	lovelier	loveliest
rapid	more rapid	most rapid
softly	more softly	most softly
common	commoner *or* more common	commonest *or* most common

Reference Note

For guidelines on **how to spell comparative and superlative forms** correctly, see page 363.

STYLE **TIP**

Most two-syllable modifiers can form their comparative and superlative forms either way. If adding *–er* or *–est* makes a word sound awkward, use *more* or *most* instead.

AWKWARD	frugaler
BETTER	more frugal
AWKWARD	rapidest
BETTER	most rapid

USAGE

8 d

USAGE

Exercise 3 **Writing Comparative and Superlative Forms**

Write the comparative and superlative forms of the following words.

EXAMPLE   **1.** bright
1. *brighter, brightest*

1. fast   **3.** happy   **5.** simple   **7.** safe   **9.** calm
2. soon   **4.** careful   **6.** hazy   **8.** wisely   **10.** pretty

(3) Modifiers that have three or more syllables form the comparative degree by using *more* and the superlative degree by using *most*.

Positive	Comparative	Superlative
energetic	more energetic	most energetic
significantly	more significantly	most significantly

(4) To show a decrease in the qualities they express, modifiers form the comparative degree by using *less* and the superlative degree by using *least*.

Positive	Comparative	Superlative
helpful	less helpful	least helpful
frequently	less frequently	least frequently

Irregular Comparison

The comparative and superlative degrees of some modifiers are irregular in form.

Positive	Comparative	Superlative
bad	worse	worst
good/well	better	best
many/much	more	most
far	further/farther	furthest/farthest
little	less	least

STYLE **TIP**

The word *little* also has regular comparative and superlative forms: *littler, littlest*. These forms are used to describe physical size (the **littlest** puppy). The forms *less* and *least* are used to describe an amount (**less** homework).

NOTE   Do not add *–er* / *–est* or *more* / *most* to irregularly compared forms. For example, use *worse*, not *worser* or *more worse*.

Exercise 4 Using Comparative and Superlative Forms

In the blank in each of the following sentences, write the correct form of the modifier in italics.

EXAMPLE *little* **1.** Both pairs of jeans are on sale, but I will buy the _____ expensive pair.

  1. less

1. *well* I can skate _____ now than I could last year.
2. *many* She caught the _____ fish of anyone in our group that day.
3. *bad* That is the _____ movie I have ever seen.
4. *much* We have _____ homework today than we had all last week.
5. *good* Felicia has the _____ attendance record of anyone.
6. *many* Are there _____ plays than poems in your literature book?
7. *good* Tyrone is the _____ pitcher on our baseball team this year.
8. *much* Of the three groups of volunteers, our group cleaned up the _____ litter.
9. *bad* My notebook looks _____ than Joshua's.
10. *little* I have _____ time to finish than he does.

Oral Practice Identifying Comparative and Superlative Forms

Read the following modifiers aloud, and give the comparative and superlative forms of each. Do not include decreasing comparisons.

EXAMPLE **1.** meaningful

  1. more meaningful, most meaningful

1. bad
2. good
3. early
4. many
5. fuzzy
6. loose
7. well
8. noisy
9. patiently
10. graceful
11. far
12. special
13. happily
14. eager
15. sleepy
16. much
17. unlikely
18. elaborate
19. quiet
20. rich

┌**HELP**──

A dictionary will tell you when a word forms its comparative or superlative form in some way other than by adding *–er* / *–est* or *more* / *most*. Look in a dictionary if you are not sure whether a word has irregular comparative or superlative forms or whether you need to change the spelling of a word before adding *–er* or *–est*.

Exercise 5 Proofreading Sentences for Correct Comparative and Superlative Forms

Identify the comparative and superlative modifiers in the following sentences. If the form of a modifier is incorrect or awkward, write the correct form. If the form is already correct, write *C*.

1. The Romany make up one of Europe's interestingest cultures.

1. *interestingest—most interesting*

1. The Romany are commonlier found in Eastern Europe than anywhere else in the world.
2. Although most Romany live in Romania, Hungary, and other European countries, the culture of the Romany suggests that they migrated to Europe from other lands.
3. The bestest theory about the origin of the Romany is that they came from India.
4. As this photograph shows, the Romany wear some of their colorfulest traditional clothing for their celebrations.
5. They also brighten their lives with the most wild violin music they can play.
6. On the move frequentlier than most other Europeans, they used to travel in brightly painted wagons.
7. The Romany usually live in groups, with the largest groups consisting of several hundred families.
8. The most high law in Romany society is the *kris*, a system of rules based on the religious beliefs of the Romany.
9. The Romany generally earn their living as migrant agricultural workers and, less frequently, as entertainers.
10. Although change has come slowlier to these wanderers than to most other ethnic groups in Europe, some Romany now are living in settled communities.

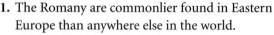

STYLE   TIP

In informal situations and in standard expressions, people sometimes use the superlative degree in comparing two things: *Put your best foot forward.* Generally, however, you should use the comparative degree in formal situations when you are comparing two things.

Use of Comparative and Superlative Forms

8e. Use the comparative degree when comparing two things. Use the superlative degree when comparing more than two.

COMPARATIVE   Writing mysteries seems **more challenging** than writing nonfiction.

In my opinion, Dorothy L. Sayers is a **better** writer than Agatha Christie.

SUPERLATIVE   Writing a mystery story is the **most challenging** assignment I've had so far.

This is the **best** Sherlock Holmes story that I have ever read.

Exercise 6 Identifying Correct Comparative and Superlative Forms

Identify the comparative and superlative modifiers in the following sentences. If the form of a modifier is incorrect, write the correct form. If the form is correct for the number of items compared, write *C*.

EXAMPLE   1. Nina's report on American Indian star legends was the more interesting report in the class.

1. *most interesting*

1. Although Nina and I both researched our reports carefully, her report was the most thorough one of the two.
2. The American Indian stories about the stars and the sky are more diverse than the Norse myths, in my opinion.
3. Nina told several stories; I found the myth that she told about the cluster of stars known as the Pleiades to be the more fascinating.
4. The stranger tale, which is from the Monache Indian people of central California, tells how a little girl and six women who wouldn't give up eating onions became the Pleiades.
5. The scariest of the tales is the Skidi Pawnee myth about six brothers and an adopted sister who fight the Rolling Skull.
6. That story was the longer legend that Nina told, and Frank said it was the more interesting.
7. Of all the earthly creatures in the stories Nina told, Coyote is perhaps the more important.
8. In fact, in some stories people often play a least important role than Coyote plays.
9. I told Nina that, compared with my report, hers was the best.
10. She said that telling the stories was easier than finding them.

8f. Include the word *other* or *else* when comparing one member of a group with the rest of the group.

NONSTANDARD   Juan is more considerate than any boy in his school.
[Juan is a boy in his school, and he cannot be more considerate than himself. The word *other* should be added.]

STANDARD   Juan is more considerate than any **other** boy in his school.

Reference Note

For a discussion of **standard and nonstandard English,** see page 223.

USAGE

| NONSTANDARD | Dana arrived earlier than anyone. [*Anyone* includes all people, and Dana is a person. Since she cannot arrive earlier than herself, *else* should be added.] |
| STANDARD | Dana arrived earlier than anyone **else.** |

Exercise 7 Correcting Faulty Comparisons

Correct each of the following sentences by adding either *other* or *else* to make the comparison logical and clear.

EXAMPLE   1. Rodney spells better than anyone in his class.

1. *Rodney spells better than anyone else in his class.*

1. Today has been colder than any day this year.
2. Kumiko eats more slowly than anybody in this cafeteria.
3. Flying is faster than any type of travel.
4. My sunflowers grew taller than any flowers I planted this year.
5. Luís enjoys swimming more than anyone in his family.
6. Dad bought that sedan because it gets better mileage than any car.
7. This hot-and-sour soup is spicier than any soup I've ever tasted.
8. Does Renee study harder than anyone?
9. Whales are bigger than any animals.
10. In my opinion, cycling is more fun than any type of exercise.

8g. Avoid using double comparisons.

A ***double comparison*** is incorrect because it contains both *–er* and *more* (*less*) or *–est* and *most* (*least*).

| NONSTANDARD | She is more funnier than he. |
| STANDARD | She is **funnier** than he. |

| NONSTANDARD | It was the least cloudiest night of the year. |
| STANDARD | It was the **least cloudy** night of the year. |

Exercise 8 Revising Modifiers to Correct Double Comparisons

Write each incorrect modifier in the following sentences. Then, correct the double comparison by crossing out the unnecessary part.

EXAMPLE   1. Today is more colder than yesterday.

1. ~~more~~ colder

1. That is the most softest sweater I have ever had.
2. You seem to be trying more harder in school this year.

USAGE

3. Is she the least tiredest runner on the team?
4. Illustrations help make the explanations more clearer to the readers.
5. Georgia is more larger in area than any other state east of the Mississippi.
6. We had the most best basketball team in our division.
7. The first day of winter is the most shortest day of the year.
8. Parrots are more smarter than other birds.
9. Cynthia's room is much less cleaner than John's.
10. Did you know that Rome is one of the most oldest capitals in the world?

8h. Be sure your comparisons are clear.

UNCLEAR   Weeds in the lawn are harder to get rid of than the garden.
          [This sentence incorrectly compares weeds to a garden.]
CLEAR   Weeds in the lawn are harder to get rid of than **weeds in** the garden.

UNCLEAR   Is the skin of the rhinoceros harder than the alligator?
CLEAR   Is the skin of the rhinoceros harder than **the skin of** the alligator?

                              or

          Is the skin of the rhinoceros harder than the **alligator's?**

Both parts of an incomplete comparison should be stated if there is any chance of misunderstanding.

UNCLEAR   Theresa called Greg more than Maria.
CLEAR   Theresa called Greg more than Maria **did.**
CLEAR   Theresa called Greg more than **she called** Maria.

Exercise 9   **Correcting Unclear Comparisons**

Rewrite the following sentences to correct unclear comparisons.

EXAMPLE   1. The annual rainfall in Seattle is higher than London.

          1. *The annual rainfall in Seattle is higher than that in London.*

1. A kangaroo's jump is higher than a rabbit.
2. The power of that truck's engine is greater than a sports car.
3. In those days, the Pottstown Panthers' winning streak was longer than the Lindale Lions.
4. Is a baboon's grip stronger than a human?

┌HELP─────
Although some sentences in Exercise 9 may be correctly revised in more than one way, you need to give only one revision for each sentence.

5. Tony's bike is as new and gleaming as Juan.
6. The canals in Venice, Italy, are wider than Venice, California.
7. Rome's climate is milder than Houston.
8. Our new windows are bigger than the Costellos' house.
9. The kudu's horns are longer than the ibex.
10. Pat's assignments are usually better written than Jessica.

Review A Correcting Modifiers in a Paragraph

Identify and correct the incorrect comparative and superlative forms in each sentence in the following paragraph. Some sentences contain more than one incorrect or unclear comparison. If a sentence is already correct, write *C*.

EXAMPLE [1] Eagles are widely regarded as more majestic than any bird in the world.

1. *Eagles are widely regarded as more majestic than any other bird in the world.*

[1] Many cultures have revered the eagle as one of their most strongest symbols of bravery and power. [2] In fact, the eagle seems to be the most popular bird used as a national symbol. [3] Mexico, Austria, and Egypt are some of the more best-known countries with eagles on their national flags. [4] In the United States, early colonial leaders thought that the bald eagle would be a more better symbol for their new country than the turkey. [5] Benjamin Franklin had argued that the turkey was the most practical choice of the two birds, but he was outvoted.

[6] I think most people would agree that the eagle is the best choice of the two. [7] While eagles are not more larger than all birds, they are among the more effective hunters and fliers. [8] As you can see from these pictures, the eagle's sharp beak and long claws are more powerful than the turkey. [9] The eagle's wings are also more strong and very wide. [10] I think the eagle is beautifuller, too.

Dangling Modifiers

8i. Avoid using dangling modifiers.

A modifying word, phrase, or clause that does not clearly and sensibly modify a word or a word group in a sentence is a ***dangling modifier.***

DANGLING	Together, the litter along the highway was picked up, bagged, and hauled away. [Was the litter together?]
CORRECT	Together, we picked up, bagged, and hauled away the litter along the highway.
DANGLING	Time seemed to stand still, watching the sunset and listening to the cicadas. [Was time watching and listening?]
CORRECT	Time seemed to stand still as we watched the sunset and listened to the cicadas.

When a modifying participial or infinitive phrase comes at the beginning of a sentence, the phrase is followed by a comma. Immediately after that comma should come the word or word group that the phrase modifies.

Reference Note

For more information on **participial phrases,** see page 79. For more information on **infinitive phrases,** see page 86.

DANGLING	Jogging in the park, a rabbit peered at me from the underbrush. [Was the rabbit jogging?]
CORRECT	Jogging in the park, **I** saw a rabbit peering at me from the underbrush.
DANGLING	Listening closely, distant thunder could be detected. [Was the thunder listening?]
CORRECT	Listening closely, **she** could detect distant thunder.
DANGLING	To master a musical instrument, practice or natural talent is usually needed. [Is practice or talent mastering an instrument?]
CORRECT	To master a musical instrument, **a musician** usually needs practice or natural talent.
DANGLING	Even when equipped with the best gear, the rock cliff was difficult to climb. [Was the rock cliff equipped?]
CORRECT	Even when equipped with the best gear, **the mountaineers** had difficulty climbing the rock cliff.

A sentence may appear to have a dangling modifier when *you* is the understood subject. In such cases, the modifier is not dangling; instead, it is modifying the understood subject.

EXAMPLE   To find the correct spelling, (you) look up the word.

Reference Note

For more about the **understood subject,** see page 51.

USAGE

Exercise 10 **Writing Sentences with Introductory Modifiers**

Write complete sentences that begin with the following introductory modifiers.

EXAMPLE   **1.** Having solved one problem,

1. *Having solved one problem, Joe Harris found that another awaited him.*

1. Leaping from branch to branch,
2. Yawning,
3. While eating our lunch,
4. Surrounded by the cheering crowd,
5. To make sure he wouldn't be late,
6. Alone,
7. Following Leila's example,
8. Not wanting to wake them up,
9. Having filled out the forms,
10. To solve this riddle,

Correcting Dangling Modifiers

To correct a dangling modifier, rearrange the words in the sentence and add or change words to make the meaning logical and clear.

DANGLING   While lighting the birthday candles, the cake started to crumble.

CORRECT   While **I was** lighting the birthday candles, the cake started to crumble.

or

While lighting the birthday candles, **I noticed** the cake **starting** to crumble.

DANGLING   To become a physicist, years of study and research are required.

CORRECT   To become a physicist, **you** must spend years studying and doing research.

or

If you want to become a physicist, **you** must spend years studying and doing research.

or

If a person wants to become a physicist, **he or she** must spend years studying and doing research.

Exercise 11 **Correcting Dangling Modifiers**

Most of the following sentences contain dangling modifiers. If a sentence has a dangling modifier, revise the sentence to correct it. If a sentence is already correct, write *C*.

EXAMPLE
1. While mopping the kitchen, my baby brother woke up from his nap.

1. *While I was mopping the kitchen, my baby brother woke up from his nap.*

1. Walking through the gate, the swimming pool is on the right.
2. Lost, the small village was a welcome sight.
3. To earn money, Mom suggested shoveling snow for our neighbors.
4. After studying hard, a long walk can be refreshing.
5. Walking in the woods, listening to the singing birds is enjoyable.
6. To understand a sentence, even little words can be important.
7. To become a great athlete, you need dedication and self-discipline.
8. Standing on the beach, a school of dolphins suddenly appeared.
9. After winning the last game of the season, the celebration lasted nearly all night.
10. Tired and sore, the job was finally finished.

Misplaced Modifiers

8j. Avoid using misplaced modifiers.

A word, phrase, or clause that seems to modify the wrong word or word group in a sentence is a *misplaced modifier.* Place modifying words, phrases, and clauses as near as possible to the words they modify.

MISPLACED	My cousin's dog was chasing the geese, yapping and barking.
CORRECT	**Yapping and barking,** my cousin's dog was chasing the geese.
MISPLACED	I read about the bank robbers who were captured in this morning's paper.
CORRECT	I read **in this morning's paper** about the bank robbers who were captured.
MISPLACED	Blackened beyond recognition, even the birds refused to eat the toast.
CORRECT	Even the birds refused to eat the toast **blackened beyond recognition.**

┌ S T Y L E   T I P ┐

Be sure to place modifiers correctly to show clearly the meaning you intend.
EXAMPLES
Only Uncle Jim sells bikes. [Uncle Jim, not anybody else, sells bikes.]

Uncle Jim **only** sells bikes. [Uncle Jim sells bikes; he does not repair them.]

Uncle Jim sells **only** bikes. [Uncle Jim does not sell cars or motorcycles.]

Exercise 12 Correcting Misplaced Modifiers

Revise the following sentences to correct misplaced modifiers. In revising a sentence, be sure not to misplace another modifier.

EXAMPLE
1. The security guard was watching for the arrival of the armored car through the window.

1. *The security guard was watching through the window for the arrival of the armored car.*

1. Michiko went outside to trim the bonsai trees with Uncle Saburo.
2. I could see the scouts marching over the hill with my binoculars.
3. As a child, my grandfather taught me how to make tortillas.
4. One advertiser handed out roses to customers with dollar bills pinned to them.
5. I borrowed a radio from my sister with a weather band.
6. Did you find any of the hats your mother used to wear in the attic?
7. Our cat waited on the porch for us to come home patiently.
8. In a tank at the aquarium, we watched the seals play.
9. She ate two peaches and a plate of strawberries watching TV.
10. We gave the boxes of cereal to the children with prizes inside.

Review B Correcting Dangling and Misplaced Modifiers

Most of the following sentences contain dangling or misplaced modifiers. If a sentence is incorrect, revise it. If a sentence is already correct, write *C*.

EXAMPLE
1. Only the American Falls are slightly higher than the Horseshoe Falls.

1. *The American Falls are only slightly higher than the Horseshoe Falls.*

1. Arriving at Niagara Falls, the sight of nature's tremendous force was awe inspiring.
2. When reading about the falls, many facts impressed me.
3. Separated by Goat Island, we discovered that the falls are in two principal parts.
4. Forming the border between Canada and the United States, most visitors admire both the Horseshoe Falls and the American Falls.
5. While climbing the tower, Niagara Falls, shown on the next page, looked magnificent to us.
6. Trying to see and do everything around Niagara Falls, the days passed quickly.

7. While riding in a tour boat called the *Maid of the Mist,* the spray from the base of the falls drenched us.
8. Roaring constantly, an awesome amount of power is generated.
9. After walking through Queen Victoria Park, a hearty lunch at the restaurant was refreshing.
10. To see the waterfalls at their most beautiful, a visit at night—when they are illuminated—was recommended by the tour guide.

Misplaced Clause Modifiers

Adjective clauses should be placed near the words they modify.

| MISPLACED | There is a car in the garage that has no windshield. |
| CORRECT | In the garage, there is a car **that has no windshield.** |

| MISPLACED | The money and tickets are still in my wallet that I meant to return to you. |
| CORRECT | The money and tickets **that I meant to return to you** are still in my wallet. |

Reference Note

For more information on **adjective clauses,** see page 101.

Exercise 13 Correcting Misplaced Clauses

Revise each of the following sentences by placing the misplaced clause near the word it modifies.

EXAMPLE
1. Alejandro searched the sand dunes for shells, which were deserted.

1. *Alejandro searched the sand dunes, which were deserted, for shells.*

1. Birds are kept away by scarecrows, many of which eat seeds.
2. The disabled truck is now blocking the overpass that suddenly went out of control.
3. There was a bird in the tree that had a strange-looking beak.
4. A huge dog chased me as I rode my bicycle that was growling and barking loudly.
5. An old log sat in the fireplace that was covered with moss.

6. We thanked the clerk at the post office that had helped us with our overseas packages.
7. There are several books on our shelves that were written by Rolando Hinojosa-Smith.
8. A boy was standing at the bus stop that looked remarkably like my cousin.
9. She crossed the river on a ferry, which was more than a mile wide.
10. There is a flower garden behind the shed that is planted with prize-winning dahlias.

Review C Correcting Dangling and Misplaced Modifiers

Revise each of the following sentences by correcting the placement of a modifier or by rephrasing the sentence.

EXAMPLE 1. Feeling nervous about flying, the twin-engine plane looked small but dependable.

1. *Feeling nervous about flying, we thought the twin-engine plane looked small but dependable.*

1. Awakening from a nap, the island of Puerto Rico came into view through my airplane window.
2. Our guide was waiting to take us to our hotel inside the baggage-claim area.
3. To understand the guide's presentation, some knowledge of both Spanish and English proved to be helpful.
4. Driving along the Panoramic Route, the scenery was breathtaking!
5. We stopped for lunch at a stall along the road that was made from palm branches.
6. Hungry, the spicy rice and beans was delicious.
7. We bought a souvenir rock from a young boy that was decorated with island scenes.
8. Look at that strange fish in the water that is puffing up!
9. Anxious to shower and unpack, our hotel room was the next stop.
10. To fully appreciate all the island had to offer, more time was needed.

Chapter Review

A. Identifying Modifiers

Identify the italicized word or word group in each of the following sentences as a *modifier* or *not a modifier*.

1. My brother is a *natural* baseball talent.
2. The elephant ambled *out of the trees* into the clearing.
3. Two well-known Mexican *authors* are Carlos Fuentes and Octavio Paz.
4. Austin, Texas, is a *pleasant* place to live.
5. As Stan *entered* the house, the cat dashed under the bed.
6. Amrit the waiter is a *very* helpful person, don't you think?
7. Jean-Marc joined the resistance to fight *against the enemy*.
8. The group Los Lobos is *well established* as a major force in the Latino music world.
9. Chi *fed* the three horses in the stables.
10. Gustav Mahler was a *gifted* Austrian composer and conductor.

B. Correcting Dangling and Misplaced Modifiers

For each of the following sentences, identify the dangling or misplaced modifier and revise the sentence to correct the error.

11. Growing up in a big family, that family movie rings true to me.
12. To paint landscapes, patience and a steady hand are helpful.
13. Almost hidden under the pile of old books, Janelle saw the letter.
14. In different parts of the world I read about unusual customs.
15. A tree was almost destroyed by a bulldozer that was two hundred years old.
16. Jogging in the park, it was a sunny day.
17. The convicts were caught by the police trying to escape from jail.
18. Rushing out the door, Ben's homework was left on the table.
19. When told of the potential threat, nothing was done.
20. The mayor pledged she would build more roads at the political rally.

C. Identifying Correct Comparative and Superlative Forms and Revising Faulty Comparisons

Identify the comparative and superlative modifiers in the following sentences. If the form of the modifier is incorrect, write the correct form. If the form is already correct, write *C*. Add words to sentences in which a faulty or unclear comparison is made.

21. Which plan is more easier to follow, his or hers?
22. My bowling was worse than usual last night.
23. This paella is more delicious than any dish I've ever eaten.
24. His problem is more worse than yours.
25. I like both shirts, but I think I like this one the most.
26. That was one of the interestingest movies he's seen.
27. The tomatoes from our garden taste sweeter than those from the store.
28. This is the nicest surprise I've ever had!
29. Which route is better—upstream, downstream, or overland?
30. The sun is brighter than anything in our solar system.
31. The water in the pond was more deep than Nicky expected.
32. Arnie is the least helpful of the two brothers.
33. Doesn't Granddad feel more better now that he's rested?
34. Did you know that the Nile is more longer than any other river in the world?
35. When Marcos was five, he was carefuller than he is now.
36. Which do you like better—Theseus Flatow's older or more recent music?
37. Ken completed the exercise faster than anyone.
38. The last problem is the most complicated one in the entire exercise.
39. Jesse is feeling more badly about the accident today than he did yesterday.
40. The tree in our yard is bigger than our neighbors.

D. Correcting Misplaced Clause Modifiers

Revise each of the following sentences by placing the misplaced clause near the word it modifies.

41. There is a magazine on the table that has no cover.

42. The test papers are still in my locker that I want to hand in to Mr. Saenz.

43. There is a vase in that display case that was made during the Ming dynasty.

44. There was a Dalmatian in the street that had a silver collar.

45. The young chestnut mare is drinking water that just won the steeplechase.

46. We called the lady at the nursing home that had been so helpful.

47. Tom inspected the cars for dents, which were on the dealer's lot.

48. A trailer sat in the empty field that was covered with rust.

49. There is a mummy in the museum that is five thousand years old.

50. A woman was running along the lake that I thought was my friend Fran.

Writing Application

Using Modifiers in a Restaurant Review

Comparative and Superlative Forms   As the restaurant critic for *Good Food* magazine, you always give a year-end summary of the best restaurants and their foods. Discuss your choices in a paragraph in which you use five comparative and five superlative forms of both adjectives and adverbs.

Prewriting   Using either real or imaginary restaurants, make a list of several places and their best dishes. Think of some ways to compare the restaurants (food, atmosphere, service, price).

Writing   As you write your first draft, use your list to help you make accurate comparisons.

Revising   Read your paragraph to a classmate to see if your comparisons are clearly stated. Revise any comparisons that are confusing.

Publishing   As you correct any mistakes in spelling, grammar, and punctuation, pay special attention to the spelling of comparative and superlative forms made by adding *–er* and *–est*. You and your classmates could prepare a *Good Food* newcomer's guide to local restaurants. Decide how you want the guide to look. Then, type the guide and make photocopies or input the guide on a computer and print it out.

Reference Note

For information about **spelling words with suffixes,** see page 363.

A Glossary of Usage

Common Usage Problems

Diagnostic Preview

Correcting Errors in Standard Usage

Each of the sentences in the following passage contains at least one error in formal, standard usage. Revise the passage, correcting all such errors.

EXAMPLE   [1] Everyone accept him joined this here club.

1. *Everyone except him joined this club.*

[1] Our school has a hiking club that learns us how to appreciate nature. [2] Our club usually goes to parks that we might not of discovered by ourselves. [3] We go hiking anywheres that can be reached by bus in a few hours. [4] Before we go, we decide what to bring with us. [5] The less things that we have to carry, the better off we are. [6] Beside water, a hat, and a jacket, little else is needed. [7] Those which pack too much soon wish they hadn't of. [8] After all, a ten-mile hike effects you differently when you are weighted down then when you are not.

[9] Our adviser, Mr. Graham, he knows where all the best hiking areas are at. [10] He always tells us that we won't see nothing interesting without we're willing to exert ourselves. [11] We can't hardly keep up with him once he starts walking.

[12] We go on this sorts of walks because we enjoy them. [13] Although we sometimes think our lungs will bust, everyone wants

to keep up with the others. [14] The real reward is when we see an unusual sight, like a fawn, a family of otters, a panoramic view, and etc. [15] Than we're sure that all of our time spent outdoors ain't been wasted. [16] We also except nature like it is and do not try to change it none. [17] When we find bottles or cans in the woods, we get upset with people who can't seem to go anywheres without leaving some mark.

[18] Everyone in the club feels the same way, so we're going to start an cleanup campaign. [19] People ought to enjoy being inside of a park without busting or changing anything there. [20] We'd rather have more hikers enjoying the wilderness and less people destroying nature.

About the Glossary

This chapter provides a compact glossary of common problems in English usage. A *glossary* is an alphabetical list of special terms or expressions with definitions, explanations, and examples. You will notice that some examples in this glossary are labeled *nonstandard, standard, formal,* or *informal.*

The label *nonstandard* identifies usage that is suitable only in the most casual speaking situations and in writing that attempts to re-create casual speech. *Standard* English is language that is grammatically correct and appropriate in formal and informal situations. *Formal* identifies usage that is appropriate in serious speaking and writing situations (such as in speeches and in compositions for school). The label *informal* indicates standard usage common in conversation and in everyday writing such as personal letters. In doing the exercises in this chapter, be sure to use only standard English.

The following are examples of formal and informal English.

Formal	Informal
angry	steamed
unpleasant	yucky
agreeable	cool
very impressive	totally awesome
accelerate	step on it

HELP

The word *diction* is often used to refer to word choice. Your choice of words affects the tone and clarity of what you say and write. When you know which usages are formal, informal, standard, and nonstandard, you can choose diction that is appropriate to any audience.

Reference Note

For a list of **words often confused,** see page 374. Use the **index** at the back of the book to find discussions of other usage problems.

USAGE

Reference Note

For more about **articles,** see page 12.

USAGE

a, an These *indefinite articles* refer to one of a general group. Use *a* before words beginning with a consonant sound; use *an* before words beginning with a vowel sound.

EXAMPLES   We saw **a** blue jay and **an** owl.

A hawk flew over us **an** hour ago. [*An* is used before *hour* because *hour* begins with a vowel sound.]

This is **a** one-way street. [*A* is used before *one-way* because *one-way* begins with a consonant sound.]

accept, except *Accept* is a verb that means "to receive." *Except* may be either a verb or a preposition. As a verb, *except* means "to leave out" or "to omit." As a preposition, it means "excluding."

EXAMPLES   I couldn't **accept** such a valuable gift!

Why should they be **excepted** from the test?

No one in my class **except** me has been to Moscow.

affect, effect *Affect* is a verb meaning "to influence." *Effect* used as a verb means "to bring about" or "to accomplish." Used as a noun, *effect* means "the result of some action."

EXAMPLES   The bright colors **affect** how the patients feel.

The treatment will **effect** a cure for the disease.

The bright colors have a beneficial **effect** on the patients.

ain't Avoid using this word in speaking or in writing; it is non-standard English.

all the farther, all the faster This expression is used in some parts of the country to mean "as far as" or "as fast as."

NONSTANDARD   This is all the faster I can go.
       STANDARD   This is **as fast as** I can go.

all right See page 375.

a lot Do not write the expression *a lot* as one word. It should be written as two words.

EXAMPLE   I have **a lot** of homework tonight.

among See **between, among.**

S T Y L E   T I P

The expression *a lot* is over-used. Try replacing *a lot* with a more descriptive, specific word or phrase.

EXAMPLES
mountains of homework

four subjects' worth of homework

and etc. *Etc.* is an abbreviation of the Latin phrase *et cetera*, meaning "and other things." Thus, *and etc.* means "and and other things." Do not use *and* with *etc.*

EXAMPLE   We'll need paint, brushes, thinner, some rags, **etc.** [not *and etc.*]

anyways, anywheres, everywheres, nowheres, somewheres Use these words without a final *s.*

EXAMPLE   That bird is described **somewhere** [not *somewheres*] in this book.

as See **like, as.**

as if See **like, as if, as though.**

at Do not use *at* after *where.*

NONSTANDARD   This is where I live at.
STANDARD   This is **where** I live.

bad, badly See page 203.

because See **reason . . . because.**

beside, besides *Beside* is a preposition that means "by the side of" someone or something. *Besides* as a preposition means "in addition to." As an adverb, *besides* means "moreover."

EXAMPLES   Sit **beside** me on the couch.

Besides songs and dances, the show featured several comedy sketches.

It's too late to rent a movie. **Besides,** I'm sleepy.

between, among Use *between* when you are referring to two things at a time, even if they are part of a group consisting of more than two. Use *among* when you are thinking of a group rather than of separate individuals.

EXAMPLES   Take the seat **between** Alicia and Noreen in the third row.

On the map, the boundaries **between** all seven counties are drawn in red. [Although there are more than two counties, each boundary lies between only two.]

Among our graduates are several prominent authors.

There was some confusion **among** the jurors about the defendant's testimony. [The jurors are thought of as a group.]

COMPUTER TIP

The spellchecker on a computer will usually catch misspelled words such as *anywheres* and *nowheres.* The grammar checker may catch errors such as double negatives. However, in the case of words often confused, such as *than* and *then* and *between* and *among,* a computer program may not be able to help. You will have to check your work yourself for correct usage.

USAGE

borrow, lend, loan *Borrow* means "to take [something] temporarily." *Lend* means "to give [something] temporarily." *Loan,* a noun in formal language, is sometimes used in place of *lend* in informal speech.

EXAMPLES   Tadzio **borrowed** a copy of *O Pioneers!* from the library.

I try not to forget to return things people **lend** me.

Could you **loan** me a dollar? [informal]

bring, take *Bring* means "to come carrying something." *Take* means "to go carrying something." Think of *bring* as related to *come, take* as related to *go.*

EXAMPLES   **Bring** that box over here.

Now **take** it down to the basement.

bust, busted Avoid using these words as verbs. Use a form of either *burst* or *break* or *catch* or *arrest.*

EXAMPLES   Even the hard freeze didn't **burst** [not *bust*] the pipes.

When aircraft **break** [not *bust*] the sound barrier, a sonic boom results.

Molly **caught** [not *busted*] Mr. Whiskers nibbling her tuna sandwich.

Did the police **arrest** [not *bust*] a suspect in the burglary?

Oral Practice **Solving Common Usage Problems**

Read each of the following sentences aloud, and identify the correct word or words in parentheses, according to standard usage.

EXAMPLE   **1.** Everyone seemed greatly (*affected, effected*) by her speech on animal rights.

    1. affected

1. There was complete agreement (*between, among*) the members of the council.
2. Is that (*all the farther, as far as*) you were able to hike?
3. The (*affects, effects*) of lasers on surgical procedures have been remarkable.
4. My schedule includes English, math, science, (*etc., and etc.*)
5. The boiler (*busted, burst*) and flooded the cellar.

6. Liza promised to (*bring, take*) me the new cassette when she comes to visit.

7. I don't know where it (*is, is at*).

8. Please (*bring, take*) this note to the manager's office when you go.

9. (*Beside, Besides*) my aunts and uncles, all my cousins are coming to our family reunion.

10. Ms. Yu (*accepted, excepted*) my excuse for being late.

Exercise 1 Proofreading Sentences for Standard Usage

The following sentences contain errors in standard English usage. Identify the error or errors you find in each sentence. Then, write the correct usage. If a sentence is already correct, write *C*.

EXAMPLE   **1.** It isn't pretty, but the fossilized skull in the picture below has caused alot of talk in the scientific world.

　　　　　 1. alot—a lot

1. Discussions between various groups of scholars focus on what killed the dinosaurs.

2. Some scientists believe an asteroid hit earth and wiped out the dinosaurs, but others think there was a severe climate change where the dinosaurs lived at.

3. Even if we don't know why the dinosaurs disappeared, most of us enjoy looking at dinosaur fossils in museums, in exhibitions, on TV, and etc.

4. The San Juan, Argentina, area is one of the best places anywheres to find dinosaur fossils.

5. In 1988, the biologist Paul Sereno's discovery there busted the old record for the most ancient dinosaur remains.

6. On a expedition with some of his students from the University of Chicago, Sereno found the oldest dinosaur fossils unearthed up to that time.

7. Besides being in good shape, Sereno's herrerasaurus fossil doesn't even look its age.

8. In fact, the 230-million-year-old skeleton was amazingly complete accept for the hind limbs.

9. That quality of find certainly ain't ordinary.

10. Sereno and his herrerasaurus have effected the work of biologists and dinosaur-lovers everywhere.

can, may Use *can* to express ability. Use *may* to express possibility or permission.

EXAMPLES   **Can** you speak German? [ability]

              Pedro **may** join us at the restaurant. [possibility]

              May I be excused? [permission]

could of Do not write *of* with the helping verb *could.* Write *could have.* Also avoid *had of, ought to of, should of, would of, might of,* and *must of.*

EXAMPLE   Diane **could have** [not *could of*] telephoned us.

discover, invent *Discover* means "to be the first to find, see, or learn about something that already exists." *Invent* means "to be the first to do or make something."

EXAMPLES   Who **discovered** those fossil dinosaur eggs?

              Robert Wilhelm Bunsen, for whom the Bunsen burner is named, **invented** the spectroscope.

don't, doesn't *Don't* is the contraction of *do not. Doesn't* is the contraction of *does not.* Use *doesn't,* not *don't,* with *he, she, it, this,* and singular nouns.

EXAMPLES   It **doesn't** [not *don't*] matter.

              The trains **don't** [not *doesn't*] stop at this station.

effect See **affect, effect.**

everywheres See **anyways,** etc.

fewer, less *Fewer* is used with plural words. *Less* is used with singular words. *Fewer* tells "how many"; *less* tells "how much."

EXAMPLES   **Fewer** students have enrolled this semester.
              Therefore, there will be **less** competition.

good, well *Good* is an adjective. Do not use *good* to modify a verb; use *well,* an adverb.

NONSTANDARD   Tiger Woods played good.
    STANDARD   Tiger Woods played **well.**

| STYLE | TIP |

Many people consider contractions informal. Therefore, it is usually best to avoid using them in formal writing and speech.

Reference Note

For more information about **formal** and **informal English,** see page 223.

While *well* is usually an adverb, it is also used as an adjective to mean "healthy."

EXAMPLE   She does not feel **well.**

NOTE   *Feel good* and *feel well* mean different things. *Feel good* means "to feel happy or pleased." *Feel well* simply means "to feel healthy."

EXAMPLES   Compliments make you feel **good.**

Do dogs and cats really eat grass when they don't feel **well**?

Exercise 2   Solving Common Usage Problems

For each sentence, choose the correct word in parentheses, according to standard usage.

EXAMPLE   **1.** Today people are using (*fewer, less*) salt than they did years ago.

            1. less

1. You should (*of, have*) written sooner.
2. Who (*discovered, invented*) what makes fireflies glow?
3. (*Don't, Doesn't*) Otis know that we're planning to leave in five minutes?
4. I usually do (*good, well*) on that kind of test.
5. Our doctor advised my uncle to eat (*fewer, less*) eggs.
6. He (*don't, doesn't*) look angry to me.
7. If I had known, I might (*of, have*) helped you with your project.
8. We had (*fewer, less*) snowstorms this year than last.
9. (*Can, May*) I please be excused now?
10. Whoever (*discovered, invented*) the escalator must have been ingenious.

Review A   Solving Common Usage Problems

Most of the following sentences contain errors in standard usage. If a sentence contains an error in standard usage, write the correct form. If a sentence is already correct, write *C*.

EXAMPLE   **1.** Don't anyone know when this game will start?

            1. Doesn't

1. Perhaps I should of called before visiting you.
2. Who discovered the cellular phone system?

USAGE

3. The beautiful weather is effecting my powers of concentration.

4. We can't decide between this movie and that one.

5. That box contains less cookies than this one.

6. We felt good because practice went so well.

7. What affect did the quiz have on your grade?

8. Why won't you except my help?

9. We stood beside the lake and watched the swans.

10. Did you bring flowers to your aunt when you went to visit her in her new home?

Review B   Solving Common Usage Problems

Choose the word or expression in parentheses that is correct according to standard usage.

EXAMPLE   Alvin Ailey significantly **[1]** (*affected, effected*) modern dance in America.

1.   *affected*

Alvin Ailey **[1]** (*could of, could have*) just dreamed of being a famous choreographer; instead, he formed **[2]** (*a, an*) interracial dance company that is known all over the world. Ailey started his dance company with **[3]** (*less, fewer*) than ten dancers in New York City in 1958. Today, the Alvin Ailey American Dance Theater has a very **[4]** (*good, well*) reputation **[5]** (*between, among*) modern-dance lovers **[6]** (*everywhere, everywheres*). Ailey also ran a dance

school and **[7]** (*discovered, invented*) many fine young dancers there. **[8]** (*Beside, Besides*) teaching, he choreographed operas, television specials, and numerous ballets. The scene shown to the left is from Ailey's ballet *Revelations*, an energetic and emotional celebration of the cultural heritage of African Americans. During his lifetime, Ailey **[9]** (*accepted, excepted*) much praise, countless compliments, numerous rave reviews, **[10]** (*and etc., etc.*), for his creativity.

had of See **could of.**

had ought, hadn't ought Unlike other verbs, *ought* is not used with *had.*

NONSTANDARD	Lee had ought to plan better; he hadn't ought to leave his packing until the last minute.
STANDARD	Lee **ought** to plan better; he **ought not** to leave his packing until the last minute.
STANDARD	Lee **should** plan better; he **shouldn't** leave his packing until the last minute.

hardly, scarcely See **The Double Negative** (page 237).

he, she, they Do not use an unnecessary pronoun after the subject of a clause or a sentence. This error is called a *double subject.*

NONSTANDARD	My mother she grows organic vegetables.
STANDARD	My mother grows organic vegetables.

hisself, theirself, theirselves Avoid using these nonstandard forms.

EXAMPLE	He bought **himself** [not *hisself*] a new notebook.

invent See **discover, invent.**

its, it's See page 379.

kind, sort, type The words *this, that, these,* and *those* should always agree in number with the words *kind, sort,* and *type.*

EXAMPLE	**This kind** of wrench is more versatile than **those** other **kinds.**

kind of, sort of In formal situations, avoid using *kind of* for the adverb *somewhat* or *rather.*

INFORMAL	We are kind of anxious to know our grades.
FORMAL	We are **somewhat** [or **rather**] anxious to know our grades.

learn, teach *Learn* means "to acquire knowledge." *Teach* means "to instruct" or "to show how."

EXAMPLE	Some of our coaches **teach** classes in gymnastics, where young gymnasts can **learn** many techniques.

leave, let *Leave* means "to go away" or "to depart from." *Let* means "to allow" or "to permit."

USAGE

NONSTANDARD	Just leave him walk in the rain if he wants.
STANDARD	Just **let** him walk in the rain if he wants.
STANDARD	**Leave** the dishes for tomorrow, and we'll take a walk.

lend, loan See **borrow, lend, loan.**

less See **fewer, less.**

lie, lay See page 167.

like, as In informal English, the preposition *like* is often used as a conjunction meaning "as." In formal English, use *like* to introduce a prepositional phrase, and use *as* to introduce a subordinate clause.

EXAMPLES   She looks **like** her sister. [The preposition *like* introduces the phrase *like her sister.*]

We should do **as** our coach recommends. [The clause *as our coach recommends* is introduced by the conjunction *as.*]

like, as if, as though In formal written English, *like* should not be used for the compound conjunctions *as if* or *as though.*

| INFORMAL | Scamp looks like he's been in the swamp again. |
| FORMAL | Scamp looks **as though** he has been in the swamp again. |

may See **can, may.**

might of, must of See **could of.**

no, none, nothing See **The Double Negative** (page 237).

nowheres See **anyways,** etc.

of Do not use *of* with prepositions such as *inside, off,* or *outside.*

EXAMPLES   He fell **off** [not *off of*] the ladder **outside** [not *outside of*] the garage.

What's **inside** [not *inside of*] that box?

ought to of See **could of.**

Exercise 3 **Solving Common Usage Problems**

For each sentence, choose the correct word or words in parentheses, according to formal, standard usage.

EXAMPLE   **1.** I (*had ought, ought*) to write my report on the Chinese inventions of paper and printing.

1. *ought*

USAGE

Reference Note

For more information about **prepositional phrases,** see Chapter 3. For more about **subordinate clauses,** see Chapter 4.

232   Chapter 9   A Glossary of Usage

1. The report must be on ancient Chinese history, (*like, as*) my teacher directed.
2. For (*this, these*) kind of report, I should start with the information that the Chinese invented paper as we know it early in the second century A.D.
3. If I (*had of, had*) seen them make paper by soaking, drying, and flattening mulberry bark, I would have been amazed.
4. (*The Chinese they, The Chinese*) didn't have the technology to mass-produce paper for another four hundred years.
5. By A.D. 200, the Chinese were using paper for writing and painting (*like, as if*) they always had done so.
6. I (*hadn't ought, ought not*) to forget that the Chinese also used paper for making umbrellas, fans, and lanterns.
7. In addition to (*this, these*) sorts of uses, the Chinese were using paper money by the seventh century.
8. You could have knocked me (*off of, off*) my chair when I learned that the Chinese were printing by A.D. 600—some eight hundred years before the invention of modern printing in Germany.
9. (*Leave, Let*) me tell you about how they used wooden blocks with characters carved on them for printing.
10. By the tenth century, the Chinese had (*learned, taught*) themselves how to print entire books with wooden blocks and had invented movable type.

reason . . . because In formal situations, do not use the construction *reason . . . because*. Instead, use *reason . . . that*.

INFORMAL   The reason for his victory is because he knew what the voters wanted.

FORMAL   The **reason** for his victory is **that** he knew what the voters wanted.

rise, raise See page 169.

sit, set See page 168.

some, somewhat In formal situations, do not use *some* for the adverb *somewhat*.

INFORMAL   I've neglected the garden some.

FORMAL   I've neglected the garden **somewhat.**

sort See **kind,** etc.

supposed to, suppose to Do not leave off the *d* when you write *supposed to.*

EXAMPLE   I am **supposed to** [not *suppose to*] clean my room.

take See **bring, take.**

teach See **learn, teach.**

than, then Do not confuse these words. *Than* is a subordinating conjunction used in comparisons; *then* is an adverb meaning *next* or *at that time.*

EXAMPLES   Algebra is easier **than** I thought it would be.

Read the directions; **then,** follow each step.

their, there, they're See page 382.

them *Them* should not be used as an adjective. Use *those.*

EXAMPLE   I like **those** [not *them*] jeans, don't you?

this here, that there The words *here* and *there* are unnecessary after *this* and *that.*

EXAMPLE   I'm buying **this** [not *this here*] cassette instead of **that** [not *that there*] one.

this kind, sort, type See **kind,** etc.

try and, try to Use *try to,* not *try and.*

EXAMPLE   We will **try to** [not *try and*] be on time.

type See **kind,** etc.

used to, use to Do not leave off the *d* when you write *used to.*

EXAMPLE   I **used to** [not *use to*] play badminton, but now I don't have time.

way, ways Use *way,* not *ways,* in referring to a distance.

EXAMPLE   We hiked a long **way** [not *ways*].

well See **good, well.**

what Do not use *what* for *that* to introduce an adjective clause.

EXAMPLE   The part of the car **that** [not *what*] lets the wheels turn at different speeds is called the differential gear.

when, where In formal situations, do not use *when* or *where* to begin a definition.

INFORMAL	In botany, a "sport" is when a plant is abnormal or has mutated in some way.
FORMAL	In botany, a "sport" is a plant **that is** abnormal or **that has** mutated in some way.

where Do not use *where* for *that* to introduce a noun clause.

EXAMPLE   I read in this magazine **that** [not *where*] Carol Clay is a champion parachutist.

which, that, who The relative pronoun *who* refers to people only; *which* refers to things only; *that* refers to either people or things.

EXAMPLES   Here is the man **who** will install the new carpet. [person]

We decided to replace our old carpet, **which** we have had for nearly ten years. [thing]

The dealer is a person **that** stands behind all of her products. [person]

It is the kind of carpet **that** will wear well. [thing]

without, unless Do not use the preposition *without* in place of the conjunction *unless.*

EXAMPLE   A rattlesnake won't strike you **unless** [not *without*] you surprise or threaten it.

would of See **could of.**

your, you're *Your* is a possessive form of *you. You're* is the contraction of *you are.*

EXAMPLES   Is that **your** bike?

I hope **you're** going to the party.

> **Exercise 4**   Solving Common Usage Problems

For each sentence, choose the correct word or words in parentheses, according to formal, standard usage.

EXAMPLE   **1.** (*That, That there*) motorcycle belongs to my cousin.

   1. That

1. Don't use more paper (*than, then*) you need.
2. (*Them, Those*) dogs have impressive pedigrees.

3. Manuel prefers (*this, these*) kind of skateboard.
4. It is only a short (*way, ways*) to the video store.
5. Tricia relaxed (*some, somewhat*) after she began to speak.
6. On the news, I heard (*where, that*) the game was called off because of rain.
7. Please set the books on (*your, you're*) desk.
8. Is she the player (*who, which*) is favored by most to win at Wimbledon this year?
9. He would not have released the report (*without, unless*) he had first verified his sources.
10. The reason we've requested your help is (*that, because*) you know the grounds better than we do.

─HELP─
Some sentences in Review C contain more than one error.

Review C Correcting Usage Errors

Identify each usage problem that you find in the sentences in the following paragraph. Then, write the usage that is correct according to formal, standard usage. If a sentence is already correct, write *C*.

EXAMPLE **[1]** The legendary statue, the Sphinx at Giza in Egypt, would of weathered away completely if it had not been rescued by modern technology.

1. *would of—would have*

[1] Some famous monuments, such as the Eiffel Tower, don't look like they need any restoration. [2] However, monuments older than the Eiffel Tower, like Egypt's Sphinx, often need alot of care. [3] The Sphinx, who has the head of a human and the body of a lion, was built around 4500 B.C. [4] Some historians think the Sphinx, shown below, might of been built at the same time as the pyramid of King Khafre, which stands beside it. [5] Those historians they believe the Sphinx's face is a portrait of Khafre. [6] The Sphinx was suffering some from old age, exposure, and bad restoration attempts, so Egyptian museum officials began a major renewal project in 1990. [7] Scientists knew that the world eventually would lose that famous statue without restoration was begun immediately. [8] Workers

dismantled many stones, set new ones in their places, and than added natural mortar to let them stones breathe. [9] Workers also stabilized the water table under the mammoth Sphinx, which towers sixty-six feet above the desert sands. [10] These kind of restorations will help to preserve the Sphinx against the harmful affects of wind, rain, and sand for many years to come.

Review D Correcting Usage Errors

Revise each of the following sentences, correcting the error or errors in usage.

EXAMPLE **1.** I saw on the news where the mayor doesn't plan to run for re-election.

  1. *I saw on the news that the mayor doesn't plan to run for re-election.*

1. Optimism is when a person look on the bright side.
2. Luanne was suppose to buy a birthday card for Jo.
3. Take this rake and them seedlings to Mae like I asked.
4. I would of begun my report sooner then I did if I had known it would need this much research.
5. I heard where people will not be allowed back in the concert hall after intermission without they show their tickets.
6. The tire came off of the truck and rolled a long ways away.
7. Heather Ruiz has promised to learn us karate.
8. The people which witnessed the crime hadn't ought to have left before the police arrived.
9. Did Thomas Edison discover the lightbulb?
10. Is it safe to leave the dog to run around the park without a leash?

The Double Negative

In a ***double negative,*** two or more negative words are used when one is sufficient. Do not use double negatives in formal writing and speaking.

hardly, scarcely The words *hardly* and *scarcely* convey a negative meaning. They should not be used with another negative word.

EXAMPLES I **can** [not *can't*] **hardly** turn the key in the lock.

  We **have** [not *haven't*] **scarcely** enough time.

© Jim Unger; distributed by United Media, 1998.

"Dropping out of school never done me no harm."

Write a short dialogue of ten lines in which the two people speaking use non-standard English. Then, go back and rewrite the dialogue, changing the non-standard usage to standard English usage.

┌─**HELP**─

Although two revisions are shown for the example in Exercise 5, you need to give only one for each sentence.

no, nothing, none Do not use these words with another negative word.

NONSTANDARD	That answer doesn't make no sense.
STANDARD	That answer **doesn't make any** sense.
STANDARD	That answer **makes no** sense.

NONSTANDARD	The field trip won't cost us nothing.
STANDARD	The field trip **won't cost** us **anything.**
STANDARD	The field trip **will cost** us **nothing.**

NONSTANDARD	We wanted grapes, but there weren't none.
STANDARD	We wanted grapes, but there **weren't any.**
STANDARD	We wanted grapes, but there **were none.**

Exercise 5 **Correcting Double Negatives**

Revise each of the following sentences, correcting the usage errors.

EXAMPLE
1. It doesn't make no difference to me.

1. *It makes no difference to me.*
   or
   It doesn't make any difference to me.

1. Rachel didn't say nothing to him.
2. There isn't hardly anything left to eat.
3. I haven't borrowed no books from the library this week.
4. Laura couldn't hardly make herself heard.
5. What you're saying doesn't make no sense to me.
6. By the time we wrote for tickets, there weren't none available.
7. Hasn't no one in the class read *And Now Miguel*?
8. There wasn't scarcely enough water to keep the fish alive.
9. Didn't you never say nothing about the noise?
10. I haven't never told no one about our discovery.

Nonsexist Language

Nonsexist language is language that applies to people in general, both male and female. For example, the nonsexist terms *humanity, human beings,* and *people* can substitute for the gender-specific term *mankind.*

In the past, many skills and occupations were generally closed to either men or women. Expressions like *seamstress, stewardess,* and *mailman* reflect those limitations. Since most jobs can now be held by both men and women, language is adjusting to reflect this change.

When you are referring generally to people, it is best to use nonsexist expressions rather than gender-specific ones. Below are some widely used nonsexist terms that you can use to replace the gender-specific ones.

Gender-specific	Nonsexist
businessman	executive, businessperson
chairman	chairperson, chair
deliveryman	delivery person
fireman	firefighter
foreman	supervisor
housewife	homemaker
mailman	mail carrier
man-made	synthetic, manufactured
manpower	workers, human resources
May the best man win!	May the best person win!
policeman	police officer
salesman	salesperson, salesclerk
seamstress	needleworker
steward, stewardess	flight attendant
watchman	security guard

If the antecedent of a pronoun may be either masculine or feminine, use both masculine and feminine pronouns to refer to it.

EXAMPLES **Anyone** who wants to enter the poster contest should bring **his or her** entry to Room 21 by Friday.

Any student may bring a poster with **him or her** to Room 21.

You can often avoid the awkward *his or her* construction (or the alternative *his/her*) by substituting an article (*a, an,* or *the*) for the construction. You can also rephrase the sentence, using the plural forms of both the pronoun and its antecedent.

EXAMPLES Any interested **student** may submit **a** poster.

All interested **students** may submit **their** posters.

STYLE TIP

You can make similar revisions to avoid using the awkward expressions *s/he* and *wo/man*.

Using Nonsexist Language

Rewrite each of the following sentences to avoid using gender-specific terms and awkward expressions.

EXAMPLE   **1.** An airline stewardess works hard to keep her passengers comfortable.

1. *Flight attendants work hard to keep their passengers comfortable.*

1. The project was short of manpower, so the management hired more staff.

2. A three-alarm fire broke out in the factory, and the firemen were soon on the scene.

3. Whether or not s/he gets a commission depends on how persuasive each salesman is.

4. May the best wo/man win!

5. Our dog growls when it sees a delivery man and barks loudly at every mailman.

6. Being a policeman is a demanding job.

7. Did you hear that Susan was elected chairman of the board?

8. The foreman of the crew will distribute the helmets.

9. When Aunt Tina and Uncle Lewis had a baby, Aunt Tina decided to become a housewife.

10. Some man-made medicines are considerably cheaper than natural medicines.

Chapter Review

A. Correcting Errors in Standard Usage

For each of the following sentences, identify and correct the error or errors in usage. If a sentence is already correct, write *C*.

1. Why don't Guadalupe try out for the team?
2. Please leave Mike solve the problem by himself.
3. The ball can't go outside of the boundary lines.
4. You are playing good now that you practice every day.
5. We sat beside the lake and fished.
6. Every spring we see less bluebirds than the year before.
7. Tyrone doesn't like this kind of frosting.
8. I read where another royal wedding is taking place.
9. Terry looked like she needed a rest after the relay.
10. They wouldn't of missed going to the mountains.

B. Proofreading a Paragraph for Standard Usage

For each sentence in the following paragraph, identify and correct the error or errors in standard English usage. If a sentence is already correct, write *C*.

[11] Please bring me a dictionary so that I can look up what *left-handed* means, like I started to do earlier. [12] Left-handedness is where the person uses the left hand more than the right hand. [13] It don't matter which hand a person mainly uses because a left-hander functions just as good as a right-hander does. [14] Being left-handed couldn't hardly be a handicap; alot of clever people have been left-handed. [15] For example, artists like Leonardo da Vinci and Michelangelo Buonarroti were left-handed. [16] Of course, less people are left-handed than right-handed. [17] Many scientists learn their students the theory that left-handedness is determined by which side of the brain is dominant. [18] Some scientists they say that the left side of the brain is more dominant in a right-handed person. [19] They also say that the right side of the brain is more dominant in a left-handed person, but there isn't nobody who knows for sure. [20] Discussions on this subject between various groups of scientists will probably continue into the distant future.

USAGE

C. Solving Common Usage Problems

For each sentence, choose the correct word in parentheses, according to formal, standard usage.

21. I looked for the library book all over the house, but I couldn't find it (*anywheres, anywhere*).
22. The deer searched the ground for food, but there wasn't (*none, any*).
23. When the temperature dropped to zero, we worried that the pipes might (*bust, burst*).
24. In the 1820s and '30s, the French scientists Louis Daguerre and Nicéphore Niépce (*discovered, invented*) photography.
25. That airline's slogan is "We fly (*everywhere, everywheres*)."
26. Dr. Mendez advised me to eat (*less, fewer*) sweets.
27. What (*affect, effect*) did the good news have on her?
28. However much you try to outrun a tornado, it doesn't make (*no, any*) difference; the best idea is to seek shelter immediately.
29. Who (*discovered, invented*) what a comet's tail is made of, Kai?
30. Nick admitted that he (*should of, should have*) told his family what time he was planning to come home.
31. "If you study hard now, you will be more confident later, and you will do (*good, well*) on the final," declared Ms. Echevarria.
32. Although it has (*fewer, less*) options than the car advertised, that car on the lot is a better deal, overall.
33. From New Orleans to Los Angeles is quite a long (*ways, way*).
34. That orchestra has a top-notch reputation (*between, among*) music lovers worldwide.
35. The author (*accepted, excepted*) the award with the grace that had long been characteristic of her.
36. Mother asked Simon to (*leave, let*) her read her book in peace.
37. I heard (*where, that*) today's discounts are the best ever.
38. Is Belle the singer (*which, that*) had that TV special last week?
39. It's hard to imagine how ice got onto the moon (*without, unless*) there had once been water there.
40. Could you (*lend, loan*) me your book?

D. Using Nonsexist Language

Rewrite each of the following sentences to avoid gender-specific terms and awkward expressions.

41. The foreman issued her first work order of the day.

42. May the best man win!

43. Caroline's friend was an airline stewardess.

44. Only the very courageous need apply to be firemen.

45. Three of the salesmen were under twenty-five.

46. The space shuttle is the most useful man-made device ever.

47. The deliverymen for that company wear brown shorts.

48. My next-door neighbor was a first-rate seamstress.

49. Fewer women become housewives these days than in the past.

50. The computer plant is advertising for a watchman, I hear.

Writing Application
Writing a Business Letter

Using Formal, Standard English After reading studies showing the benefits of school uniforms, the school board in your district has proposed requiring students to wear uniforms. One study found that schools that require uniforms experience less violence. Another study concluded that students who wore uniforms made better grades. Write a letter to the school board, telling why your district should or should not require students to wear uniforms.

Prewriting If you already have an opinion about school uniforms, jot down some reasons to support your view. If you are undecided, you may want to make two lists—one pro and one con. Give several reasons to support each position. Then, choose the more persuasive side.

Writing As you write your first draft, keep focused on your topic. Choose only the best reasons from your list, and expand on these.

Revising Add, delete, or rearrange details to support your argument. Also, see that the tone and word choice of your letter conform to the standards of a polite business letter.

Publishing Proofread your paper for any errors in spelling and punctuation. Then, use the glossary entries in this chapter to correct common usage errors. You and your classmates may wish to have a debate on the school uniform issue. You might also like to post your letter on the class bulletin board or Web page.

Capital Letters
The Rules for Capitalization

Diagnostic Preview

A. Correcting Sentences That Contain Errors in Capitalization

Correct the errors in capitalization in the following sentences by capitalizing or lowercasing letters as needed. If a sentence contains no errors, write *C*.

EXAMPLE   **1.** My Aunt and I visited the White house in Washington, D.C.

         1. aunt, House

1. Val's new schwinn bike had a flat tire.

2. My father is taking a course in public speaking.

3. The atmosphere on venus is one hundred times denser than the atmosphere on earth.

4. Has your favorite team ever won the rose bowl?

5. The opossum can be found as far south as Argentina and as far north as Canada.

6. For our Spring project, our Club raised money for the American heart association.

7. The maya of the Yucatán peninsula worshiped nature Gods such as chac, a god of rain, and Itzamná, a sky god.

8. My uncle Scott works at Apex hardware store.

9. In drama 2, we staged a production of Denise Chávez's *The flying tortilla Man*.

10. The U.S. senate and the house of representatives may pass a bill into law, but the president can veto it.
11. Mr. Williams is a Reporter for United Press international.
12. We went to Sea World over easter vacation.
13. Both rabbi Frankel and reverend Stone organized aid for the many victims of the fire.
14. The Winter Games of the 1998 olympics were held in Nagano, Japan.
15. Michelangelo's *The creation of the World* and *The Last Judgment* are paintings that depict scenes from the bible.

B. Correcting Capitalization Errors in a Paragraph

Correct the errors in capitalization in the following paragraph by capitalizing or lowercasing letters as needed. If a sentence contains no errors, write *C*.

EXAMPLE   **[1]** A gentle elephant named jumbo was once the largest, most popular captive animal in the World.

     1. *Jumbo, world*

[16] When p. t. barnum bought Jumbo in 1882, the elephant had already become a star with the London royal circus. [17] All of england protested the sale when the unhappy elephant refused to board the ship for New York city. [18] however, even queen Victoria and the Prince of wales could not prevent Jumbo's going, since the sale had been completed. [19] Jumbo's Trainer, Matthew Scott, kept the elephant content on the journey across the atlantic ocean. [20] In april, the new addition to the Show arrived in New York, and the 13,500-pound Star marched up broadway to the cheers of a huge crowd. [21] Soon Jumbo-mania swept across the United States. [22] The elephant was so popular that his name became a common word in the english language—*jumbo,* meaning "extra large." [23] He died tragically on September 15, 1885, in the canadian town of St. Thomas, Ontario. [24] The big-hearted giant, seeing a train bearing down on a baby elephant, pushed the youngster to safety but could not save himself. [25] To keep Jumbo's memory alive, Barnum donated the skeleton of his beloved elephant to the American Museum of natural history.

Using Capital Letters Correctly

A capital letter at the beginning of a word is an important signal to the reader. A capital letter may indicate the beginning of a sentence and also may mark a significant difference in meaning, such as the difference between *may* (as in *you may*) and *May* (as in *May 3, 2002*).

10a. Capitalize the first word in every sentence.

EXAMPLES   **T**he world of computers has its own vocabulary. **C**omputer equipment is called *hardware,* and the programs are called *software.*

Exercise 1 Capitalizing Sentences in a Paragraph

Rewrite the following paragraph. Capitalize the ten words that should begin with a capital letter. Add the appropriate punctuation mark to the end of each sentence.

EXAMPLE   1. what are some new developments in science

             1. *What are some new developments in science?*

   work has begun on a new kind of laser radar this instrument would be especially useful for people with visual impairments how does the radar work a laser device that is small enough to fit onto an eyeglass frame emits invisible infrared light beams when the light strikes an object, it bounces back to a receiver placed in the wearer's ear the receiver, in turn, sounds a small tone with this sort of device, the person can "hear" any object nearby the device is very promising in fact, it may one day replace the cane or the guide dog as an aid for people who are blind there are few better examples of how beneficial laser research can be

10b. Traditionally, the first word of a line of poetry is capitalized.

EXAMPLES   **A** bird came down the walk:
            He did not know I saw;
            He bit an angleworm in halves
            And ate the fellow, raw.

                        Emily Dickinson, "A Bird Came Down
                              the Walk"

10c. Capitalize the first word of a directly quoted sentence.

EXAMPLE   Eduardo wondered, "**W**here did I put my backpack?"

Reference Note

For more information on using **capital letters in quotations,** see page 315.

MECHANICS

10d. Capitalize the first word in both the salutation and the closing of a letter.

EXAMPLES   **D**ear Service Manager: **S**incerely,

                       Dear Amy,   **Y**ours truly,

10e. Capitalize the pronoun *I* and the interjection *O*.

Although it is rarely used, *O* is always capitalized. Generally, it is reserved for invocations and is followed by the name of the person or thing being addressed. You will more often use the interjection *oh*, which is generally not capitalized unless it is the first word in a sentence.

EXAMPLES   "Exult **O** shores! and ring **O** bells!" is a line from Walt Whitman's poem "**O** Captain! My Captain!"

                   The play was a hit, but **o**h, how nervous I was!

                   Oh, I forgot my book.

BORN LOSER reprinted by permission of Newspaper Enterprise Association, Inc.

Exercise 2   **Correcting Capitalization Errors in Sentences**

Correct the errors in capitalization in the following sentences. If a sentence contains no errors, write *C*.

EXAMPLE   1. in "Jazz Fantasia," the speaker tells the Musicians, "Go to it, o jazzmen."

          1. *In, musicians, O*

1. yesterday i learned two psalms that begin, "Bless the Lord, o my soul."
2. Ms. Jones asked, "can anyone name the author of that poem?"
3. I haven't decided, but Oh, how I'd like to be an astronaut!
4. "you must be careful of the coral snake," said the guide, "because it is the most poisonous snake in our region."
5. In the poem "The Fool's Prayer," the jester pleads, "O Lord, be merciful to me, a fool!"
6. do you know that the fifth of May is a Mexican American holiday?
7. most trucks have rear-wheel drive.
8. Two days ago—oh, such a short time!—I left without a care.
9. The car stopped suddenly, and Oh, was i glad for my seat belt!
10. My favorite verses from that scene are

      see how she leans her cheek upon her hand!

      oh, that i were a glove upon that hand,

      that i might touch that cheek!

MECHANICS

Reference Note

For more about **common** and **proper nouns,** see page 3. For a discussion of **proper adjectives,** see page 11.

┌HELP───

Proper nouns and proper adjectives sometimes lose their capitals through frequent usage.

EXAMPLES

watt   **t**itanic   **s**andwich

To find out whether a noun should be capitalized, check in a dictionary. The dictionary will tell you whether a word should always be capitalized or whether it should be capitalized only in certain uses.

10f. Capitalize proper nouns and proper adjectives.

A *common noun* names any one of a group of persons, places, things, or ideas. A *proper noun* names a particular person, place, thing, or idea. A *proper adjective* is an adjective formed from a proper noun.

Proper nouns are capitalized. Common nouns are generally not capitalized unless they

- begin a sentence

    or

- begin a direct quotation

    or

- are part of a title

Common Nouns	Proper Nouns	Proper Adjectives
a **p**atriot	**T**homas **J**efferson	**J**effersonian ideals
a **c**ountry	**T**urkey	**T**urkish border
a **q**ueen	**Q**ueen **E**lizabeth	**E**lizabethan drama
a **r**eligion	**I**slam	**I**slamic beliefs
a **r**egion	the **S**outhwest	**S**outhwestern cooking

In proper nouns of more than one word, do not capitalize

- short prepositions (generally, ones with fewer than five letters, such as *in, on,* and *with*)

- articles (*a, an, the*)

- coordinating conjunctions (*and, but, for, nor, or, so, yet*)

- the sign of the infinitive (*to*)

EXAMPLES   Mary, Queen **of** Scots

Eric **the** Red

*Romeo **and** Juliet*

"Writing **t**o Persuade"

(1) Capitalize the names of persons and animals.

│ **COMPUTER TIP**

The spellings of personal names can challenge even the best spellchecking software. However, you may be able to customize your spellchecker. If your software allows, add to it any names that you use frequently but have difficulty spelling or capitalizing.

Given Names	**A**lana	**M**ark	**L**a**V**erne
Surnames	**D**iaz	**C**ollins	**W**illiams
Animals	**T**rigger	**S**ocks	**R**over

NOTE For names having more than one part, capitalization may vary.

EXAMPLES
De Vere   **d**e la **G**arza

McGregor   **O'L**eary

Ibn-**K**haldun   **v**on **B**raun

Always check the spelling of such a name with the person who has that name, or look in a reference source.

(2) Capitalize initials in names and abbreviations that come before or after names.

EXAMPLES
A. E. Roosevelt   Lewis **F.** Powell, **Jr.**   **Sr.** Gomez

Ms. Sonstein   Sabra Santos, **M.D.**   **Dr.** Alan Berg

(3) Capitalize geographical names.

Type of Name	Examples	
Towns and Cities	**P**ortland **D**etroit	**M**exico **C**ity **R**io de **J**aneiro
Counties, Townships, and Provinces	**K**ane **C**ounty **H**ayes **T**ownship **P**lum **B**orough	**E**ast **B**aton **R**ouge **P**arish **Q**uebec **P**rovince **W**illiamson **C**ounty
States	**I**owa **M**issouri	**A**laska **N**orth **C**arolina
Countries	**E**l **S**alvador **N**ew **Z**ealand	**U**nited **A**rab **E**mirates **S**witzerland
Continents	**A**sia	**S**outh **A**merica
Islands	**W**ake **I**sland the **W**est **I**ndies	the **I**sle of **P**alms the **F**lorida **K**eys
Mountains	**M**ount **A**rarat **H**imalayas	the **A**lps the **M**ount of **O**lives
Bodies of Water	**I**ndian **O**cean **A**driatic **S**ea	**R**ed **R**iver **L**ake of the **W**oods

(continued)

Reference Note

For more about **capitalizing titles used with names,** see Rule 10h(1). For information on **punctuating abbreviations** that come before or after names, see page 267.

Reference Note

Abbreviations of the names of states are capitalized. See page 268 for more about **using and punctuating such abbreviations.**

STYLE   TIP

Words such as *north, west,* and *southeast* are not capitalized when they indicate direction.

EXAMPLES
farther **n**orth
traveling **s**outheast

However, these words are capitalized when they name a particular region.

EXAMPLES
states in the **N**orthwest
driving in the **S**outh

MECHANICS

(continued)

Type of Name	Examples	
Parks and Forests	**C**leburne **S**tate **P**ark the **E**verglades **N**ational **P**ark	**P**almetto **S**tate **P**ark **O**uachita **N**ational **F**orest
Regions	the **W**est the **S**outheast	**G**reat **P**lains **C**orn **B**elt
Other Geographical Names	**S**inai **P**eninsula **C**arlsbad **C**averns	**H**arding **I**cefield **B**ryce **C**anyon
Roads, Streets, and Highways	**S**tate **R**oad 17 **I**nterstate 787	**M**o-**P**ac **E**xpressway **W**est **F**irst **S**treet

NOTE In a street name that is a hyphenated number, the second word begins with a lowercase letter.

EXAMPLE   Twenty-**s**econd Street

Words like *city, island, river, street,* and *park* are capitalized when they are part of a name. When words like these are not part of a proper name, they are common nouns and are not capitalized.

Common Nouns	Proper Nouns
life in a big **c**ity	life in **N**ew **Y**ork **C**ity
the **r**iver	the **S**pokane **R**iver
a small **i**sland	**L**iberty **I**sland
on a narrow **s**treet	on **S**tate **S**treet

Exercise 3 **Recognizing the Correct Use of Capital Letters**

Write the letter of the correctly capitalized sentence in each of the following pairs.

EXAMPLE   1. a. Drive Northeast until you get to New Haven.
           b. Drive northeast until you get to New Haven.

1. *b*

Reference Note

In addresses, abbreviations such as *St., Blvd., Ave., Dr.,* and *Ln.* are capitalized. For information about **punctuating abbreviations,** see page 267.

STYLE TIP

Since *rio* is Spanish for "river," *Rio de la Plata River* is redundant. Use only *Rio de la Plata.*

Other terms to watch for are

- *sierra,* Spanish for "mountain range" [Use only *Sierra Nevada,* not *Sierra Nevada Mountains.*]

- *yama,* Japanese for "mountain" [Use only *Fujiyama* or *Mount Fuji,* not *Mount Fujiyama.*]

- *sahara,* Arabic for "desert" [Use only *Sahara,* not *Sahara Desert.*]

- *gobi,* Mongolian for "desert" [Use only *Gobi,* not *Gobi Desert.*]

MECHANICS

1. **a.** We went canoeing on the Ohio river.
   b. We went canoeing on the Ohio River.
2. **a.** I read the article on south America.
   b. I read the article on South America.
3. **a.** Farewell Bend State Park is in Oregon.
   b. Farewell Bend State park is in Oregon.
4. **a.** Her address is 1614 Robin Street.
   b. Her address is 1614 Robin street.
5. **a.** I will be at Forty-Second Street and Park Avenue.
   b. I will be at Forty-second Street and Park Avenue.
6. **a.** The North Sea is east of Great Britain.
   b. The North sea is East of great Britain.
7. **a.** Atlanta is a fast-growing City in the south.
   b. Atlanta is a fast-growing city in the South.
8. **a.** Pensacola is on the gulf of Mexico.
   b. Pensacola is on the Gulf of Mexico.
9. **a.** The Hawaiian Islands are southwest of California.
   b. The Hawaiian islands are Southwest of California.
10. **a.** Laredo is on the Mexican Border in Webb county.
    b. Laredo is on the Mexican border in Webb County.

(4) Capitalize the names of organizations, teams, government bodies, and institutions.

Type of Name	Examples	
Organizations	United Nations	Boy Scouts of America
	National Weather Service	Millersville Orchid Society
Teams	Green Bay Packers	River City Allstars
	Golden State Warriors	Lady Lobos
		Pitt Panthers
Government Bodies	Congress	Peace Corps
	Federal Trade Commission	State Department
		Austin City Council
Institutions	Smithsonian Institution	New College
		North High School
	Stanford University	Bellevue Hospital

STYLE TIP

The names of organizations, businesses, and government bodies are often abbreviated to a series of capital letters.

EXAMPLES

National Organization for Women	NOW
American Telephone & Telegraph	AT&T
National Science Foundation	NSF

Usually the letters in such abbreviations are not followed by periods, but always check an up-to-date dictionary or other reliable source to be sure.

MECHANICS

EXAMPLES   The new regime promises to institute **d**emocratic reforms.

The **D**emocratic candidate will debate the **R**epublican candidate tonight.

The word *party* in the name of a political party may be capitalized or not; either way is correct. Be consistent in the use of the word throughout a particular piece of writing.

EXAMPLES   Libertarian **p**arty *or* **P**arty

Federalist **p**arty *or* **P**arty

(5) Capitalize the names of historical events and periods, special events, holidays, and other calendar items.

Type of Name	Examples	
Historical Events and Periods	**F**rench **R**evolution	**W**orld **W**ar II
	Age of **R**eason	**B**attle of **B**ritain
Special Events	**S**pecial **O**lympics	**G**ulf **C**oast **T**rack-and-**F**ield **C**hampionship
	Parents' **D**ay	
Holidays and Other Calendar Items	**T**hursday	**V**alentine's **D**ay
	December	**L**abor **D**ay
	New **Y**ear's **D**ay	**A**ugust

Oral Practice   **Creating Sentences Using Lowercase and Capital Letters**

Correctly use each of the following words in a sentence spoken aloud.

EXAMPLE   **1.** river

1. *The river is rising.*

1. river	**3.** hotel	**5.** street	**7.** march	**9.** west
2. River	**4.** Hotel	**6.** Street	**8.** March	**10.** West

(6) Capitalize the names of nationalities, races, and peoples.

EXAMPLES   **C**anadian, **K**orean, **C**aucasian, **A**sian, **K**urds, **Z**ulu, **S**eminole

(7) Capitalize the names of religions and their followers, holy days and celebrations, sacred writings, and specific deities.

Type of Name	Examples		
Religions and Followers	**J**udaism **B**uddhism	**M**uslim **T**aoist	**B**aptist **Q**uaker
Holy Days and Celebrations	**L**ent **D**iwali	**P**assover **E**piphany	**R**amadan **R**osh **H**ashanah
Sacred Writings	**B**ible **T**almud	**U**panishads **D**euteronomy	**K**oran **D**ead **S**ea **S**crolls
Specific Deities	**A**llah	**B**rahma	**G**od

NOTE The words *god* and *goddess* are not capitalized when they refer to the deities of ancient mythology. However, the names of specific mythological gods and goddesses are capitalized.

EXAMPLE   The Greek poet paid tribute to the **g**od **Z**eus.

(8) Capitalize the names of businesses and the brand names of business products.

BUSINESSES   **M**otorola, **I**nc., **B**ank of **A**merica, **S**am's **S**hoes

BRAND NAMES   **F**ormica, **C**hevrolet, **A**ce, **K**leenex, **W**hirlpool

NOTE Do not capitalize a common noun that follows a brand name: Formica **c**ountertop, Chevrolet **v**an, Ace **b**andage.

(9) Capitalize the names of planets, stars, constellations, and other heavenly bodies.

Type of Name	Examples		
Planets and Other Heavenly Bodies	**S**aturn the **M**ilky **W**ay	**O**rion **V**ega	**J**upiter **P**roxima **C**entauri

STYLE   TIP

The words *black* and *white* may or may not be capitalized when they refer to races. However, within a particular piece of writing, be consistent in the way you capitalize these words.

STYLE   TIP

In some writings, you may notice that pronouns referring to deities are always capitalized as a sign of respect. In other cases, writers capitalize such pronouns only to prevent confusion.

EXAMPLE
The Lord called upon Moses to lead **H**is people out of Egypt. [*His* is capitalized to show that it refers to *the Lord*, not *Moses*.]

STYLE   TIP

The word *earth* is not capitalized unless it is used along with the names of other heavenly bodies that are capitalized. The words *sun* and *moon* generally are not capitalized.

MECHANICS

(10) Capitalize the names of ships, trains, aircraft, and spacecraft.

Type of Name	Examples		
Ships, Trains, Aircraft, and Spacecraft	**A**rgo **S**putnik	**Y**ankee **C**lipper **F**lying **S**cotsman	**C**olumbia **T**hunder **B**ird

(11) Capitalize the names of awards, memorials, and monuments.

Type of Name	Examples	
Awards, Memorials, and Monuments	**N**obel Prize **S**ilver **S**tar	**L**incoln **M**emorial **T**omb of the **U**nknown **S**oldier

(12) Capitalize the names of particular buildings and other structures.

Type of Name	Examples		
Buildings and Other Structures	**T**ower of **L**ondon **G**olden **G**ate **B**ridge	**P**laza **H**otel the **A**lamo **F**ort **K**nox	**S**hasta **D**am **G**reat **W**all of **C**hina

NOTE Generally, do not capitalize words like *hotel, theater, college, high school,* and *courthouse* unless they are part of a proper name.

EXAMPLES   Jackson **H**igh **S**chool   a **h**igh **s**chool principal

Copley Square **H**otel   a **h**otel in Boston

Fox **T**heater   a **t**heater in Dallas

Victoria County **C**ourthouse   a **c**ourthouse hallway

Exercise 4   **Correcting the Capitalization of Words and Phrases**

Correct the following words and phrases, using capital letters as needed.

EXAMPLE   **1.** a methodist minister

1. *a Methodist minister*

1. somewhere between mars and jupiter

2. a shopping center on twenty-third street

3. lafayette park in tallahassee, florida
4. some wheaties cereal
5. jefferson racquet club
6. harvard university
7. at the new jewish synagogue
8. on memorial day
9. an african american
10. the sinking of the *lusitania*
11. making easter baskets for the children
12. a visit to the washington monument
13. seeing venus through a telescope
14. reading a passage from the koran
15. flying in the *spruce goose*
16. to the ritz hotel
17. stories about the Egyptian god ra
18. a hammer from Ridgeway hardware store
19. passed by a dodge minivan
20. taking pictures of the eiffel tower

Review A **Identifying and Correcting Errors in Capitalization**

Correct the capitalization errors in each of the following sentences by capitalizing and lowercasing letters as needed.

EXAMPLE   1. The earliest African American Folk tales have their roots in africa.

1. *folk, Africa*

1. Africans who first came to the americas enjoyed folk tales that blended their own african songs with stories they heard here.
2. Before the civil war, African Americans created new tales that reflected their experiences as Slaves and their desire for Freedom.
3. Many of these tales are about Animals, especially the small but clever character named brer rabbit.
4. Zora neale hurston collected a number of these animal stories and published them in *Mules and Men.*
5. Brer rabbit, a character that was especially popular in the south in the 1800s, constantly plays tricks on brer fox and brer wolf.
6. In some later tales, the main Character isn't a rabbit but a slave, john, who outsmarts the slave owner.

THE PEOPLE COULD FLY
American Black Folktales
told by VIRGINIA HAMILTON
Illustrated by LEO *and* DIANE DILLON

7. The author virginia hamilton, winner of the newbery medal and the national book award, tells other tales in *The People Could Fly: American Black Folktales.*

8. Both the title of that Book and the Painting on its cover refer to another popular kind of black folk tale that developed during the years of slavery.

9. Can you tell that the People on the book's cover are flying above the Earth?

10. "The People Could Fly" is one of many fantasy tales about enslaved people who use Magic Powers to fly away from their troubles.

10g. Do not capitalize the names of school subjects, except the names of language classes or course names that contain a number.

EXAMPLES   This year I am taking **g**eometry, **E**nglish, **c**ivics, **D**rafting **I**, and a **f**oreign **l**anguage. Next year I plan to take **A**merican **g**overnment, **E**nglish, **t**rigonometry, **B**iology **I**, and **S**panish.

Review B **Correcting Capitalization Errors in Sentences**

Correct the following sentences by changing lowercase letters to capital letters as needed.

EXAMPLE   1. mi kyung's mother told us that buddhism and confucianism have a long history in korea.

    1. *Mi Kyung's mother told us that Buddhism and Confucianism have a long history in Korea.*

1. in tuesday's class, mrs. garcía explained that the diameter of earth is only 405 miles greater than that of venus.

2. this year's freshmen will be required to take more courses in english, science, and math than prior freshmen at briarwood county high school were.

3. in chicago we visited soldier field and the museum of science and industry, which are known all over the world.

4. Aboard the space shuttle *columbia* in january 1986, franklin Chang-Díaz became the first astronaut to send a message in spanish back to earth.

5. are latin and biology the most helpful courses for someone planning to go into medicine?

6. after i went to the mall and the hardware store, i stopped at quik mart on twenty-second street.

┌H E L P──

Do not capitalize the class names *freshman, sophomore, junior,* or *senior* unless they are part of a proper noun.

EXAMPLES
All **f**reshmen should meet after school to discuss the **F**reshman-**S**ophomore **B**anquet.

MECHANICS

7. we vacationed in the west, stopping to see pikes peak and to go camping and fishing in colorado.
8. in kentucky, one of the border states between the north and the south, you can visit mammoth cave, churchill downs, and the lincoln birthplace national historic site.
9. after labor day last fall, the columbus youth fellowship sponsored a softball tournament at maxwell field.
10. augustus saint-gaudens, a great sculptor who came to the united states from ireland as a child, portrayed abraham lincoln as a tall, serious man standing with his head bowed.

10h. Capitalize titles.

(1) Capitalize a person's title when the title comes before the person's name.

EXAMPLES   **P**resident Kennedy   **M**r. Nakamura

                 Dr. Dooley   **F**riar Tuck

                 Professor Simmons   **P**rincipal Phillips

                 Mrs. Robinson   **L**ady Jane Grey

Generally, a title that is used alone or following a person's name is not capitalized, especially if the title is preceded by *a* or *the*.

EXAMPLES   We saw the **m**ayor at the park.

                 Daniel Inouye was first elected **s**enator in 1962.

                 Who was the **q**ueen of England during the Victorian Age?

Titles used alone in direct address, however, generally are capitalized.

EXAMPLES   Well, **D**octor, what is your diagnosis?

                 There's a message for you, **A**dmiral.

                 Good morning, **M**a'am [or *ma'am*].

(2) Capitalize a word showing a family relationship when the word is used before or in place of a person's name, unless the word follows a possessive noun or pronoun.

EXAMPLES   **U**ncle Jack, **C**ousin Joshua, **G**randfather,
                 my **u**ncle Jack, your **c**ousin Joshua, Kim's **g**randfather

Reference Note

For information about **capitalizing** and **punctuating abbreviations,** see pages 249 and 267.

STYLE   **TIP**

For special emphasis or clarity, writers sometimes capitalize a title used alone or following a person's name.

EXAMPLES

Many young people admire the **M**ayor.

How did the **S**enator vote on this issue?

At the ceremony, the **Q**ueen knighted Paul McCartney.

MECHANICS

Reference Note

For information on using **italics with titles,** see page 312. For information on using **quotation marks with titles,** see page 320.

─HELP─

The official title of a book is found on the title page. The official title of a newspaper or other periodical is found on the masthead, which usually appears on the editorial page or the table of contents.

MEETING THE CHALLENGE

Write a one-page biography about your favorite author, artist, filmmaker, or song-writer. Mention at least five titles by your subject, being careful to use proper capitalization. (Also, make sure that the titles are properly italicized or placed in quotation marks.)

(3) Capitalize the first and last words and all important words in titles and subtitles.

Unimportant words in a title include

- articles: *a, an, the*
- short prepositions (fewer than five letters): *of, to, for, from, in, over*
- coordinating conjunctions: *and, but, for, nor, or, so, yet*
- the sign of the infinitive: *to*

NOTE Capitalize an article (*a, an,* or *the*) at the beginning of a title or subtitle only if it is the first word of the official title or subtitle.

EXAMPLES "**A**n Ancient Gesture"   **t**he *Saturday Review*

The *Miami Herald*   **t**he *Houston Chronicle*

A *Christmas Carol*   **t**he *Odyssey*

Type of Name	Examples	
Books	*The **S**ea **A**round **U**s*	*Nisei **D**aughter*
	***U**ltimate **V**isual Dictionary*	*Island of the **B**lue **D**olphins*
Chapters and Other Parts of Books	"**T**he **C**irculatory **S**ystem"	**C**hapter 11
	"**L**esson 5: **M**anifest **D**estiny"	"**U**nit 3: **P**oetry"
Periodicals	*The **N**ew **Y**ork **T**imes*	the *Hispanic **R**eview*
Poems	"**W**oman **W**ork"	*The **S**ong of **H**iawatha*
	"**M**ending **W**all"	
Stories	"**T**he **P**it and the **P**endulum"	"**R**aymond's **R**un"
		"**T**he **E**clipse"
Historical Documents	**T**reaty of **P**aris	**M**agna **C**arta
	The **D**eclaration of **I**ndependence	**T**he **E**mancipation **P**roclamation
Movies and Videos	*It's a **W**onderful **L**ife*	*Fly **A**way **H**ome*
	*Willy **W**onka and the **C**hocolate **F**actory*	*Yoga: **B**eginners' **L**evel*

Type of Name	Examples	
Television and Radio Programs	*Ancient Mysteries*	*60 Minutes*
	Meet the Press	*All Things Considered*
	Law and Order	*Sesame Street*
Plays	*The Three Sisters*	*A Doll's House*
Works of Art	*The Rebel Slave*	*La Primavera*
Musical Works	"The Flight of the Bumblebee"	*Liverpool Oratorio*
		Sweeney Todd
Albums and CDs	*Romantic Adagio*	*Blue*
	Left of the Middle	*This Fire*
	Dos Mundos	*Ray of Light*
Computer Games and Video Games	Sonic the Hedgehog	Sim City
	Logical Journey	Frogger
	Legend of Zelda	X-Men
Cartoons and Comic Strips	*Jump Start*	*Dilbert*
	For Better or Worse	*Daria*
	Scooby Doo	*Peanuts*

Review C   Correcting Capitalization Errors

If the capitalization in a word group below is incorrect, rewrite it correctly. If a word group contains no errors, write *C*.

EXAMPLE   1. watched the classic movie *casablanca*

1. *watched the classic movie* Casablanca

1. mayor Cartwright
2. "Home on The Range"
3. the *Reader's Digest*
4. visiting Yosemite national park
5. the president of the United States
6. was a hindu priest
7. saying hello to grandma higgins
8. my Cousin's parents
9. N. Scott Momaday won the Pulitzer Prize.
10. *the Mystery of Edwin Drood*

Review D **Correcting Capitalization Errors in Paragraphs**

Correct the sentences in the following paragraphs by capitalizing or lowercasing letters as needed. If a sentence is already correct, write *C*.

EXAMPLE   **[1]** Louis armstrong was one of america's most gifted Jazz Vocalists and Performers.

1. *Louis Armstrong was one of America's most gifted jazz vocalists and performers.*

[**1**] In social studies last week, we learned all about Louis Armstrong. [**2**] Nicknamed "satchmo," Armstrong was born in poverty in new Orleans in august 1901. [**3**] He learned to play the Cornet, a kind of small trumpet, while serving a sentence for delinquency. [**4**] While growing up, he also played the trumpet on the paddleboats that sailed on the Mississippi river.

[**5**] In 1922, his favorite bandleader, king Oliver, asked him to play second trumpet in a band in chicago. [**6**] King Oliver's band was called the creole jazz band. [**7**] While performing with the Creole Jazz band, Armstrong was coached by the band's classically trained pianist, Lil hardin, who became mrs. Armstrong in 1924. [**8**] Armstrong soon left Oliver and joined the Fletcher henderson band in New York city.

[**9**] Louis Armstrong soon established himself as a great Trumpeter and Vocalist. [**10**] One of his innovations was scat, a vocal technique in which a Musician's rhythmic, wordless voice imitates the sound of instruments. [**11**] This technique first appeared in recordings such as "Heebie jeebies," issued under the band name hot Five. [**12**] The scat technique was later imitated by other famous african american singers such as ella Fitzgerald and Al jarreau.

[**13**] As a Composer, Armstrong was known for such classic jazz songs as "dippermouth blues" and "Wild Man Blues." [**14**] Armstrong's outgoing personality and Style attracted new audiences to jazz. [**15**] By the Mid-1930's, Armstrong had become a popular entertainer. [**16**] He retained his brilliance as a jazz trumpeter, however. [**17**] After world war II, he formed a series of small bands. [**18**] When the U.S. state department made Armstrong a goodwill ambassador, it honored his worldwide reputation as a generous and well-liked personality. [**19**] In his capacity as Ambassador, he traveled widely around the world. [**20**] Louis Armstrong died at his home in queens, New York, in July 1971.

Chapter Review

A. Correcting Sentences That Contain Errors in Capitalization

Most of the following sentences contain at least one error in capitalization. Write each sentence, capitalizing or lowercasing letters where necessary. If a sentence is already correct, write *C*.

1. The only U.S. President who was never elected was Gerald Ford.
2. The program was titled *Animals of the serengeti plain.*
3. Would you say that the South and the Northeast are the regions of the United States with the most distinctive accents?
4. Although the wheel was unknown to the inca people, their Empire contained many miles of roads.
5. Students at a yeshiva, or Jewish Seminary, study the torah.
6. The highest peak in the alps is Mont Blanc, on the French-italian border, or so I'm told.
7. I later learned that uncle Steve had been taking three courses in night school.
8. Henri Matisse's early paintings include *A glimpse of Notre Dame in the late afternoon* and *Green stripe.*
9. My aunt Terry is an Editor at a large textbook Publishing Company in Texas.
10. The united nations building is on the east River in New York city.
11. The letter was mistakenly delivered to 1408 West Twenty-third Street instead of 1408 east Twenty-third Street.
12. Dr. Mendoza served in the Vietnam war before he studied medicine at Iowa state university.
13. While recovering from surgery, Mr. Gomez watched *Good morning, America* every day on television.
14. What is the date of easter Sunday this year?
15. The woman from the U.S. department of labor was sent to our community hospital when she became sick.
16. The *Queen Elizabeth 2* was delayed by serious storms while crossing the Atlantic ocean.
17. Last Thursday, July 4, we Americans celebrated Independence Day.

MECHANICS

18. The tenor sang "America the beautiful" at the dedication of the new monument.
19. Did you know, professor, that the *Mona Lisa* will be shown this year at the Metropolitan Museum of Art?
20. On Thanksgiving day, my family thanks god for many blessings.

B. Correcting Errors in Capitalization

Correct the errors in capitalization in the following paragraph by capitalizing or lowercasing words as needed.

[**21**] almost everybody has heard of pasteurization, but how many people know what it is, or who originated it? [**22**] The French Chemist Louis Pasteur developed the process, which involves destroying disease-causing microorganisms by applying heat. [**23**] That was only one of many accomplishments of this Scientific Genius. [**24**] Born in 1822 in a small town in Eastern France, he made his first scientific discovery at the age of 26. [**25**] As his reputation grew, he was elected to the academy of Scientists in Paris and named Director of Scientific studies at one of the Capital City's most prestigious schools. [**26**] Pasteur's discovery that Microorganisms can cause disease led to recognition of the importance of vaccination. [**27**] The Great Scientist developed vaccines for rabies, anthrax, and a form of Cholera found in farmyard fowl. [**28**] Thanks to the support of emperor Napoleon III, a special laboratory was created for Pasteur. [**29**] In 1874, the French parliament granted him a lifetime stipend, and the Pasteur institute was inaugurated in Paris a few years before he died. [**30**] His discoveries were crucial, but perhaps Pasteur's greatest contribution to Science was his new way of looking at things.

C. Proofreading for Correct Capitalization

Correct the following word groups, using capital letters as needed.

31. the cities of san miguel and cuernavaca
32. an irish american
33. the great ship *titanic*
34. at the hotel bristol
35. on christmas day

MECHANICS

36. a call from uncle Ernesto

37. smith and garcia, inc.

38. gulf of mexico

39. southwest texas state university

40. whoever won the nobel prize

41. driving a dodge colt

42. zilker park in austin, texas

43. sarge's deli on third avenue

44. on labor day

45. the greek god apollo

Writing Application

Using Capital Letters Correctly in a Paragraph

Proper Nouns   Your school's language club plans to publish a booklet about foreign cities that most interest students. Write a paragraph telling about one city and its major attractions.

Prewriting   Choose a foreign city that interests you, and jot down the reasons you find it interesting. You may want to gather some information about it from encyclopedias, travel books or brochures, and magazine or newspaper articles. Make a list of the city's major attractions.

Writing   As you write your first draft, be sure to include information about the city's location and historical or cultural importance.

Revising   Ask a friend who is unfamiliar with the city to read your paragraph. Does the information you have presented make your friend want to visit the city? Add or delete details to make your writing more interesting and informative.

Publishing   Be sure that you have correctly capitalized geographical names and the names of businesses, institutions, places, and events. Pay particular attention to the spelling of foreign words. With your teacher's permission, post your paragraph on the class bulletin board or Web page.

Punctuation
End Marks, Abbreviations, and Commas

Diagnostic Preview

Correcting Sentences by Adding Periods, Question Marks, Exclamation Points, and Commas

Write the following paragraphs, adding periods, question marks, exclamation points, and commas where necessary.

EXAMPLE   **[1]** Inventing I have found can be fun

1.   *Inventing, I have found, can be fun.*

[1] My science teacher announced yesterday that our school is hosting an Invention Convention [2] What is an Invention Convention [3] Ms. Sanchez explained that students will be thinking of ideas for a new product [4] The invention can be an original product an improvement on an existing product or something totally unusual [5] I am really excited [6] After thinking of an idea students will be building or making the product [7] It can be a model a drawing or the actual product [8] Inventors are expected to keep a journal about their experiences [9] The deadline for the invention is soon

[10] Wow, we only have three weeks for the whole process [11] Students will bring their invention to school by Friday November 11 [12] There will be awards for first- second- and third-place winners [13] I had better get started

[**14**] The first thing I did naturally is go to the library to research my product idea [**15**] Great, it hasn't been invented yet [**16**] What would happen I wonder if you submitted an idea that had already been invented [**17**] My idea while practical is quite unique [**18**] I have invented a nose mitten [**19**] Have you ever had a cold nose in the wintertime [**20**] My only problem is how to get the mitten to stick to my nose

End Marks

Sentences

End marks—periods, question marks, and exclamation points—are used to indicate the purpose of a sentence.

11a. A statement (or declarative sentence) is followed by a period.

EXAMPLES   Nancy López won the golf tournament.

What Balboa saw below was the Pacific Ocean.

Flora wondered who had already gone.

NOTE Notice in the third example that a declarative sentence containing an indirect question is followed by a period. (An **indirect question** is one that does not use the speaker's exact words.) Be sure to distinguish between a declarative sentence that contains an indirect question and an interrogative sentence, which asks a direct question.

INDIRECT QUESTION   I wondered what makes that sound. [declarative]
DIRECT QUESTION   What makes that sound? [interrogative]

11b. A question (or interrogative sentence) is followed by a question mark.

EXAMPLES   Do you know American Sign Language?

Why don't you ask Eileen?

Who wrote this note? Did you?

STYLE   TIP

As you speak, the tone and pitch of your voice, the pauses in your speech, and the gestures and expressions you use all help make your meaning clear. In writing, marks of punctuation, such as end marks and commas, show readers where these verbal and nonverbal cues occur.

Punctuation alone won't clarify the meaning of a confusing sentence, however. If you have trouble punctuating a sentence, check to see whether rewording it would help express your meaning more clearly.

MECHANICS

Reference Note

For information about how **sentences** are **classified according to purpose,** see Chapter 2.

STYLE **TIP**

Sometimes declarative and interrogative sentences show such strong feeling that they are more like exclamations than like statements or questions. In such cases, an exclamation point should be used instead of a period or a question mark.

EXAMPLES
Here comes the bus!
Can't you speak up!

STYLE **TIP**

An interjection is generally set off from the rest of the sentence by a comma or an exclamation point.

EXAMPLES
Well, I guess so.
Ouch! That hurt.

Reference Note

For more about **interjections,** see page 33.

STYLE **TIP**

Sometimes a command or request is expressed as if it were a question. The meaning, however, may be imperative, in which case a period or exclamation point is used.

EXAMPLES
May I say a few words now.
Will you leave me alone!

A direct question may have the same word order as a declarative sentence. Since it is a question, it is followed by a question mark.

EXAMPLES   You know American Sign Language?

You're not asking Eileen?

11c. An exclamation (or exclamatory sentence) is followed by an exclamation point.

EXAMPLES   Hurrah! The rain stopped!

Ouch!

Look out!

11d. A command or request (or imperative sentence) is followed by either a period or an exclamation point.

When an imperative sentence makes a request, it is generally followed by a period. When an imperative sentence expresses a strong command, an exclamation point is generally used.

EXAMPLES   Please answer my question. [request]

Turn off your radio. [command]

Answer me right now! [strong command]

Exercise 1 **Using Periods, Question Marks, and Exclamation Points**

Write the following sentences, adding periods, question marks, and exclamation points where they are needed. Identify each sentence as *declarative, imperative, interrogative,* or *exclamatory.*

EXAMPLE   1. Are you familiar with lacrosse, a field game

1. *Are you familiar with lacrosse, a field game?—interrogative*

1. Do you know how to play lacrosse
2. On TV last night there was a segment on teams playing lacrosse
3. What a rough sport lacrosse must be
4. Did you know that North American Indians developed this game
5. Before Columbus came to the Americas in A.D. 1492, the Iroquois were playing lacrosse in what is now upper New York State and Canada
6. Do you realize that this makes lacrosse the oldest organized sport in America

7. Lacrosse is played by two opposing teams
8. Use a stick to catch, carry, and throw the ball
9. The name of the game comes from *la crosse*, French for a bishop's staff, which the lacrosse stick resembles
10. Lacrosse is especially popular in Canada, the British Isles, and Australia, and it is played in the United States, too

Abbreviations

11e. Use a period after certain abbreviations.

An **abbreviation** is a shortened form of a word or word group. Notice how periods are used with abbreviations in the examples in this part of the chapter.

Personal Names

Abbreviate given names only if the person is most commonly known by the abbreviated form of the name.

EXAMPLES   Ida **B.** Wells   **T. H.** White   **M.F.K.** Fisher

Titles

(1) Abbreviate social titles whether used before the full name or before the last name alone.

EXAMPLES   **Mr.** Tom Evans   **Ms.** Jody Aiello   **Mrs.** Dupont

                Sr. (Señor) Cadenas   **Sra.** (Señora) Garza   **Dr.** O'Nolan

(2) You may abbreviate civil and military titles used before full names or before initials and last names. Spell such titles out before last names used alone.

EXAMPLES   **Sen.** Kay Bailey Hutchison   **Senator** Hutchison

                Prof. E. M. Makowski   **Professor** Makowski

                Gen. Norman Schwarzkopf   **General** Schwarzkopf

(3) Abbreviate titles and academic degrees that follow proper names.

EXAMPLES   Ira Knox, **Jr.**   Peter Garcia, **M.D.**

MECHANICS

STYLE TIP

Only a few abbreviations are appropriate in the text of a formal paper written for a general audience. In tables, notes, and bibliographies, abbreviations are used more freely in order to save space.

STYLE TIP

Leave a space between two initials, but not between three or more.

HELP

If a statement ends with an abbreviation, do not use an additional period as an end mark. However, do use a question mark or an exclamation point if one is needed.

EXAMPLES

Mrs. Tavares just received her Ph.D.

When did she receive her Ph.D.?

Do not include the titles *Mr., Mrs., Ms.,* or *Dr.* when you use a professional title or degree after a name.

EXAMPLE **Dr.** Joan West *or* Joan West, **M.D.** [*not* Dr. Joan West, M.D.]

Agencies and Organizations

An ***acronym*** is a word formed from the first (or first few) letters of a series of words. Acronyms are written without periods. After spelling out the first use of the names of agencies and organizations, abbreviate these names and other things commonly known by their acronyms.

EXAMPLE My older sister works for the **National Institute of Mental Health (NIMH).** She is compiling data for one of **NIMH**'s behavioral studies.

AMA American Medical Association	**USAF** United States Air Force
HUD (Department of) Housing and Urban Development	**UN** United Nations
CPU Central Processing Unit	**NEA** National Endowment for the Arts
RAM random-access memory	**FM** Frequency Modulation

A few acronyms, such as *radar, laser,* and *sonar,* are now considered common nouns. They do not need to be spelled out on first use and are no longer capitalized. When you're not sure whether an acronym should be capitalized, look it up in a recent dictionary.

Geographical Terms

In text, spell out names of states and other political units whether they stand alone or follow other geographical terms. Abbreviate such names in tables, notes, and bibliographies.

TEXT On our vacation to Canada, we visited Victoria, the capital of British Columbia.

CHART

London, U.K.	Tucson, Ariz.
Victoria, B.C.	Fresno, Calif.

FOOTNOTE	³The Public Library in Annaville, Mich., has an entire collection of Smyth's folios.
BIBLIOGRAPHY ENTRY	"The Last Hurrah." Editorial. *Star-Ledger* [Newark, N.J.] 29 Aug. 1991: 30.

NOTE Include the traditional abbreviation for the District of Columbia, *D.C.,* with the city name *Washington* to distinguish it from the state of Washington.

In text, spell out every word in an address. Such words may be abbreviated in letter and envelope addresses and in tables and notes.

TEXT	We live at 413 West Maple Street.

ENVELOPE   413 W. Maple St.

NOTE Two-letter state abbreviations without periods are used only when the ZIP Code is included.

EXAMPLE   Cincinnati, **OH** 45233

Time

Abbreviate the frequently used era designations *A.D.* and *B.C.* The abbreviation *A.D.* stands for the Latin phrase *anno Domini*, meaning "in the year of the Lord." It is used with dates in the Christian era. When used with a specific year number, *A.D.* precedes the number. When used with the name of a century, it follows the name.

EXAMPLES	In **A.D.** 476, the last Western Roman emperor, Romulus Augustulus, was overthrown by Germanic tribes.
	The legends of King Arthur may be based on the life of a real British leader of the sixth century **A.D.**

The abbreviation *B.C.*, which stands for "before Christ," is used for dates before the Christian era. It follows either a specific year number or the name of a century.

EXAMPLES	Homer's epic poem the *Iliad* was probably composed between 800 and 700 **B.C.**
	The poem describes battles that probably occurred around the twelfth century **B.C.**

STYLE   TIP

In your reading, you may come across the abbreviations *C.E.* and *B.C.E.* These abbreviations stand for *Common Era* and *Before Common Era*. These terms are sometimes used in place of *A.D.* and *B.C.*, respectively, and are written after the date.

EXAMPLES
752 **C.E.**

1550 **B.C.E.**

In regular text, spell out the names of months and days whether they appear alone or in dates. Both types of names may be abbreviated in tables, notes, and bibliographies.

TEXT   Please join us on Thursday, March 21, to celebrate Grandma and Grandpa's anniversary.

NOTE   Thurs., Mar. 21

Abbreviate the designations for the two halves of the day measured by clock time. The abbreviation *A.M.* stands for the Latin phrase *ante meridiem,* meaning "before noon." The abbreviation *P.M.* stands for *post meridiem,* meaning "after noon." Both abbreviations follow the numerals designating the specific time.

EXAMPLE   My mom works four days a week, from 8:00 **A.M.** until 6:00 **P.M.**

Units of Measurement

Abbreviations for units of measurement are usually written without periods. However, do use a period with the abbreviation for *inch* (*in.*) to prevent confusing it with the word *in.*

EXAMPLES   mm, kg, ml, tsp, doz, yd, ft, lb

In regular text, spell out the names of units of measurement whether they stand alone or follow a spelled-out number or a numeral. Such names may be abbreviated in tables and notes when they follow a numeral.

TEXT   The speed limit here is fifty-five **miles per hour** [not *mph*].

The cubicle measured ten **feet** [not *ft*] by twelve.

TABLE

1 **tsp** pepper	97° **F**
12 **ft** 6 **in.**	2 **oz** flour

Exercise 2   **Using Abbreviations**

Rewrite the following sentences, correcting errors in the use of abbreviations.

EXAMPLE   1.   Hillary Clinton was born in Chicago, IL.

1.   *Hillary Clinton was born in Chicago, Illinois.*

1. The flight for Montevideo departs at 11:15 A.M. in the morning.

2. Julius Caesar was assassinated in the Roman Forum in B.C. 44.
3. Harun ar-Rashid, whose reign is associated with the Arabian Nights, ruled as caliph of Baghdad from 786 to 809 A.D.
4. The Mississippi River flows from Lake Itasca, MN, all the way to the Gulf of Mexico at Port Eads, LA.
5. I will be leaving soon to visit Mr. Nugent on Elm St. in New Paltz, NY.
6. The Fbi. is the chief investigative branch of the U.S. Department of Justice.
7. The keynote speaker was Dr. Matthew Villareal, Ph.D.
8. We will meet at 4:00 P.M..
9. I wrote "56 in" in the blank labeled "height."
10. G. Washington was the first president of the United States.

Review A **Correcting Sentences by Adding Periods, Question Marks, and Exclamation Points**

Write the following sentences, adding periods, question marks, and exclamation points as needed.

EXAMPLE   1. Does Josh come from Chicago

          1. *Does Josh come from Chicago?*

1. What a great car that is
2. Whose car is that
3. We asked who owned that car
4. Roman troops invaded Britain in 54 BC.
5. By AD. 809, Baghdad was already an important city
6. Dr Edward Jenner gave the first vaccination against smallpox in 1796
7. Why do so many children enjoy using computers
8. Please explain why so many children enjoy using computers
9. When did Alan Keyes run for president
10. Terrific Here's another coin for my collection

Commas

If you fail to use necessary commas, you may confuse your reader.

CONFUSING   The friends I have invited are Ruth Ann Jerry Lee Derrick Martha and Julie. [How many friends?]

CLEAR   The friends I have invited are Ruth Ann, Jerry Lee, Derrick, Martha, and Julie. [five friends]

Items in a Series

11f. Use commas to separate items in a series.

Notice in the following examples that the number of commas in a series is one fewer than the number of items in the series.

EXAMPLES   All my cousins, aunts, and uncles came to our family reunion. [words in a series]

The children played in the yard, at the playground, and by the pond. [phrases in a series]

Those who had flown to the reunion, who had driven many miles, or who had even taken time off from their jobs were glad that they had made the effort to be there. [subordinate clauses in a series]

STYLE **TIP**

Because using the final comma is never wrong, some writers prefer always to use the comma before the *and* in a series. Follow your teacher's instructions on this point.

When the last two items in a series are joined by *and,* the comma before the *and* is sometimes omitted if the comma is not necessary to make the meaning clear.

CLEAR WITH COMMA OMITTED	The salad contained lettuce, tomatoes, onions, cucumbers, carrots and radishes.
NOT CLEAR WITH COMMA OMITTED	Our school newspaper has editors for news, sports, humor, features and art. [How many editors are there, four or five? Does one person serve as a features and art editor, or is an editor needed for each job?]
CLEAR WITH COMMA INCLUDED	Our school newspaper has editors for news, sports, humor, features, and art. [five editors]

NOTE Some words—such as *bread and butter, rod and reel, table and chairs*—are used in pairs and may be considered one item in a series.

EXAMPLE   Our collection includes pop, reggae, mariachi, **rhythm and blues,** and hip-hop music.

(1) If all items in a series are joined by *and, or,* or *nor,* do not use commas to separate them.

EXAMPLES   I need tacks **and** nails **and** a hammer.

Sam **or** Carlos **or** Yolanda will be able to baby-sit tomorrow.

Neither horses **nor** elephants **nor** giraffes are carnivorous.

MECHANICS

(2) Short independent clauses may be separated by commas.

EXAMPLE   The engine roared, the wheels spun, and a cloud of dust
            swirled behind the sports car.

> NOTE Sentences that contain more than one independent clause are
> *compound* or *compound-complex sentences.*

  COMPOUND   The Wilsons grow organic vegetables, and they sell them
               at the farmers' market.

  COMPOUND-   When the weather is bad, the dog hides under the bed,
  COMPLEX   and the cat retreats to my closet.

Reference Note
Independent clauses in a series can be separated by semicolons. For more about this use of **semi-colons,** see page 298.

(3) Use commas to separate two or more adjectives preceding a noun.

EXAMPLE   Are you going to that hot, crowded, noisy mall?

When the last adjective in a series is thought of as part of the
noun, the comma before the adjective is omitted.

EXAMPLES   I study in our small **dining room.**

             Let's have our picnic under that lovely, shady **fruit tree.**

Compound nouns like *dining room* and *fruit tree* are considered single
units—the two words act as one part of speech.

Reference Note
For more information about **compound** and **compound-complex sentences,** see page 109.

> NOTE If one of the words modifies another modifier, do not separate
> those two words with a comma.
>
> EXAMPLE   Do you like this **dark blue** sweater?

Reference Note
For more information on **compound nouns,** see page 4.

MECHANICS

Exercise 3 Correcting Sentences by Adding Commas

Write each series in the following sentences, adding commas where
needed.

EXAMPLE   **1.** Rita plays soccer volleyball and softball.
            1. soccer, volleyball, and softball

1. Dr. Charles Drew worked as a surgeon developed new ways of
   storing blood and was the first director of the Red Cross blood
   bank program.
2. I am going to take English science social studies and algebra.
3. The loud insistent smoke alarm woke us just before dawn.

When two or more adjectives precede a noun, you can use two tests to determine whether the last adjective and the noun form a unit.

TEST 1
Insert the word *and* between the adjectives. If *and* fits sensibly between the adjectives, use a comma.

EXAMPLE
A juicy, tangy apple makes a good snack. [*Juicy and tangy* makes sense, so the comma is correct.]

TEST 2
Change the order of the adjectives. If the order of the adjectives can be reversed sensibly, use a comma.

EXAMPLE
The quiet, polite girl sat next to her mother. [*Polite, quiet girl* makes sense, so the comma is correct.]

4. Please pass those delicious blueberry pancakes the margarine and the syrup.
5. My twin sister can run faster jump higher and do more push-ups than I can.
6. Where is the nearest store that sells newspapers magazines and paperbacks?
7. Horns tooted tires screeched a whistle blew and sirens wailed.
8. Steel is made from iron other metals and small amounts of carbon.
9. The clown wore a long blue raincoat; big red plastic gloves; and floppy yellow tennis shoes.
10. Robert Browning says that youth is good that middle age is better and that old age is best.

Exercise 4 Using Commas Correctly in Series

Your school's new counselor wants to get to know the students better. He has developed the following personality questionnaire, and today he has given a copy to all the students in your class. Answer each question by writing a sentence that includes a series of words, phrases, or clauses. Use commas where needed in each series.

EXAMPLE 1. What do you consider your most outstanding traits?
1. *I am considerate, thoughtful, and loyal.*

Personality Questionnaire

1. What do you consider your most outstanding traits?
2. What qualities do you admire most in a person?
3. Who are the people who have influenced you most?
4. What are your favorite hobbies?
5. What famous people would you like to meet?
6. What countries would you most like to visit?
7. For what reasons do you attend school?
8. What are your favorite subjects in school?
9. What things about the world would you most like to change?
10. What goals do you hope to achieve during the next ten years?

Independent Clauses

11g. Use a comma before *and, but, for, nor, or, so,* or *yet* when it joins independent clauses.

EXAMPLES   Hector pressed the button**, and** the engine started up.

She would never argue**, nor** would she complain to anyone.

Are you going to the football game**, or** do you have other plans for Saturday?

He is an accomplished actor**, yet** he's very modest.

    Do not be misled by compound verbs, which can make a sentence look like a compound sentence.

SIMPLE SENTENCE   Mara **cleared** the table and **did** the dishes.
            [one subject with a compound verb]

COMPOUND SENTENCE   **Mara cleared the table,** and **Roland did the dishes.** [two independent clauses]

> NOTE   The comma joining two independent clauses is sometimes omitted before *and, but, or,* or *nor* when the independent clauses are very short and when there is no possibility of misunderstanding.
>
> CLEAR   The dog barked and the cat meowed.
> AWKWARD   Bill bathed the dog and the cat hid under the bed.
>   [confusing without comma]
> CLEAR   Bill bathed the dog**,** and the cat hid under the bed.

Reference Note

For more about **compound sentences,** see page 109. For information on **compound subjects** and **compound verbs,** see page 52.

STYLE TIP

For clarity, some writers prefer always to use the comma before a conjunction joining independent clauses. Follow your teacher's instructions on this point.

MECHANICS

Exercise 5   **Correcting Sentences by Adding Commas Between Independent Clauses**

Where a comma should be used, write the word preceding the comma, the comma, and the conjunction following it. If a sentence is already correct, write *C*.

EXAMPLE   **1.** Accident-related injuries are common and many of these injuries can be prevented.

    1. common, and

1. It is important to know first aid for an accident can happen at almost any time.
2. More than 83,000 people in the United States die in accidents each year and many millions are injured.

3. Many household products can cause illness or even death but are often stored where small children can reach them.
4. Biking accidents are common wherever cars and bicycles use the same road so many communities have provided bicycle lanes.
5. Car accidents are the leading cause of childhood fatalities but seat belts have saved many lives.
6. Everyone should know what to do in case of fire and different escape routes should be tested.
7. If you need to escape a fire, you should stay close to the floor and be very cautious about opening doors.
8. Holding your breath, keep low and protected behind a door when opening it for a blast of superheated air can be fatal.
9. An injured person should not get up nor should liquid be given to someone who is unconscious.
10. Always have someone with you when you swim or you may find yourself without help when you need it.

Nonessential Clauses and Phrases

11h. Use commas to set off nonessential subordinate clauses and nonessential participial phrases.

Reference Note

For more information about **subordinate clauses,** see page 99. For more about **participial phrases,** see page 79.

A *nonessential* (or *nonrestrictive*) clause or participial phrase adds information that is not necessary to the main idea in the sentence.

NONESSENTIAL CLAUSES   Eileen Murray, **who is at the top of her class,** wants to go to medical school.

Texas, **which has the most farms of any state in this country,** produces one fourth of our oil.

NONESSENTIAL PHRASES   Tim Ricardo, **hoping to make the swim team,** practiced every day.

The Lord of the Rings, **written by J.R.R. Tolkien,** has been translated into many languages.

Omitting each boldface clause or phrase in the preceding examples does not change the main idea of the sentence.

EXAMPLES   Eileen Murray wants to go to medical school.

Texas produces one fourth of our oil.

Tim Ricardo practiced every day.

The Lord of the Rings has been translated into many languages.

When a clause or phrase is necessary to the meaning of a sentence—that is, when it tells *which one(s)*—the clause or phrase is **essential** (or **restrictive**), and commas are not used.

Notice how the meaning of each of the following sentences changes when the essential clause or phrase is omitted.

"SURE I GOT ALL THE PUNCTUATION: COMMA, COMMA, PERIOD, PERIOD, QUESTION MARK, COMMA, SEMI-COLON, COMMA, EXCLAMATION POINT, PERIOD..."

© 1998 by Sidney Harris.

ESSENTIAL CLAUSE   All students **whose names are on that list** must report to Ms. Washington this afternoon. [All students must report to Ms. Washington this afternoon.]

ESSENTIAL PHRASE   A Ming vase **displayed in the museum** was once owned by Chiang Kai-shek. [A Ming vase was once owned by Chiang Kai-shek.]

Depending on the writer's meaning, a participial phrase or clause may be either essential or non-essential. Including or omitting commas tells the reader how the clause or phrase relates to the main idea of the sentence.

NONESSENTIAL CLAUSE   LaWanda's brother, who is a senior, works part time at the mall. [LaWanda has only one brother. He works at the mall.]

ESSENTIAL CLAUSE   LaWanda's brother who is a senior works part time at the mall. [LaWanda has more than one brother. The one who is a senior works at the mall.]

NOTE   An adjective clause beginning with *that* is usually essential.

EXAMPLE   Was Hank Aaron the first major league baseball player **that** broke Babe Ruth's home run record?

Exercise 6   **Correcting Sentences with Essential and Nonessential Clauses by Adding or Deleting Commas**

The following sentences contain essential and nonessential clauses. Add or delete commas as necessary to punctuate each of these clauses correctly. If a sentence is already correct, write *C*.

EXAMPLE   1. My mother who is a Celtics fan has season tickets.

   1. *My mother, who is a Celtics fan, has season tickets.*

MECHANICS

MEETING THE CHALLENGE

Write a one-page short story on any topic you like. In your story, use two nonessential subordinate clauses and three nonessential participial phrases. Be sure to punctuate the phrases and clauses correctly.

MECHANICS

1. *Jump Start* which is my favorite comic strip makes me think as well as laugh.

2. Ms. Lopez, who teaches social studies and gym will leave at the end of the year.

3. The amusement rides that are the most exciting may be the most dangerous.

4. Many of the first Spanish settlements in California were founded by Father Junípero Serra who liked to take long walks between them.

5. People, who carry credit cards, should keep a record of their account numbers at home.

6. Amy Kwan who is our class president plans to go to Yale after she graduates from high school.

7. A town like Cottonwood which has a population of five thousand seems ideal to me.

8. All dogs that pass the obedience test get a reward; those that don't pass get to take the test again later.

9. Have you tried this pemmican which my mother made from an old Cree recipe?

10. "The Gift of the Magi" is a story, in which the two main characters who are deeply in love make sacrifices in order to buy gifts for each other.

Exercise 7 **Correcting Sentences with Participial Phrases by Adding or Deleting Commas**

Add or delete commas as necessary to punctuate the following sentences correctly. If a sentence is already correctly punctuated, write *C*.

EXAMPLE   1. Our dog startled by the noise began to bark.

1. *Our dog, startled by the noise, began to bark.*

1. People, visiting the reservation, will be barred from burial sites, which are considered holy by American Indians.

2. Players breaking training will be dismissed from the team.

3. Students, planning to go on the field trip, should bring their lunches.

4. When Tony holding up a parsnip asked whether parsnips are related to carrots, I said, "Well, they certainly look alike."

5. Joe told me that kudzu introduced into the United States in the 1800s now grows in much of the South.

6. Elizabeth Blackwell completing her medical studies in 1849 became the first female doctor in the United States.

7. Pressure and heat acting on the remains of plants and animals turn those remains into gas or oil or coal.
8. Every child, registering for school for the first time, must present evidence of certain vaccinations.
9. The astronauts living in the space station studied the effects of weightlessness.
10. Windsor Castle built during the reigns of Henry III and Edward III stands twenty-one miles west of London.

Review B **Correcting Sentences with Nonessential Clauses and Participial Phrases by Adding Commas**

Some of the following sentences contain clauses and phrases that need to be set off by commas. If a sentence is incorrect, add the necessary comma or commas. If a sentence is already correctly punctuated, write *C*.

EXAMPLE   1. Hanukkah which is also called the Feast of Lights is a major Jewish celebration.

1. *Hanukkah, which is also called the Feast of Lights, is a major Jewish celebration.*

1. The picture on this page shows a part of the Hanukkah celebration that is very beautiful.
2. The girl following an ancient custom is lighting the menorah.
3. The menorah which is an eight-branched candlestick symbolizes the original festival.
4. Hanukkah which means "dedication" celebrates the rededication of the Temple of Jerusalem in 165 B.C.
5. This event followed the Jewish people's victory over Syria, which was led by a pagan king.
6. During the first Hanukkah, according to traditional lore, the Jews had a one-day supply of lamp oil that lasted for eight days.
7. Today celebrating the memory of this miraculous event modern Jews light one candle on themenorah each day of the eight-day festival.
8. Hanukkah starts on the twenty-fifth day of the Hebrew month of Kislev which is usually in December on the Gregorian calendar.

9. The festival celebrated all over the world is a time of feasting, gift giving, and happiness.

10. During Hanukkah, children play a game with a dreidel which is a four-sided toy that is like a top.

Review C **Correcting Sentences by Adding Commas**

Add commas where they are needed in the following sentences. If a sentence does not require any commas, write *C*.

EXAMPLE   1. The emu is a large flightless bird from Australia.

          1. *The emu is a large, flightless bird from Australia.*

1. The students sold crafts used books and baked goods at the bazaar.
2. John Wayne whose real name was Marion Morrison won an Academy Award for *True Grit*.
3. Add flour mix the ingredients and stir the batter.
4. People who come to the game early will be allowed to take pictures of the players.
5. *Exiles* written by James Joyce will be performed by the Grantville Community Players and will run for three weeks.
6. The float in the homecoming parade was covered with large pink rose petals and small silvery spangles.
7. Members of the committee met for three hours but they still have not chosen a theme for the dance.
8. Helium which is used by balloonists deep-sea divers and welders is an inert gas.
9. An eclipse that occurs when the earth prevents the sun's light from reflecting off the moon is called a lunar eclipse.
10. In one month our little town was hit by a tornado and a flood and a fire yet we managed to survive.

Introductory Elements

11i. Use commas after certain introductory elements.

(1) Use a comma to set off a mild exclamation such as *well*, *oh*, or *why* at the beginning of a sentence. Other introductory words such as *yes* and *no* are also set off with commas.

EXAMPLES   **Why,** you're Andy's brother, aren't you?

             Yes, she's going to the cafeteria.

MECHANICS

(2) Use a comma after an introductory participial phrase.

EXAMPLES   **Switching on a flashlight,** the ranger led the way down the path to the caves.

               Disappointed by the high prices, we made up a new gift list.

               Given a choice, I would rather work in the yard early in the morning.

(3) Use a comma after two or more introductory prepositional phrases or after a long one.

EXAMPLES   **Near the door to the garage,** you will find hooks for the car keys.

               Inside the fence at the far end of her property, she built a potting shed.

               By the time they had finished, the boys were exhausted.

> **NOTE** One short introductory prepositional phrase does not require a comma unless the comma is necessary to make the meaning clear.
>
> EXAMPLES   **At our house** we share all the work.
>
>   **At our house,** plants grow best in the sunny, bright kitchen. [The comma is necessary to avoid reading *house plants.*]

(4) Use a comma after an introductory adverb clause.

EXAMPLES   **After Andrés Segovia had played his last guitar concert,** the audience applauded for more than fifteen minutes.

               If you see smoke, you know there is a fire.

> **NOTE** An adverb clause in the middle or at the end of a sentence is generally not set off by a comma.
>
> EXAMPLES   Miranda, please remember to phone me **when you get home this evening.** [No comma is necessary between *me* and *when.*]
>
>   We stayed a long time **because we were having fun.** [No comma is necessary between *time* and *because.*]

Reference Note

For information on **participial phrases,** see page 79. For information on **prepositional phrases,** see page 70.

MECHANICS

Reference Note

For information on **adverb clauses,** see page 104.

Correcting Sentences with Introductory Elements by Adding Commas

Add commas where they are needed after introductory elements in the following sentences. If a sentence is already correct, write *C*.

EXAMPLE
1. When Marco Polo visited China in the thirteenth century he found an advanced civilization.

1. *When Marco Polo visited China in the thirteenth century, he found an advanced civilization.*

1. Although there was a great deal of poverty in China the ruling classes lived in splendor.
2. Valuing cleanliness, Chinese rulers took baths every day.
3. Instead of using coins as currency the Chinese used paper money.
4. After marrying a Chinese woman usually lived in her mother-in-law's home.
5. After one Chinese emperor had died he was buried with more than eight thousand statues of servants and horses.
6. Respected by their descendants elderly people were highly honored.
7. Built around 200 B.C. the main part of the Great Wall of China is about four thousand miles long.
8. Why until modern freeways were built, the Great Wall was the world's longest construction.
9. In the picture on this page you can see that Asian landscapes look different from those created by Western artists.
10. In Asian art people are often very small and are usually shown in harmony with nature.

Interrupters

11j. Use commas to set off elements that interrupt the sentence.

Two commas are used around an interrupting element—one before and one after.

EXAMPLES
His guitar, **according to him,** once belonged to Bo Diddley.

Mr. Gonzales, **my civics teacher,** encouraged me to enter my essay in the contest.

Sometimes an "interrupter" comes at the beginning or at the end of a sentence. In such cases, only one comma is needed.

EXAMPLES   **Nevertheless,** you must go with me.

I need the money, **Josh.**

(1) Nonessential appositives and nonessential appositive phrases should be set off with commas.

A *nonessential* (or *nonrestrictive*) *appositive* or *appositive phrase* provides information that is unnecessary to the basic meaning of the sentence.

EXAMPLES   Their new parrot, **Mina,** is very gentle. [The sentence means the same thing without the appositive.]

Elizabeth Peña, **my favorite actress,** stars in the movie I rented. [The sentence means the same thing without the appositive phrase.]

An *essential* (or *restrictive*) *appositive* or *appositive phrase* adds information that makes the noun or pronoun it identifies more specific.

EXAMPLES   My friend **Tamisha** lost her wallet. [The writer has more than one friend. *Tamisha* identifies which friend. The meaning of the sentence changes without the appositive.]

He recited the second stanza of "Childhood" by the poet **Margaret Walker.** [The appositive *Margaret Walker* identifies which poet.]

We **art club members** made the decorations. [The appositive phrase *art club members* explains who is meant by *We.*]

Reference Note

For more information on **appositives** and **appositive phrases,** see page 89.

(Exercise 9) **Correcting Sentences with Appositives and Appositive Phrases by Adding Commas**

Correctly use commas to punctuate the appositives in the following sentences. If a sentence needs no commas, write *C.*

EXAMPLE   **1.** My cousin consulted Dr. Moniz an allergy specialist about the harmful effects of pollution.

     1. My cousin consulted Dr. Moniz, an allergy specialist, about the harmful effects of pollution.

1. *Ecology* an obscure word forty years ago is now a popular term.
2. The word *ecology* comes from *oikos,* the Greek word meaning "house."

MECHANICS

3. Ecology is the study of an enormous "house" the world of all living things.

4. Ecologists study the bond of a living organism to its environment the place in which it lives.

5. Humans one kind of living organism affect their environment in both beneficial and harmful ways.

6. My twin sister Margaret Anne is worried about the future of the environment.

7. She and many of her friends attended Earth Day a festival devoted to ecology.

8. An amateur photographer my cousin prepared a slide show on soil erosion in Grant Park.

9. One of many displays at the Earth Day Festival my cousin's presentation attracted wide attention and won a prize.

10. The mayor a member of the audience promised to appoint a committee to study the problem.

(2) Words used in direct address are set off by commas.

EXAMPLES   **Linda,** you know the rules.

I did that exercise last night, **Ms. Ryan.**

Sir, are these your keys?

Your room, **Bernice,** needs cleaning.

Oral Practice   **Correcting Sentences with Words in Direct Address by Adding Commas**

Read the following sentences aloud, and say where commas are needed.

EXAMPLE   1. Annabella when will you be at the station?

    1. *Annabella, when will you be at the station?*

1. Dad why can't I go to the movies tonight?
2. As soon as you're ready Virginia we'll leave.
3. Yes Mom I washed the dishes.
4. What we need Mayor Wilson is more playgrounds.
5. Will you answer the last question Jim?
6. Rex fetch the ball!
7. I think ma'am that my piano playing has improved this year.

8. We left some for you Bella.
9. José how far from here is the teen recreation center that has the heated swimming pool?
10. May I help you with the gardening Grandma?

(3) Parenthetical expressions are set off by commas.

Parenthetical expressions are side remarks that add information or relate ideas.

Reference Note

For information on using **parentheses** and **dashes** to set off parenthetical expressions, see Chapter 15.

Commonly Used Parenthetical Expressions		
after all	generally speaking	nevertheless
at any rate	however	of course
consequently	I believe	on the contrary
for example	in the first place	on the other hand
for instance	moreover	therefore

EXAMPLES **Of course,** I am glad that he called me about the extra movie tickets.

She is, **in fact,** a dentist.

You should try out for quarterback, **in my opinion.**

Some expressions may be used either parenthetically or not parenthetically. Do not set them off with commas unless they're truly parenthetical.

EXAMPLES Sandra will, **I think,** enjoy the program. [parenthetical]
I think Sandra will enjoy the program. [not parenthetical]

However, Phuong Vu finished her report on time. [parenthetical]
However did Phuong Vu finish her report on time? [not parenthetical—similar to "How did she finish?"]

To tell the truth, he tries. [parenthetical]
He tries **to tell the truth.** [not parenthetical]

After all, we've been through this situation before. [parenthetical]
After all we've been through, we need a vacation. [not parenthetical]

MECHANICS

NOTE A contrasting expression introduced by *not* is parenthetical and should be set off by commas.

EXAMPLES The divisor**, not the dividend,** is the bottom number of a fraction.

The coach and I believe the winner of the long jump will be Rachel**, not her.**

Exercise 10 Correcting Sentences with Parenthetical Expressions by Adding Commas

Correctly punctuate the parenthetical expressions in the following sentences.

EXAMPLE 1. In my opinion my little sister Iona has great taste in music.

1. *In my opinion, my little sister Iona has great taste in music.*

1. For instance her favorite collection of songs is called *Gift of the Tortoise.*
2. Performed I believe by Ladysmith Black Mambazo, the lyrics of the songs are a blend of English and Zulu words and phrases.
3. The South African performers in fact sing a cappella (without musical instruments accompanying them).
4. Not surprisingly their powerful style of music is known by millions of people worldwide.
5. Fudugazi by the way is the storytelling tortoise who explains the meaning of the songs.
6. By listening to the song "Finger Dance," Iona has learned believe it or not to count to five in Zulu.
7. She has not yet learned to sing any of her favorite songs in Zulu however.
8. Of course our whole family enjoys listening to these lovely South African songs.
9. The spirited music and moving sound effects moreover seem to transport us to a faraway land and culture.
10. Everyone should I think follow Fudugazi's advice: "There is magic in these songs; close your eyes and listen, and you will feel the magic, too!"

Conventional Uses of Commas

11k. Use commas in certain conventional situations.

(1) Use commas to separate items in dates and addresses.

EXAMPLES After Tuesday, November 24, 2009, address all orders to Emeryville, CA 94608.

Please send your cards by November 23, 2009, to 7856 Hidalgo Way, Emeryville, CA 94608.

Notice that no comma divides the month and day (November 23) or the house number and the street name (7856 Hidalgo Way) because each is considered one item. Also, the ZIP Code is not separated from the abbreviation of the state by a comma (Emeryville, CA 94608).

> NOTE Commas are not needed if the day precedes the month or if only the month and year are given.
>
> EXAMPLES President Bill Clinton took office on **20 January 1993.**
>
> Hurricane Andrew hit southern Florida in **August 1992.**

(2) Use a comma after the salutation of a personal letter and after the closing of any letter.

EXAMPLES Dear Mr. Arpajian,   Sincerely yours,

My dear Anna,   Yours very truly,

┌HELP
Use a colon after the salutation of a business letter.

EXAMPLE
Dear Service Manager:

(3) Use commas to set off abbreviations such as *Jr., Sr.,* or *M.D.* when they follow persons' names.

EXAMPLES Please welcome Allen Davis, Sr.

Carol Ferrara, M.D., is our family physician.

Reference Note

For more about using **colons,** see page 303.

Review D   **Correcting Sentences by Adding Commas**

Add commas where they are needed in the following sentences. If a sentence is already correct, write *C.*

EXAMPLE 1. On July 14 1789 the people of Paris stormed the Bastille.
1. *On July 14, 1789, the people of Paris stormed the Bastille.*

1. Please address the envelope to Ms. Marybeth Correio 1255 S.E. 56th Street Bellevue WA 98006.

MECHANICS

2. Sources claim that on April 6 1909 Matthew Henson, assistant to Commander Robert E. Peary, reached the North Pole.

3. I glanced quickly at the end of the letter, which read, "Very sincerely yours Alice Ems Ph.D."

4. The Constitution of the United States was signed on September 17 1787 eleven years after the adoption of the Declaration of Independence on July 4 1776.

5. Did you go on a field trip to the desert in March or April of 1999?

6. We used to live in Monterrey but now we live at 100 Robin Road Austin Texas.

7. Tony watch out for that spider.

8. My grandmother a Russian learned English late in life.

9. That man is the governor by the way.

10. The gauchos crossed the hot windy vast expanse of the pampas.

Unnecessary Commas

11l. Do not use unnecessary commas.

Have a reason for every comma and other mark of punctuation that you use. When there is no rule requiring punctuation and when the meaning of the sentence is clear without it, do not insert any punctuation mark.

INCORRECT My friend, Jessica, said she would feed my cat, and my dog while I'm away, but now, she tells me, she will be too busy.

CORRECT My friend Jessica said she would feed my cat and my dog while I'm away, but now she tells me she will be too busy.

Review E Correcting Sentences by Adding Commas

For each of the following sentences, write all the words that should be followed by a comma. Place a comma after each of these words.

EXAMPLE 1. Yes Phyllis I know that you want to transfer to Bayside the high school that has the best volleyball team in the city.

1. *Yes, Phyllis, Bayside,*

1. Scuttling across the dirt road the large hairy spider a tarantula terrified Steve Ellen and me.

2. Whitney not Don won first prize.

3. German shepherds are often trained as guide dogs; other breeds that have also been trained include Labrador retrievers golden retrievers and Doberman pinschers.

4. According to her official birth certificate Mary Elizabeth was born September 7 1976 in Juneau Alaska but she does not remember much of the city.

5. Angela and Jennifer are you both planning to write poems to enter in the contest?

6. All entries for the essay-writing competition should be submitted no later than Friday to Essay Contest 716 North Cliff Drive Salt Lake City UT 84103.

7. The best time to plant flower seeds of course is just before a rainy season not in the middle of a hot dry summer.

8. Our next-door neighbor Ms. Allen manages two large apartment buildings downtown.

9. As a matter of fact most horses can run four miles without having to stop.

10. The Comanches like some other nomadic American Indians once traveled throughout the states of Kansas New Mexico Texas and Oklahoma.

11. My favorite story "The Most Dangerous Game" was written back in 1924.

12. Even though I ran quickly around the base of the tree the squirrel always stayed on the opposite side of the tree from me.

13. We planted irises because they are perennials flowers that bloom year after year.

14. One of Cleopatra's Needles famous stone pillars from ancient Egypt stands in Central Park in New York City New York.

15. In April 1976 a fifth-grader in Newburgh New York released a helium balloon; it was found in Strathaven Scotland on the other side of the Atlantic Ocean two days later.

16. Danny's father just bought a 1967 Ford Mustang with green white and red stripes on the sides.

17. Before we begin reading *The Odyssey* we will see a movie about ancient Greece.

18. Mount Waialeale, Hawaii, receives an average of 460 inches of rain each year making it the rainiest place in the world.

19. A light frost was on the ground the leaves were falling the air was cool and the wind was blowing stronger; autumn had arrived overnight.

20. The performance of our school's spring musical has been sold out for weeks but those of us who helped build the set will get free tickets.

Review F Adding End Marks and Commas

Add end marks and commas where they are needed in each sentence in the following paragraph.

EXAMPLE **[1]** As you can see from the map below Cabeza de Vaca explored areas in North America and South America

1. *As you can see from the map below, Cabeza de Vaca explored areas in North America and South America.*

[1] Did you know that Álvar Núñez Cabeza de Vaca a Spanish explorer participated in two trips to this region [2] To tell the truth neither trip ended successfully [3] In the summer of 1527 he was treasurer of an expedition that was sent to conquer and colonize Florida [4] However the invasion didn't work out as planned and he was one of a handful of survivors [5] These men intended to sail to Mexico but their ship wrecked off the coast of Texas [6] What an unlucky expedition that was [7] Cabeza de Vaca was captured by a native people but he later escaped and wandered through Texas and Mexico for eight years [8] He tells about his Florida expedition in the book *Naufragios* which has the Spanish word for "shipwrecks" as its title. [9] In 1541 this adventurer led an expedition to South America and he became governor of Paraguay [10] When the colonists revolted Cabeza de Vaca returned to Spain under arrest but he was later pardoned.

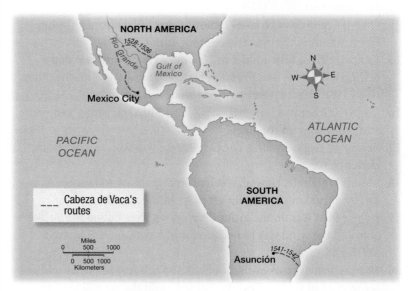

Chapter Review

A. Correcting Sentences by Adding End Marks and Commas

Most of the following sentences contain errors in the use of end marks and commas. Write each sentence, adding end marks and commas where needed. If no additional punctuation is needed, write *C*.

1. She says tae kwon do a Korean martial art improves concentration

2. Well that's the last time that I'll ever ride in one of those taxis

3. Is the card addressed to Robert Danieli Jr or to Robert Danieli

4. The batter hoping to advance the runners laid down a perfect bunt

5. Use light colors by the way to make a small room seem larger

6. We used to live in Lansing but now we live at 457 Cleveland Road Huntsville Alabama

7. Did you ask Joe to bring the forks plates and cups to the picnic

8. What an interesting enjoyable book that is

9. When we complained to Mrs Finch about the remark she apologized to us

10. Reva look out for that pothole in the road

11. If the worn tire had not been replaced it could have caused an accident.

12. The green flag the signal to begin the race was seen by thousands

13. Send your application to Box 36 New York NY before June 30 2009

14. Your homework of course must be finished before you go hiking

15. Sitting on their front porch my grandparents talk to the children who pass

16. We looked after our neighbors' dog while they toured Canada for two weeks and they offered to feed our cat next Thanksgiving

17. Wow this movie is exciting

18. People watching the parade were sitting on curbs and standing on sidewalks.

19. At the convenience store on the corner my sister bought juice

20. Désirée I would like to know your secret for a beautiful complexion

B. Using Periods, Commas, Question Marks, and Exclamation Points

Add commas, periods, question marks, and exclamation points where needed in the following sentences. Identify each sentence as *declarative, imperative, interrogative,* or *exclamatory.*

21. Did the author Willa Cather write about life on the prairie

22. Angelo had cereal a muffin a boiled egg and toast for breakfast

23. How long did that project take

24. Well, wouldn't hearing Domingo sing be worth the trip

25. Oh boy what a great idea

26. Students, sign up in the office if you are going on the field trip

27. You will find the test on my desk which is near the bookcase

28. Rita wants to invite Ingrid Ingrid's cousin and their friend Jamila

29. My younger sister who will be twelve wants to have a birthday party

30. Turn down the radio

C. Using Abbreviations

Rewrite the following sentences, correcting errors in the use of abbreviations.

31. The guest of honor was Dr. Steve Welch, M. D.

32. Maj. Gen. McCambridge, the base commander, was on TV.

33. This statue was probably sculpted between B.C. 500 and 400.

34. At 9:35 A.M. in the morning, the race started.

35. Following family custom, Samuel Brandt, Junior, named his first-born son Samuel Brandt III.

36. The interns working in the ER enjoyed the challenges and the unpredictability of life in an emergency room.

37. In 1271 A.D., the Italian adventurer Marco Polo left Venice on his long voyage to China.

38. My parents spent their early years in Wilmington, DE, and Miami, FL.

39. The explorers set up camp in what would later become Seattle, Wash.

40. The speeding car was clocked at seventy-five m.p.h.

D. Proofreading a Paragraph for End Marks and Commas

In the following paragraph, insert end marks and commas as needed.

[41] As I took photos last Saturday with an instant camera I became increasingly curious about the origin of this type of camera [42] Being the persistent seeker after knowledge that I am how could I not spend time the next day researching the topic [43] The results of my research needless to say were quite interesting [44] Apparently Edwin Land's daughter once asked him why a camera couldn't immediately produce pictures [45] Land who had taught himself physics quickly worked out the basic principles and design of an instant camera [46] What a tremendous achievement that was [47] He became head of Polaroid Corp and that company produced the first Polaroid Land camera in 1948 [48] Did you know that Land later made important contributions to the study of lasers and color vision [49] Land died on March 1 1991 [50] Among his honors were the Presidential Medal of Freedom and of course the National Medal of Science

Writing Application
Writing Clear Directions

Using Commas   A friend asks you for directions from your school to a particular destination. In your instructions, use commas to separate items in a series, to join independent clauses, to set off an introductory adverb clause, to set off a noun of direct address, and to separate items in an address.

Prewriting   Choose a destination (real or imagined), and then outline on paper the way to get there.

Writing   As you write your first draft, concentrate on making the directions clear and easy to follow.

Revising   Read your directions to be sure they are arranged in a logical order. Check to see that you have used commas in the five ways specified in the instructions for this writing activity.

Publishing   Proofread your directions for correct grammar and punctuation. You and your classmates may want to collect your directions into a newcomers' guide for new students at your school.

Punctuation
Semicolons and Colons

Diagnostic Preview

A. Correcting Sentences by Adding Semicolons and Colons

For the following sentences, write each word or numeral that should be followed by a semicolon or colon, and then insert the missing semicolon or colon. If a sentence is already correct, write *C*.

EXAMPLE
1. Someday, robots may do many simple household chores, wash windows, answer the telephone, make repairs, and serve dinner.

1. *chores:*

1. I didn't go to the game last night, instead, I took care of my baby brother, Carl.
2. The band members will perform at the civic center on Tuesday, January 15, at the Kiwanis Club on Saturday, January 19, and at the Oak Nursing Home on Friday, January 25.
3. For the lesson on figures of speech, we had to find examples of similes, metaphors, personification, and hyperbole.
4. Dr. Enríquez has traveled to rain forests in many parts of the world, Borneo, Brazil, Costa Rica, and Sri Lanka.
5. The first Spaniards who settled in America built forts, missions, and pueblos, evidence of Spanish influence on American architecture can be found throughout the Southwest.

6. The Tower of Babel, as described in Genesis 11 1–9, resembled a ziggurat, or terraced pyramid.
7. Erica seldom misses a football playoff on TV, last Saturday, for example, she watched the NFC championship game from noon to 3 00 P.M.
8. I invited Peggy, Josefina, and Sonya, and Beth, Errol, and Randy are coming too.
9. My brother doesn't like many TV shows; instead of watching TV, he prefers to read books.
10. The events for the annual Ironman Triathlon, which is held in Hawaii and is open to men and to women, are as follows, swimming in the ocean 2.4 miles, bicycling 112 miles, and running 26.2 miles.

B. Proofreading a Letter for Correct Use of Semicolons and Colons

Find the ten places where a semicolon or a colon should be used in the following letter. Write each word or number that should be followed by a semicolon or a colon; then, add the necessary punctuation mark.

EXAMPLE   [1] Last summer we stayed home during summer vacation, this summer we took a trip in the car.

1. *vacation;*

290 Eureka Street
Dallas, TX 76012

August 15, 2009

Director
California Department of Parks and Recreation
Box 2390
Sacramento, CA 95811

[11] Dear Sir or Madam,

[12] While on vacation this summer, my family and I visited the following states Washington, Oregon, and California. [13] We wanted you to know that we especially enjoyed our stay in California, we learned a lot and are planning to return soon.

[14] What we liked best was visiting the Spanish missions in the Los Angeles area they gave us a real sense of history. [15] My favorite places were Mission San Fernando Rey de España, located in Mission Hills, Mission San Gabriel Arcangel, located in San Gabriel, and El Pueblo de Los Angeles. [16] The Old Plaza Church, Nuestra Señora la

Reina de Los Angeles, which dates from 1822, was especially wonderful, we stayed there from noon to 500 P.M., when the mission closed.

[17] Our stay in California was great, we hope to return next summer when we will have more time. [18] I would like to visit some of the missions around San Francisco therefore, I would appreciate it if you could send me some information on that area. Thank you very much.

Yours truly,

Angie Barnes

Angie Barnes

Semicolons

12a. Use a semicolon between independent clauses that are closely related in meaning if they are not joined by *and, but, for, nor, or, so,* or *yet.*

Notice in the following pairs of examples that the semicolon takes the place of the comma and the conjunction joining the independent clauses.

EXAMPLES First, I had a sandwich and a glass of milk**, and** then I called you for the homework assignment.

First, I had a sandwich and a glass of milk**;** then I called you for the homework assignment.

Patty likes to act**, but** her sister gets stage fright.
Patty likes to act**;** her sister gets stage fright.

Similarly, a semicolon can take the place of a period to join two or more clauses that are closely related.

EXAMPLES Manuel looked out at the downpour**.** **T**hen he put on his raincoat and boots. [two simple sentences]

Manuel looked out at the downpour**;** then he put on his raincoat and boots. [one compound sentence]

Rain soaked the earth**.** **P**lants became green**.** **F**ragrant flowers bloomed. [three simple sentences]

Rain soaked the earth**;** plants became green**;** fragrant flowers bloomed. [one compound sentence]

STYLE TIP

Use a semicolon to join independent clauses only if the ideas in the clauses are closely related.

INCORRECT
Josh wants to go to Venezuela; Elaine wants to swim.

CORRECT
Josh wants to go to Venezuela**;** Elaine wants to go to Paraguay.

Reference Note

For information on **simple and compound sentences,** see page 109.

MECHANICS

Exercise 1 **Correcting Sentences by Adding Semicolons Between Independent Clauses**

Indicate where a semicolon should be placed in each of the following sentences. In some instances, you may prefer to use a period. Be prepared to explain your choice.

EXAMPLE   **1.** Great earthquakes usually begin gently only one or two slight shocks move the earth.

    1. *Great earthquakes usually begin gently; only one or two slight shocks move the earth.*

┌**HELP**──

In the example for Exercise 1, a semicolon is used because the two independent clauses are closely related.

1. Pressure builds along faults, or cracks, in the earth's crust the weight of this pressure causes earthquakes.
2. The San Andreas fault, shown here, extends nearly the entire length of California earthquakes often occur all along this fault.
3. During an earthquake, huge chunks of the earth's crust begin to move The San Francisco earthquake of 1906, pictured here, was one of the most destructive earthquakes recorded in history.
4. Energy released during an earthquake is tremendous it can equal the explosive force of 180 metric tons of TNT.
5. Scientists study the force of earthquakes they measure this force on a scale of numbers called the Richter scale.
6. An earthquake measuring less than 5 on the Richter scale is not serious more than 1,000 earthquakes measuring 2 or less occur daily.
7. In 1906, one of the most powerful earthquakes in history occurred in the Pacific Ocean near Ecuador it measured 8.9 on the Richter scale.
8. Tidal waves are a dangerous result of earthquakes geologists use the Japanese word *tsunami* for these destructive ocean waves.
9. Predicting when earthquakes will occur is not yet possible predicting where they will occur is somewhat more certain.
10. Earthquakes seem to strike in a regular time sequence in California, for example, a major earthquake usually occurs every fifty to one hundred years.

MECHANICS

Semicolons   **297**

12b. Use a semicolon between independent clauses joined by a conjunctive adverb or transitional expression.

EXAMPLES Emma felt shy; **however,** she soon made some new friends.

My bird does unusual tricks; **for example,** he rings a bell and says "Wow."

Commonly Used Conjunctive Adverbs			
accordingly	furthermore	meanwhile	otherwise
also	however	moreover	still
besides	indeed	nevertheless	then
consequently	instead	next	therefore

Commonly Used Transitional Expressions			
as a result	for instance	in fact	on the other hand
for example	in addition	that is	in other words

Notice in the examples under Rule 12b that the conjunctive adverb and the transitional expression are preceded by semicolons and followed by commas.

NOTE When a conjunctive adverb or transitional expression appears within one of the clauses and not between clauses, it is usually punctuated as an interrupter (set off by commas). The two clauses are still separated by a semicolon.

EXAMPLES Our student council voted to have a Crazy Clothes Day; the principal, **however,** vetoed the idea.

That quilt is quite old; it is, **in fact,** filled with cotton, not polyester, batting.

12c. A semicolon (rather than a comma) may be needed to separate independent clauses joined by a coordinating conjunction when the clauses contain commas.

CONFUSING Alana, Eric, and Kim voted for her, and Scott, Roland, and Vanessa voted for Jason.

CLEAR Alana, Eric, and Kim voted for her; and Scott, Roland, and Vanessa voted for Jason.

STYLE   TIP

Use a semicolon between clauses joined by a coordinating conjunction only when a semicolon is needed to prevent misreading, as in the examples of confusing sentences given for Rule 12c. If a sentence is clear without a semicolon, don't add one just because the clauses contain commas.

EXAMPLE
Lana, you are the best musician I know, and you're a great dancer, too. [clear without semicolon]

CONFUSING   Scanning the horizon for the source of the whirring sound, Pedro saw a huge, green cloud traveling in his direction, and, suddenly recognizing what it was, he knew that the crops soon would be eaten by a horde of grasshoppers.

CLEAR   Scanning the horizon for the source of the whirring sound, Pedro saw a huge, green cloud traveling in his direction; and, suddenly recognizing what it was, he knew that the crops soon would be eaten by a horde of grasshoppers.

Exercise 2) Correcting Sentences by Adding Semicolons Between Independent Clauses

Write each word that should be followed by a semicolon in the following sentences and add the semicolon. In some cases, you may prefer to use a period. Be prepared to explain your choice.

EXAMPLE   1. Cape Cod is only one of many attractions in Massachusetts, Boston and the Berkshires are also worth visiting.
    1. *Massachusetts;*

┌HELP─
In the example for Exercise 2, a semicolon is used because the independent clauses are closely related.

1. My mother and I sometimes go to Massachusetts in late summer, however, last year we went in July.
2. We visit Cape Cod once a year, my grandparents live there, so we always have a place to stay.
3. I miss my friends and sometimes find the yearly trip to Cape Cod boring, Besides, my cousins in Massachusetts are all older than I am.
4. To my great surprise, we had a very good time last year, we even did some sightseeing in Boston, Plymouth, and Marblehead.
5. One hot day my mother, my grandparents, and I went to the beach, and my grandfather, the most active man I know, immediately went down to the water for a swim.
6. My grandfather loves the water and is a strong swimmer, nevertheless, because the currents are strong and tricky, we worried when we saw that he was swimming out farther and farther.
7. Grandpa, to our great relief, finally turned around and swam back to shore, he was astonished that we had been worried about him.
8. While he was in the water, Mom had gathered driftwood, dug a shallow pit in the sand, and built a fire in it, and Grandma had put lobster, corn, and potatoes on the coals.
9. By the time we had finished eating, it was quite late, consequently, everyone else on the beach had gone home.
10. We didn't leave for home right away, instead, we spent the evening watching the darkening ocean, listening to the whispering waves, and watching the stars come out.

MECHANICS

12d. Use a semicolon between items in a series if the items contain commas.

EXAMPLES   I would like to introduce Mrs. Boyce, our mayor**;** Mr. Bell, her secretary**;** Ms. Lincoln, the editor of our newspaper**;** and Mr. Quinn, our guest of honor.

The Photography Club will meet on Wednesday, September 12**;** Wednesday, September 19**;** and Tuesday, September 25**.**

Review A Correcting Sentences by Adding Semicolons

Write each word or numeral that should be followed by a semicolon in the following sentences and add the semicolon. If a sentence needs no semicolons, write *C*.

EXAMPLE   **1.** Tina likes playing basketball, I prefer hockey.
           1. basketball;

1. The first passenger jet was Britain's *Comet*, first flown in 1949, it had some problems at first but later became a quite popular plane.
2. On our trip to Paris, my sister wanted to visit the Louvre, but I was more interested in the Eiffel Tower.
3. Africa's kingdoms included Mali, on the Niger River, Benin, in what is now Nigeria, and Mwanamutapa, in southern Africa.
4. Formerly, most cars had carburetors, the newer models have fuel injectors.
5. Many words in modern Japanese come from English, for instance, the word *doonatsu* comes from *doughnut*.
6. The Incas planted crops, such as corn, they domesticated animals, such as the llama, and they developed crafts, such as weaving.
7. Many scientists believe that one of the elephant's closest living relatives is not a large animal at all surprisingly, it is a small rodentlike creature called the hyrax.
8. Mrs. Gillis said that we could write about Dekanawidah, the Huron founder of the Iroquois League, Mansa Musa, the Muslim emperor of Mali, or Tamerlane, the Mongol conqueror of the Ottoman Turks.
9. Most of Grandmother's belongings were packed away in the attic, however, Mother discovered another suitcase in the cellar, and there were things locked up in the safe-deposit box, too.
10. In the fifteenth century, the kings of France, England, and Spain grew stronger as they unified their lands.

Oral Practice **Correcting Sentences by
Adding Semicolons**

Most of the following sentences contain an error in the use of semicolons. Read each sentence aloud. Then, say where a semicolon should
be added. If a sentence is already correct, say "correct."

EXAMPLE   **1.** The largest animal in the world today is the blue whale
the largest blue whale ever caught measured slightly
more than 112.5 feet and weighed about 170 tons.

    1. whale; the

1. Each of the more than seventy-five species of whales is different
   however, all whales migrate with the seasons.
2. Whales, which are warmblooded marine mammals, are divided
   into two main families, these families are the toothed whales (the
   larger family) and the toothless whales.
3. The biggest toothed whale, the sperm whale, hunts giant squid
   along the bottom of the ocean, like all toothed whales, it uses its
   teeth for catching food, not chewing it.
4. The sperm whale is a record holder in the animal kingdom; it has
   the largest brain and the thickest skin.
5. Other species of whales include the gray whale, which is probably
   the best-known toothless whale, the Baird's beaked whale, which is
   also called the giant bottlenose whale, the bowhead whale, which
   is also known as the arctic whale, and the killer whale, which is
   also called *orca.*

6. Whales take very full, deep breaths consequently, they can dive almost a mile below the surface of the ocean and remain underwater for more than an hour at a time.

7. Some whale species exhibit remarkable social behavior; for example, members of a group may stay with a wounded animal or even support it in the water.

8. During the past 250 years, whalers have nearly wiped out many species of whales, the whaling industry continues to threaten those species that have managed to survive.

9. Several countries, including the United States, have banned the killing of certain whale species; but the blue whale, which is close to extinction, remains an endangered species.

10. Whale-watching cruises originated with the public's growing concern over the survival of whales today whalewatching attracts as many as 350,000 people a year.

Review B   Correcting Sentences by Adding Semicolons

Most of the following sentences need at least one semicolon. For each incorrectly punctuated sentence, write the word preceding each missing semicolon, the semicolon, and the word following the semicolon. If a sentence needs no semicolon, write *C*.

EXAMPLE   1. American Indian pottery fascinates me, whenever I can, I watch potters like this woman at the Tigua (pronounced TEE-wah) Indian Reservation and Pueblo in El Paso, Texas.

1. *me; whenever*

1. I could have watched for hours as this artist painted designs on the vases, however, I knew that the rest of my family was eager to see more of the reservation.

2. There is much to see there, and they were determined to see it all!

3. The Tiguas have a large adobe visitors center, where they display their arts and crafts and have dance demonstrations, and my younger brothers, Jaime and Lucas, ran all around it.

4. Of course, we had to sample the Tigua specialties at the restaurant, otherwise, we would have missed a unique experience.

5. I've eaten American Indian dishes in Phoenix, Arizona, Muskogee, Oklahoma, and Taos, New Mexico, but the food at the Tigua Reservation was my favorite.

6. I especially enjoyed the *gorditas,* which are a little like tacos, the bread, which was fresh out of the oven, and the chili, which was very spicy.

7. After lunch, a guide told us that the community was established in 1682 by Tiguas who were displaced from northern New Mexico; he said the reservation is the oldest inhabited community in Texas today.

8. The Tiguas are especially proud of their mission they certainly should be.

9. Now known as the Ysleta Mission, it is a beautiful restored building, we enjoyed seeing it.

10. It is the oldest mission in Texas moreover, it is one of the oldest in all of North America.

Colons

12e. Use a colon to mean "note what follows."

(1) Use a colon before a list of items, especially after expressions like *the following* and *as follows.*

EXAMPLES   You will need to bring **the following equipment:** a sleeping bag, a warm sweater, and extra socks.

Additional supplies are **as follows:** a toothbrush, toothpaste, a change of clothes, and a pillow.

Sometimes the items that follow a colon are used as appositives. If a word is followed by a list of appositives, the colon makes the sentence clear.

EXAMPLES   At the air base we saw three signs: To Norway, To Paris, and To Lisbon.

You need to shop for several items: brown shoelaces, a quart of milk, and five or six carrots.

Reference Note

For more on **appositives** and **appositive phrases,** see page 89.

NOTE Do not use a colon between a verb and its complements or between a preposition and its objects.

INCORRECT	Additional supplies are: a toothbrush and toothpaste, a change of clothes, a towel, a pillow, and an air mattress.
CORRECT	Additional supplies are a toothbrush and toothpaste, a change of clothes, a towel, a pillow, and an air mattress.

INCORRECT	You need to shop for: brown shoelaces, a quart of milk, and five or six carrots.
CORRECT	You need to shop for brown shoelaces, a quart of milk, and five or six carrots.

Reference Note

For more about using **long quotations,** see page 318.

(2) Use a colon before a long, formal statement or a long quotation.

EXAMPLE   Horace Mann had this to say: "Do not think of knocking out another person's brains because he differs in opinion from you. It would be as rational to knock yourself on the head because you differ from yourself ten years ago."

(3) Use a colon between independent clauses when the second clause explains or restates the idea of the first.

EXAMPLE   Thomas Jefferson had many talents: He was a writer, a politician, an architect, and an inventor.

NOTE The first word of a sentence following a colon is capitalized.

EXAMPLE   Lois felt that she had done something worthwhile: She had designed and sewn her first quilt.

─HELP─

Use a comma after the salutation of a personal letter.

EXAMPLES
  Dear Kim,

  Dear Uncle Remy,

12f. Use a colon in certain conventional situations.

(1) Use a colon between the hour and the minute.

EXAMPLES   10:30 A.M.   6:30 P.M.

(2) Use a colon between the chapter and the verse in Biblical references and between titles and subtitles.

EXAMPLES   Exodus 1:6–14   *Whales: Giants of the Sea*

(3) Use a colon after the salutation of a business letter.

EXAMPLES   Dear Ms. González: Dear Dr. Fenton:

            Dear Sir or Madam: To Whom It May Concern:

Exercise 3 Correcting Sentences by Adding Colons

Correct the following sentences by adding necessary colons. If a sentence does not need a colon, write *C*.

EXAMPLE 1. When I came into class at 9 15 A.M., everyone was writing an essay based on this West African proverb "To know nothing is bad; to learn nothing is worse."

1. *When I came into class at 9:15 A.M., everyone was writing an essay based on this West African proverb: "To know nothing is bad; to learn nothing is worse."*

1. Last summer I read "Choices A Tribute to Dr. Martin Luther King, Jr.," by Alice Walker.
2. Mrs. Hughes named the three students who had completed extra projects Marshall, Helena, and Regina.
3. At the festival we bought tacos and refried beans.
4. The qualities she likes most in a person are as follows reliability, a good sense of humor, and willingness to work.
5. Learn to spell the following new words *aneurysm, fluoroscope, peregrination,* and *serendipity.*
6. An enduring statement of loyalty, found in Ruth 1 16, begins as follows "Entreat me not to leave thee or to return from following after thee, for whither thou goest, I will go."
7. The desk was littered with papers, pencils, paperback books, food wrappers, and dirty socks.
8. From 8 00 A.M. until 6 00 P.M., Mr. Brooks sells brushes, brooms, and cleaning products.
9. Alone in the house at night, I heard some scary sounds the creaking of a board, the scratching of tree branches against a window, and the hissing of steam in the radiator.
10. Tomorrow's test will include the punctuation marks that we have studied so far commas, semicolons, and colons.

COMPUTER TIP

Some software programs can evaluate your writing for common errors in the use of end marks, commas, semicolons, and colons. Such grammar-checking programs can help you proofread your drafts.

MEETING THE CHALLENGE

Create a recipe listing ingredients and directions. You may wish to create a recipe for your favorite dish or for an abstract idea, such as happiness or success. Write the recipe directions in complete sentences. Correctly use at least one colon and at least three semicolons in your directions.

MECHANICS

DILBERT reprinted by permission of United Feature Syndicate, Inc.

Correct the following sentences, using semicolons and colons where they are needed.

EXAMPLE **1.** We didn't have time to go to Michigan, instead, we went to New Mexico.

1. *We didn't have time to go to Michigan; instead, we went to New Mexico.*

1. A small, windowless log cabin stood against the rail fence directly behind it ran a muddy stream.
2. Because the club has run out of funds, the following supplies must be brought from home pencils, erasers, paper, and envelopes.
3. Other jobs take too much time for example, if I worked in a store, I probably would have to work most nights.
4. I enjoy the following hobbies fly-fishing, reading, and riding my bike.
5. American cowhands used the ten-gallon hat as protection from the sun and as a dipper for water the leather chaps they wore served as protection from thorny bushes.
6. A rabbi, a Lutheran minister, and a Catholic priest discussed their interpretations of Isaiah 2 2 and 5 26.
7. In his speech Dr. Fujikawa quoted from several poets Rudyard Kipling, David McCord, and Nikki Giovanni.
8. Sojourner Truth, a former slave, could neither read nor write however, this accomplished woman spoke eloquently against slavery and for women's rights.
9. From 1853 to 1865, the United States had three presidents Franklin Pierce, a Democrat from New Hampshire James Buchanan, a Democrat from Pennsylvania and Abraham Lincoln, a Republican from Illinois.
10. From 12 30 to 1 00 P.M., I was so nervous that I could not sit still I paced up and down, swinging my arms and taking deep breaths, while I rehearsed my lines in my mind.

Chapter Review

A. Correcting Sentences by Adding Semicolons Between Independent Clauses

The following sentences are missing semicolons. Write each sentence, adding semicolons where needed.

┌─HELP─┐

In Part A of the Chapter Review, you may need to delete some commas and replace them with semicolons.

1. Irma likes cats, her sister is allergic to them.
2. First I cleaned my room, then I called the movie theater to find out the time of the next show.
3. Two of the world's longest railway tunnels are in Italy, moreover, one of the longest motor-traffic tunnels is also located there.
4. My brother Manuel enjoys cooking, I prefer eating.
5. Marty decided to invite Adam, Oliver, and Dorian, and Don, Guy, and Sarah would be there, too.
6. On our first trip to Houston, I wanted to see the Astrodome, my little brother wanted to visit the Johnson Space Center.
7. Tim and Maria often spend Christmas at home however, this year they are going to visit Maria's family in Guanajuato.
8. The popular names of certain animals are misleading, for example, the koala bear is not really a bear.
9. French and Spanish were Charlotte's most difficult subjects, accordingly, she gave them more time than any of her other subjects at school.
10. The teacher settled the argument, he told us we each had to give a presentation.

B. Correcting Sentences by Adding Colons

Correct the following sentences by adding necessary colons. If a sentence is already correct, write *C*.

11. You will need to bring the following equipment a hammer, a screwdriver, and safety goggles.
12. At the crossroads we saw three signs To Quebec, To Montreal, and To Ottawa.
13. We need to shop for several items salad greens, milk, and a loaf of bread.

MECHANICS

14. Exodus 1 6–14 is my favorite passage in the Old Testament.

15. The corner store is open from 6 00 A.M. until 11 00 P.M.

16. Last year I read the following novels *David Copperfield,* by Charles Dickens; *The Joy Luck Club,* by Amy Tan; and *Bel-Ami,* by Guy de Maupassant.

17. The desert floor was strewn with rocks, pebbles, tumbleweed, and mineral shards.

18. This evening's program will focus on what we have discussed so far the changes in the West over the last two centuries.

19. Especially challenging were the following spelling words *fluorescent, dissuade, annotate,* and *fortuitous.*

20. At 11 45 A.M. the flight to Mexico City, Bogotá, Brasilia, and Buenos Aires will depart from Gate 2.

C. Proofreading for Correct Use of Semicolons and Colons

The following advertisement contains errors in the use of semicolons and colons. Write the word or number preceding the error, and add the needed punctuation mark.

┌HELP─

In Part C of the Chapter Review, you may need to delete some commas and replace them with semicolons and colons.

[21] Your pet probably loves to watch TV, therefore, it should have the best in quality entertainment. [22] Forcing your dog or cat to watch only what humans watch is not only boring for the pet it is somewhat inconsiderate on your part. [23] Buy your faithful friend the new *Rockin' and Rollin' Pets* video it will change your pet's life. [24] No dog or cat will be bored with this movie on the contrary, Fidos and Tabbies everywhere have been sitting up and taking notice. [25] With this video, your pet will get the exciting, up-to-date entertainment it has been craving, as a concerned owner, you will feel good about what your pet is watching. [26] Science has proven that dogs and cats like the movement and music on television, moreover, they like human contact while watching TV. [27] Ask yourself this question, Are you thinking about your pet's happiness when you turn on the set at 7 00 or 8 00 in the evening? [28] Do you think your pet really likes to watch situation comedies, which are about families it doesn't know, movies, which are too long, and news programs, which are too serious? [29] You already know the answer order your pet a *Rockin' and Rollin' Pets* video today! [30] To place your order, call the following toll-free number 1-000-PET-ROCK.

MECHANICS

Writing Application

Punctuating a Business Letter

Semicolons and Colons   You have volunteered to order the items that the members of your school band will sell to raise money for road trips. Write a short letter to order these items.

Prewriting   First, decide what kinds of items to sell (for example, ballpoint pens, dried fruit, candles, or book covers) and how many to order. Also, decide on each item's price and make up a name and address for the company from which you will purchase the items.

Writing   As you write your first draft, try to keep the body of your letter short and to the point.

Revising   Be sure that you have followed the correct form for a business letter. Make sure that you have included all the information necessary for the order.

Publishing   Check that you have used a colon after the salutation and before the list of items that you are ordering. Slowly read your letter, focusing on spelling and punctuation. Have you capitalized all proper names, company names, addresses, and brand names? You may want to put your letter-writing abilities to use for your school band or for another school or community organization that holds fund-raisers.

Punctuation
Italics and Quotation Marks

Diagnostic Preview

A. Correcting Sentences by Adding Underlining (Italics) and Quotation Marks

Add underlining (italics) and quotation marks where they are needed in each of the following sentences.

EXAMPLE   1. Don't forget your umbrella, said Jody. I read in the Sun Times that it's going to rain today.

1. *"Don't forget your umbrella," said Jody. "I read in the Sun Times that it's going to rain today."*

1. My grandmother asked me which one I wanted for my birthday, Laura said, a subscription to Time or one to Popular Mechanics.
2. Welcome aboard the Elissa, said the skipper. It was built in the 1800s, but it has been restored and is still a seaworthy ship.
3. Emerson once said, The only way to have a friend is to be one; I think he's right.
4. In the book The Complete Essays of Mark Twain, you'll find an essay titled Taming the Bicycle.
5. Jennifer said, I never can remember how many c's and s's the word necessary has.
6. Beth finally figured out that when Tranh used the Vietnamese phrase không biết, he was telling her that he didn't understand.

7. The 18 on her uniform looks like a 13, Earl said.

8. Alexandra replied, I'm surprised you watched Gone with the Wind. Two days ago you said, I don't want to see the movie until I've read the book.

9. Every week the whole family gathered in front of the television to watch 7th Heaven.

10. The Beatles' song Yesterday has been a favorite of several generations.

B. Correcting Paragraphs of Dialogue by Adding Underlining (Italics) and Quotation Marks

The following dialogue contains errors in the use of underlining (italics) and quotation marks. Correct these errors by adding appropriate marks of punctuation. If a sentence is already correct, write *C*.

EXAMPLES   **[1]** I thought the poetry unit in English class would be dull, Ella said, but it's not. **[2]** We're studying Langston Hughes, and he's great!

1.   *"I thought the poetry unit in English class would be dull,"* Ella said, *"but it's not. 2. We're studying Langston Hughes, and he's great!"*

[11] Oh, I've heard of him, Chet said. [12] Didn't he write a poem called The Dream Keeper?

[13] Yes, that's one of my favorites, Ella said. [14] An entire book of his poems is called The Dream Keeper, too. [15] Another one of his best-known poems is called Dreams.

[16] I guess he dreamed a lot, Chet replied.

[17] Ella said, He did much more than that! [18] Mrs. Berry told us that Langston Hughes traveled extensively. [19] For a time, he was on the crew of a steamer that sailed around Africa and Europe. [20] In fact, one of his autobiographies is called The Big Sea.

┌─ **HELP** ─

In Part B of the Diagnostic Preview, each error in the use of quotation marks involves a pair of single or double quotation marks.

Italics

Italic letters slant to the right, *like this*. When writing or typing, indicate italics by underlining. If your composition were to be printed, the typesetter would set the underlined words in italics. For example, if you typed the sentence

```
Helen Keller wrote The Story of My Life.
```

it would be printed like this:

Helen Keller wrote *The Story of My Life.*

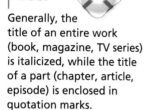
MECHANICS

13a. Use italics (underlining) for titles and subtitles of books, periodicals, long poems, plays, films, television series, long musical works and recordings, and works of art.

Type of Title	Examples
Books	*Vanity Fair: A Novel Without a Hero*
Periodicals	*Seventeen, The New York Times*
Long Poems	*Evangeline, Beowulf*
Plays	*The Piano Lesson, King Lear*
Films	*Casablanca, Harvey*
Television Series	*60 Minutes, Home Improvement*
Long Musical Works and Recordings	*The Magic Flute, Sinfonia Antarctica, The Three Tenors, Dos Mundos*
Works of Art	*The Thinker, Birth of Venus*

The words *a, an,* and *the* written before a title are italicized only when they are part of the title. The official title of a book appears on the title page. The official title of a newspaper or other periodical appears on the masthead, which is usually found on the editorial page or the table of contents.

EXAMPLES   I am reading John Knowles's ***A*** *Separate Peace.*

An *Incomplete Education* is a book that tries to summarize everything you should have learned in college.

My parents subscribe to ***The*** *Wall Street Journal* and **the** *Atlantic.*

NOTE   A long poem is one that is long enough to be published as a separate volume. Such poems are usually divided into titled or numbered sections, such as cantos, parts, or books. Long musical compositions include operas, symphonies, ballets, oratorios, and concertos.

EXAMPLES   In my report on Coleridge, I plan to quote from the seventh stanza of ***The Rime of the Ancient Mariner.***

At her recital, she will play a selection from ***Swan Lake.***

13b. Use underlining (italics) for the names of ships, trains, aircraft, and spacecraft.

Type of Name	Examples
Ships	*Titanic, Queen Elizabeth 2*
Trains	*Orient Express, City of New Orleans*
Aircraft and Spacecraft	*Spirit of Saint Louis, Apollo 1*

13c. Use italics (underlining) for words, letters, symbols, and numerals referred to as such and for foreign words that are not yet a part of the English vocabulary.

EXAMPLES   The word ***Mississippi*** has four ***s***'s and four ***i***'s.

           The ***8*** on that license plate looks like an ***&.***

           The ***corrido,*** a fast-paced ballad, evolved from a musical form brought to the Americas by early Spanish explorers and settlers.

NOTE   English has borrowed many words from other languages. Once such words are considered a part of the English vocabulary, they are no longer italicized.

EXAMPLES amoeba (Greek)   judo (Japanese)

             boss (Dutch)   kibbutz (Modern Hebrew)

             canyon (Spanish)   okra (West African)

             chimpanzee (Bantu)   résumé (French)

             chipmunk (Algonquian)   vermicelli (Italian)

┌HELP┐

If you are not sure whether to italicize a word of foreign origin, look in a recently published dictionary to see if the word is italicized there.

MECHANICS

Exercise 1 Correcting Sentences by Adding Underlining (Italics)

Rewrite the following sentences. Then, underline all the words and word groups that should be italicized.

EXAMPLE   1. We gave Mom a subscription to Working Woman.
            1. *We gave Mom a subscription to <u>Working Woman</u>.*

1. Jason named his ship Argo because Argos had built it.
2. The motto of the United States Marine Corps is Semper Fidelis, which means "always faithful."
3. Have you read the novel Great Expectations by Charles Dickens?
4. When I spelled occurrence with one r, I was eliminated from the spelling contest.
5. The Gilbert and Sullivan comic opera The Mikado and the Puccini opera Madama Butterfly are both set in Japan.
6. Shari asked if she could borrow my copy of Sports Illustrated.
7. Mrs. Hopkins said that if she had to describe me in one word, the word would be loquacious.
8. My grandmother, who grew up in Chicago, still subscribes to the Chicago Tribune.
9. My favorite painting is Georgia O'Keeffe's Black Iris; my favorite sculpture is Constantin Brancusi's Bird in Space.
10. My parents own a set of the Encyclopaedia Britannica; and my aunt, who lives within walking distance of us, just bought a set of The World Book Encyclopedia.

Quotation Marks

13d. Use quotation marks to enclose a *direct quotation*—a person's exact words.

EXAMPLES   Melanie said, "This car is making a very strange noise."
              "Maybe we should pull over," suggested Amy.

Always be sure to place quotation marks at both the beginning and the end of a direct quotation.

INCORRECT   She shouted, "We can win, team!
CORRECT   She shouted, "We can win, team!"

Do not use quotation marks for an *indirect quotation*—a rewording of a direct quotation.

DIRECT QUOTATION	Stephanie said, "I'm going to wash the car." [the speaker's exact words]
INDIRECT QUOTATION	Stephanie said that she was going to wash the car. [not the speaker's exact words]

An interrupting expression is not a part of a quotation and therefore should not be inside quotation marks.

INCORRECT	"Let's sit here, Ann whispered, not way down there."
CORRECT	"Let's sit here," Ann whispered, "not way down there."

When two or more sentences by the same speaker are quoted together, use only one set of quotation marks.

INCORRECT	Brennan said, "I like to sit close to the screen." "The sound is better there."
CORRECT	Brennan said, "I like to sit close to the screen. The sound is better there."

13e. A direct quotation generally begins with a capital letter.

EXAMPLES	Explaining the lever, Archimedes said, "Give me a place to stand, and I can move the world."
	Miss Pérez answered, "The rest of the chapter, of course." [Although this quotation is not a sentence, it is Miss Pérez's complete remark.]

Reference Note

For more about **capitalizing quotations,** see page 246.

NOTE If the direct quotation is obviously a fragment of the original quotation, it may begin with a lowercase letter.

EXAMPLE	Are our ideals, as Scott says, mere "statues of snow" that soon melt? [The quotation is obviously only a part of Scott's remark.]

13f. When an interrupting expression divides a quoted sentence into two parts, the second part begins with a lowercase letter.

EXAMPLES	"I wish," she said, "that we went to the same school."
	"I know," I answered, "but at least we are friends."

If the second part of a quotation is a new sentence, a period (not a comma) follows the interrupting expression, and the second part begins with a capital letter.

EXAMPLE	"I requested an interview," the reporter said. "She told me she was too busy."

MECHANICS

13g. A direct quotation can be set off from the rest of a sentence by a comma, a question mark, or an exclamation point, but not by a period.

EXAMPLES   Delores explained, "You know how much I like chicken," as she passed her plate for more.

                 "When will we be leaving?" asked Tony.

                 The plumber shouted, "Turn off that faucet!" when the water started gushing out of the pipe.

13h. When used with quotation marks, other marks of punctuation are placed according to the following rules:

(1) Commas and periods are placed inside closing quotation marks.

EXAMPLES   "I haven't seen the movie," remarked Jeannette, "but I understand that it's excellent."

(2) Semicolons and colons are placed outside closing quotation marks.

EXAMPLES   Socrates once said, "As for me, all I know is that I know nothing"; I wonder why everyone thinks he was such a wise man.

                 The following actresses were nominated for the award for "best performance in a leading role": Helen Hunt, Meryl Streep, Cher, and Jodie Foster.

(3) Question marks and exclamation points are placed inside the closing quotation marks if the quotation itself is a question or an exclamation; otherwise, they are placed outside.

EXAMPLES   "Is it too cold in here?" the manager asked as I shivered.

                 "Yes!" I answered. "Please turn down the air conditioner!"

                 Can you explain the saying "Penny wise, pound foolish"?

                 It's not an insult to be called a "bookworm"!

NOTE   When both a sentence and the quotation at the end of that sentence are questions or exclamations, only one question mark or exclamation point is used. It goes inside the closing quotation marks.

EXAMPLE   Did Elizabeth Barrett Browning write the poem that begins with "How do I love thee?"

Exercise 2 | **Writing Sentences with Direct and Indirect Quotations**

If a sentence contains a direct quotation, change it to an indirect quotation. If a sentence contains an indirect quotation, change it to a direct quotation. Make sure your answers are correctly punctuated.

EXAMPLES
1. "Where should we go for vacation?" asked my mother.
1. *My mother asked where we should go for vacation.*

2. My little brother Jason said that he wanted to see castles like the ones in the brochures.
2. *My little brother Jason said, "I want to see castles like the ones in the brochures."*

1. When we planned our trip to England, Mom said, "Our stops should include some castles."
2. Our tour book says that Colchester Castle, begun in 1076, is a good place to start.
3. Jason asked whether the castles were haunted.
4. "No," said Mom, "and, besides, we'll stay close together."
5. In England, Jason told Mom that he wanted to swim in a moat.
6. "Warwick Castle," said our guide, "is one of the most beautiful."
7. "One of its towers," he went on to say, "was built in 1066."
8. The guide said that the castle contains many works of art.
9. "I like the collection of suits of armor best," said Jason.
10. "Is it still the home of the Earls of Warwick?" I asked.

13i. When you write dialogue (a conversation), begin a new paragraph every time the speaker changes.

EXAMPLE

"What's that?" Sally demanded impatiently.

Luisa seemed surprised. "What's what?"

"That thing, what you got in your hand."

"Oh this . . ." and she held it up for Sally to inspect. "A present."

"A what?"

"A present I picked up."

"Oh." Sally moved her eyes to the house. "Looks like his place burned down. What d'you find inside?"

"Just this," Luisa said, gazing blankly at the house.

"What d'you want that for?"

Ron Arias, "El Mago"

STYLE TIP

In dialogue, a paragraph may be only one line long and may consist of one or more sentence fragments.

MECHANICS

13j. When a quoted passage consists of more than one paragraph, put quotation marks at the beginning of each paragraph and at the end of the entire passage. Do not put quotation marks after any paragraph but the last.

EXAMPLE
"At nine o'clock this morning someone entered the Mill Bank by the back entrance, broke through two thick steel doors guarding the bank's vault, and escaped with sixteen bars of gold.

"No arrests have been made, but state police are confident the case will be solved within a few days."

NOTE   A long passage (not dialogue) quoted from a book or another printed source is usually set off from the rest of the text. The entire passage is usually indented and double-spaced. When a quoted passage has been set off in one of these ways, no quotation marks are necessary.

EXAMPLE
In his autobiography The Interesting Narrative of the Life of Olaudah Equiano, or Gustavus Vassa, the African, Olaudah Equiano describes encountering African languages other than his own:

> From the time I left my own nation I always found somebody that understood me till I came to the sea coast. The languages of different nations did not totally differ, nor were they so copious as those of the Europeans, particularly the English. They were therefore easily learned; and while I was journeying thus through Africa, I acquired two or three different tongues.

13k. Use single quotation marks to enclose a quotation within a quotation.

EXAMPLES
Annoyed, Becky snapped, "Don't tell me, 'That's not the way to do it.'"

My uncle said, "Remember the words of Chief Joseph: 'I have heard talk and talk, but nothing is done. Good words do not last long unless they amount to something.' This is good advice."

Tiffany exclaimed, "How dare you say, 'Yuck!'"

Review A Correcting Sentences by Adding Quotation Marks for Dialogue

Correct each of the following passages, adding quotation marks where necessary. Remember to begin a new paragraph each time the speaker changes.

EXAMPLE   **1.** Is Rio de Janeiro the capital of Brazil, asked Linda, or is Brasília?

     1. "Is Rio de Janeiro the capital of Brazil," asked Linda, "or is Brasília?"

1. Retired race-car driver Janet Guthrie, said Chet, reading from his notes, was a trained physicist who spent many years working at an aircraft corporation.

2. Who shot that ball? Coach Larsen wanted to know. I did, came the reply from the small, frail-looking player. Good shot, said the coach, but always remember to follow your shot to the basket. I tried, but I was screened, the player explained.

3. The *Brownsville Beacon,* the editorial began, will never support a candidate who tells the taxpayers, Vote for me, and I will cut taxes. The reason is simple. Taxes, just like everything else in this inflationary society, must increase. Any candidate who thinks otherwise is either a fool or a liar.

4. In the interview, the candidate said, I am a very hospitable person. Yes, her husband agreed, Ralph Waldo Emerson must have been thinking of you when he said, Happy is the house that shelters a friend.

" WOULD YOU STOP PUTTING QUOTES AROUND EVERYTHING I SAY ?! "

Reference Note

Remember that the **titles of long poems and long musical works are italicized,** not enclosed in quotation marks. See the examples on page 312.

13l. Use quotation marks to enclose titles and subtitles of articles, essays, short stories, poems, songs, individual episodes of TV series, and chapters and other parts of books and periodicals.

Type of Title	Examples
Articles	"What Teenagers Need to Know About Diets" "Satellites That Serve Us"
Essays	"Charley in Yellowstone" "An Apartment in Moscow"
Short Stories	"The Man to Send Rain Clouds" "The Pit and the Pendulum"
Poems	"Fog" "Incident" "The End of My Journey"
Songs	"The Ballad of Gregorio Cortez" "Peace Train"
Episodes of TV Series	"The Sure Thing" "Monarch in Waiting"
Chapters and Other Parts of Books and Periodicals	"Life in the First Settlements" "The Talk of the Town"

NOTE   When titles listed in 13l appear within quotations, use single quotation marks.

EXAMPLE   "Did Thomas Hardy write 'The Dynasts'?" asked Terri.

Oral Practice   **Correcting Sentences by Adding Quotation Marks for Titles**

Read each of the following sentences aloud, and tell which word or word group should be enclosed in quotation marks. If a sentence is already correctly punctuated, say *correct*.

EXAMPLE   1. Did O. Henry write the story The Last Leaf?
           1. *Did O. Henry write the story "The Last Leaf"?*

1. That address to the United Nations can be found in our literature book, in the chapter titled Essays and Speeches.
2. One popular Old English riddle song is Scarborough Fair.

3. Have you read the story Split Cherry Tree by Jesse Stuart?
4. Which Eve Merriam poem is that, Cheers or How to Eat a Poem?
5. Have you read Fran Lebowitz's essay Tips for Teens?
6. One of Pat Mora's poems about being bilingual and bicultural is titled Legal Alien.
7. I read Kurt Vonnegut's short story "Harrison Bergeron" last week.
8. In his essay Misspelling, Charles Kuralt examines some of the difficulties people have with spelling.
9. Fiona said, "My favorite Irish ballad is Cliffs of Dooneen."
10. The whole class enjoyed reading Naomi Shihab Nye's poem Daily.

Review B **Correcting Sentences by Adding Underlining (Italics) and Quotation Marks**

Write the following sentences, adding underlining (italics) and quotation marks where needed.

EXAMPLE   1. Please turn to the chapter titled A Walk in the Highlands.

1. *Please turn to the chapter titled "A Walk in the Highlands."*

1. The Bay Area Youth Theater is presenting Bernard Shaw's play Major Barbara.
2. Tyrone announced that he is going to sing Some Enchanted Evening from the musical South Pacific.
3. I have tickets to the opera Carmen, said Karen, and I would like you to be my guest.
4. Does the Swahili word kwa heri mean the same thing that the Spanish word adiós does?
5. My favorite story by Sir Arthur Conan Doyle is The Adventure of the Dying Detective, which is included in the anthology The Complete Sherlock Holmes.
6. Ms. Loudon said, I enjoyed your report on Ernest Hemingway. Remember, however, that the name Ernest is spelled without an a.
7. In her review of The King and I, the drama critic for the Los Angeles Times commented, This production is an excellent revival of a play that never seems to wear thin.
8. In my paper, which I titled The Hispanic Soldier in Vietnam, I cited several passages from Luis Valdez's play The Buck Private.
9. Mrs. Howard asked, In the play Julius Caesar, who said, This was the noblest Roman of them all? Which Roman was being described?
10. Have you read Hannah Armstrong, one of the poems in the Spoon River Anthology by Edgar Lee Masters?

Correct the following paragraphs by adding underlining (italics) and quotation marks where necessary.

EXAMPLE **[1]** Are all of these books by or about Benjamin Franklin? asked Bonnie Lou.

1. *"Are all of these books by or about Benjamin Franklin?" asked Bonnie Lou.*

[1] Yes, Bonnie Lou, Mr. Reyes answered. [2] There's even one, Ben and Me by Robert Lawson, that's a biography written from the point of view of Amos, Franklin's pet mouse.

[3] This one, The Many Lives of Benjamin Franklin by Mary Pope Osborne, sounds really interesting, said Jasmine.

[4] It is, Mr. Reyes said. [5] That's exactly what we're going to talk about today—the many lives of this early American genius. [6] Who can tell me about one of them?

[7] He invented electricity, didn't he? asked Liam.

[8] Well, he didn't invent electricity, corrected Mr. Reyes, but his experiments proved that lightning is a form of electricity.

[9] Franklin, he continued, also helped draft some of our important historical documents, and he was a diplomat, a printer, and a publisher. [10] Franklin's writings, especially his Autobiography and Poor Richard's Almanack, have given us many well-known sayings.

MECHANICS

Chapter Review

A. Correcting Sentences by Adding Underlining (Italics) and Quotation Marks

The following sentences contain errors in the use of underlining (italics) and quotation marks. Write each sentence, adding underlining and quotation marks where needed.

1. The concert ended with a stirring rendition of The Stars and Stripes Forever.
2. There's Still Gold in Them Thar Hills, an article in Discover, describes attempts to mine low-grade gold deposits on Quartz Mountain in California.
3. Mozart's opera The Magic Flute is being performed tonight.
4. The fifth episode in the TV series The African Americans is titled The Harlem Renaissance.
5. I Am Joaquín is an epic poem about Mexican American culture.
6. As a baby sitter I have read the children's book The Pokey Little Puppy at least a dozen times.
7. The journalist Horace Greeley founded the New York Tribune, an influential newspaper.
8. Although the poem When You Are Old has three stanzas, it contains only one sentence.
9. The word recommended has two m's but only one c.
10. Robert Fulton's steamboat, Claremont, was the first one that could be operated without losing money.
11. My father always swore by Newsweek, but Mother preferred U.S. News & World Report.
12. In his novel David Copperfield, Dickens draws a vivid picture of Victorian life.
13. In Spanish, sí means yes; in French, si is also used to mean yes, but only in answer to a negative statement.
14. Tim asked, What time did they say they would be here?
15. Usually, they read the Daily News on Sundays.
16. Those b's look like 6's.
17. I didn't think I would be able to sit through an opera, said Brittany, but I really enjoyed Hansel and Gretel.

18. On Mondays during football season, the entire family watches Monday Night Football on television.

19. How many m's and t's does the word committee have? asked Betty.

20. One of Kathryn's favorite novels is Martin Chuzzlewit by Charles Dickens.

B. Punctuating Dialogue by Adding Quotation Marks

The following dialogue contains errors in the use of quotation marks. Write each sentence, adding quotation marks where needed.

[21] Before our field trip begins, continued Mrs. Garcia, be sure that you have a notebook and a collection kit.

[22] Will we need binoculars? asked Melvin.

[23] Leave your binoculars at home, answered Mrs. Garcia. Your ears will be more helpful than your eyes on this trip.

[24] What will we be able to hear out there? asked Arnold.

[25] What a question! exclaimed Felicia. This time of year, you can hear all sorts of sounds.

[26] I hope that we hear and see some birds, said Koko. Didn't someone once say, The birds warble sweet in the springtime?

[27] When, asked James, do we eat lunch? My mom packed my favorite kinds of sandwiches.

[28] Don't worry, said Mrs. Garcia. Most birds are quiet at midday. We can have our lunch then.

[29] Ruth Ann said, Mrs. Garcia, would you believe that I don't know one birdcall from another?

[30] That's all right, Ruth Ann, laughed Mrs. Garcia. Some birds call out their own names. For example, the bobolink repeats its name: Bob-o-link! Bob-o-link!

C. Correcting Paragraphs by Adding Underlining (Italics) and Quotation Marks

The following paragraph contains errors in the use of underlining (italics) and quotation marks. Write each sentence, adding underlining and quotation marks where necessary. Be sure to start a new paragraph each time the speaker changes.

[31] As most of you probably know, said Mr. Sundaresan, our geography teacher, Everest, on the border of Tibet and Nepal, is the

world's highest mountain; does anyone know the name of the world's second-highest peak? Yes, Elaine? [**32**] It's K2. [**33**] Yes, said Mr. Sundaresan, impressed. How did you know? [**34**] Well, said Elaine, for Christmas my parents gave me a book called K2: Challenging the Sky by Roberto Mantovani. I just finished reading it last night. [**35**] Very good, said Mr. Sundaresan. Now can anyone tell me the name of the highest mountain in Europe? I'll give you a hint: It's not in Switzerland. Elaine's hand shot up again. [**36**] Isn't it Mont Blanc, on the border of France and Italy? she asked. [**37**] Quite right, said Mr. Sundaresan. May I ask how you knew that? [**38**] For my birthday I got a copy of The Alps and Their People by Susan Bullen. It's a really interesting book. [**39**] Well, have you read any books on the Rockies, Elaine? asked Mr. Sundaresan. [**40**] As a matter of fact, I just started reading The Rockies by David Muench, and before you ask, I can tell you that Mount Elbert is the highest peak in the Rockies!

Writing Application
Writing a Dialogue

Using Quotation Marks   Write a page of dialogue in which characters tell a story, either fact or fiction, through a conversation.

Prewriting   Decide on a story and a few characters to tell it. You could retell a favorite anecdote, report the exact words of an amusing conversation, or write an imaginary interview with a famous person.

Writing   As you write your first draft, think about making the characters sound different from one another.

Revising   First, ask a classmate to read your dialogue. Revise any parts that are unclear or uninteresting to your reader. Be sure that you have begun a new paragraph every time the speaker changes. Also, check that you have followed the rules for punctuating direct quotations and quotations with interrupting expressions.

Publishing   Read through your dialogue again, this time concentrating on correcting errors in grammar, spelling, and punctuation. You and your classmates may want to work in small groups to present your dialogues to the class.

Punctuation
Apostrophes

Diagnostic Preview

Revising Sentences in a Journal Entry by Using Apostrophes Correctly

In the following journal entry, Josh often incorrectly uses contractions and possessive forms. Write the correct form of each incorrect word or expression used.

EXAMPLE [1] Im still working on todays assignment.

1. *I'm; today's*

[1] Ive just finished tonights homework. [2] Writing a composition is usually two hours hard work for me, but Im pleased with this one. [3] Ill read it over in the morning to make sure that my handwritings legible. [4] My teacher has trouble reading my *d*s, *t*s, and *o*s. [5] He also objects to my overuse of *and*s and *so*s. [6] If theres an error, Ill have to revise my composition. [7] Thats one good reason for being careful, isnt it?

[8] My compositions title is "The Reign of Animals." [9] Moms friend suggested that I call it "Whose in Charge Here?" [10] My familys love for animals is well known in the neighborhood and among our friends'. [11] At the moment were owned by two inside cats; three outside cats; our resident dog, Pepper; and a visiting dog we call Hugo.

[12] During Peppers walks, Im usually followed by at least one other dog. [13] Some owners care of their dogs never seems to go beyond feeding them. [14] The city councils decision to fine owners'

who let they're dogs run loose makes sense. [**15**] Hugos a huge dog who's always wandering loose in my neighborhood. [**16**] We took him in several times after hed narrowly escaped being hit by a car. [**17**] In fact, Hugos and Peppers feeding dishes sit side by side in our kitchen.

[**18**] Peter, our senior cat, who was once one of our neighborhoods strays, isnt about to run from anyones dog. [**19**] At times weve seen him safeguarding other cats of ours' by running in front of them and staring down an approaching dog and it's owner. [**20**] Our dogs and cats different personalities never cease to fascinate me.

Possessive Case

The *possessive case* of a noun or pronoun shows ownership or possession.

EXAMPLES **Larry's** friend Dana uses a wheelchair.

You need a good **night's** sleep.

Can I count on **their** votes?

I appreciate **your** waiting so long.

14a. To form the possessive case of most singular nouns, add an apostrophe and an *s.*

EXAMPLES Yuki**'s** problem   a bus**'s** wheel

the mayor**'s** desk   this evening**'s** paper

Mrs. Ross**'s** job   a dollar**'s** worth

NOTE For a proper name ending in *s,* add only an apostrophe if the name has two or more syllables and if the addition of *'s* would make the name awkward to pronounce.

EXAMPLES **Ulysses'** plan   **West Indies'** export

Mrs. Rawlings' car   **Texas'** governor

For a singular common noun ending in *s,* add both an apostrophe and an *s* if the added *s* is pronounced as a separate syllable.

EXAMPLES the actress**'s** costumes   the dress**'s** sleeves

the class**'s** teacher   a platypus**'s** tail

Exercise 1 Using Apostrophes to Form the Possessive Case of Singular Nouns

Form the possessive case of each of the following nouns. After each possessive word, give an appropriate noun.

EXAMPLE   **1.** Teresa

            1. Teresa's pencil

1. baby	**8.** mouse	**15.** horse
2. uncle	**9.** Mr. Chan	**16.** Paris
3. year	**10.** Miss Reynolds	**17.** system
4. cent	**11.** plane	**18.** judge
5. class	**12.** boss	**19.** Mr. Jones
6. Terry	**13.** child	**20.** synagogue
7. Ellen	**14.** Ms. Sanchez	

14b. To form the possessive case of a plural noun ending in *s*, add only the apostrophe.

EXAMPLES   two bird**s'** feathers   all three cousin**s'** vacation

                  the Garza**s'** patio   the Girl Scout**s'** uniforms

Although most plural nouns end in *s*, some are irregular. To form the possessive case of a plural noun that does not end in *s*, add an apostrophe and *s*.

Reference Note

For more examples of **irregular plurals,** see page 368.

EXAMPLES   children**'s** shoes   those deer**'s** food

Exercise 2 Forming the Possessive Case of Plural Nouns

Form the possessive case of each of the following plural nouns.

EXAMPLE   **1.** knives

            1. knives'

1. men	**8.** cattle	**15.** runners
2. cats	**9.** mice	**16.** attorneys
3. teachers	**10.** parents	**17.** allies
4. enemies	**11.** the Smiths	**18.** friends
5. princesses	**12.** sheep	**19.** women
6. dollars	**13.** wives	**20.** bats
7. elves	**14.** O'Gradys	

Exercise 3 Revising Phrases by Forming the Possessive Case of Nouns

Revise the following phrases by using the possessive case.

EXAMPLE   **1.** the parties for seniors

1. *the seniors' parties*

1. prizes for winners
2. manners for teenagers
3. yokes of oxen
4. duties of nurses
5. names of players

6. suits for women
7. ideas of inventors
8. medals for veterans
9. routines for dancers
10. roles for actresses

> NOTE In general, you should not use an apostrophe to form the plural of a noun.
>
> INCORRECT   Two player's left their gym suits on the locker room floor.
>
> CORRECT   Two **players** left their gym suits on the locker room floor. [plural]
>
> CORRECT   Two **players'** gym suits were left on the locker room floor. [The apostrophe shows that the gym suits belong to the two players.]

© 1993 by Sidney Harris.

Review A Recognizing Correct Forms of Nouns

Choose the correct form of each noun in parentheses in the following paragraph.

EXAMPLES   Several **[1]** (*photographs, photograph's*) taken by *Voyagers 1* and *2* were combined into the illustration on the next page to show a few of **[2]** (*Saturns, Saturn's*) many satellites.

1. *photographs*

2. *Saturn's*

At least eighteen natural satellites, or celestial **[1]** (*bodies, body's*), revolve around the planet Saturn. Seven of our solar **[2]** (*systems, system's*) nine planets have satellites, but Saturn and Jupiter have the most. **[3]** (*Scientists, Scientists'*) figures on the true number of **[4]** (*satellites, satellite's*) vary, and new space **[5]** (*probes, probe's*) sometimes reveal more satellites. Two **[6]** (*planets, planets'*), Earth and Pluto, have only one satellite each. Of course, you are already familiar with our

own **[7]** (*planets, planet's*) satellite, the moon. As you can see from this illustration, **[8]** (*satellite's, satellites'*) sizes and features vary greatly. Titan, a satellite of Saturn, is the largest of that **[9]** (*planets, planet's*) satellites. Another of **[10]** (*Saturns, Saturn's*) satellites, Mimas, has a crater that covers about one third of its diameter.

14c. Possessive personal pronouns do not require an apostrophe.

Reference Note

For more about **using pronouns correctly,** see Chapter 7.

Possessive Personal Pronouns	
Singular	**Plural**
my, mine	our, ours
your, yours	your, yours
his, her, hers, its	their, theirs

My, your, her, its, our, and *their* are used before nouns or pronouns. *Mine, yours, hers, ours,* and *theirs,* on the other hand, are not used before a noun or pronoun; they are used as subjects, subject complements, or objects in sentences. *His* may be used in either way.

EXAMPLES   Lee has **your** sweater.   Lee has a sweater of **yours.**

That is **your** watch.   That watch is **yours.**

Her idea was wonderful.   **Hers** was the best idea.

This is **our** plant.   This plant is **ours.**

There is **his** CD.   There is a CD of **his.**

Reference Note

For more about **whose, its,** and **their,** see pages 384, 379, and 382.

NOTE   The possessive form of *who* is *whose,* not *who's.* Similarly, do not write *it's* for *its,* or *they're* for *their.*

EXAMPLES   **Whose** [not *Who's*] book is this?

Its [not *It's*] cover is torn.

Is that **their** [not *they're*] copy?

MECHANICS

Exercise 4 Choosing Correct Forms of Possessive Personal Pronouns

Choose the correct pronoun in parentheses in each of the following sentences.

EXAMPLE **1.** Ralph Ellison, (*who's, whose*) book *Invisible Man* won a National Book Award, studied music at Tuskegee Institute.

  1. whose

1. Did you know, Sumi, that two poems of (*yours, yours'*) have been chosen for the literary magazine?
2. When I first read that book, I was surprised by the high quality of (*its, it's*) artwork.
3. (*Hers, Her's*) is the bicycle with the reflectors on (*its, it's*) fenders.
4. Eudora Welty, (*who's, whose*) short stories often involve eccentric characters, is my favorite writer.
5. "The trophy is (*ours, our's*)!" shouted the captain as the *Flying S* crossed the finish line.
6. (*Theirs, Theirs'*) is the only house with blue shutters.
7. Penny and Carla worked as gardeners this summer and saved (*their, they're*) money for a ski trip.
8. The students (*who's, whose*) names are called should report backstage.
9. (*Their, They're*) schedule calls for a test on Tuesday.
10. (*Who's, Whose*) signature is this?

14d. Indefinite pronouns in the possessive case require an apostrophe and *s*.

EXAMPLES   nobody**'s** wishes   another**'s** viewpoint

  someone**'s** license   neither**'s** school

Exercise 5 Choosing Correct Forms of Possessive Pronouns

Choose the correct pronoun in parentheses in each of the following sentences.

EXAMPLE **1.** That Mozart CD is (*hers, her's*).

  1. hers

1. (*No ones, No one's*) guess was correct.
2. (*Ours, Our's*) works better than (*theirs, their's*).
3. (*Who's, Whose*) game is that?

Reference Note
For a list of **indefinite pronouns,** see page 9.

┌─HELP─
For the expressions *everyone else* and *nobody else,* the correct possessives are *everyone else's* and *nobody else's.*

MECHANICS

4. (*Theirs, Their's*) is the best frozen yogurt in town.

5. Your car needs to have (*its, it's*) oil changed.

6. It wasn't (*anyone's, anyones'*) fault that we missed the bus.

7. (*Her's, Hers*) is the best project in the Science Fair.

8. (*Someones, Someone's, Someones'*) choir robe was left on the bus.

9. (*Everybodys, Everybody's, Everybodys'*) morale suffered.

10. That dog of (*their's, theirs*) should be on a leash.

Reference Note

For information on **forming the plurals of nouns,** see Chapter 16.

Review B — Writing the Singular, Plural, and Possessive Forms of Nouns

On a piece of paper, make four columns headed *Singular, Singular Possessive, Plural,* and *Plural Possessive.* Write each of those forms of the following nouns. Add a suitable noun to follow each word in the possessive case. If you do not know how to spell a plural form, use a dictionary.

EXAMPLE

	Singular	Singular Possessive	Plural	Plural Possessive
1.	dog	dog's owner	dogs	dogs' owners

1. friend

2. typist

3. bicycle

4. referee

5. sheep

6. woman

7. penny

8. dress

9. musician

10. lioness

11. actor

12. mechanic

13. deer

14. artist

15. purse

16. man

17. truck

18. dish

19. window

20. mouse

Review C — Correcting the Forms of Nouns and Pronouns

Identify and correct the ten incorrect possessive forms in the following paragraph.

EXAMPLE   [1] The women shown in these photographs welcomed us to the Shaker village of Pleasant Hill, Kentucky, during our history class' field trip last spring.

1. *class's*

[1] As you can see, the style of the womens dresses is quite old. [2] In fact, the villages history goes back to 1806. [3] That was the year that the religious group known as the Shakers founded they're own community. [4] We learned that the Shaker's lively way of dancing gave the group it's name. [5] Everyones life in the Shaker village was supposed to be orderly, simple, and productive. [6] This basic harmony was true of even the childrens' routines. [7] During the days tour of the village, we saw several people practicing Shaker crafts. [8] One guide of our's

told us that the Shakers invented the common clothespin and the flat broom and designed useful furniture and boxes. [9] I enjoyed visiting the gardens and the Centre Family House and imagining what a Shakers' life must have been like.

14e. Generally, in compound words, names of organizations and businesses, and words showing joint possession, only the last word is possessive in form.

COMPOUND WORDS	community **board's** meeting
	vice-president's contract
	her brother-in-**law's** gifts
ORGANIZATIONS	the Museum of **Art's** budget
	United **Fund's** drive
BUSINESSES	Berkeley Milk **Company's** trucks
JOINT POSSESSION	Peggy and **Lisa's** tent [The tent belongs to both Peggy and Lisa.]
	children and **parents'** concerns [The children and the parents have the same concerns.]

When one of the words showing joint possession is a pronoun, both words should be possessive in form.

EXAMPLE   **Peggy's** and **my** tent [not *Peggy and my tent*]

Reference Note

For more about **acronyms** see page 268.

NOTE The possessive of an acronym (NASA, DOS) or an abbreviation (CIA, CBS) is formed by adding an apostrophe and *s*.

EXAMPLES NASA**'s** latest space probe

CBS**'s** hit television series

14f. When two or more persons possess something individually, each of their names is possessive in form.

EXAMPLES **Mrs. Martin's** and **Mrs. Blair's** cars [the cars of two different women]

Asha's and **Daniella's** tennis rackets [individual, not joint, possession]

Exercise 6 Using the Possessive Case

Use the possessive case to rewrite the following word groups.

EXAMPLE 1. the book owned by Natalie and Stan

1. *Natalie and Stan's book*

1. the ticket of Sylvia and the ticket of Eric
2. an investigation by the FBI
3. the duet of Gwen and Carlos
4. a uniform belonging to the master sergeant
5. the history of the Grand Canyon
6. the job shared by Isabel and me
7. an agent for the Acme Life Insurance Company
8. one tractor belonging to my uncle and one to us
9. the award received by the Sales Department
10. the business of her mother-in-law and the business of her cousin

Review D Identifying Words That Require Apostrophes

Identify the ten words requiring apostrophes in the following paragraph. Then, write the words, inserting the apostrophes.

EXAMPLE [1] Have you ever heard of the U.S. Patent Offices Hall of Fame for inventors?

1. *Offices—Office's*

[1] The Hall of Fames members, who are both American and foreign, include many people that you've probably heard of as well as some you haven't. [2] Vladimir Kosma Zworykin's picture tube helped

lead to televisions development. [3] Charles Richard Drew changed peoples lives all over the world with his work on blood plasma in transfusions. [4] Luther Burbanks accomplishment was the development of more than eight hundred new plant varieties. [5] Heart patients pacemakers were invented by Wilson Greatbatch. [6] You'll probably recognize such famous inventors as the Ford Motor Companys founder, Henry Ford. [7] Of course, Thomas Edisons and Alexander Graham Bells achievements assured their enduring fame. [8] No ones pleasure is greater than mine that Orville and Wilbur Wrights invention of the airplane landed them in such good company, too.

Contractions

14g. Use an apostrophe to show where letters, numerals, or words have been omitted in a contraction.

A **contraction** is a shortened form of a word, a group of words, or a numeral. The apostrophes in contractions indicate where letters, numerals, or words have been left out.

EXAMPLES		
who is . . . who**'s**		I am . . . I**'m**
1991 . . . **'91**		you are . . . you**'re**
of the clock . . . o**'**clock		we had . . . we**'d**
let us . . . let**'s**		she has . . . she**'s**
she will . . . she**'ll**		I had . . . I**'d**
Bill is . . . Bill**'s**		we have . . . we**'ve**

Ordinarily, the word *not* is shortened to *n't* and added to a verb without any change in the spelling of the verb.

EXAMPLES		
is not . . . isn**'t**		were not . . . weren**'t**
are not . . . aren**'t**		has not . . . hasn**'t**
does not . . . doesn**'t**		have not . . . haven**'t**
do not . . . don**'t**		had not . . . hadn**'t**
did not . . . didn**'t**		would not . . . wouldn**'t**
EXCEPTIONS will not . . . won**'t**		cannot . . . can**'t**

STYLE   TIP

Many people consider contractions informal. Therefore, it is usually best to avoid using them in formal writing and speech.

INFORMAL
    The Founding Fathers couldn't foresee the mobility of modern life.

FORMAL
    The Founding Fathers **could not** foresee the mobility of modern life.

MECHANICS

Do not confuse contractions with possessive pronouns.

Contractions	Possessive Pronouns
Who's at bat? [Who is]	**Whose** bat is that?
It's roaring. [It is]	Listen to **its** roar.
You're too busy. [You are]	**Your** friend is busy.
There's a kite. [There is]	That kite is **theirs**.
They're tall trees. [They are]	**Their** trees are tall.

MEETING THE CHALLENGE

Writers sometimes have trouble with the following pairs of words: *it's/its, they're/their, who's/whose,* and *you're/your. It's, they're, who's,* and *you're* all have apostrophes and are contractions (of *it is/has, they are, who is/has,* and *you are*). Possessive pronouns make up the other set. How can writers remember which word to use at which time? For each pair of words, write a sentence to help you distinguish between the two words. For example, for *it's/its,* you could write "It's time to feed the puppy its food." Share your four sentences with your classmates.

Exercise 7 **Correcting Sentences by Using Apostrophes for Contractions**

Write each incorrect contraction in the following sentences, adding an apostrophe as necessary. If a sentence is already correct, write *C*.

EXAMPLE   **1.** Hes pleased by his promotion.

　　　　　1. He's

1. "Youve changed," she said.
2. World War II ended in 45.
3. Whos coming to the party?
4. "The stores about to close," said the clerk.
5. Several stores were closed because of the storm.
6. Well have to try to make it there on time.
7. Whose telescope is that, Richard?
8. She gets up at 6 oclock.
9. Im very glad to meet you.
10. Don't you play chess?

Oral Practice **Recognizing the Correct Use of Apostrophes**

Read aloud each sentence in the following paragraph, and say which choice in parentheses is correct.

EXAMPLE   **[1]** (*Your, You're*) likely to see fiesta scenes like the one on the next page in Mexican American communities across the United States each year on September 16.

　　　　　1. You're

[1] (*It's, Its*) a day of celebration that includes parades, speeches, music, and, as you can see, even colorful folk dances. Of course, [2] (*theirs, there's*) plenty of food, including stacks of tortillas and bowls of beans and soup. [3] (*Who's, Whose*) to say how late the merry-making will last? [4] (*It's, Its*) a joyful holiday of fun, but everyone remembers [5] (*it's, its*) importance, too. Mexican Americans know that

MECHANICS

[6] (*they're, their*) celebrating the beginning of Mexico's rebellion to gain independence from Spain. On September 16, 1810, Father Miguel Hidalgo y Costilla gathered his forces for the rebellion and uttered [7] (*it's, its*) first battle cry. Father Hidalgo, [8] (*who's, whose*) parish was in west central Mexico, led an army across the country. If [9] (*your, you're*) in Mexico City on the eve of September 16, you can hear the president of Mexico ring what is believed to be the bell that Hidalgo rang to summon his people for [10] (*they're, their*) historic march.

Plurals

14h. To prevent confusion, use an apostrophe and an *s* to form the plurals of lowercase letters, some capital letters, numerals, symbols, and some words that are referred to as words.

EXAMPLES   Grandma always tells me to mind my *p*'**s** and *q*'**s.**

I got A'**s** on both tests I took last week. [An apostrophe is used because without one the plural spells the word *As.*]

The *1*'**s** in this exercise look like *l*'**s.**

Two different Web site addresses began with ##'**s** and ended with *.com*'**s.**

His *hi*'**s** are always cheerful. [An apostrophe is used because without one the plural spells the word *his.*]

> **MECHANICS**

> STYLE TIP
>
> Many writers add only *s* when forming the kinds of plurals listed in Rule 14h. However, using both an apostrophe and *s* is not wrong and may be necessary to make your meaning clear. Therefore, it is a good idea always to include the apostrophe.

Exercise 8   Forming Plurals by Using Apostrophes

Use an apostrophe to form the plural of each of the italicized items in the following word groups.

EXAMPLE   **1.** margins filled with *?*

    1. *?*'s

1. *s* that look like *f*
2. to put *U* at the end
3. two *r* and two *s*
4. adding columns of *$* and *%*

> **Reference Note**
>
> For more information on **forming these kinds of plurals,** see page 371.

5. these *q* or *g*
6. all *C* and *B*
7. replace all the *his* with *its*
8. too many *her* and *their*
9. your *i* and your *t*
10. two *I* in the sentence

—HELP—
You may need
to change the spelling of
some words in Review F.

Review E **Using Apostrophes Correctly**

Add or delete apostrophes as needed in the following sentences.

EXAMPLE   **1.** Summers here, but because of air conditioning its more
bearable than it used to be.

    1. Summer's; it's

1. Dont you wonder when people started cooling they're homes
with air conditioning?
2. Air cooling isnt a new practice; in fact, in ancient Rome, wet grass
mat's were hung over window's to cool incoming air by evaporation.
3. In the early sixteenth century, one of the greatest Italian artist's
and engineer's, Leonardo da Vinci, built historys first
mechanical fan.
4. The British scientist David B. Reid's air-ventilation system's were
installed in the British House of Commons in 1838.
5. However, modern technique's of air conditioning werent
invented until the early twentieth century in Buffalo, New York.
6. One of Buffalos most famous citizen's, Willis Carrier, who's name
is still on many air conditioners, invented the first air-condition-
ing unit in 1902.
7. By 1928, the technologys' rapid development had produced the
first fully air-conditioned office building, the Milam Building in
San Antonio, Texas.
8. Wasnt Texas—where in summer the temperature can reach
90 degrees by eleven oclock in the morning—a logical place to
have the first air-conditioned office building?

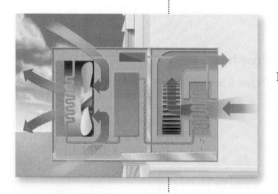

9. By the late 1950's, more and more homes' had
window air conditioner's, and smaller unit's
for motor vehicle's were becoming increasingly
common.
10. Arent you glad air conditioning is so common
nowaday's?

Chapter Review

A. Correcting Sentences by Using Apostrophes Correctly

In the following sentences, apostrophes are either missing or incorrectly used. Write the correct form of each incorrect word. In some cases, an apostrophe must be added or deleted; in others, the spelling of the word also must be changed.

1. Ancient peoples felt that writing had a magic power of it's own.
2. Writing was practiced by the elders' of a tribe to preserve the tribes lore as well as its laws.
3. Were not sure when or how writing began, but we do know that it existed several century's before 3000 B.C.
4. Theres plenty of evidence that people communicated through they're drawings long before they had a system of writing.
5. Spain and France's wonderful cave drawings were painted more than thirty thousand year's ago.
6. The ancient Peruvians message system was a complicated arrangement of knots.
7. Someones research has shown that *W*'s and *J*'s werent used in English writing until the late Middle Ages.
8. In China, ones mastery of basic reading depends on learning one thousand character's.
9. Hardwick Book Stores window display features early system's of writing, such as cuneiform.
10. Bess and Robert, who's reports were on the history of writing, asked one of Mr. Hardwicks clerks for permission to examine the stores display.

B. Proofreading a Paragraph for Correct Use of Apostrophes

The following paragraph contains errors in the use of apostrophes. For each sentence, write the correct form of each incorrect word.

[11] Despite many years work, scholars were not able to decipher hieroglyphics until the early nineteenth century. [12] In 1799, one of Napoleons soldiers serving in Egypt discovered a stone tablet. [13] The

MECHANICS

tablet came to be known as the Rosetta Stone after the town in which it was found: Rashid, which European's called Rosetta. [**14**] The tablets surface was inscribed in three ancient language's: Greek, Egyptian hieroglyphics, and Coptic, a language derived from ancient Egyptian. [**15**] The experts translations of the Greek text revealed that the same information had been written in all three languages in 196 B.C. [**16**] They're next step was to use their knowledge of Greek and Coptic to identify how names' of specific people and places were written in hieroglyphics. [**17**] It wasnt until 1822, however, that a Frenchman named Jean-François Champollion deciphered the ancient Egyptians' writing. [**18**] Following another scholars' theory that hieroglyphic symbols represent sounds, Champollion figured out which symbols represent which sounds. [**19**] He also established that the stones' hieroglyphics were a translation from the Greek—not, as had been thought, the other way around. [**20**] Though many door's remained to be opened, a key to ancient Egyptian history had been found.

C. Using Apostrophes to Form Possessive Nouns

Write the possessive form for each of the following nouns. After each possessive word, give an appropriate noun.

21. Humble Oil Company   **26.** Massachusetts

22. buffalo   **27.** Northern Ireland

23. anything   **28.** bishops

24. geese   **29.** NBC

25. Lori   **30.** mosque

D. Using Apostrophes Correctly

The following sentences contain errors in the use of apostrophes. Write each incorrect word or expression, adding or deleting apostrophes where needed. You may need to change the spelling as well.

31. Havent you ever wondered when the first refrigerator's were used?

32. Wealthy Romans main method of refrigeration was to cool food in snow cellars.

33. Snow cellar's were pit's dug in the ground, insulated with straw, and filled with snow and ice.

34. Didnt ancient India and Egypts' cooling techniques include using evaporative cooling to freeze perishable products?

35. Evaporative cooling means placing water in shallow tray's and using the ice thats formed during rapid evaporation.

36. In the sixteenth century, Italians' discovered that a mixture of water and potassium nitrate could be used to cool bottled liquids.

37. During the 1850's, Ferdinand Carré, a French inventor, developed the worlds' first absorption system using ammonia.

38. Absorption system's use the direct application of heat to initiate the refrigeration cycle by changing refrigerant's from liquid to gas and back again.

39. Another system that produces refrigeration is compression, in which compressor's are used to bring about refrigeration cycles.

40. In 1876, the scientific world learned the name of Carl von Linde, a German engineer who's compression system using ammonia was the foundation of modern refrigeration.

Writing Application
Using Apostrophes in a Paragraph

Possessive Case   Write a paragraph about the musical preferences of one or more family members or friends. Use at least two singular possessive nouns, two plural possessive nouns, and one indefinite pronoun in the possessive case.

Prewriting   First, make a list of family members or friends, and beside each name write what you know about that person's musical tastes. If you are not sure about someone's preferences, ask him or her.

Writing   As you write your first draft, think about ways of organizing your information by type of music, age of listener, and so on.

Revising   Ask a family member or friend to read your paragraph. Is it clear whose preferences are discussed? Are the preferences accurately expressed?

Publishing   Check your placement of apostrophes. As you read through your paragraph, correct errors in spelling, grammar, and punctuation. With the permission of the person or persons whose musical tastes you have discussed in your paragraph, post your piece on a class bulletin board, or use it as a basis for a class discussion.

MECHANICS

Punctuation

Hyphens, Dashes, Parentheses, Brackets, Ellipsis Points

Diagnostic Preview

A. Using Hyphens, Dashes, and Parentheses

Use hyphens, dashes, and parentheses to punctuate the following sentences. Do not add commas to these sentences.

┌HELP┐

If there are multiple ways to correct a sentence, give only one.

EXAMPLE   **1.** Henry Viscardi he founded the National Center for Disability Services dedicated his life to creating opportunities for people who have disabilities.

1. *Henry Viscardi—he founded the National Center for Disability Services—dedicated his life to creating opportunities for people who have disabilities.*

1. The soup was three fourths water and one fourth vegetables.
2. Twenty six students most of them from the advanced math class represented our school at the all state chess match.
3. The Battle of Bunker Hill June 17, 1775 damaged the confidence of the British.
4. The ex treasurer of our club he's an extremely self confident person is now running for class president.
5. My sister she lives in Boston now is studying pre Columbian art.
6. If you have ever dreamed of finding buried treasure and who hasn't? your search could begin on Padre Island.
7. George Grinnell was a self taught expert on the American West and helped negotiate treaties with three American Indian peoples the Blackfoot, the Cheyenne, and the Pawnee.
8. Aunt Jo murmured, "Please turn out the" and then fell asleep.

9. Rachel Carson was working for the U.S. Fish and Wildlife Service created in 1940 when she first recognized the threat of pesticides.
10. Her book *Silent Spring* copyright 1962 alerted the public to the dangers of environmental pollution.

B. Using Hyphens, Dashes, Brackets, and Parentheses

Use hyphens, dashes, brackets, and parentheses to punctuate the following sentences. If a sentence is already correct, write *C*. Do not add commas.

EXAMPLE   **1.** There are several countries Senegal, Gambia, Guinea, Guinea-Bissau, Sierra Leone, and Liberia along the west-central coast of Africa.

       1. There are several countries—Senegal, Gambia, Guinea, Guinea-Bissau, Sierra Leone, and Liberia—along the west-central coast of Africa.

11. Liberia's history its founding, that is is unique.
12. Liberia was settled in pre Civil War days by freed slaves from the United States.
13. An antislavery group known as the American Colonization Society it was officially chartered by the U.S. Congress started sending freed slaves to a colony in Africa in 1822.
14. Twenty five years later, the colonists how proud they must have been! declared Liberia independent.
15. They named their capital Monrovia in honor of President James Monroe in office 1817–1825.
16. They also modeled their country's constitution and government not surprisingly on those of the United States.
17. The first president of Liberia, Joseph Jenkins Roberts (he originally served for eight years 1848–1856 and again during an economic crisis 1872–1876), was born in Virginia.
18. Roberts began his political career as an aide to the colonial governor, Thomas H. Buchanan a white member of the American Colonization Society.
19. During Liberia's early years, the United States provided financial aid.
20. However, the U.S. government didn't officially recognize Liberia until President Lincoln's administration 1862.

MECHANICS

Hyphens

Word Division

15a. Use a hyphen to divide a word at the end of a line.

EXAMPLE   The new governor's victory celebration will be organized by her campaign committee.

When you divide a word at the end of a line, keep in mind
the following rules:

(1) Do not divide a one-syllable word.

INCORRECT   The line of people waiting to buy tickets stretched halfway down the block.

CORRECT   The line of people waiting to buy tickets stretched
halfway down the block.

CORRECT   The line of people waiting to buy tickets
stretched halfway down the block.

(2) Divide a word only between syllables.

INCORRECT   The stars Betelgeuse and Rigel are in the conste-
llation known as Orion.

CORRECT   The stars Betelgeuse and Rigel are in the constel-
lation known as Orion.

CORRECT   The stars Betelgeuse and Rigel are in the constella-
tion known as Orion.

(3) A word containing double consonants usually may be divided
between those two consonants.

EXAMPLES   con-nect   drum-mer

(4) Divide a word with a prefix or a suffix between the prefix and
the base word (or root) or between the base word and the suffix.

EXAMPLES   pre-judge   post-pone   half-back

fall-ing   frag-ment   con-fusion

(5) Divide an already hyphenated word only at a hyphen.

INCORRECT   The speaker this morning is my mother-in-law.

CORRECT   The speaker this morning is my mother-
in-law.

HELP

If you need to
divide a word and are not
sure about its syllables,
looking it up in a dictionary may help. Many
dictionaries show how to
break words into syllables.

(6) Do not divide a word so that one letter stands alone.

INCORRECT The utility company built a new turbine to generate e-
lectricity.

CORRECT The utility company built a new turbine to generate elec‑
tricity.

> **Exercise 1** **Using Hyphens to Divide Words at the Ends of Lines**

Write each of the following words, using hyphens to indicate where the word may be divided at the end of a line. If a word should not be divided, write *one-syllable word*.

EXAMPLES **1.** thoroughly **2.** cooked
     1. *thor-ough-ly* 2. *one-syllable word*

1. Olympics
2. library
3. fourth
4. unchanged
5. impolite
6. tomorrow
7. breathe
8. corporation
9. through
10. merry-go-round

┌─**HELP**─
If you are uncertain of the proper syllabication of the words in Exercise 1, check a dictionary that shows how to break words into syllables.

Compound Words

Some compound words are hyphenated (*red-hot*); some are written as one word (*redhead*); and some are written as two or more words (*red tape*). Whenever you need to know whether a word is hyphenated, look it up in a current dictionary.

15b. Use a hyphen with compound numbers from *twenty-one* to *ninety-nine* and with fractions used as modifiers.

EXAMPLES **seventy-six** trombones

     three-quarters cup [but *three quarters* of a cup]

15c. Use a hyphen with the prefixes *ex–, self–, all–,* and *great–;* with the suffixes *–elect* and *–free;* and with all prefixes before a proper noun or proper adjective.

EXAMPLES **ex**-coach **great**-aunt **mid**-July

     self-made president-**elect** **pro**-American

     all-star   fat-**free**   **pre**-Columbian

│ **S T Y L E** **T I P** │

The prefix *half–* often requires a hyphen, as in *half-life, half-moon,* and *half-truth.* However, sometimes *half* is used without a hyphen, either as a part of a single word (*halftone, halfway, halfback*) or as a separate word (*half shell, half pint, half note*). If you are not sure how to spell a word containing *half,* look up the word in a dictionary.

MECHANICS

15d. Hyphenate a compound adjective when it precedes the noun it modifies.

EXAMPLES   a **well-written** book [but *a book that is well written*]

                 a **small-town** boy [but *a boy from a small town*]

Do not use a hyphen if one of the modifiers is an adverb that ends in *–ly.*

EXAMPLE   a **bitterly cold** day

NOTE   Some compound adjectives are always hyphenated, whether they precede or follow the nouns they modify.

EXAMPLES   a **brand-new** shirt
                 a shirt that is **brand-new**

                 a **down-to-earth** person
                 a person who is **down-to-earth**

┌─ **HELP** ─

If you are unsure about whether a compound adjective is hyphenated, look up the word in a current dictionary.

Exercise 2   Hyphenating Words Correctly

Insert hyphens in the words that should be hyphenated in the following sentences. If a sentence is already correct, write *C.*

EXAMPLE   1. The world famous speaker was very well informed.

            1. *The world-famous speaker was very well informed.*

1. The exgovernor presented the all American trophy at the competition.
2. Until 1959, the United States flag had forty eight stars.
3. In twenty five days my great grandparents will celebrate their seventy fifth wedding anniversary; about three fourths of the family will attend the celebration.
4. The exambassador's lecture focused on the post Napoleonic era.
5. He added one half teaspoon of sugar free vanilla extract to the mixture and set the timer for thirty five minutes.
6. A documentary called "The Self Improvement Culture" was on TV last night.
7. Herman's new mountain bike was very up to date.
8. Well designed buildings have clearly marked fire escapes.
9. Sally has always been very down-to-earth.
10. The President elect gathered his Cabinet to discuss future policy.

MECHANICS

Oral Practice **Identifying the Correct Use of Hyphens**

You have just received the following e-mail message from your friend Eduardo. His computer is acting up and putting in hyphens that are not supposed to be there. Read each numbered item aloud, and list words containing incorrectly used hyphens and words containing correctly used ones.

EXAMPLE   [1] My brother-in-law says that the early-bird catches the worm.

Incorrect	Correct
early-bird	*brother-in-law*

Hey there!

    [1] So, how have you-been? [2] I can't believe it's mid-April. [3] I've really been running myself ragged with home-work, club-meetings, sports, and ninety-nine other things. [4] You wouldn'-t believe how busy I've been!

    [5] I've got a role in our spring-play. [6] It's not a big role, but I'm part of an all-star cast. [7] We're doing *Our Town*. [8] I am managing the props, too.

    [9] Enclosed is a good recipe that I used last week to make pop-corn topping. [10] I'm president-elect of the foreign language-club, and it was once again my turn to host the monthly meeting. [11] Thirty-three members came to my house on Friday (we have a total of fifty-one members). [12] Of course, I served refreshments, and every-one loved this topping.

    [13] Recipe for Mexican Popcorn Topping: In a small bowl, mix one-fourth cup of chili-powder and one-half teaspoon of salt. Then, add one-teaspoon each of garlic powder, cilantro, and cumin. [14] (Those last two are herbs.) [15] Sprinkle mixture over plain-popcorn.

Take care, and write soon.

Eduardo

YOU CORRECT MY GRAMMAR, MY SPELLING, MY PUNCTUATION! I CAN'T STAND THE PRESSURE OF LIVING WITH A PERFECTIONIST!

Parentheses

15e. Use parentheses to enclose material that is added to a sentence but is not considered to be of major importance.

Notice in the following examples that parenthetical material may be omitted without changing the basic meaning and construction of the sentence.

EXAMPLES   During the Middle Ages (from about A.D. 500 to A.D. 1500), both Moors and Vikings invaded parts of Europe.

The music of Liszt (always a favorite of mine) was quite popular in the nineteenth century.

Material enclosed in parentheses may range from a single word to a short sentence. A short sentence in parentheses may stand by itself or be contained within another sentence.

Use punctuation marks within the parentheses when the punctuation belongs to the parenthetical matter. Do not use punctuation within the parentheses if such punctuation belongs to the sentence as a whole.

EXAMPLES   Fill in the application carefully. (Use a pen.)

That old house (it was built at the turn of the century) may soon become a landmark.

After we ate dinner (we had leftovers again), we went to the mall.

Exercise 3   Using Parentheses Correctly

Use parentheses to set off the parenthetical elements in the following sentences.

EXAMPLE   1. A fly-specked calendar it was five years out-of-date hung on the kitchen wall.

1. *A fly-specked calendar (it was five years out-of-date) hung on the kitchen wall.*

1. I have read all the *Oz* books that I own a considerable number.
2. Edna St. Vincent Millay 1892–1950 began writing poetry as a child.
3. In 1850, California entered the Union as a free state read more about free states in Chapter 5.
4. Gwendolyn Brooks her first book was *A Street in Bronzeville* has received high praise from critics.

5. Killer whales they're the ones with the black-and-white markings often migrate more than one thousand miles annually.

6. We arrived in Poland through the port city of Gdańsk called Danzig in German.

7. The black rat scientific name *Rattus rattus* is found on every continent.

8. During the French Revolution and the Terror 1789–1793, France underwent dramatic changes.

9. Paulo Coelho born 1947 is a bestselling Brazilian author.

10. The cooking of New Mexico my home state is rich and varied.

Dashes

Sometimes words, phrases, and sentences are used *parenthetically;* that is, they break into the main thought of a sentence.

EXAMPLES The penguin, **however,** has swum away.

Her worry **(how could she explain the mix-up?)** kept her up all night.

Most parenthetical elements are set off by commas or parentheses. Sometimes, however, parenthetical elements are such an interruption that a stronger mark is needed. In such cases, a dash is used.

15f. Use a dash to indicate an abrupt break in thought or speech or an unfinished statement or question.

EXAMPLES There are a thousand reasons—well, not a thousand, but many—that we should go.

Our dog—he's a long-haired dachshund—is too affectionate to be a good watchdog.

"Why—why can't I come, too?" Janet asked hesitatingly.

"You're being—" Tina began and then stopped.

15g. Use a dash to indicate *namely, that is,* or *in other words* or to otherwise introduce an explanation.

EXAMPLES I know what we could get Mom for her birthday—a new photo album. [namely]

She could put all those loose pictures—the ones she's taken since Christmas—in it. [that is]

NOTE Either a dash or a colon is acceptable in the first example above.

STYLE **TIP**

Do not overuse dashes. When you evaluate your writing, check to see that you have not used dashes carelessly for commas, semicolons, and end marks. Saving dashes for instances in which they are most appropriate will make them more effective.

MECHANICS

COMPUTER TIP

When you use a word processor, you can type two hyphens to make a dash. Do not leave a space before, between, or after the hyphens. When you write by hand, use an unbroken line about as long as two hyphens.

Reference Note

For information on using **colons,** see page 303.

MEETING THE CHALLENGE

Writers sometimes set off asides in sentences with dashes; other times they use parentheses. Each punctuation mark assigns a slightly different emphasis to the words set off. Which type of mark makes the words stand out? Which mark pushes them into the background? Write one sentence that contains words that are set off. Punctuate it first with parentheses, then with dashes. Read both sentences aloud. What effect does the punctuation have on meaning? Finally, try using commas to set off the words. Do commas work? Why or why not?

Exercise 4 **Inserting Dashes in Sentences**

Insert dashes where they are appropriate in the following sentences.

EXAMPLE
1. The winner is but I don't want to give it away yet.
1. The winner is—but I don't want to give it away yet.

2. It was an exciting game Brazil had taken the lead, but Italy scored in overtime.
2. It was an exciting game—Brazil had taken the lead, but Italy scored in overtime.

1. Tom said, "I'd like to thank" and then blushed and sat down.
2. We were surprised in fact, amazed to learn that the game had been called off.
3. The valedictorian that is, the student with the highest average will be given a scholarship.
4. She remembered what she wanted to tell them the plane was leaving at seven, not eight.
5. My brother's engagement it's been kept a secret till now will be announced Sunday.
6. The ancient Mediterranean seafaring cultures the Phoenician, the Greek, and the Roman all used versions of the trireme, a ship driven by three rows of oars.
7. The truth is and I'm sure you realize this we have no way of getting to the airport.
8. The manager of the restaurant I can't remember his name said he would reserve a table for us.
9. Because Maria she's the one who accompanies us will be away next week, choral practice will be postponed until the following week.
10. Very few carmakers three, to be precise offer models exclusively with full-time all-wheel drive.

┌HELP──
Although some sentences in Review B can be corrected in more than one way, you need to give only one revision for each.

Review A **Using Hyphens, Dashes, and Parentheses Correctly**

Rewrite each of the following sentences, inserting hyphens, dashes, and parentheses where they are needed. If a sentence is already correct, write C.

EXAMPLE
1. State flags you can tell by looking at those shown on the next page are as different as the states themselves.
1. State flags—you can tell by looking at those shown on the next page—are as different as the states themselves.

1. I think the shield on the Oklahoma flag reflects that state's pre statehood years as the territorial home of the Osage, the Cherokee, and other American Indian peoples.
2. "What kind of tree is in the center of the South Carolina flag?" Emilio asked. "Is it oh, it's a palmetto."
3. Two goddesses Ceres, or the goddess of agriculture, and Liberty are in the center of New Jersey's flag.
4. On the Colorado flag, one third of the background is white and the rest is blue.
5. Arkansas by the way, a major diamond-producing state has a large diamond on its flag.
6. An ancient Pueblo symbol of the all important sun is on New Mexico's flag.
7. The Union Jack of the United Kingdom look closely is on a corner of the Hawaiian flag.
8. "The Texas flag is red, white, and blue and contains one lone star because" Megan said before she was interrupted.
9. Blue is a dominant color in forty one state flags.
10. Only one state flag Washington's has a green background.

Review B Using Hyphens, Dashes, and Parentheses Correctly

Insert hyphens, dashes, and parentheses where they are needed in the following sentences. Do not add commas. If a sentence is already correct, write *C*.

EXAMPLE
    1. You might be able to tell from the photograph on the next page that the Comanche chief Quanah Parker 1845–1911 was a man of strong character.

    1. *You might be able to tell from the photograph on the next page that the Comanche chief Quanah Parker (1845–1911) was a man of strong character.*

1. Parker can you tell this from the photograph? was both a great war chief and a great peace chief.
2. He was the son of a Comanche tribal leader and a young woman Cynthia Ann Parker who was captured during a raid on a Texas homestead.
3. In the 1870s, Parker himself led a band of Comanche warriors in the Texas Panhandle.
4. Parker surrendered with his band the Quahadi in 1875; they were the last Comanches on the southern plains to surrender.
5. After surrendering, Parker became a prosperous rancher quite a change of lifestyle and even owned railroad stock.
6. In fact, he embodied the ideal of the self made man.
7. Parker encouraged his people to learn modern ways and to farm.
8. Parker guided the Comanches his title was principal chief during difficult times after the war ended.
9. In later years, he went to Washington, D.C., and this fact may surprise you became a friend of President Theodore Roosevelt.
10. The Texas city called Quanah a Comanche word meaning "sweet smelling" was named after this chief.

Ellipsis Points

15h. Use ellipsis points (. . .) to mark omissions from quoted materials and pauses in a written passage.

ORIGINAL   The streetlights along Toole Street, which meandered down-hill from the Language Academy to the town, were already lit and twinkled mistily through the trees. Standing at the gates were small groups of students, clustered together according to nationality. As Myles passed by, he could not help overhearing intense conversation in Spanish, German, and Japanese; all of his students had momentarily abandoned English in the urgency of deciding where to go for the weekend and how to get there.

(1) When you omit words from the middle of a sentence, use three spaced ellipsis points.

EXAMPLE   The streetlights along Toole Street **. . .** were already lit and twinkled mistily through the trees.

NOTE   Be sure to include a space before the first ellipsis point and after the last one.

(2) When you omit words at the beginning of a sentence within a quoted passage, keep the previous sentence's end punctuation and follow it with the ellipsis points.

EXAMPLE   Standing at the gates were small groups of students, clustered together according to nationality. . . . [A]ll of his students had momentarily abandoned English in the urgency of deciding where to go for the weekend and how to get there.

NOTE   Be sure not to begin a quoted passage with ellipsis points.

(3) When you omit words at the end of a sentence within a quoted passage, keep the sentence's end punctuation and follow it with the ellipsis points.

EXAMPLE   Standing at the gates were small groups of students. . . . As Myles passed by, he could not help overhearing intense conversation in Spanish, German, and Japanese; all of his students had momentarily abandoned English in the urgency of deciding where to go for the weekend and how to get there.

(4) When you omit one or more complete sentences from a quoted passage, keep the previous sentence's end punctuation and follow it with the ellipsis points.

EXAMPLE   The streetlights along Toole Street, which meandered downhill from the Language Academy to the town, were already lit and twinkled mistily through the trees. . . . As Myles passed by, he could not help overhearing intense conversation in Spanish, German, and Japanese; all of his students had momentarily abandoned English in the urgency of deciding where to go for the weekend and how to get there.

(5) To show that a full line or more of poetry has been omitted, use an entire line of spaced periods.

ORIGINAL   Half a league, half a league,
Half a league onward,
All in the valley of Death
Rode the six hundred.
"Forward the Light Brigade!
Charge for the guns!" he said.
Into the valley of Death
Rode the six hundred.

Alfred, Lord Tennyson,
"The Charge of the Light Brigade"

┌HELP┐
Notice in the example to the left that the *a* beginning *all* has been capitalized because it begins the sentence following the ellipsis points. Brackets are used around the *A* to show that it was not capitalized in the original passage.

MECHANICS

WITH OMISSION	Half a league, half a league,
	Half a league onward,
	• • • • • • • • • •
	Into the valley of Death
	Rode the six hundred.

Notice that the line of periods is as long as the line above it.

(6) To indicate a pause in dialogue, use three spaced ellipsis points with a space before the first point and a space after the last point.

EXAMPLE   "Well, I could **• • •** I can't honestly say," he hedged.

Brackets

15i. Use brackets to enclose an explanation within quoted or parenthetical material.

EXAMPLES   In her acceptance speech, the star said: "I am honored by this award **[**the Oscar**]**, and I want to thank my parents and everybody who worked with me." [The words are enclosed in brackets to show that they have been inserted into the quotation and are not the exact words of the speaker.]

The growth of the Irish economy in recent years is a great success story. (See page 15 **[**Graph 1A**]** for a time line.)

Exercise 5 **Using Ellipsis Points and Brackets Correctly**

Revise the following sentences, using ellipsis points and brackets correctly.

EXAMPLE   **1.** Franklin said, "That cat just . . . . . flew up to the top of the refrigerator!"

     1. Franklin said, "That cat just . . . flew up to the top of the refrigerator!"

1. At the committee meeting, Judy said, "We have to make this (the Homecoming Dance) the most memorable event of the year."
2. "I . . I can't believe she would have said that!" Aaron exclaimed.
3. The levels of photosynthesis activity varied drastically with the different cycles of light and darkness. (See page 347 (Chart 17D) for details.)
4. "Do you really believe they have a chance to win the (Stanley) Cup this year?" asked Martin skeptically.
5. "But . . . . . then how can we be sure it's true?" Carla asked.

Chapter Review

A. Using Hyphens to Divide Words at the Ends of Lines

Write each of the following words, using a hyphen to indicate where the word may be divided at the end of a line. If a word should not be divided, write *do not divide.*

1. baked
2. complete
3. input
4. unexpected
5. yo-yo

6. bagel
7. thorough
8. divide
9. away
10. whale

B. Using Hyphens, Dashes, and Parentheses Correctly

Use hyphens, dashes, and parentheses to punctuate the following sentences. Do not add commas to these sentences.

┌HELP┐

Some sentences in Part B may be correctly punctuated in more than one way, but you need to give only one answer per item.

11. Yuri, our Russian exchange student, will be twenty one on the first of September this year.
12. "That sounds like" gasped Jeff as he dashed for the window.
13. A former all state quarterback, our coach insists that there is no such thing as a self made star.
14. A dog I think it was a poodle jumped into the lake.
15. The Historical Society the local members, that is will conduct a tour of the harbor.
16. My sister Patricia she is in college now wants to be a marine biologist.
17. This recipe for savory bread calls for one and one half cups of whole wheat flour.
18. At the auction someone bid one thousand dollars for a pre Revolutionary desk.
19. The Inca empire flourished during the reign of the emperor Pachacuti 1438–1471.
20. Next month of course, I'll write you before then we're going on an overnight trip.

MECHANICS

21. John F. Kennedy 1917–1963 was the first Roman Catholic president of the United States.

22. Four of our former classmates yes, Beth was among them traveled to Australia with the U.S. athletes.

23. My grandparents will celebrate their fiftieth wedding anni versary on the third of October.

24. My friend Juan he went back to Puerto Rico has always wanted to be a veterinarian.

25. Linda Wing she is the ex champion will award the trophies.

26. Doing homework and seeing their improvement raised their self esteem.

27. Add exactly one half tablespoon of sugar to that recipe.

28. Napoleon's reign as emperor of France 1804–1815 was marked by great achievements and great setbacks.

29. "You don't mean to" exclaimed Renata.

30. The Friends of Silesia the Midwestern chapter, of course will have their annual dinner in Chicago this year.

31. Four players have been chosen for the state's all star team.

32. Beth I don't know her last name plays the lead role in the play.

33. She said wearily she often sounded weary "I'll go tomorrow."

34. By mid January twenty four inches of snow had fallen.

35. Mr. Brandt our neighbor of twelve years moved back to Germany after that country's reunification.

36. Franklin D. Roosevelt 1882–1945 was the thirty second president.

37. The ex governor of Kansas will speak at the reception.

38. Blake Ricky Blake, I mean was waiting for me downstairs.

39. Reggae music I heard it in the West Indies is popular here.

40. We all grew up in the same town Boise, Idaho.

C. Using Hyphens, Dashes, Parentheses, Ellipsis Points, and Brackets Correctly

Correctly use hyphens, dashes, parentheses, ellipsis points, and brackets where needed in the following sentences. If a sentence is already correct, write *C*.

41. The Italian flag red, white, and green is similar in design to the French tricolor flag red, white, and blue.

42. "Well, I'll try . . . . . or maybe not," she stammered.

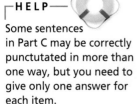

┌HELP┐

Some sentences in Part C may be correctly punctutated in more than one way, but you need to give only one answer for each item.

43. The large building on the corner of Elm Street is the headquarters of the organization.

44. The Battle of Verdun February–July 1916 was a crucial French victory over the Germans in World War I.

45. In Mexico, San Miguel de Allende population approximately 80,000 is a popular destination for American artists and retirees.

46. [See page 100 (Map 2) for a more detailed look at the developing military situation.]

47. "My goodness!" exclaimed Grandpa. "Isn't that the?" and he hurriedly consulted his program.

48. The museum's preColumbian artifacts are well worth seeing.

49. I can think of dozens of people well, maybe not dozens, but quite a few who would agree with me.

50. Lorenzo Da Ponte was the man who wrote the libretto for Mozart's opera *Don Giovanni* and later and this came as a surprise to me taught Italian in New York City.

Writing Application
Writing a Report

Using Punctuation Write a short report of no more than three paragraphs on your favorite author. Use at least three of the five elements of punctuation (hyphens, dashes, parentheses, ellipsis points, and brackets) discussed in this chapter.

Prewriting First, gather biographical information on your chosen author. Include any details you find interesting or unusual.

Writing As you write your first draft, think about how you plan to organize your information: by type of writing (fiction, nonfiction, poetry) or chronologically; or you could focus on a particular story, novel, or poem. Compare your draft to other short treatments of the author.

Revising Read through your draft. Is the organization clear? If not, add, cut, or rearrange information to make it clearer.

Publishing Proofread your essay for errors in grammar, spelling, and punctuation. You and your classmates may want to post the finished report on the class bulletin board or on a school Web page.

Spelling
Improving Your Spelling

Diagnostic Preview

A. Choosing Correct Spelling

Choose the correct word from the pair in parentheses.

EXAMPLE   **1.** I was very careful not to (*brake, break*) the vase.

        1. break

1. After the Paris-Lyon high-speed train (*past, passed*) the waving onlookers and raced (*threw, through*) the tunnel, it reached a maximum speed of more than 180 miles per hour.

2. When the new (*principle, principal*) talked to her staff, she tried to get (*there, their, they're*) honest opinions.

3. The auctioneer (*led, lead*) the bidding on the original White House (*stationary, stationery*) on which was written President Roosevelt's actual signature.

4. Cuenca, near Madrid, is a lovely old town that is known for its (*piece, peace*) and (*quite, quiet*).

5. My aunt (*who's, whose*) picture appeared in yesterday's paper was (*formerly, formally*) a vice-president at First State Bank.

6. (*Altogether, All together*), the guitar music, the songs, and the aroma of *pan dulce* were a wonderful (*compliment, complement*) to the relaxed atmosphere.

7. Of (*course, coarse*), I found it nearly impossible to (*choose, chose*) between those two movies.

8. I took a (*plain, plane*) to Houston, and I visited family members who live (*there, their, they're*).
9. Although (*its, it's*) smaller than both Geneva and Zurich, Bern is the (*capital, capitol*) of Switzerland.
10. The new British (*council, consul, counsel*) and her husband returned to the embassy after having coffee and (*desert, dessert*) with the emir.

B. Proofreading a Paragraph for Spelling Errors

Identify any misspelled or misused words in the following paragraph, and then write the words correctly. If all the words in a sentence are already correct, write *C*.

EXAMPLE   **[1]** I have read about Santa Fe, but I have never been their.
    1.   their—there

[11] Santa Fe, New Mexico, is an all together charming and unusual city. [12] It is not only the capitol of the state but also a major tourist center. [13] The city lies in the north-central part of New Mexico at a hieght of about 7,000 feet and enjoys outstanding whether year-round. [14] The altitude sometimes has a bad affect on first-time visitors. [15] They are adviced not to exert themselves for the first day or so. [16] Santa Fe is one of the oldest citys in the United States. [17] It was founded in 1610 as the seat of government of the Spanish colony of New Mexico. [18] In 1912, New Mexico joined the United States as the 47th state. [19] I think the food in Santa Fe is awsome. [20] I suggest sampleing Southwestern cuisine, some of which is very spicy.

Good Spelling Habits

16a. To learn the spelling of a word, pronounce it, study it, and write it.

(1) Pronounce words carefully.

Mispronunciation can lead to misspelling. For instance, if you say *mis • chē • vē • əs* instead of *mis • chə • vəs*, you will be more likely to spell the word incorrectly.

• First, make sure that you know how to pronounce the word correctly, and then practice saying it.

┌HELP┐
If you are not sure how to pronounce a word, look in a dictionary. In the dictionary, you will usually find the pronunciation given in parentheses after the word. The information in parentheses generally shows the sounds used, the syllable breaks, and any accented syllables. A guide to the pronunciation symbols is usually found at the front of the dictionary.

- Second, study the word. Notice especially any parts that might be hard to remember.
- Third, write the word from memory. Check your spelling.
- If you misspelled the word, repeat the three steps of this process.

(2) Use a dictionary.

Whenever you find that you have misspelled a word, look it up in a dictionary. Don't guess about correct spelling.

(3) Spell by syllables.

A *syllable* is a word part that is pronounced as one uninterrupted sound.

EXAMPLES   thor • ough [two syllables]

              sep • a • rate [three syllables]

Instead of trying to learn how to pronounce a whole word, break it up into its syllables whenever possible. It's easier to learn a few letters at a time than to learn all of them at once.

Oral Practice   **Pronouncing Spelling Words Correctly**

Study the correct pronunciations in parentheses after each of the following words. Then, pronounce each word correctly three times.

1. athlete (ath′ • lēt′)
2. children (chil′ • drən)
3. drowned (drournd)
4. escape (e • skāp′)
5. library (lī′ • brer • ē)
6. lightning (līt′ • ning)
7. perhaps (pər • haps′)
8. probably (prŏb′ • ə • blē)

Exercise 1   **Spelling by Syllables**

Look up the following words in a dictionary, and divide each one into syllables. Pronounce each syllable correctly, and learn to spell the word by syllables.

EXAMPLE   1. possibility

             1. *pos • si • bil • i • ty*

1. representative
2. awkward
3. candidate
4. temperature
5. apparent
6. similar
7. definition
8. benefit
9. acquaintance
10. fascinate

(4) Proofread for careless spelling errors.

Re-read your writing carefully, and correct any mistakes and unclear letters. For example, make sure that your *i*'s are dotted, your *t*'s are crossed, and your *g*'s don't look like *q*'s.

(5) Keep a spelling notebook.

Divide each page into four columns:

COLUMN 1   Correctly spell the word you missed. (Never enter a misspelled word.)

COLUMN 2   Write the word again, dividing it into syllables and marking its accents.

COLUMN 3   Write the word once more, circling the letters that give you trouble.

COLUMN 4   Jot down any comments that might help you remember the correct spelling.

Here is an example of how you might make entries for two words that are often misspelled.

Correct Spelling	Syllables and Accents	Trouble Spot	Comments
probably	prob'•a•bly	prob(ab)ly	Pronounce both b's.
usually	u'•su•al•ly	usua(ll)y	usual+ly (Study rule 16f.)

COMPUTER TIP

Spellcheckers can help you proofread your writing. Even the best spellcheckers aren't foolproof, however. Many accept British spellings, obsolete words, archaic spellings, and words that are spelled correctly but used incorrectly (such as *affect* for *effect*). Always double-check your writing to make sure that your spelling is error-free.

Exercise 2   Spelling Commonly Misspelled Words

Copy each of the following words or expressions, paying special attention to the italicized letters. Then, without looking at this page or the copy you made of the correctly spelled words, write the words as a friend dictates them to you.

1. ans*w*er
2. a*w*kward
3. *wh*ole
4. to*w*ard
5. *kn*ow
6. knowle*d*ge
7. writt*en*
8. of*t*en
9. condem*n*
10. colum*n*
11. r*h*ythm
12. use*d* to
13. in*s*tead
14. *mea*nt
15. *a*isle
16. toni*gh*t
17. su*r*ely
18. tho*ugh*
19. thro*ugh*
20. ninety

MECHANICS

Spelling Rules

ie and *ei*

TIPS & TRICKS

Remember this rhyme:
I before *e* except after *c*
or when sounded like *a*
as in *neighbor* and
weigh.

16b. Write *ie* when the sound is long *e*, except after *c*.

EXAMPLES
achieve	chief	niece	shield	ceiling
believe	field	piece	thief	deceit
brief	grief	relief	yield	receive

EXCEPTIONS either, leisure, neither, seize, protein

16c. Write *ei* when the sound is not long *e*.

EXAMPLES
counterfeit	height	reign	forfeit
foreign	heir	veil	weigh

EXCEPTIONS friend, mischief, kerchief

NOTE Rules 16b and 16c apply only when the *i* and the *e* are in the same syllable.

EXAMPLES de • i • ty   sci • ence

–cede, –ceed, and *–sede*

16d. Only one English word ends in *–sede: supersede.* Only three words end in *–ceed: exceed, proceed,* and *succeed.* Almost all other words with this sound end in *–cede.*

EXAMPLES
accede	intercede	recede
concede	precede	secede

Exercise 3 Proofreading Sentences to Correct Spelling Errors

The following sentences contain errors involving the use of *ie, ei, –ceed, –cede,* and *–sede.* For each sentence, identify the misspelled word or words and then write them correctly. If a sentence has no spelling errors, write *C.*

EXAMPLE 1. On my birthday I recieved a wonderful gift.

1. *recieved—received*

1. My neighbor, who is a good freind of mine, went on a trip out West.
2. He sent me a Dream Catcher like those used by the Sioux to sheild themselves from bad dreams.

MECHANICS

3. Charms like this once hung in each tepee, and mine hangs from the cieling near my bed.

4. According to legend, bad dreams get caught in the web and only good ones succede in reaching the sleeper.

5. I do not really believe that my Dream Catcher can interceed on my behalf, but I have not had one bad dream since my birthday!

6. The Plains Indians moved their homes often, so their possessions could be niether bulky nor heavy.

7. Consequently, the Sioux who made the Dream Catcher used common, lightweight materials.

8. The twig bent into a ring is willow wood, and tiny glass beads represent nightmares siezed by the web.

9. Gracefully hanging from either side is a beautiful feather or a horsehair tassel.

10. Wonderful peices of workmanship like this help ensure that the culture of the Sioux will never resede into the past.

Adding Prefixes

16e. When a prefix is added to a word, the spelling of the original word itself remains the same.

EXAMPLES   im + mobile = im**mobile**   mis + spell = mis**spell**
             un + certain = un**certain**   over + rule = over**rule**

Adding Suffixes

16f. When the suffix *–ness* or *–ly* is added to a word, the spelling of the original word itself remains the same.

EXAMPLES   time + ly = **time**ly   even + ness = **even**ness
             real + ly = **real**ly   late + ness = **late**ness

EXCEPTIONS   1. Words ending in *y* usually change the *y* to *i* before *–ness* and *–ly:* empty—empt**i**ness; easy—eas**i**ly

             2. However, most one-syllable adjectives ending in *y* follow Rule 16f: shy—**shy**ly; dry—**dry**ness

             3. *True, due,* and *whole* drop the final *e* before *–ly:* truly, duly, wholly.

Exercise 4 **Spelling Words with Prefixes and Suffixes**

Spell each of the following words, including the prefix or suffix that is given.

EXAMPLE   **1.** un + common

            1. uncommon

1. un + necessary

2. il + legal

3. occasional + ly

4. cleanly + ness

5. mean + ness

6. im + moral

7. sly + ly

8. speedy + ly

9. same + ness

10. un + usual

16g. Drop the final silent *e* before adding a suffix that begins with a vowel.

EXAMPLES   tame + ing = **tam**ing   loose + est = **loos**est

            noble + er = **nobl**er   admire + ation = **admir**ation

            tickle + ish = **tickl**ish   move + able = **mov**able

EXCEPTIONS **1.** Keep the final silent *e* in most words ending in *ce* or *ge* before a suffix that begins with *a* or *o*:

            *knowledg**e**able, courag**e**ous.*

            Sometimes the *e* becomes *i*, as in *grac**i**ous* and *spac**i**ous*.

            2. To avoid confusion with other words, keep the final silent *e* in some words:

            *dy**e**ing* and *dying, sing**e**ing* and *singing*

            3. mile + age = mil**e**age

Exercise 5 **Spelling Words with Suffixes**

Spell each of the following words, including the suffix that is given.

EXAMPLE   **1.** write + ing

            1. writing

1. become + ing

2. guide + ance

3. continue + ous

4. surprise + ed

5. determine + ation

6. sense + ible

7. save + ing

8. advantage + ous

9. dine + ing

10. hope + ed

16h. Keep the final silent *e* when adding a suffix that begins with a consonant.

EXAMPLES   safe + ty = saf**e**ty   large + ly = larg**e**ly

                   hope + ful = hop**e**ful   awe + some = aw**e**some

                   care + less = car**e**less   pave + ment = pav**e**ment

EXCEPTIONS   awe + ful = **aw**ful   true + ly = **tru**ly

                   nine + th = **nin**th   argue + ment = **argu**ment

---

Review A **Spelling Words with Suffixes**

Spell each of the following words, including the suffix that is given.

EXAMPLE   **1.** use + less

              1. *useless*

1. announce + ment   **6.** station + ary

2. use + age   **7.** hope + less

3. imagine + ary   **8.** type + ing

4. care + ful   **9.** advertise + ment

5. write + ing   **10.** use + ful

16i. When a word ends in *y* preceded by a consonant, change the *y* to *i* before any suffix except one beginning with *i*.

EXAMPLES   tidy + er = tid**i**er   glory + ous = glor**i**ous

                   worry + ed = worr**i**ed   terrify + ing = terrif**y**ing

EXCEPTIONS   **1.** Some one-syllable words:

                      shy + ness = sh**y**ness   sky + ward = sk**y**ward

                  2. *lady* and *baby* with most suffixes:

                      lad**y**like   lad**y**ship   bab**y**hood

16j. When a word ends in *y* preceded by a vowel, simply add the suffix.

EXAMPLES   play + ful = **play**ful   boy + hood = **boy**hood

                   array + ed = **array**ed   gray + est = **gray**est

                   pray + ing = **pray**ing   pay + ment = **pay**ment

EXCEPTIONS   day + ly = **dai**ly   pay + ed = **pai**d

                   say + ed = **sai**d   lay + ed = **lai**d

MECHANICS

Exercise 6   Spelling Words with Suffixes

Spell each of the following words, including the suffix that is given.

EXAMPLE   **1.** ply + able

      1. pliable

1. extraordinary + ly   **6.** baby + ish
2. try + ing   **7.** say + ing
3. deny + al   **8.** joy + ful
4. satisfy + ed   **9.** bray + ing
5. rely + able   **10.** fly + ing

Doubling Final Consonants

16k. When a word ends in a consonant, double the final consonant before a suffix that begins with a vowel only if the word:

- has only one syllable or is accented on the last syllable

and

- ends in a *single* consonant preceded by a *single* vowel

EXAMPLES   dim + est = di**mm**est   red + ish = re**dd**ish

            plan + ed = pla**nn**ed   propel + er = prope**ll**er

            sit + ing = si**tt**ing   refer + ed = refe**rr**ed

Otherwise, simply add the suffix.

EXAMPLES   jump + ed = **jump**ed   tunnel + ing = **tunnel**ing

            sprint + er = **sprint**er   appear + ance = **appear**ance

HELP

The final consonant in some words may or may not be doubled. In such cases, both spellings are equally correct.

EXAMPLES

travel + er = trave**ler** *or* trave**ller**

shovel + ed = shove**led** *or* shove**lled**

Exercise 7   Spelling Words with Suffixes

Spell each of the following words, including the suffix that is given.

EXAMPLE   **1.** rebel + ed

      1. rebelled

1. swim + er   **6.** prepare + ing
2. accept + ance   **7.** control + ed
3. number + ing   **8.** slim + er
4. excel + ed   **9.** prefer + ing
5. riot + ous   **10.** glamor + ous

MECHANICS

Review B **Spelling Words with Prefixes and Suffixes**

The following paragraph contains spelling errors involving the use of prefixes and suffixes. For each sentence, write the misspelled word or words correctly. If a sentence is already correct, write *C*.

EXAMPLE **[1]** Few people know that a teenage boy helped create the awsome Mount Rushmore monument.

1. *awesome*

┌ **HELP** ─

No proper nouns in Review B are misspelled.

[1] Begining when he was fifteen, Lincoln Borglum helped his famous father, Gutzon Borglum, who planed and made this gigantic sculpture. [2] First, Gutzon Borglum built a plaster model one-twelfth as large as the completted sculpture would be. [3] On top of this model Borglum attached the equipment from which he controlled a plumb line. [4] The plumb line could be dangled in front of each president's likness to record carefuly each feature. [5] Lincoln Borglum helped in making these mea-surments. [6] Then, on top of the cliff, they fastenned an identical machine twelve times as large. [7] Lincoln Borglum was one of the workers who operatted this machine. [8] Using it, he copied the movements of the smaller machine and marked exactly where to cut away the rock. [9] The closer the workers got to finishing the faces, the more carefully the Borglums studied the heads. [10] There were numerous problems, but the monument was finally inaugurated in 1941.

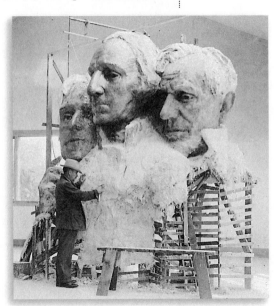

Forming Plurals of Nouns

16l. To form the plurals of most English nouns, simply add *s*.

SINGULAR	boat	care	storm	radio	Jim
PLURAL	boat**s**	care**s**	storm**s**	radio**s**	Jim**s**

16m. To form the plurals of other nouns, follow these rules.

(1) If the noun ends in *s*, *x*, *z*, *ch*, or *sh*, add *es*.

SINGULAR	moss	fox	Sanchez	clutch	dish
PLURAL	moss**es**	fox**es**	Sanchez**es**	clutch**es**	dish**es**

NOTE Some one-syllable words ending in *z* double the final consonant when forming plurals.

EXAMPLES   quiz   fez

               qui**zz**es   fe**zz**es

Exercise 8   Spelling the Plurals of Nouns

Spell the plural of each of the following nouns.

EXAMPLE   **1.** Evans

            1. Evanses

1. guess	**6.** boss
2. ax	**7.** student
3. tongue	**8.** Owens
4. cafeteria	**9.** box
5. wash	**10.** ditch

(2) If the noun ends in *y* preceded by a consonant, change the *y* to *i* and add *es*.

SINGULAR	fly	pony	cry	story
PLURAL	fl**ies**	pon**ies**	cr**ies**	stor**ies**

EXCEPTION   plurals of proper nouns: the Hard**ys,** the Car**ys**

TIPS & TRICKS

Noticing how the plural is pronounced will help you remember whether to change the *f* to *v*.

(3) For some nouns ending in *f* or *fe*, add *s*. For other nouns ending in *f* or *fe*, change the *f* to *v* and add *s* or *es*.

EXAMPLES	giraffe	roof	self	life	elf	thief	wolf
	giraffe**s**	roof**s**	sel**ves**	li**ves**	el**ves**	thie**ves**	wol**ves**

NOTE Some nouns can correctly form their plurals either way.

EXAMPLES   hoof   scarf

               hoo**ves**   scar**ves**

                 or   *or*

               hoof**s**   scarf**s**

MECHANICS

Exercise 9 Spelling the Plurals of Nouns

Spell the plural of each of the following nouns.

EXAMPLES   **1.** shelf
     1. shelves

     2. poppy
     2. poppies

1. thief   **6.** wife
2. chef   **7.** loaf
3. theory   **8.** comedy
4. gulf   **9.** trophy
5. ally   **10.** self

(4) **If the noun ends in *o* preceded by a vowel, add *s*.**

SINGULAR	radio	cameo	kangaroo	Julio
PLURAL	radio**s**	cameo**s**	kangaroo**s**	Julio**s**

(5) **If the noun ends in *o* preceded by a consonant, add *es*.**

SINGULAR	echo	hero	tomato	veto
PLURAL	echo**es**	hero**es**	tomato**es**	veto**es**

EXCEPTIONS Some common nouns ending in *o* preceded by a consonant (especially musical terms) and proper nouns form the plural by adding only *s*.

SINGULAR	peso	sombrero	photo	alto
	piano	solo	Sotho	Sakamoto
PLURAL	peso**s**	sombrero**s**	photo**s**	alto**s**
	piano**s**	solo**s**	Sotho**s**	Sakamoto**s**

NOTE A number of nouns that end in *o* preceded by a consonant have two correct plural forms.

SINGULAR	cargo	grotto	mosquito
PLURAL	cargo**s**	grotto**s**	mosquito**s**
	or	*or*	*or*
	cargo**es**	grotto**es**	mosquito**es**

The best way to determine the plurals of words ending in *o* preceded by a consonant is to check their spellings in a dictionary.

HELP

To correctly complete Exercise 9, you may wish to refer to a recent dictionary.

MECHANICS

HELP

To correctly
complete Exercise 10,
you may wish to refer to
a recent dictionary.

Exercise 10 · Spelling the Plurals of Nouns

Spell the plural of each of the following nouns.

EXAMPLE   **1.** stereo

     1. *stereos*

1. igloo	**6.** banjo
2. soprano	**7.** taco
3. patio	**8.** cello
4. veto	**9.** Romeo
5. torpedo	**10.** studio

(6) The plurals of some nouns are formed in irregular ways.

SINGULAR	child	foot	goose	man	tooth
PLURAL	child**ren**	**fee**t	ge**e**se	m**e**n	t**ee**th

(7) Some nouns have the same form in both the singular and the plural.

SINGULAR and PLURAL	Japanese	spacecraft	sheep

Compound Nouns

(8) For most compound nouns, form the plural of only the last word in the compound.

SINGULAR	spoonbill	smashup	icebox	six-year-old
PLURAL	spoonbill**s**	smashup**s**	icebox**es**	six-year-old**s**

(9) For many compound nouns in which one of the words is modified by the other word or words, form the plural of the word modified.

SINGULAR	sister-in-law	notary public	attorney at law
PLURAL	sister**s**-in-law	notar**ies** public	attorney**s** at law

NOTE   Whenever you are not sure about how to spell the plural form of a compound noun, check a recent dictionary.

Exercise 11 · Spelling the Plurals of Nouns

Spell the plural form of each of the following nouns.

EXAMPLE   **1.** ox

     1. *oxen*

1. Vietnamese
2. earmuff
3. mouse
4. cross-reference
5. goose

6. brother-in-law
7. aircraft
8. woman
9. runner-up
10. twenty-year-old

Latin and Greek Loan Words

(10) Some nouns borrowed from Latin and Greek form the plural as in the original language.

SINGULAR	PLURAL
alumn**us** [male]	alumn**i**
alumn**a** [female]	alumn**ae**
analy**sis**	analy**ses**
cri**sis**	cri**ses**
dat**um**	dat**a**
phenomen**on**	phenomen**a**

NOTE A few Latin and Greek loan words have two correct plural forms.

SINGULAR	appendix	formula
PLURAL	append**ices** *or* append**ixes**	formul**as** *or* formul**ae**

Check a dictionary to find the preferred spelling of a plural loan word. The preferred spelling is generally the one listed first.

Numerals, Letters, Symbols, and Words Used as Words

(11) To form the plurals of numerals, most capital letters, symbols, and words used as words, add either an *s* or an apostrophe and an *s*.

EXAMPLES   Put the **4's** (*or* **4s**) and the **T's** (*or* **Ts**) in the second column.

Change the **&'s** (*or* **&s**) to **and's** (*or* **ands**).

My parents were teenagers during the **'60's** (*or* **'60s**).

Many immigrants came to this country during the **1800's** (*or* **1800s**).

BORN LOSER reprinted by permission of Newspaper Enterprise Association, Inc.

HELP

Even though some of the items in Exercise 12 and Review C have two correct plural forms, you need to give only one form for each. You may wish to refer to an up-to-date dictionary.

HELP

When corrected, some lines of the poem in Review C will no longer rhyme.

To prevent confusion, always use an apostrophe and an *s* to form the plurals of lowercase letters, certain capital letters, and some words used as words.

EXAMPLES   What do these **a's** in the margins mean?

Ramon got **A's** last semester.

Her muffled **tee-hee's** did not interrupt the speaker.

Exercise 12 **Spelling the Plurals of Nouns, Numerals, Letters, Symbols, and Words Used as Words**

Give the plural form of each of the following words, numerals, symbols, and words used as words.

EXAMPLE   **1.** *o*

1. *o's*

1. +   6. *C*
2. parenthesis   7. 1840
3. *so*   8. index
4. *9*   9. *!*
5. fulcrum   10. *ho-ho-ho*

Review C **Spelling the Plurals of Nouns**

Most lines in the following silly poem contain misspelled words. Correct each misspelled word. If a line contains no misspellings, write C.

EXAMPLES   **1.** A group of mans and womens started up a local zoo.

1. *men; women*

2. They bought a lot of animales and put them all on view.

2. *animals*

1. They caged the oxes with the gooses, the lion with the calfs,
2. The butterflys and mouses with the burroes and giraffs.
3. Armys of people soon arrived. In jalopys they were piled,
4. With wifes and husbands, son-in-laws, and lots of little childs.
5. The boys and girls rode poneys, and they fed the sheeps and deer,
6. And thought their folks were heros to bring them all right here.
7. The mosquitoses had a fine time feasting on the kangarooes;
8. Most of the other animals minded their *ps* and *qs*.
9. The moon shone brightly through the leafs as night began to fall.
10. Why do you think the lion had the nicest day of all?

Spelling Numbers

16n. Spell out a number that begins a sentence.

EXAMPLE **One thousand five hundred** band members attended this year's State Marching Band Festival.

16o. Within a sentence, spell out numbers that can be written in one or two words; use numerals for other numbers.

EXAMPLES I have only **one** week in which to write **four** reports.

We picked **twenty-one** quarts of peaches.

Agnes has sold **116** magazine subscriptions.

EXCEPTION 1 If you use some numbers that have one or two words and some that have more than two words, use numerals for all of them.

EXAMPLE Our school had **563** freshmen, **327** sophomores, **143** juniors, and **90** seniors.

EXCEPTION 2 Use numerals for dates when you include the name of the month. Always use numerals for years.

EXAMPLES School closes on June **6.** [This example could also be correctly written as *the sixth of June,* but not *June 6th.*]

Egypt fell to the Romans in **30** B.C.

16p. Spell out numbers used to indicate order.

EXAMPLE My brother graduated **second** [not *2nd*] in his class.

Reference Note

For more about **writing dates,** see page 287.

Write five original sentences, following the directions given below.

EXAMPLE   **1.** Write a sentence giving the year in which your best friend was born.

      1. *Rudy Garza was born in 1986.*

1. Write a sentence beginning with a number.
2. Write a sentence containing two numbers, both of which can be written in one or two words.
3. Write a sentence containing three numbers, two of them with one or two words and one of them with more than two words.
4. Write a sentence using a number to indicate the order in which a person placed in a race.
5. Write a sentence giving the month and date of your birthday.

Words Often Confused

You can prevent many spelling errors by learning the difference between the words grouped together in this section. Some of them are confusing because they are *homonyms*—that is, they are pronounced alike. Others are confusing because they are spelled the same or nearly the same.

advice	[noun] *counsel* Why don't you ask your father for *advice*?
advise	[verb] *to give advice* The weather service *advises* boaters.
affect	[verb] *to influence* Do sunspots *affect* the weather?
effect	[verb] *to bring about, to accomplish*; [noun] *result, consequence* Our new boss *effected* some startling changes in our use of technology. Name three *effects* of the Industrial Revolution on family life.
all ready	[adjective] *everyone or everything prepared* We were *all ready* to go.
already	[adverb] *previously* Sharon has *already* gone.

all right	[This is the only acceptable spelling. Although the spelling *alright* is in some dictionaries, it has not become standard usage.]
all together	[adjective or adverb] *everyone or everything in the same place* *All together* at last, the travelers relaxed. The band simply must play *all together*.
altogether	[adverb] *entirely* You're *altogether* mistaken, I fear.
altar	[noun] *a table used for a religious ceremony* The *altar* was draped with a white cloth.
alter	[verb] *to change* This actor can *alter* his appearance.
brake	[noun] *a stopping device*; [verb] *to stop* The *brakes* on our car are good. I *brake* for deer.
break	[verb] *to shatter, sever* A high-pitched sound can *break* glass.
capital	[noun] *center of government*; *money or property used in business*; [adjective] *punishable by death*; *of major importance*; *excellent*; *uppercase* Raleigh is the *capital* of North Carolina. We need more *capital* to buy the factory. Is killing a police officer a *capital* crime? I made a *capital* error in judgment. This is a *capital* detective story. You need a *capital* letter here.
capitol	[noun] *building, statehouse* The *capitol* is on East Edenton Street.
choose	[verb, used for present and future tense] *select* You may *choose* your own partner.
chose	[verb, past tense, rhymes with *nose*] *selected* They *chose* to postpone the meeting.

(continued)

Reference Note

In the Glossary of Usage, Chapter 9, you can find many other words that are often confused or misused. You can also look them up in a dictionary.

MECHANICS

TIPS & TRICKS

To remember the correct spelling of *capitol,* use this memory aid: There is a d**o**me on the capit**o**l.

(continued)

coarse	[adjective] *rough, crude* This *coarse* fabric is very durable. He never uses *coarse* language.
course	[noun] *path of action or progress; unit of study; track or way; part of a meal;* [also used with *of* to mean *naturally* or *certainly*] The airplane strayed off its *course* in the storm. I'm taking an algebra *course*. She's at the golf *course*. The main *course* at the banquet was roasted turkey with dressing. Cats, of *course*, are predators.

Exercise 14 Distinguishing Between Words Often Confused

Choose the correct word or expression from the pair in parentheses.

EXAMPLE **1.** I was proud to (*accept, except*) the award.

1. *accept*

1. Betty has (*all ready, already*) handed in her paper.
2. (*All right, Alright*), I'll wrap the package now.
3. The mechanic adjusted the (*brakes, breaks*).
4. Do you know which city is the (*capital, capitol*) of your state?
5. They were (*all together, altogether*) at dinner.
6. The rule goes into (*affect, effect*) today.
7. His (*coarse, course*) manners offended everyone.
8. A fragile piece of china (*brakes, breaks*) easily.
9. Our state (*capital, capitol*) is built of limestone and marble.
10. When will they (*choose, chose*) the winners?

Exercise 15 Proofreading for Words Often Confused

Correct the errors in word choice in the following sentences.

EXAMPLE **1.** After taking that class, we were already to shoot our own videos.

1. *all ready*

1. The best moviemaking advise I ever received came from Ms. Herrera.

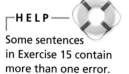

┌HELP─

Some sentences in Exercise 15 contain more than one error.

MECHANICS

2. She taught the video coarse that I choose as an elective last semester.
3. Once we would-be moviemakers were altogether, she said simply, "Rule number one: Take the lens cap off."
4. Everyone laughed, but she said, "It's no joke—in every class at least one person brakes this one basic rule."
5. "Of coarse," she added, "forgetting to put a videocassette in the camera has much the same affect."
6. If you chose to make your own home videos, I'd advice you to remember Ms. Herrera's words.
7. They will seriously effect you.
8. I remembered her advice when I went to the steps of the capital for my first shoot.
9. I checked the lighting and angle and chose a subject that was all together satisfactory.
10. When I started to shoot, I realized I had made a capitol error—I had forgotten to take the lens cap off!

complement	[noun] *something that completes or makes perfect;* [verb] *to complete or make perfect* The office now has a full *complement* of personnel. The rug *complemented* the cozy room.
compliment	[noun] *a remark that expresses approval, praise, or admiration;* [verb] *to pay a compliment* Ms. Garcia paid me a *compliment.* The review *complimented* Rosemary on her performance.
consul	[noun] *the representative of a foreign country* Did you meet the Greek *consul* at the reception?
council	[noun] *a group called together to accomplish a job* Our town *council* meets next Tuesday.
counsel	[noun] *advice;* [verb] *to give advice* Her *counsel* is invaluable to the president. The engineers *counsel* them to use additional support for the crossbeams.

(continued)

TIPS & TRICKS

To remember the correct spelling of *complement,* use this memory aid: A compl**e**ment compl**e**tes.

(continued)

councilor	[noun] *a member of a council* At the council meeting, my mother plans to introduce Dr. Watkins, the new *councilor*.
counselor	[noun] *one who gives advice* I don't think I'm qualified to act as your *counselor*.
desert	[noun, pronounced des'•ert] *a dry region* The Sahara is the world's largest *desert*.
desert	[verb, pronounced de•sert'] *to leave* She would never *desert* her comrades.
dessert	[noun, pronounced des•sert'] *a sweet, final course of a meal* What would you like for dessert tonight?

Exercise 16 Distinguishing Between Words Often Confused

Choose the correct word from the choices in parentheses.

EXAMPLE   **1.** The town (*counselor, councilor*) voted on the bill.

1. councilor

1. The funds are for a (*desert, dessert*) irrigation project.
2. The Security (*Consul, Council, Counsel*) of the United Nations consists of fifteen members.
3. The new tie will (*complement, compliment*) my suit.
4. Miss Jee is my guidance (*councilor, counselor*).
5. The house looks (*deserted, desserted*).
6. Listen to your parents' (*consul, council, counsel*).
7. I passed on your charming (*complement, compliment*) to Isabel.
8. All the members of the city (*council, counsel*) agreed.
9. Frozen yogurt is my favorite (*desert, dessert*).
10. The American (*consul, counsel*) in Bahrain announced the recent trade agreement.

formally	[adverb] *properly, according to strict rules* Should he be *formally* introduced?
formerly	[adverb] *previously, in the past* The new consul was *formerly* a professor.

hear	[verb] *to receive sounds through the ears* Did you *hear* the president's speech?
here	[adverb] *at this place* The bus will be *here* soon.
its	[possessive of *it*] *belonging to it* The lion stopped in *its* tracks.
it's	[contraction of *it is* or *it has*] *It's* snowing! *It's* started snowing!
lead	[verb, present tense, rhymes with *deed*] *to go first* I'll *lead* the way.
led	[verb, past tense of *lead*] *went first* Last week she *led* us to victory.
lead	[noun, rhymes with *red*] *a heavy metal; graphite in a pencil* We made fishing sinkers out of *lead*. Use a sharp *lead* to draw fine lines.
loose	[adjective, rhymes with *noose*] *not tight, not securely fastened; not close together* The string on the package is too *loose*.
lose	[verb, rhymes with *choose*] *to suffer loss* Don't *lose* your ticket.
moral	[adjective] *having to do with good or right;* [noun] *a lesson in conduct* It's a *moral* question. These fables all have a *moral*.
morale	[noun] *mental condition, spirit* Letters from home raised our *morale*.
passed	[verb, past tense of *pass*] *went by* He *passed* us in the corridor.
past	[noun] *history, what has gone by;* [adjective] *former;* [preposition] *farther than; after* I didn't ask him about his *past*. Her *past* employer recommended her. I went *past* the house. It's ten minutes *past* noon.

(continued)

(continued)

peace	[noun] *absence of conflict* Only after war is *peace* truly appreciated.
piece	[noun] *a part of something*; [verb] *to assemble slowly* Have a *piece* of my homemade bread. We *pieced* together the puzzle.

┌─ **TIPS** & **TRICKS** ─┐

To remember the correct spelling of *piece*, use the following memory aid: a **pie**ce of **pie**.

Exercise 17 Distinguishing Between Words Often Confused

Choose the correct word of the pair in parentheses.

EXAMPLE   **1.** The two countries settled their dispute and now live in (*piece, peace*).

1. *peace*

1. The coach's praise after the game raised the team's (*morale, moral*).
2. It's already (*passed, past*) nine o'clock.
3. The searchers hoped that the search dog would (*lead, led*) them to the missing skier.
4. The two forwards (*led, lead*) the team to victory.
5. I'm more interested in math than I (*formally, formerly*) was.
6. Several children asked what the (*moral, morale*) of the story was.
7. I need a pencil with soft (*led, lead*).
8. Everyone at the dance was dressed (*formally, formerly*).
9. Molly (*past, passed*) the open doorway.
10. Is the bank offering good interest rates on (*it's, its*) savings accounts and loans?

Exercise 18 Proofreading for Words Often Confused

Correct the errors in word choice in the following sentences.

EXAMPLE   **1.** My dad's promotion lead to a move for our family.

1. *led*

1. Sometimes relocating can feel like abandoning everything and everyone you formally cared about.
2. However, before my family and I moved, one of my friends gave me very good council.
3. "Moving away," she said, "doesn't mean that you are desserting your old friends."

4. After my family moved across the country, I remembered that peace of advice.
5. For the first few months after we moved hear, I felt as though I'd been cut lose from everything I loved.
6. To boost my morale, my parents told me something that I needed to here.
7. If you dwell on the passed, you will loose out on the present.
8. They both moved often when they were young, so I guess they know what its like.
9. Now that a year has past, I understand that every place has it's good points.
10. I've made quite a few new friends, and I'm finally at piece with myself—and with my parents.

plain	[adjective] *clear, not fancy;* [noun] *a flat area of land*
	She made her point of view *plain.*
	Steven wears very *plain* clothes.
	The storm lashed the open *plain.*
plane	[noun] *a flat surface; a level; a tool; an airplane*
	Each *plane* of the granite block was smooth.
	The debate was conducted on a high *plane.*
	Chris smoothed the wood with a *plane.*
	The *plane* arrived on time.
principal	[noun] *head of a school;* [adjective] *main, most important*
	Our new *principal* addressed the assembly.
	Product design is my *principal* responsibility.
principle	[noun] *a rule of conduct; a law*
	His *principles* do not allow compromise.
	Please explain the *principle* of gravity.
quiet	[adjective] *silent, still*
	The library is usually fairly *quiet.*
quite	[adverb] *to a great extent or degree, completely*
	My little brother is *quite* clever for his age.
	I'm not *quite* finished.

(continued)

TIPS & TRICKS

To remember the correct spelling of *principal,* use the following memory aid: The princi**pal** is your **pal**.

(continued)

shone	[verb, past tense of *shine*] *emitted light* The sun *shone* brightly this morning.
shown	[verb, past participle of *show*] *revealed, displayed* Li Hua has just *shown* me her scrapbook.
stationary	[adjective] *in a fixed position* These chairs are *stationary*.
stationery	[noun] *writing paper* Use white *stationery* for business letters.
than	[conjunction, used for comparisons] Jimmy enjoys tennis more *than* golfing.
then	[adverb] *at that time; next* Did you know Bianca *then*? I revised my paper, and *then* I proofread it.
their	[possessive of *they*] *belonging to them* The girls gave *their* opinions.
there	[adverb] *at that place;* [also an expletive used to begin a sentence] I'll be *there* on time. *There* isn't any milk left.
they're	[contraction of *they are*] *They're* at the station now.

┌─ T I P S & T R I C K S ─┐

To remember the correct spelling of *stationery*, use the following memory aid: "You write a lett**er** on station**ery**."

Reference Note

For information on **possessive pronouns**, see page 184. For information on **adverbs**, see page 200. For information on **forming contractions**, see page 335.

MECHANICS

Exercise 19 Distinguishing Between Words Often Confused

Choose the correct word from the pair in parentheses.

EXAMPLE   1. Mrs. Tanaka is our school's (*principal, principle*).

1. *principal*

1. An elephant eats more vegetation (*then, than*) any other animal does.
2. One scene of the movie was not (*shone, shown*) on TV.
3. The deer was (*stationary, stationery*) for a full minute.
4. Gossiping is against his (*principals, principles*).
5. Last night many stars (*shone, shown*) brightly.
6. I wrote the letter on blue (*stationary, stationery*).
7. Rosa learned how to use a (*plain, plane*) in industrial arts class.

8. My (*principal, principle*) problem is learning to spell.
9. I hope they remembered (*there, their*) homework.
10. Is he (*quite, quiet*) sure?

Review D Proofreading for Words Often Confused

Correct each error in word choice in the following sentences.

┌─**H E L P**─

Some sentences
in Review D contain
more than one error.

EXAMPLE 1. Our principle let us out of class early to welcome home
our victorious volleyball team.

1. *principal*

1. King High School won quiet a victory last year—the girls' regional
   volleyball championship.
2. Everyone wanted to complement the team's abilities.
3. The victory had a positive affect on the whole student body.
4. Hundreds of students went to the airport to meet the team's plain.
5. The flight arrived on time, but than it took more then an hour for
   the aircraft to reach the gate.
6. Finally someone shouted, "Their they are!"
7. "There coming up the ramp!"
8. Coach Janos asked for quite and introduced each of the girls.
9. They're were loud cheers for each of them, even though quite a few
   hadn't played in the final game.
10. It was plane that they were quite excited about there success and
    were looking forward to the official victory rally the next day.

threw	[verb] *tossed; pitched* Freddy *threw* three strikes.
through	[preposition] *in one side and out the opposite side* The firetruck raced *through* the heavy traffic.
to	[preposition; also used before the infinitive form of a verb] They've gone *to* the store. She told us *to* wash the windows.
too	[adverb] *also; excessively* I like soccer, and Ted does, *too.* He was *too* tired to think clearly.
two	[adjective or noun] *the sum of one + one* I noticed *two* packages on the sofa.

(continued)

waist	[noun] *the middle part of the body* This skirt is too big in the *waist*.
waste	[noun] *unused material*; [verb] *to squander* *Waste* is a major problem in the United States. Don't *waste* your money on that.
weak	[adjective] *feeble, lacking force, not strong* The fawn is still too *weak* to walk.
week	[noun] *seven days* Carol has been gone a *week*.
weather	[noun] *conditions outdoors* The *weather* suddenly changed.
whether	[conjunction indicating alternative or doubt] She wondered *whether* to enter the contest.
who's	[contraction of *who is* or *who has*] I can't imagine *who's* at the door now. *Who's* been marking in my book?
whose	[possessive of *who*] *belonging to whom* *Whose* bicycle is this?
your	[possessive of *you*] *belonging to you* What is *your* idea?
you're	[contraction of *you are*] R.S.V.P. so that I'll know whether *you're* planning to be there.

MECHANICS

(Exercise 20) **Distinguishing Between Words Often Confused**

Choose the correct word from the ones given in parentheses.

EXAMPLE   1. Lourdes speaks Portuguese, (*to, two, too*).

   1. *too*

1. Next (*weak, week*) the Bearcats will play the Wolverines.
2. The ball crashed (*threw, through*) the window.
3. (*Your, You're*) up next, Leshe.
4. Giving a speech makes me (*weak, week*) in the knees.
5. (*Your, You're*) sleeve is torn.
6. Each band member wore a gold sash around the (*waist, waste*).
7. (*Whose, Who's*) bat is this?

8. (*Whose, Who's*) going to be first?
9. No, this isn't a (*waist, waste*) of time.
10. (*Whose, Who's*) seen my black sweater?

Exercise 21 **Proofreading for Words Often Confused**

Correct the errors in word choice in the following sentences.

EXAMPLE   **1.** Have you ever had the whether ruin you're plans?

        1. weather, your

1. Last Labor Day weekend, my brother Jorge and I got up early Saturday morning and rode our bikes four miles too the beach.
2. The two of us were to busy talking too notice that the sky was growing darker as we rode along.
3. Just as we through our towels on the sand, it started to rain heavily.
4. We waisted the next hour huddled under one of the beach shelters, arguing about weather to stay or to go home.
5. We also got into an argument about who's fault it was.
6. "Your the one who had the bright idea," said Jorge.
7. "Whose the one who said it would be sunny?" I retorted.
8. Finally, we pedaled back home threw the driving rain.
9. It rained all day Sunday and Monday, to.
10. We spent the weekend cooped up in the house while whether forecasters predicted sunny skies for the next weak.

Review E **Identifying Correctly Spelled Words**

Choose the correct word or expression from the pair in parentheses.

EXAMPLE   **1.** a (*stationary, stationery*) exercise bicycle

        1. stationary

1. a (*brief, breif*) talk
2. (*neither, niether*) one
3. (*course, coarse*) cloth
4. some good (*advice, advise*)
5. fruit for (*desert, dessert*)
6. many (*heros, heroes*)
7. on the (*cieling, ceiling*)
8. two (*copies, copys*)
9. looking (*passed, past*) him
10. (*weather, whether*) to stay
11. the (*altar, alter*) boys
12. building (*patioes, patios*)
13. recycled (*34, thirty-four*) cans
14. we will go (*than, then*)
15. a (*mispelled, misspelled*) word
16. (*happyly, happily*) ever after
17. that's (*awsome, awesome*)
18. a (*week, weak*) voice
19. this sharp pencil (*led, lead*)
20. (*their, they're*) his

Chapter Review

A. Proofreading Sentences to Correct Spelling Errors

Most of the following sentences contain spelling errors. Write the misspelled words correctly. If a sentence is already correct, write *C*.

1. Silas has no doubt that his favorite neice will succede in whatever career she chooses to follow.
2. The winter snow and ice damaged the eveness of the road surface.
3. Some critics' reviews were largely favorable; others said the movie was awful.
4. Occasionaly, we stay home on Saturdays to clean the yard.
5. Cousin Mark bought that car because he thinks it is a senseible compromise between style and economy.
6. I read all the recommended books from cover to cover for the finals, and now that exams are over, the books are safely back on the library bookshelfs where they belong.
7. I asked Patrick O'Daniel how long the O'Daniel's had lived in Texas.
8. In his twenties, Grandpa was an awsome swimer.
9. Extraordinaryly quickly, the snake disappeared into the undergrowth.
10. "As you know," said Ms. Garza, "February 15th—that is, tomorrow—is Colleen's birthday."
11. My cheif objection to attending the ceremony was having to listen to all those speech's.
12. "Alright, then," said Mom. "You can go outside, but be careful on those icey sidewalks."
13. How many boxs were stacked near the door?
14. The members of the United Nations Security Counsel are the United States, Russia, China, France, and the United Kingdom.
15. The engineer accidentally shut down the transmitter.
16. Vivian's account of her experiences in New Guinea was breif but vivid.
17. What do you call the passage that preceeds the main body of our Constitution?
18. The paper is delivered dayly, except on Mondays.

19. The elephant was considerring coming into the clearing.

20. I'm grumpy because I just had an arguement with a friend.

B. Distinguishing Between Words Often Confused

Choose the correct word from the pair in parentheses.

21. Last night I went (*too, to*) the theater.

22. How did the news (*effect, affect*) him?

23. We need to order some letterhead (*stationary, stationery*) and paper for the photocopier.

24. At the graduation ceremony, Mr. Garcia, the (*principle, principal*), gave a short speech.

25. The (*plain, plane*) finally took off after a two-hour delay.

26. First we sketched the outline, and (*than, then*) we filled in the features of the house.

27. Her duties in her old job were (*quiet, quite*) different from those in the new job.

28. "Son," said Dad, "I'd (*advice, advise*) you to keep at it. Quitters never get anywhere."

29. For (*desert, dessert*) they had frozen yogurt and shredded pineapple.

30. We were all very pleased when we heard that Shawna's dad had been named U.S. (*Counsel, Consul*) in Pretoria, South Africa.

31. Please permit me to introduce (*formerly, formally*) Dr. Villanueva, my sponsor.

32. When parking on an incline, always remember to set the (*break, brake*).

33. I think that tonight's debate is on the subject of (*capital, capitol*) punishment.

34. "(*All together, Altogether*) now," said the choir director.

35. Going to the Christmas concert with the whole family certainly raised my (*morale, moral*).

36. The (*capital, capitol*) of New York State is not New York City, but Albany.

37. 1 wonder (*who's, whose*) parka this is.

38. From Fran's point of view, volunteering to help clean up the city park was as much a question of (*principal, principle*) as goodwill.

39. "Was that really (*you're, your*) best effort?" asked Ms. Yokoyama impatiently.

40. He opened his mouth to reply, but Babs had (*all ready, already*) gone.

41. Friends never (*dessert, desert*) each other.

42. Use a (*led, lead*) pencil to sketch the outlines.

43. "How could you (*loose, lose*) an entire bag of groceries?" asked Belinda incredulously.

44. The same truck (*past, passed*) us three times on the same stretch of highway.

45. Please remember that every journey has (*it's, its*) good and bad points.

46. "Improving communication, as many of you will find out, can boost (*moral, morale*)," said Ms. Lockheed.

47. The amber harvest moon (*shown, shone*) through the rustling branches and onto the badger's burrow.

48. "All the caddies will be paid in full, of (*course, coarse*)," said Mr. Glendinning.

49. When the office workers go home, a strange (*quiet, quite*) descends on the downtown business district.

50. The tornadoes raced across the barren (*plane, plain*).

DILBERT reprinted by permission of United Feature Syndicate, Inc.

Writing Application
Using Correct Spelling in a Letter

Spelling Words Correctly   The junior varsity volleyball team is having its best season in several years, but no one else in school seems to know about it. Write a letter to the coach explaining the three best things the team can do to raise awareness and interest throughout the school. Use at least five words from the spelling lists and five words from the lists of words that are often confused.

Prewriting   Begin by making a list of all the ideas you can think of to promote the team. Look at the other successful sports and activities at your school. What do they do to promote themselves? Narrow your list down to the three ideas that are most likely to work.

Writing   Begin your letter by clearly explaining your purpose. Then, list each of your ideas and explain why you think they may help. Include estimates of how much money and time each of the ideas might involve. Conclude by offering to take charge of one part of the effort.

Revising   First, read your letter to make sure all of your ideas are clearly and completely explained. Ask yourself if you have thought about all of your ideas thoroughly. Have you considered all the expenses that each plan may involve? Would anyone be offended or hurt by any of your plans? You may want to have an adult friend or family member look at your ideas to see if they are appropriate. Make sure you have used at least five words from the spelling lists and five words from the lists of words that are often confused.

Publishing   Check your letter carefully for errors in grammar, usage, and punctuation. Then, think about a sport or other activity at school that does not get the recognition and support you think it deserves. Show your letter to the coach or sponsor of the activity, and offer to help carry out some of the ideas to get the activity more recognition.

MECHANICS

75 Commonly Misspelled Words

The following list contains seventy-five words that are often misspelled. To find out which words give you difficulty, ask someone to read you the list in groups of ten. Write down each word, and then check your spelling. In your spelling notebook, make a list of any words you misspelled. Keep reviewing your list until you have mastered the correct spelling.

ache	friend	speak
across		speech
again	grammar	straight
all right	guess	sugar
almost		surely
always	half	
answer	having	tear
	heard	though
belief	hour	through
built		tired
business	instead	together
busy		tomorrow
buy	knew	tonight
	know	tough
can't		trouble
color	laid	truly
coming	likely	Tuesday
cough		
could	making	until
country	meant	
	minute	wear
doctor		Wednesday
doesn't	often	where
don't	once	which
		whole
eager	ready	women
easy	really	won't
every		write
	safety	
February	said	
forty	says	
	shoes	
	since	

300 Spelling Words

Learn to spell the following words this year if you don't already know how.

absence	accommodate	accustomed
absolutely	accompany	achievement
acceptance	accomplish	acquaintance
accidentally	accurate	actually

administration
affectionate
agriculture
amateur
ambassador
analysis
analyze
announcement
anticipate
apology
apparent
appearance
approach
approval
arguing
argument
assurance
attendance
authority
available

basically
beginning
believe
benefit
benefited
boundary

calendar
campaign
capital
category
certificate
characteristic
chief
circuit
circumstance
civilization
column
commissioner
committee
comparison
competent
competition
conceivable

concept
confidential
conscience
conscious
consistency
constitution
continuous
control
cooperate
corporation
correspondence
criticism
criticize
cylinder

debtor
decision
definite
definition
deny
description
despise
diameter
disappearance
disappointment
discipline
disgusted
distinction
distinguished
dominant
duplicate

economic
efficiency
eighth
elaborate
eligible
embarrass
emergency
employee
encouraging
environment
equipped
essential
evidently

exaggerate
exceedingly
excellent
excessive
excitable
exercise
existence
expense
extraordinary

fascinating
fatal
favorably
fictitious
financier
flourish
fraternity
frequent
further

glimpse
glorious
grabbed
gracious
graduating
grammatically
gross
gymnasium

happiness
hasten
heavily
hindrance
humorous
hungrily
hypocrisy
hypocrite

icy
ignorance
incidentally
indicate
imagination
immediately
immense
indispensable

MECHANICS

inevitable
innocence
inquiry
insurance
intelligence
interfere
interrupt
interpretation
investigation

jealous

knowledge

leisure
lengthen
lieutenant
likelihood
liveliness
loneliness

magazine
maneuver
marriage
marvelous
mechanical
medieval
merchandise
minimum
mortgage
multitude
muscle
mutual

narrative
naturally
necessary
negligible
niece
noticeable

obligation
obstacle

occasionally
occurrence
offense
official
omit
operation
opportunity
oppose
optimism
orchestra
organization
originally

paid
paradise
parallel
particularly
peasant
peculiar
percentage
performance
personal
personality
perspiration
persuade
petition
philosopher
picnic
planning
pleasant
policies
politician
possess
possibility
practically
precede
precisely
preferred
prejudice
preparation
pressure

primitive
privilege
probably
procedure
proceed
professor
proportion
psychology
publicity
pursuit

qualities
quantities

readily
reasonably
receipt
recognize
recommendation
referring
regretting
reign
relieve
remembrance
removal
renewal
repetition
representative
requirement
residence
resistance
responsibility
restaurant
rhythm
ridiculous

sacrifice
satire
satisfied
scarcely
scheme
scholarship

scissors
senate
sensibility
separate
sergeant
several
shepherd
sheriff
similar
skis
sponsor
solemn
sophomore
source
specific
straighten

substantial
substitute
subtle
succeed
successful
sufficient
summary
superior
suppress
surprise
survey
suspense
suspicion

temperament
tendency

thorough
transferring
tremendous
truly

unanimous
unfortunately
unnecessary
urgent
useful
using

vacancies
vacuum
varies

MECHANICS

Correcting Common Errors

Key Language Skills Review

This chapter reviews key skills and concepts that pose special problems for writers.

- **Sentence Fragments and Run-on Sentences**
- **Subject-Verb and Pronoun-Antecedent Agreement**
- **Verb Forms**
- **Clear Pronoun Reference**
- **Comparison of Modifiers**
- **Dangling and Misplaced Modifiers**
- **Standard Usage**
- **Capitalization**
- **Punctuation—End Marks, Commas, Quotation Marks, Apostrophes, Semicolons, and Colons**
- **Spelling**

Most of the exercises in this chapter follow the same format as the exercises found throughout the grammar, usage, and mechanics sections of this textbook. You will notice, however, that two sets of review exercises are presented as standardized tests. These exercises are designed to provide you with practice not only in solving usage and mechanics problems but also in dealing with these kinds of problems on standardized tests.

Each of the following word groups is a sentence fragment. Rewrite each fragment to make it a complete sentence. Add whatever words are necessary to make the meaning of the sentence complete.

Reference Note

For information on **correcting sentence fragments,** see page 434.

EXAMPLE   1. having already read the book

      1. *Having already read the book, I was not surprised by the film's end.*

1. television, radio, newspapers, billboards, magazines, and now the World Wide Web
2. beside the cold, clear spring tumbling down the rocky slopes
3. when we passed through the turnstile
4. to appreciate adequately the complexity of these drum rhythms
5. according to the most recent experiments
6. exercising regularly for thirty minutes at least three times a week
7. trained as a lab assistant at the local junior college
8. who had once actually stood on the Great Wall of China
9. one of the first women of that rank in the Navy
10. where the laundry had been hung on a line in full sunlight

Exercise 2 **Identifying Sentences and Revising Sentence Fragments**

Identify each numbered word group in the following paragraph as either a sentence fragment (*F*) or a complete sentence (*S*). Then, make each fragment part of a complete sentence either by adding words to it or by combining it with another fragment or sentence in the paragraph. Change the punctuation and capitalization as necessary.

EXAMPLES   [1] I discovered that the jacket was made of linen.

      [2] When I got home.

      1. *S*

      2. *F—When I got home, I discovered that the jacket was made of linen.*

[1] Before you spend your money on that expensive shirt. [2] Read the label carefully! [3] Because some clothes must be sent to the dry cleaner. [4] They will cost you extra money. [5] A lot of money in the long run. [6] Other clothes must be washed by hand. [7] Requiring extra time and care for their upkeep. [8] If you are looking for quality clothes. [9] That are both attractive and inexpensive to own. [10] It pays to read the label.

Reference Note

For information on **correcting run-on sentences,** see page 441.

Exercise 3 **Revising Run-on Sentences**

Each of the following numbered items is a run-on sentence. Revise each run-on, using the method given in brackets after it. Be sure to change punctuation and capitalization as necessary.

EXAMPLE 1. Today's world offers many kinds of popular entertainment earlier Americans relied mainly on music and dancing. [*Use a comma and coordinating conjunction.*]

  1. *Today's world offers many kinds of popular entertainment, but earlier Americans relied mainly on music and dancing.*

1. Just imagine your life without TV, audio and video recordings, and movies surely you would spend your time quite differently from the way you do now. [*Make two sentences.*]

2. In a world without recorded music, a musician could often attract a crowd even today, good musicians can make a living on the streets of a large city. [*Use a semicolon.*]

3. Music was important to the early settlers they often made their own instruments. [*Use a comma and a coordinating conjunction.*]

4. Many of the settlers owned fiddles, dulcimers, flutes, and guitars music could be a part of everyday life. [*Use a semicolon, a conjunctive adverb, and a comma*]

5. Long before the settlers arrived, there was already plenty of music in North America American Indians prized music and song. [*Use a semicolon.*]

6. The Seneca used rattles similar to the instruments known as maracas Northern Plains Indians used the hand drum. [*Use a comma and a coordinating conjunction.*]

7. The Maidu played flutes and whistles musicians today often incorporate such American Indian instruments into popular music. [*Make two sentences.*]

8. The banjo is widely regarded as a traditional American musical instrument, the banjo originated in Africa. [*Use a semicolon, a conjunctive adverb, and a comma*]

9. West Africans made banjo-like instruments out of gourds for strings, they used dried animal gut. [*Use a semicolon.*]

10. Early banjos had no frets and only four strings frets are the ridges positioned at intervals on the necks of banjos and guitars. [*Make two sentences.*]

Exercise 4 Revising Sentence Fragments and Run-on Sentences

Most of the following word groups are either run-on sentences or sentence fragments. Identify and correct each sentence fragment and run-on sentence. If a word group is already a complete sentence, write *C*.

EXAMPLE **1.** The area where I live used to be a prehistoric sea, some-times my friends and I find fossilized sharks' teeth.

  1. The area where I live used to be a prehistoric sea, and sometimes my friends and I find fossilized sharks' teeth.

1. Walking slowly over the rocky terrain.
2. A strange rock caught our attention Jackie broke it open.
3. Inside were rows and rows of brilliant quartz crystals, we gasped at our discovery.
4. Gold lies hidden in the West, many people still seek their fortune there.
5. Is one of the best places in the world for prospectors.
6. When rainfall, a landslide, or some other act of nature alters the landscape.
7. Easier to find gold, silver, platinum, and other precious metals.
8. Although most commonly used for jewelry, gold has numerous industrial uses.
9. You can grow your own crystals, some grow quite quickly.
10. With a kit from a hobby shop only two blocks away from my house in Colorado Springs.

Oral Practice Choosing Verbs That Agree in Number with Their Subjects

Read each of the following sentences aloud, and choose the correct form of the verb in parentheses.

EXAMPLE **1.** One of the customs most readily shared among cultures (*is, are*) games.

  1. is

1. Almost everybody (*has, have*) played games that originated in faraway places.
2. Few of these games (*is, are*) difficult to play.

Reference Note

For information on **subject-verb agreement,** see page 121.

COMMON ERRORS

3. Pictures on ancient Greek pottery (*show, shows*) people playing with yo-yos.
4. (*Was, Were*) the first people who ever played the game lacrosse American Indian?
5. Arctic peoples, Africans, the Maori of New Zealand, and others as well (*plays, play*) cat's cradle.
6. Somewhere, somebody in one of the world's cultures probably (*is, are*) spinning a top right now.
7. Not all card games (*uses, use*) a standard deck of cards.
8. Most of these games (*requires, require*) at least two players, and some require four.
9. Several ancient African games still (*enjoys, enjoy*) popularity among children.
10. None of those colorful Chinese tangrams (*turns, turn*) out to be easy to solve.

Exercise 5 **Proofreading a Paragraph for Subject-Verb Agreement**

Identify the errors in subject-verb agreement in the following paragraph. Then, change each incorrect verb to agree with its subject.

EXAMPLE   **[1]** Many a building design don't meet the needs of people with disabilities.

  1. *don't—doesn't*

[1] Ordinary houses or a public building sometimes present problems for people with disabilities. [2] For example, a person using a wheelchair or crutches often have difficulty maneuvering in narrow halls. [3] Flights of stairs and a front stoop makes access difficult for anyone using a wheelchair or a walker. [4] Moreover, inadequate shower access or high counters needlessly poses problems for people with wheelchairs. [5] One homebuilder and solver of these problems are Craig Johnson. [6] Johnson, with a team of advisors and decorators, seek to make life easier for people with various disabilities. [7] Johnson recognizes that easy access and freedom from barriers is becoming both an issue for our aging population and a growing business opportunity. [8] Creating designs and making modifications for people with disabilities helps others, too. [9] For instance, doesn't most people find that levers are easier to operate than doorknobs are? [10] Also, neither a handrail nor a ramp give anyone any difficulty; in fact, both can come in handy for everyone.

Exercise 6 Identifying Antecedents and Writing Pronouns

Each of the following sentences contains a blank where a pronoun should be. Identify the antecedent for each missing pronoun. Then, complete the sentence with a pronoun that agrees with that antecedent.

Reference Note

For information on **pronoun-antecedent agreement,** see page 135.

EXAMPLE
    1. At about the age of fifteen, Janet Collins followed _____ dream to the Ballet Russe de Monte Carlo.

    1. *Janet Collins—her*

1. Until Janet Collins, nobody of African heritage had ever made _____ debut on the stage of the Metropolitan Opera House.
2. While waiting to audition, she saw other ballerinas on a winding staircase backstage doing _____ warm-up exercises.
3. All of the people who saw Janet at her audition clapped _____ hands.
4. However, because of Collins's color, Mr. Massine, the choreographer, could not hire her for _____ production.
5. Collins continued practicing, and in the end _____ was rewarded.
6. The Metropolitan Opera opened _____ doors to the prima ballerina.
7. Rudolph Bing admired her adagio dancing so much that _____ gave her many opportunities to leap and jump.
8. Two of her roles were in *Carmen* and *Aida,* and _____ helped to make her famous.
9. To be successful, a ballerina must discipline _____.
10. Either Ms. Lawton or Ms. Vicks will show the class _____ autographed picture of Collins.

Exercise 7 Proofreading for Pronoun-Antecedent Agreement

Proofread the following sentences, and identify pronouns that do not agree with their antecedents. Give the correct form of each incorrect pronoun. If a sentence is already correct, write *C.*

EXAMPLE
    1. From the earliest times, people all over the world have decorated himself or herself.

    1. *himself or herself—themselves*

1. Whether for war, religious rituals, or beauty, cosmetics have always had its place in human society.
2. In ancient Egypt, both men and women used various kinds of cosmetics to make himself or herself more attractive.

3. In addition, nearly all Egyptians painted their eyelids with green paste to prevent sunburn.

4. One of the Egyptian kings was even buried with rouge and lip color in their tomb.

5. Ancient cosmetics were usually made from natural ingredients, some of which were poisonous to its users.

6. Arsenic and mercury were two of the most dangerous, and it ruined many lives.

7. The Roman man or woman who used cosmetics containing arsenic was slowly killing themselves.

8. Similarly, in Queen Elizabeth I's time, the English girl or woman who used a skin whitener containing mercury risked having their teeth fall out.

9. Since before the time of Cosmis—who sold makeup during the reign of Julius Caesar—to the present, enterprising people have made their fortunes by providing products that help others meet their cultures' standards of beauty.

10. Galen, a man of science in ancient Rome, would be pleased to find that today's cold cream is based on the formula they invented.

Exercise 8 **Revising Sentences for Agreement**

Each of the following sentences contains either an error in subject-verb agreement or an error in pronoun-antecedent agreement. Revise the sentences to correct each error in agreement.

EXAMPLE 1. Either Mr. Baker or Mr. Perez have promised to drive his van on the field trip.

 1. *Either Mr. Baker or Mr. Perez has promised to drive his van on the field trip.*

1. Many a girl has taken Shirley Chisholm as their model of success.
2. Here, class, is several classic examples of Aztec art.
3. Each member of the cast knows all of their lines for the play.
4. Beautifully illustrated and written, *Saint George and the Dragon* were awarded the Caldecott Medal.
5. Have Ms. Ivy and Mr. Lee played her and his music for the school?
6. Two dollars were once considered generous pay for an hour's work.
7. All of the travelers were surprised when he or she saw the old purple-and-yellow bus.
8. An international team of archaeological researchers is assembling, one by one, at the site of this exciting discovery.

9. Do Cindy and Brenda practice her dance routine here every day?

10. The two performers has become one of the most popular teams in the history of comedy.

Exercise 9 **Writing Correct Verb Forms**

Complete each sentence with the correct past or past participle form of the verb in italics.

EXAMPLE   **1.** *do*   Have you _____ any research on the Cajun culture?

          1. *done*

1. *visit*   Last year, we _____ Louisiana, where most Cajuns live.

2. *begin*   The Cajun culture _____ after French immigrants to Acadia, Canada, traveled south.

3. *come*   While in Canada, these immigrants _____ to be known as Acadians.

4. *take*   In Louisiana, the name Acadian _____ on a different pronunciation—"Cajun."

5. *choose*   The Cajuns _____ to befriend the Choctaws, as well as settlers from Germany and Spain.

6. *put*   Cajun cooks _____ to their own use what they learned from the Choctaws about native plants and animals.

7. *eat*   They _____ seafood seasoned with the Choctaws' filé, which is powdered sassafras leaves.

8. *drink*   They _____ coffee flavored with chicory.

9. *raise*   German settlers in the bayou country _____ the beef and pork that the Cajuns used in their tasty dishes.

10. *bring*   The Cajuns were also delighted with okra, called gumbo by the Bantu, who had _____ it with them from Africa.

Exercise 10 **Identifying Correct Forms of Irregular Verbs**

Choose the correct form of the verb in parentheses in each of the following sentences.

EXAMPLE   **1.** For many years, teams of scientists have (*took, taken*) the opportunity to study the Antarctic Peninsula during the summer.

          1. *taken*

1. The scientists (*went, gone*) there to study the delicate balance of the ecosystem.

Reference Note

For information on **using verbs correctly,** see Chapter 6.

Reference Note

For information on **using irregular verbs,** see page 147.

COMMON ERRORS

Grammar and Usage   **401**

2. These scientists (*knew, knowed*) that worldwide weather patterns are influenced by events in Antarctica.

3. Before the twentieth century, few people (*choosed, chose*) to brave the frigid voyage to the Antarctic.

4. However, new means of transportation have (*brought, brung*) more people, especially scientists, to Antarctica.

5. Such countries as Chile, Britain, and Russia have (*began, begun*) exploring what's beneath Antarctica's ice and snow.

6. No one knows how long Antarctica's waters have (*ran, run*) red with krill, tiny creatures at the bottom of the food chain.

7. Many times, the Ross Ice Shelf has (*shook, shaken*) as a huge iceberg known as B9 has crashed into it.

8. An oil rig could have (*fallen, fell*) if struck by a roving iceberg.

9. If that had happened, a huge oil spill would likely have (*did, done*) major damage to Antarctica's ecosystem.

10. In Antarctica, the nations of the world have been (*gave, given*) an opportunity to work together in peace.

Exercise 11 Proofreading for Correct Verb Forms

Most of the following sentences contain incorrect verb forms. If a form of a verb is wrong, write the correct form. If a sentence already is correct, write *C*.

EXAMPLE   **[1]** The brave galleon had rode the waves to an icy grave.

    1. ridden

[1] Over thousands of years of seafaring, many a ship has been broke on the rocks or lost in a storm. [2] Thirst for the treasure of these sunken ships has drove opportunists and scholars alike to the dark bottoms of the world's oceans. [3] The invention of scuba equipment in 1943 rung in a new era in underwater exploration. [4] Since then, treasure hunters and scientists have dove into waters all over the world and surfaced with gold and historical artifacts. [5] Expeditions have successfully rose entire ships, such as the *Vasa,* a seventeenth-century Swedish vessel. [6] Astonishingly, divers have swum down and inspected the remains of crafts more than forty centuries old! [7] Not only ships but also towns set on the ocean floor. [8] One such site is the community of Port Royal, which lays near Jamaica. [9] Ironically, although many treasures have been found, the search for treasure has not shrinked. [10] On the contrary, as technology has improved, the number of underwater expeditions has growed.

Proofreading for Correct Verb Forms

Most of the following sentences contain an incorrect verb form. If the form of a verb is wrong, write the correct form. If a sentence is already correct, write *C*.

EXAMPLE   **1.** His horse weared a braided bridle.

        1. *wore*

1. Luis Ortega has been describe as history's greatest rawhide braider.
2. For years, collectors and cowhands alike have spoke of him with respectful awe.
3. Ortega was lucky to have had a fine teacher; many braiders do not teach their craft because students have stole their secrets.
4. However, even after a generous American Indian taught Ortega to braid, it taked young Luis many years of practice to perfect his skill.
5. Ortega has never shrinked from hard work.
6. Once a vaquero himself, he throwed many a lasso in his younger days.
7. Since the 1930s, Ortega has wore the title of professional braider.
8. Ortega not only mastered the traditional craft, but also striked out on his own by adding color to braiding.
9. Unlike whips, which have stinged many a runaway steer, a riata is a type of lariat used for roping.
10. Pity the cowhand whose heart must have sunk as a steer ran off with his treasured Ortega riata!

Exercise 13 **Identifying Correct Forms of Pronouns**

Choose the correct pronoun in parentheses in each of the following sentences. Then, tell whether the pronoun is used as a *subject*, a *predicate nominative*, a *direct object*, an *indirect object*, an *object of a preposition*, or an *appositive*.

Reference Note

For information on **using pronouns correctly,** see Chapter 7.

EXAMPLE   **1.** Mr. Kwan and (*we, us*) members of the recycling club picked up all the litter along the highway last Saturday.

        1. *we—subject*

1. Do you know (*who, whom*) safely disposes of old batteries?
2. The two Earth Club members who collect items for recycling are James and (*she, her*).
3. (*Who, Whom*) threw these cans in the garbage?
4. Save all recyclable material for (*we, us*) club members.

COMMON ERRORS

5. Give the co-chairpersons, Lisa and (*she, her*), all of the cans that you have collected.
6. Ask (*whoever, whomever*) you know to save old newspapers for us to collect.
7. (*Who, Whom*) could the next recycling team leader be?
8. To (*whom, who*) do we give this cardboard?
9. The city gave Mr. Kwan, (*who, whom*) everyone in the school respects, an award.
10. Please give Carl and (*he, him*) the maps you three drew yesterday.

> ### Exercise 14 Correcting Inexact Pronoun References
>
> Correct each inexact pronoun reference in the following sentences. If a sentence is already correct, write *C*.
>
> EXAMPLE   1. When you take medication for your allergies, be sure to read them carefully.
>
> 1. *When you take medication for your allergies, be sure to read the directions carefully.*

1. Annie said that she must have sneezed two dozen times today and that it was really bothering her.
2. Annie asked Heather several good questions about her new allergy medication.
3. Everyone knows that Heather has more problems with pollen allergies than I have.
4. Pollen, molds, and animal dander are widespread in our environment; they are three of the most common causes of allergies.
5. Different plants release pollen at different times of the year, which is why people have discomfort at various times.
6. Annie asked Sarah about summer allergies because she is especially uncomfortable during July.
7. To take a pollen count, they place a glass slide coated with oil outside for twenty-four hours.
8. The slide is then placed under a microscope, and the grains of pollen sticking to it are counted.
9. When it rains, the pollen count drops because the rain washes the pollen grains from the air.
10. In the news reports, they often give the pollen count.

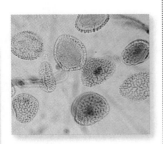

Pollen Grains

Proofreading for Clear Pronoun Usage

Most of the following sentences contain inexact pronoun references. Revise each incorrect sentence. If a sentence is already correct, write *C*.

Reference Note

For information on **using pronouns correctly,** see Chapter 7.

EXAMPLES

    1. In India, they belong to laughing clubs.

    1. In India, some people belong to laughing clubs.

    2. These clubs are popular with the people of India because of the conflicts they face every day.

    2. C

1. Scientists believe that long ago an island slammed into Asia; it created the Himalayas and joined the island to the continent.

2. That landmass is now India, and worlds still collide there, which is seen in the contradictions and conflicts of modern India.

3. India has been independent for more than fifty years, and it has caused many changes in this growing nation.

4. For instance, the famous city of Bombay has been renamed Mumbai, which honors the Hindu goddess Mumba.

5. However, British influences still exist, and that is apparent in English-language street signs.

6. Free-market policies have now been adopted, and many people have taken advantage of that; small, independent businesses are booming.

7. To the refugees who come to Kolkata from Bangladesh, it offers a little hope.

8. There are as many as thirty-seven laughing clubs in Mumbai (members believe it fights stress).

9. At the same time, beside the wall of an alleyway in Kolkata, a woman prepares food for her daughter while she sits in a nearby tree.

10. A country with ample natural resources and millions of highly educated people, India is taking its place on the world stage.

COMMON ERRORS

Reference Note

For information on **using modifers correctly,** see Chapter 8.

Exercise 16 **Using Comparative and Superlative Forms**

Complete each sentence with the correct comparative or superlative form of the word given in italics.

EXAMPLE   1. *well*   Carl can perform CPR _____ than I can.

   1. *better*

1. *few*   Bicyclists who wear helmets have _____ serious injuries from accidents than bicyclists who do not wear helmets.

2. *many*   Our family follows _____ safety procedures than we used to follow in the past.

3. *bad*   Some of the _____ accidents are more likely to happen in the home than anywhere else.

4. *much*   Is it _____ common to have an accident in the kitchen or in the bathroom?

5. *well*   Emergency crews can spot luminous house numbers _____ than numbers that do not glow in the dark.

6. *bad*   A grease fire will become _____ if you put water on it.

7. *good*   Do you know the _____ way to extinguish an electrical fire?

8. *many*   Smoke detectors are found in _____ homes than ever before.

9. *much*   In many small fires, smoke causes _____ of the damage.

10. *good*   Of course, the _____ safety procedure of all is preventing fires from starting in the first place.

Exercise 17 **Proofreading Sentences for Correct Comparative and Superlative Forms**

Correct each error in the use of comparative and superlative forms in the following sentences. If no modifiers need to be corrected, write *C*.

EXAMPLE   1. Most oftenest, I plan my day in the morning.

   1. *Most often*

1. One of the importantest skills is the ability to set priorities.

2. You can establish your priorities more easily if you know your goals.

3. Owning a good car, having a rewarding job, and owning a house are three of the most commonest goals people share.

4. You, however, may want a pilot's license, a medical degree, an eighteen-wheeler, or just a comfortabler bed.

5. Whatever your goal, you will be much more likelier to achieve it if you plan your time carefully.

6. Look at even the most small unit of your time.

7. Can you think of ways that you could use your time more better than you do?

8. Try every day to work on your most highest priority.

9. Try more hard to stick to your schedule.

10. With a plan, you can meet your goals quicklier than you could without one.

Exercise 18 **Writing Comparative and Superlative Forms**

Write the comparative and superlative forms of the following modifiers.

EXAMPLE   **1.** kind

    1. *kinder, kindest; less kind, least kind*

1. alone	**6.** bad	**11.** natural	**16.** contentedly
2. loudly	**7.** delightful	**12.** wet	**17.** green
3. late	**8.** fiercely	**13.** mysterious	**18.** bravely
4. secretly	**9.** exact	**14.** gleefully	**19.** poor
5. lucky	**10.** childishly	**15.** timid	**20.** cautiously

Exercise 19 **Correcting Double Negatives**

Revise each of the following sentences to correct the double negative that it contains.

EXAMPLE   **1.** The jurors couldn't say nothing about the trial.

    1. *The jurors could say nothing about the trial.*

             or

    The jurors couldn't say anything about the trial.

1. Those machines don't take no dollar bills.

2. My grandfather doesn't hardly let anything bother him.

3. Don't never accept a ride from a stranger!

4. Why didn't no one take a message when Mom called?

5. Never use none of those microwave oven pans in a regular oven.

6. The movie hadn't scarcely started when the power went off.

7. I can't see nothing from here.

8. There aren't none of those tamales left now.

9. Don't let nobody tell you that you can't win!

10. Neither cold nor heat nor nothing else discouraged them.

┌HELP──

Although two possible answers are shown, you need to give only one answer for each item in Exercise 19.

Reference Note

For information on **double negatives,** see page 237.

COMMON ERRORS

Exercise 20 **Correcting Misplaced Modifiers**

Revise the following sentences to correct errors in the use of modifiers.
You may need to rearrange or add words to make the meaning clear.

EXAMPLE   **1.** Cold and overcast, the tour group left the city.

         1. *The tour group left the cold and overcast city.*

1. I watched the hawk swoop down and grab its prey with my new pair of binoculars.
2. He is such a hard-working student that he did every bit of his homework when he even got the flu.
3. Running through town, soft moonlight fell on the freight train.
4. You should accept rides from people only you know.
5. A kingfisher sat alertly on the fence post that had been hunting by the creek.
6. I figured out the answer studying the problem.
7. Bulky and dusty, we moved all of the boxes out of the attic.
8. Filled with wildflowers, Amy put that vase on her desk.
9. Suddenly, the bats swarmed out of the cave that we had awakened.
10. A package sat on the doorstep with Michael's name on it.

Exercise 21 **Correcting Dangling Modifiers**

Most of the following sentences contain a dangling modifier. If a
sentence is incorrect, revise it to correct the dangling modifier. If a
sentence is already correct, write *C*.

EXAMPLE   **1.** Following the path, a tiny cottage came into view.

         1. *As we were following the path, a tiny cottage came into view.*

1. Rounding third base, the coach and the fans in the stands cheered and applauded.
2. To manage time better, making a schedule will help.
3. Modified to allow space for an additional bedroom, the floor plan's lack of closets became a problem.
4. While studying for exams, a storm knocked out the electricity.
5. Before beginning your library research, a specific topic or category must be selected.
6. Right in the middle of making a copy of my report, the out-of-paper message flashed.
7. Tired from the long hike, our camp was a welcome sight.

8. After hanging the new plants, the room appeared larger.
9. To save money, a realistic budget is necessary.
10. While we watched the children play, our problems seemed small.

Exercise 22 **Correcting Misplaced and Dangling Modifiers**

The following sentences contain misplaced and dangling modifiers. Revise each sentence to correct the misplaced or dangling modifier.

EXAMPLE   1. Seeing the rescue helicopter, shouts of joy burst out.

       1. *Seeing the rescue helicopter, the crew burst out with shouts of joy.*

1. Customers lined up for copies of the new film about extra-terrestrials in the video store.
2. To save a file, a name must be given to it.
3. The spaceship drifted toward the small moon that had lost its engines.
4. Dozens of white daisies decorated the tables, which had been grown in our own garden.
5. Marked by signs saying "Reserved," we couldn't find anywhere to park.
6. Did George Washington ever meet Robert E. Lee, whose face is on our dollar?
7. Following the trail, camp was quickly found.
8. Having advertised all week, all the tickets had been sold.
9. Patient hawks watched for fish soaring over the lake.
10. Mother packed a picnic lunch humming quietly.

Exercise 23 **Correcting Errors in Standard Usage**

Identify and correct each error in the use of formal, standard English in the following sentences.

EXAMPLE   1. I ain't going to the movies on Saturday.

       1. *ain't—am not*

1. Please bring this note to Ms. Nichols in the gym.
2. Who else was late to the party beside Ronnie and Ed?
3. My science project took alot of time last weekend.
4. Oh, no! I can't find my raincoat anywheres.
5. Common elements include oxygen, hydrogen, iron, and etc.
6. The weather can effect people's moods.
7. Starting next year, each student will wear an uniform.

Reference Note

For more on **common usage problems,** see Chapter 9. For information about **formal, standard English,** see page 223.

COMMON ERRORS

8. Look out! You almost busted my CD player!
9. Gradually, our dog excepted the new kitten.
10. The little steam engine pulled all the faster it could.

Exercise 24 Correcting Errors in Standard Usage

Revise the following sentences to correct all errors in the use of formal, standard English.

EXAMPLE
1. Like you would expect, the use of color is very important to artists.

1. *As you would expect, the use of color is very important to artists.*

1. Artists which study color know that color, value, and contrast form the foundation of a good painting.
2. Many artists would not even begin no painting without they first planned how they would use these elements.
3. One of the basics that nearly all artists learn is where color is divided into warm colors and cool colors.
4. Like you might of guessed, red is a warmer color then blue, while green is cooler than orange.
5. The value, or darkness, of a color can indicate that objects differ some in distance from the viewer.
6. For example, a dark color may be used to indicate that something is a long ways off.
7. Contrast is when two very different colors are placed besides each other.
8. Contrasting values help to show detail, as does the contrast among this here white page and black type.
9. For them artists that work only in black and white, contrast and value are major concerns.
10. Many people feel that the affect of a painting can depend more on color then on other elements.

Grammar and Usage Test: Section 1

DIRECTIONS Either part or all of each of the following sentences is under-lined. Using the rules of formal, standard English, choose the answer that correctly expresses the meaning of the underlined word groups. If there is no error, choose A. Indicate your response by shading in the appropriate oval on your answer sheet.

EXAMPLE 1. In 1990, restoration began on the Sphinx, it is an ancient Egyptian statue.

      (A) Sphinx, it is an ancient Egyptian statue

      (B) Sphinx because it is an ancient Egyptian statue

      (C) Sphinx, an ancient Egyptian statue

      (D) Sphinx, being an ancient Egyptian statue

      (E) Sphinx when it was an ancient Egyptian statue

ANSWER 1.    (A) (B) (C) (D) (E)

1. The magnificent glass pyramids at the Louvre, which were designed by the American architect I. M. Pei.

    (A) The magnificent glass pyramids at the Louvre, which were designed by the American architect I. M. Pei.

    (B) Being designed by the American architect I. M. Pei, the magnificent glass pyramids at the Louvre.

    (C) The American architect I. M. Pei, who designed the magnificent glass pyramids at the Louvre.

    (D) The American architect I. M. Pei designed the magnificent glass pyramids at the Louvre.

    (E) I. M. Pei, an American architect, designing the magnificent glass pyramids at the Louvre.

2. Have you read about the tornado that damaged so many homes in today's paper?

    (A) about the tornado that damaged so many homes in today's paper

    (B) in today's paper about the tornado that damaged so many homes

    (C) about the tornado in today's paper that damaged so many homes

    (D) about the destructive tornado in today's paper

    (E) today about the destructive tornado in the paper

3. Most people believe that the Loch Ness monster is just a <u>myth, sightings of the monster continue to be reported.</u>

   (A) myth, sightings of the monster continue to be reported
   (B) myth, and people report still seeing the monster
   (C) myth. Sightings of the monster continue to be reported
   (D) myth; sightings of the monster continue to be reported
   (E) myth; however, sightings of the monster continue to be reported

4. Tamara told Jenny <u>that she probably made an A.</u>

   (A) that she probably made an A
   (B) that an A was probably what she made
   (C) that Jenny probably made an A
   (D) about her making an A probably
   (E) that her grade was probably an A

5. To fully appreciate many of Gary Soto's stories, <u>some knowledge of Mexican American culture is necessary.</u>

   (A) some knowledge of Mexican American culture is necessary
   (B) the reader needs some knowledge of Mexican American culture
   (C) you must learn all about Mexican American culture
   (D) knowing something about Mexican American culture
   (E) the necessity is to know about Mexican American culture

6. <u>In this article, it says that the Chinese were using paper money by the thirteenth century.</u>

   (A) In this article, it says that the Chinese were using paper money by the thirteenth century.
   (B) According to this article, it says that the Chinese were using paper money by the thirteenth century.
   (C) By the thirteenth century, the Chinese in this article were using paper money.
   (D) In this article, they say that the Chinese were using paper money by the thirteenth century.
   (E) According to this article, the Chinese were using paper money by the thirteenth century.

7. <u>The capital of Liberia, Monrovia, which was named by freed slaves in honor of President James Monroe.</u>

   (A) The capital of Liberia, Monrovia, which was named by freed slaves in honor of President James Monroe.
   (B) Monrovia, the capital of Liberia, named by freed slaves in honor of President James Monroe.

(C) Named by freed slaves, Monrovia, the capital of Liberia, in honor of President James Monroe.

(D) In honor of President James Monroe, freed slaves named the capital of Liberia Monrovia.

(E) In honor of President James Monroe, freed slaves who named Monrovia the capital of Liberia.

8. I bought a collar <u>for my kitten that has a reflective tag and a breakaway buckle.</u>

 (A) for my kitten that has a reflective tag and a breakaway buckle

 (B) for my kitten with a reflective tag and a breakaway buckle

 (C) that has a reflective tag and a breakaway buckle for my kitten

 (D) for my kitten having a reflective tag and a breakaway buckle

 (E) for my kitten, and it has a reflective tag and a breakaway buckle

9. <u>Henry Ford wanted to make his cars affordable to everyone; that is why he developed an efficient assembly-line method for manufacturing them.</u>

 (A) Henry Ford wanted to make his cars affordable to everyone; that is why he developed an efficient assembly-line method for manufacturing them.

 (B) Henry Ford wanted to make his cars affordable to everyone so that he could develop an efficient assembly-line method for manufacturing them.

 (C) Henry Ford wanted to make his cars affordable to everyone because he developed an efficient assembly-line method for manufacturing them.

 (D) Henry Ford developed an efficient assembly-line method for manufacturing his cars because he wanted to make them affordable to everyone.

 (E) To develop an efficient assembly-line method for manufacturing his cars, Henry Ford wanted to make them affordable to everyone.

10. <u>Having seen that people in some countries were denied basic civil rights, my uncle's appreciation for the Bill of Rights grew.</u>

 (A) Having seen that people in some countries were denied basic civil rights, my uncle's appreciation for the Bill of Rights grew.

 (B) My uncle, having seen the Bill of Rights, knew that people in some countries were denied basic civil rights.

 (C) When basic civil rights are denied people in some countries, my uncle's appreciation for the Bill of Rights grows.

 (D) My uncle's appreciation for people denied basic civil rights in some countries grew as he read the Bill of Rights.

 (E) My uncle's appreciation for the Bill of Rights grew after he had seen that people in some countries were denied basic civil rights.

Grammar and Usage Test: Section 2

DIRECTIONS Read the paragraph below. For each numbered blank, select the word or word group that best completes the sentence. Indicate your response by shading in the appropriate oval on your answer sheet.

EXAMPLE More powerful than optical microscopes, electron microscopes __(1)__ researchers to study extremely small objects.

> 1. (A) has enabled
>   (B) is enabling
>   (C) enabling
>   (D) enable
>   (E) enables

ANSWER 1.

An electron microscope, using a beam of electrons, __(1)__ a magnified image. Unlike an optical microscope, __(2)__ instrument does not depend on __(3)__ light rays. Instead, an electron lens __(4)__ a system of electromagnetic coils that focus the electron beam. The electrons __(5)__ , of course, aren't visible to the naked eye. Rather, __(6)__ are directed at a specimen to form __(7)__ image on a photographic plate. The wavelength of an electron beam is __(8)__ than the wavelength of light. Therefore, __(9)__ magnification is possible with an electron microscope __(10)__ optical microscope.

1. (A) create
   (B) is creating
   (C) creates
   (D) will create
   (E) will have created

2. (A) this here
   (B) this
   (C) these
   (D) these kind of
   (E) that there

3. (A) any
   (B) not one
   (C) no
   (D) hardly any
   (E) barely some

4. (A) use
   (B) has used
   (C) will use
   (D) uses
   (E) had been using

5. (A) themself
   (B) themselves
   (C) theirself
   (D) theirselves
   (E) itself

6. (A) them
   (B) it
   (C) that
   (D) this
   (E) they

7. (A) its
   (B) their
   (C) they're
   (D) its'
   (E) it's

8. (A) short
   (B) shorter
   (C) more short
   (D) more shorter
   (E) shortest

9. (A) good
   (B) gooder
   (C) better
   (D) more better
   (E) more good

10. (A) then with an
    (B) then with a
    (C) than with an
    (D) than with a
    (E) then a

BURE-U OF
MIS-ING
LET-ERS

COMMON ERRORS

Reference Note

For information on **capital letters,** see Chapter 10.

Exercise 25 Correcting the Capitalization of Words and Phrases

Correct the following words and phrases by either changing lowercase letters to capital letters or changing capital letters to lowercase letters.

EXAMPLE   1. Hank's poem "Waiting for morning in july"

            1. *Hank's poem "Waiting for Morning in July"*

1. geometry I, latin, and civics
2. *national geographic* magazine
3. the god of abraham, isaac, and jacob
4. an Island in the gulf of mexico
5. liberty bell
6. during the great depression
7. readings from "the scarlet ibis"
8. internal revenue service forms
9. mother's day
10. an episode of *party of five*
11. Grandfather Ben and my Cousin
12. Hiroshige's painting *The Moon Beyond The Leaves*
13. an italian custom
14. bill of rights
15. a passage from the koran
16. is that an okidata® printer?
17. dr. and mrs. Dorset
18. a congressional medal of honor recipient
19. chief joseph
20. *King Of The Wind*

Exercise 26 Proofreading for Correct Capitalization

Each of the following sentences contains at least one capitalization error. Correct each error by changing capital letters to lowercase letters or lowercase letters to capital letters.

EXAMPLE   1. In the barn my Dad is building an ultralight plane that we have named the *hummingbird*.

            1. *dad, Hummingbird*

1. The slave knelt at the feet of the statue and said, "Zeus, o, Zeus, Oh please, help me."
2. long ago, Africans shaped tools from stones; we find these stones wherever they lived.

3. My grandma told me that she used to go to Wrigley field with her father and mother.

4. This saturday, instead of going to eagle lake, let's go to the Riverdale High School Festival.

5. A Yale student laid out the plans for a submarine that was used in the American revolution.

6. Fred started sewing kites for himself and his friends and now has a small business known as Fred's fliers.

7. "Have you read *Changes in Latitudes*?" i asked.

8. Because the Panama Canal is too narrow for some supertankers, they sometimes must pass through the waters of the strait of Magellan at the Southern tip of south america.

9. The chess club meets every day after school in the large room East of the auditorium.

10. We think our team, the Kennedy middle school bobcats, is the best in Baker county.

Exercise 27 Proofreading for Correct Capitalization

Each of the following sentences contains errors in capitalization. Correct each error by changing capital letters to lowercase letters or lowercase letters to capital letters.

EXAMPLE   1. Often, i feel like a World traveler in my hometown.

       1. *I, world*

1. When I ride the bus down central avenue, I can hear people speaking spanish, hindi, japanese, arabic, and some other languages I don't even recognize.

2. On independence day, my Mother and I drove our old ford thunderbird to Taylor park.

3. Near there we saw mr. Narazaki and Ms. white eagle talking.

4. They were in front of the Lincoln building, where the federal bureau of investigation has offices.

5. On that same Saturday, we also saw several muslim women wearing long robes and veils in front of hill medical center next to the Park.

6. After the band played John philip Sousa's "the Stars And Stripes Forever," people stood beside a statue of the Greek deity Athena and gave readings from the declaration of independence and the bible.

7. Later, mayor Mendoza read a telegram from the president of the united states, gave a speech, and awarded Medals to several people for their public service.

8. As soon as the big dipper was clearly visible, the fireworks started, and I thought, "this is definitely the greatest place on Earth!"
9. Next year, I plan to take United States history II at West creek high school.
10. I am going to look in my new history book for a list of all the peoples that make up our country, from the inuits of alaska to the hawaiians of hilo bay.

Exercise 28 Using Commas Correctly

Reference Note

For information on **using commas correctly,** see page 271.

Add and delete commas to punctuate the following sentences correctly.

EXAMPLE　　1.　A first-aid kit should contain adhesive tape scissors antiseptic and a variety of bandages.

　　　　　　1.　*A first-aid kit should contain adhesive tape, scissors, antiseptic, and a variety of bandages.*

1. Yes I have a screwdriver and some screws and wood glue.
2. On the balcony of a second-floor apartment a large macaw sat watching us.
3. We moved on October 15; our new address is 5311 East Baker Street, Deerfield Illinois, 60015.
4. All you need to bring are a change of clothes shoes socks a toothbrush and toothpaste.
5. Phobos is I believe one of the moons around Mars Mrs. Farris.
6. Fire damaged a number of houses yet no one was injured not even any pets.
7. Because acrylic a type of water-based paint dries rapidly you must work quickly with it.
8. Birds sang frogs jumped and children played on that hot sunny day.
9. Malfunctioning dangerously the robot moved jerkily toward the table picked up a dish dropped it on the floor and rolled out the door.
10. Easing up on the throttle she coasted in for a smooth landing.

Exercise 29 Using Commas Correctly

Add and delete commas to punctuate the following sentences correctly.

EXAMPLE　　1.　They made beads out of small white seashells Ed.

　　　　　　1.　*They made beads out of small, white seashells, Ed.*

1. Deer thrived sea life flourished and all manner of edible plants grew in the region, that is now California.

2. Up and down the coastline of California communities of American Indians have lived for centuries.

3. The Karok Pomo Yurok and Modoc are just four of the dozens of peoples living in this area.

4. Skilled in basketwork the Pomo became known for the decoration variety and intricate weaving of their baskets.

5. The Yurok developed an elaborate monetary system which they used in fixing a price on every privilege or offense.

6. While many peoples favored dentalium shells as currency they also exchanged other items in trade.

7. Yurok marriages were arranged with care for marriage was an important public and historic alliance.

8. Yes Helen, the Gabrielino hunted with a stick that is similar to the boomerang the famous Australian weapon.

9. Traditionally, the Coast Miwok peoples were each represented by a male chief, and a female chief and a female ceremonial leader called a *maien.*

10. Kintpuash who was also called Captain Jack was the Modoc leader, who escaped capture on November 29 1872.

Exercise 30 Proofreading for Correct Use of Semicolons and Colons

Add or delete semicolons and colons to correct the punctuation in the following sentences.

EXAMPLE
1. The party starts at 7 30, we will need to leave our house by 7 00.

1. *The party starts at 7:30; we will need to leave our house by 7:00.*

1. John is bringing the drinks, ice, and cups, and Wanda is bringing the plates, knives, and forks.

2. Compare these three translations of King David's famous song, Psalm 23 1–6.

3. Don't forget to pick up: Carlos, Kam, Lisa, and Mary at 7 15 sharp.

4. Twin koalas are rare in captivity, consequently, Australia's Yanchep National Park prized Euca and Lyptus, the two born there in 1996.

5. The dance committee still needs to get the following equipment a CD player, outdoor speakers, and a microphone.

6. During our party on the Fourth of July last year, a huge storm forced everyone inside, then lightning knocked the power out.

HELP

In Exercise 30, you may need to use colons and semicolons to replace incorrectly used commas.

Reference Note

For information on **semicolons and colons,** see Chapter 12.

COMMON ERRORS

7. California's seagulls will eat just about anything clams, chicks, berries, and even the occasional starfish.
8. We have invited exchange students from Dublin, Ireland, Paris, France, and Tokyo, Japan.
9. At 10 30 P.M., he neatly printed the title page, which read "Alfredo in Wonderland A Tale of an Exchange Student in New York."
10. Bamboo is a versatile and flexible building material, in Indonesia, as in many countries, it has a wide variety of uses.

Exercise 31 Using Punctuation Correctly in Sentences

Add periods, question marks, commas, semicolons, and colons to correct the punctuation in the following sentences.

EXAMPLE
1. In almost every corner of the world dogs do useful work for people

1. *In almost every corner of the world, dogs do useful work for people.*

1. Herding flocks collies and briards and other varieties of sheepdog are on the job wherever there are sheep.
2. Did you know that German shepherds which make good guard dogs can also herd sheep
3. Dogs guard our homes assist people with disabilities herd sheep_ and hunt game.
4. Sled dogs include the following breeds Samoyeds, huskies, Alaskan malamutes, and a few other strong breeds with thick fur.
5. Partners with police the world over bloodhounds are feared by criminals and praised by the parents of lost children whom these dogs have found.
6. The basenji comes from Africa and is in fact called the Congo dog many people share their homes with these animals whose ancestors date back to 3000 B C
7. Although Mexican Chihuahuas are tiny they fiercely take on any foe they don't back down even when facing a larger dog.
8. Brave little Chihuahuas ignore the good advice given in Ecclesiastes 9 4
9. Those famous lines make an obvious point "A living dog is better than a dead lion."
10. My favorite neighbor Edward Nichols Jr bought his Pekingese on Wednesday January 9 2008.

Correcting Errors in the Use of Quotation Marks and Other Punctuation

For each of the following sentences, correct any error in the use of quotation marks, commas, and end marks.

Reference Note

For information on **using quotation marks,** see page 314.

EXAMPLE   **1.** The troop leader said that we should bring the 'barest essentials': a change of clothes, a toothbrush, and a comb.

  1. The troop leader said that we should bring the "barest essentials": a change of clothes, a toothbrush, and a comb.

1. James seemed excited and said, "Did you see the news last night?

2. "Sorry, Emma" Becky began "but I'm late already."

3. When Coach Myers announced the tryouts this morning, she said, "that anyone could try out."

4. Ms. Waters asked us to read The Tell-Tale Heart and one other short story of our choice this weekend.

5. They are watching reruns of *The Magic School Bus;* this episode is Lost in the Solar System.

6. For tomorrow's assignment, read The Price of Freedom, the next chapter in your textbook.

7. My favorite part of *Reader's Digest* is Humor in Uniform.

8. Why don't you title your poem "Words and Music"? Tom asked

9. The recent article Carbon Monoxide: The Silent Killer details the effects of this deadly gas.

10. Didn't you hear me yell Call 911! asked Erik.

Punctuating and Capitalizing Quotations

For each of the following sentences, correct any error in the use of quotation marks, commas, end marks, and capitalization.

EXAMPLE   **1.** Larry told me that "you were sitting in the library."

  1. Larry told me that you were sitting in the library.

1. "I can't decide which selection to use for my project" sighed Fran.

2. Mary nodded and said "I haven't made up my mind either." "Are you going to choose a poem or a story"?

3. "I'm going to make a diorama of "Stopping by Woods on a Snowy Evening," interrupted Greg.

4. What if Ms. Hill says 'that you can't'? asked Mary.

5. Didn't she say "anything goes?" Greg answered.

6. "You're right." The instructions say 'write a song, present a play, or draw a picture, added Mary.

7. You play the guitar, Fran pointed out. Maybe you could write a song."

8. Mary smiled and said, "great idea!

9. What I'd really like to do is write extra verses for Woody Guthrie's song This Land Is Your Land, Fran said.

10. Perhaps even," Mary added "make a video of it"!

Exercise 34 Using Apostrophes Correctly

Reference Note

For more information on **using apostrophes,** see Chapter 14.

Add or delete apostrophes to punctuate the following items correctly. If an item is already correct, write C.

EXAMPLE   **1.** Weve got Matts tickets'.

    1. We've got Matt's tickets.

1. Dont use so many *so*s.
2. Its time for Janes report.
3. Ronnies and Eriks desks
4. Mom and Dads only car
5. PBSs most popular show
6. Who's your brother?
7. my sister's-in-laws cars
8. geeses caretaker
9. that baby birds' beak
10. Kerrys and your project
11. anyone's guess
12. Russs' *U*s look like *N*s.
13. Youre right!
14. those foxes dens
15. The blame is theirs'.
16. Lets eat at six oclock.
17. my March of Dimes donation
18. She says that shell bring ours'.
19. There's still time.
20. Bobs dog

Exercise 35 Proofreading for Spelling Errors

Reference Note

For information on **spelling rules,** see Chapter 16.

Correct each spelling error in the following sentences.

EXAMPLE   **1.** To succede, you must keep triing.

    1. succeed; trying

1. I cannot easily make dayly visits, even though I would surly like to.

2. The judge finaly conceded that the other driver had been exceding the speed limit.
3. The members of the procession carried one hundred twenty-five baskets of beautiful flowers.
4. The desert heat and dryness stoped both armys.
5. My neighbor's childs are always getting into mischeif.
6. A word with two *es*, such as *deer,* has a long vowel sound.
7. The children truely enjioed hearing thier echoes bounce off the canyon walls.
8. The candidate siezed the opportunity to give a breif statement of his beleifs.
9. Leafs fluttered off the trees and down the desertted beachs during that 1st day of winter.
10. 5 years ago, each of my brother-in-laws was working two jobs.

Exercise 36 **Proofreading for Spelling Errors**

For each of the following sentences, write the misspelled word or words correctly.

Reference Note

For information on **spelling rules,** see Chapter 16.

EXAMPLE   1. Six concrete elfs guarded the doorway to my nieghbor's house.

        1. *elves, neighbor's*

1. Leisure activities may be wholely unecessary for survival, but they make life enjoyable.
2. On the way to Japan, his neice met a Chinese man who spoke perfect English.
3. After the clouds receeded, the sun glinted on the wet rooves.
4. Three ranch hands were teaching ropeing to the tourists who had payed for lessons.
5. These attachments are interchangeable, I beleive.
6. While my freinds and I were siting on the porch, we saw a white rabbit hoping across the street.
7. Place two heaping spoonsful of flour in a saucepan; then, slice three small tomatos.
8. Yes, several attorney-at-laws at our offices are alumnuses of the state university.
9. There must have been over one hundred and fifty people standing in line longer than that.
10. Mr. Brady said that suddenly the terrifing possibility of going to school all year had not seemed so bad to the Bradies.

Exercise 37 Proofreading for Words Often Confused

For each of the following sentences, correct any error in word usage.

EXAMPLE 1. A camel caravan in the dessert is a noble sight.
1. *A camel caravan in the desert is a noble sight.*

1. The roar of the plain's engine broke the quite of the night.
2. Its time to get you're suitcase packed.
3. I put my desert right here on the kitchen table, and now its gone.
4. As the mustangs picked they're way through the canyon, they unknowingly past a cougar hiding in the rocks.
5. Who was the warrior who lead the Zulus in there famous battle against the Boers?
6. Be careful, or you will brake that mirror into a million peaces.
7. Every knight choose his own way threw the forest.
8. First, the pigs got lose; then we spent all day trying too catch them.
9. He couldn't here us; he was too week from the fever.
10. Who's biography did you chose to read?

Exercise 38 Distinguishing Between Words Often Confused

Choose the correct word in parentheses in each of the following sentences.

EXAMPLE 1. Is Korean food for dinner (*all right, alright*) with you?
1. *all right*

1. I believe that Andrew Young began his political career during the 1960s; (*than, then*) he became a U.S. representative before being named ambassador to the United Nations.
2. Millie, would you care to explain the first (*principle, principal*) of thermodynamics to the class?
3. A (*stationery, stationary*) cold front has been responsible for this week's wonderful weather.
4. Recycling helps cut down on the (*waist, waste*) of resources.
5. Did you (*all ready, already*) qualify for the race?
6. How would you (*council, consul, counsel*) someone in this situation?
7. What (*effects, affects*) will the Internet have on your future career?
8. There's nothing (*plain, plane*) about these stylized medieval reliefs.
9. I think that when it came to scat singing, Sarah Vaughan really was (*all together, altogether*) the best.
10. Designing a golf (*coarse, course*) must be a challenging task.

Proofreading a Business Letter

For each numbered item in the following business letter, correct any errors in mechanics. An item may contain more than one error. If an item is already correct, write *C*.

EXAMPLE   **[1]** 813 E Maple St

       1. 813 E. Maple St.

---

     813 East Maple Street
[1] Belleville IL, 62223

[2] February 12th, 2009

[3] Customer Service
Super Sport Shoes
14 Magenta Road
Woodinville WA, 98072

[4] Dear Sir or Madam,

[5] Thank you for your prompt response to my order (number 51238) for two pairs of white jogging shoes. **[6]** These shoe's are the most comfortable ones I have ever worn.

[7] However, one of the pairs that I recieved is the wrong size. **[8]** This pair is to small; consequently, I am returning these shoes with this letter. **[9]** Please exchange them for one pair of white joggers two sizes larger.

[10] Your's truly

Neville Walters

Neville Walters

Mechanics Test: Section 1

DIRECTIONS Each of the following sentences contains an underlined word or word group. Choose the answer that shows the correct capitalization, punctuation, and spelling of the underlined part. If there is no error, choose answer E (Correct as is). Indicate your response by shading in the appropriate oval on your answer sheet.

EXAMPLE 1. Marla <u>asked, "did</u> you see the meteor shower last night?"

     (A) asked, "Did

     (B) asked "Did

     (C) asked "did

     (D) asked did you

     (E) Correct as is

ANSWER 1.

1. We keep a variety of emergency equipment in the trunk of our <u>car, a first-aid</u> kit, jumper cables, a blanket, a flashlight, and road flares.

     (A) car a first-aid   **(D)** car: a 1st-aid

     (B) car: a first-aid   **(E)** Correct as is

     (C) car; a first-aid

2. Alvin <u>Ailey, who's choreography</u> thrilled audiences for years, formed the dance company that still bears his name.

     (A) Ailey who's choreography   **(D)** Ailey, whose choreography

     (B) Ailey whose choreography   **(E)** Correct as is

     (C) Ailey who's choreography,

3. Jerome <u>said, "I cant believe</u> that Ben Franklin wanted the turkey to be the symbol for the United States!"

     (A) said, "I can't believe   **(D)** said, 'I can't believe

     (B) said "I can't believe   **(E)** Correct as is

     (C) said, "I can't beleive

4. "Do <u>you," asked Kay 'Know</u> the story of Icarus?"

     (A) you, asked Kay, "know   **(D)** you," asked Kay, 'know

     (B) you?" asked Kay. "Know   **(E)** Correct as is

     (C) you," asked Kay, "know

5. I often struggle to open my gym <u>locker; its</u> lock is probably rusty.

   (A) locker, its   (D) locker: It's
   (B) locker; Its   (E) Correct as is
   (C) locker. It's

6. Please <u>bring too tomatos,</u> a head of lettuce, and some feta cheese from the market.

   (A) bring: two tomatoes,   (D) bring to tomatoes,
   (B) bring 2 tomatoes   (E) Correct as is
   (C) bring two tomatoes,

7. "Did Principal Reeves really say, 'We need *less* <u>discipline?"</u> asked Cassandra.

   (A) discipline,'"   (D) discipline'"?
   (B) discipline'?"   (E) Correct as is
   (C) discipline?'

8. Grandfather enjoyed the <u>childrens storys</u> about their visit to the wildlife sanctuary.

   (A) childrens story's   (D) children's stories
   (B) childrens' stories   (E) Correct as is
   (C) childrens stories

9. The Leonards <u>visited: Rome, Italy,</u> Athens, Greece; and Istanbul, Turkey, on their vacation.

   (A) visited Rome, Italy;   (D) visited Rome; Italy;
   (B) visited: Rome, Italy;   (E) Correct as is
   (C) visited, Rome, Italy;

10. Did <u>aunt Susan,</u> bring the coleslaw?

    (A) aunt Susan   (D) Aunt, Susan,
    (B) aunt, Susan,   (E) Correct as is
    (C) Aunt Susan

Mechanics Test: Section 2

DIRECTIONS   Each numbered item below contains an underlined group of words. Choose the answer that shows the correct capitalization, punctuation, and spelling of the underlined part. If there is no error, choose answer E (Correct as is). Indicate your response by shading in the appropriate oval on your answer sheet.

EXAMPLE   **[1]** 200 north Vine Street

        (A) 200 North Vine street

        (B) 200 North Vine Street

        (C) Two-Hundred North Vine Street

        (D) 200, North Vine Street

        (E) Correct as is

ANSWER   1.   Ⓐ **Ⓑ** Ⓒ Ⓓ Ⓔ

---

200 North Vine Street
Austin, TX 78741

[1] May, 5 2009

Athena Wilson
Worldwide Travel, Inc.
4135-A Anderson Avenue
[2] San Antonio, Tex. 78249

[3] Dear Ms. Wilson:

[4] Thank you for you're prompt response to my request for information about traveling to Australia. The color brochures describing the **[5]** different, Australian tours were especially helpful. My family and I are interested in the "Natural Wonders" **[6]** package, that includes day trips to **[7]** the great Barrier reef. **[8]** Well also want to schedule a three-day stay in Sydney. How much will the entire package **[9]** cost, for three adults and one child?

[10] Yours truly

Naomi Baskin

Naomi Baskin

1. **(A)** May 5 2009
   (B) May Fifth 2009
   (C) May 5th 2009
   (D) May 5, 2009
   (E) Correct as is

2. **(A)** San Antonio, Tex 78249
   (B) San Antonio Texas 78249
   (C) San Antonio, TX 78249
   (D) San Antonio TX 78249
   (E) Correct as is

3. **(A)** Dear Ms. Wilson,
   (B) Dear ms. Wilson:
   (C) Dear Ms Wilson,
   (D) Dear Ms. Wilson;
   (E) Correct as is

4. **(A)** Thank you for youre
   (B) Thank you for youre'
   (C) Thank you for your
   (D) Thank you for your'
   (E) Correct as is

5. **(A)** different australian
   (B) different Australian
   (C) different, Australian,
   (D) different, australian,
   (E) Correct as is

6. **(A)** package that includes
   (B) package that, includes
   (C) package: that includes
   (D) package that includes:
   (E) Correct as is

7. **(A)** the Great Barrier Reef
   (B) the great Barrier Reef
   (C) the Great Barrier reef
   (D) The great Barrier reef
   (E) Correct as is

8. **(A)** Well, also
   (B) We'll, also,
   (C) We'll also
   (D) We'll, also
   (E) Correct as is

9. **(A)** cost for 3
   (B) cost? For three
   (C) cost: for three
   (D) cost for three
   (E) Correct as is

10. **(A)** Yours' truly,
    (B) Yours truly:
    (C) Your's truly,
    (D) Yours truly,
    (E) Correct as is

Sentences

GO TO: go.hrw.com

Writing Complete Sentences

Diagnostic Preview

A. Identifying Sentences and Sentence Fragments

Identify each of the following word groups as a *sentence* or a *sentence fragment*.

EXAMPLE   **1.** Falling into a deep, dreamless sleep.

1. sentence fragment

1. To begin on page 10 and read the rest of the chapter.
2. Because we did not have any other homework over the weekend.
3. Learning to speak a second language is one of my goals.
4. If you will be allowed to leave class early next Tuesday afternoon.
5. Irritable from lack of sleep, the child began to whine.
6. Lettuce, a cucumber, a bell pepper, and some shredded carrots.
7. The full moon, rising above the trees, illuminated the snowy fields.
8. These muffins, which are made with whole-wheat flour and buttermilk.
9. As we entered the cave, our guide pointed to some interesting formations.
10. Max, who is one of my cousins from Michigan.

B. Revising Sentence Fragments

Rewrite each of the following sentence fragments to create a complete sentence.

EXAMPLE   1. Underneath one of the cushions on the couch.

            1. *I found ten pennies underneath one of the cushions on the couch.*

11. Encouraging her to become a doctor.
12. Excited about the approaching vacation.
13. The fishing boats that were tied up at the dock.
14. After he finished folding the clothes.
15. One of the most thoughtful essays I have ever read.

C. Identifying and Revising Run-on Sentences

Identify each of the following word groups as a *sentence* or a *run-on sentence*. Then, revise each run-on sentence to make it one or more complete sentences.

EXAMPLE   1. Don't leave your lunch on that table, did I tell you what happened to me at the park last week?

            1. *run-on sentence Don't leave your lunch on that table. Did I tell you what happened to me at the park last week?*

16. The morning was warm and sunny, I agreed to take my younger sister and her friends to the park.
17. While I packed lunch, Sarah, Ellen, and Annie put on their bike helmets and checked the air pressure in their tires.
18. The park is only a mile from our house, the ride was easy and pleasant.
19. When we reached the park, we locked our bikes and walked over to the playground, we put our helmets and lunch on a nearby picnic table.
20. The girls climbed on the playscape while I sat under a tree and read.
21. After an hour, Sarah announced that she was hungry, and we all agreed to stop and eat lunch.
22. As we approached the picnic table, we heard squealing and chattering, a family of squirrels had started lunch without us.
23. A big squirrel was perched on one of the bike helmets, in its paws was a piece of one of our sandwiches.
24. One squirrel was eating an apple, and another was tearing at a paper bag, searching for more good things to eat.
25. The squirrels ran away when we appeared, of course, we had to go back home to eat lunch.

Sentence Fragments

A ***sentence*** is a word group that has a subject and a verb and that expresses a complete thought. A ***sentence fragment*** is a word group that is missing a subject or a verb or that does not express a complete thought.

Sentence fragments usually occur when you write in a hurry or become a little careless. You may leave out a word, or you may chop off part of a sentence by putting in a period too soon.

To find out whether you have a complete sentence or a sentence fragment, you can use a simple three-part test:

1. Does the group of words have a subject?
2. Does it have a verb?
3. Does it express a complete thought?

If you answer *no* to any of these questions, your word group is a fragment. It is missing at least one basic part.

FRAGMENT	Was the best sharpshooter in the United States. [The subject is missing. Who was the best sharpshooter in the United States?]
SENTENCE	Annie Oakley was the best sharpshooter in the United States.
FRAGMENT	Annie Oakley with Buffalo Bill Cody's Wild West show. [The verb is missing. What did she do with the Wild West show?]
SENTENCE	Annie Oakley performed with Buffalo Bill Cody's Wild West show.
FRAGMENT	As it fell through the air ninety feet away. [This group of words has a subject (*it*) and a verb (*fell*), but it does not express a complete thought. What happened as something fell through the air?]
SENTENCE	Annie could shoot a playing card as it fell through the air ninety feet away.

Annie Oakley

NOTE By itself, a fragment does not express a complete thought. However, fragments can make sense if they are clearly related to the sentences that come before or after them. These sentences give the fragments meaning by helping the reader fill in the missing parts.

The following passage is from an essay that describes the death and the cutting down of a great white oak on the writer's family homestead. The author's grandfather has carefully cut at the dead tree and is about to aim the final blows. See how the author uses fragments to describe the fall of the great tree.

> Then came the great moment. A few last, quick strokes. A slow, deliberate swaying. The crack of parting fibers. Then a long "swoo-sh!" that rose in pitch as the towering trunk arced downward at increasing speed.
>
> Edwin Way Teale, "The Death of a Tree"

Experienced writers like Teale sometimes use sentence fragments to achieve a certain effect. As a developing writer, however, you need to practice and master writing complete sentences before you begin to experiment with writing fragments.

Oral Practice **Identifying Sentence Fragments**

Some of the following items are sentence fragments. Read each item aloud. Then, tell whether the item is a complete sentence, is missing a subject, is missing a verb, or does not express a complete thought.

EXAMPLE   **1.** After he wrote "A Christmas Memory."

  1. Not a complete thought

1. Truman Capote was an American author.
2. Was born in New Orleans in 1924.
3. Grew up in Alabama.
4. Because he hated attending boarding schools.
5. A movie version of *Breakfast at Tiffany's,* probably his most famous novel.
6. When he moved to New York City.
7. Capote's short story "A Christmas Memory" was made into a television movie.
8. His characters lively and eccentric.

9. Is one of his most moving stories.

10. Spent six years researching the nonfiction book titled *In Cold Blood.*

┌─────────────────────┐
│ TIPS & TRICKS │
└─────────────────────┘
To find phrase fragments in your writing, read the sentences in your paragraphs from the last to the first. Reading this way helps you to listen for complete thoughts that make sense.

Phrase Fragments

A *phrase* is a group of words that does not have a subject and a verb and that is used as a single part of speech. Three kinds of phrases that can easily be mistaken for complete sentences are *verbal phrases, appositive phrases,* and *prepositional phrases.*

Verbal Phrases

Verbals, forms of verbs that are used as other parts of speech, sometimes fool us into thinking that a group of words has a verb when it really does not. Some verbals end in *–ing, –d,* or *–ed* and are used the same way adjectives are. Other verbals have the word *to* in front of the base form (*to go, to play*).

Reference Note

For more on **verbals** (participles, gerunds, and infinitives), see page 77.

A *verbal phrase* is a phrase containing a verbal and its modifiers and complements. By itself, a verbal phrase is a fragment because it does not express a complete thought.

FRAGMENT   Learning about the Civil War.
SENTENCE   I enjoy learning about the Civil War.

FRAGMENT   Gaining glory for itself and for all black soldiers.
SENTENCE   Gaining glory for itself and for all black soldiers, the 54th Massachusetts Regiment led the attack on Fort Wagner.

FRAGMENT   Inspired by the 54th Massachusetts Regiment.
SENTENCE   Inspired by the 54th Massachusetts Regiment, other black soldiers fought bravely.

FRAGMENT   To become good soldiers.
SENTENCE   Black volunteers trained hard to become good soldiers.

Appositive Phrases

An *appositive* is a noun or pronoun placed beside another noun or pronoun to identify or describe it. An *appositive phrase,* a phrase made up of an appositive and its modifiers, is a fragment. It does not contain the basic parts of a sentence.

FRAGMENT   A twenty-five-year-old soldier.
SENTENCE   The 54th Massachusetts Regiment was commanded by
            Colonel Shaw, a twenty-five-year-old soldier.

Prepositional Phrases

A *prepositional phrase* is a group of
words containing a preposition and a
noun or pronoun object. A prepositional
phrase cannot stand alone as a sentence
because it does not express a complete
thought.

FRAGMENT   With great courage on the
            battlefield.
SENTENCE   The 54th Massachusetts
            Regiment acted with great
            courage on the battlefield.

The 54th Massachusetts Regiment

Exercise 1 **Revising Phrase Fragments**

Use your imagination to create sentences from the following phrases.
You can either (1) attach the fragment to a complete sentence or
(2) develop the phrase into a complete sentence by adding a subject, a
verb, or both.

EXAMPLE   1. landing on the planet
              1. *Landing on the planet, the astronauts immediately
                  began to explore.*

                            or

              The astronauts were landing on the planet.

 1. in a huge spaceship
 2. setting foot on the planet
 3. to explore the craters
 4. walking around in a spacesuit
 5. finding no sign of life
 6. the astronauts' spaceship
 7. checking the spaceship for damage
 8. the planet's moon
 9. to return to Earth
10. on a successful mission

**MEETING THE
CHALLENGE**

You may have already
noticed that many adver-
tisements use fragments
rather than complete sen-
tences. Search through a
popular magazine, and clip
out an ad that uses frag-
ments. Then, revise the ad
so that it contains only
complete sentences. How
does the ad change when
you revise the fragments?
Do you think the new ad
would appeal to the same
audience that the original
ad did? Write a brief paragraph in which you explain
your conclusions.

Subordinate Clause Fragments

A *clause* is a group of words that has a subject and a verb. One kind of clause, an **independent clause,** expresses a complete thought and can stand on its own as a sentence. For example, the group of words *I ate my lunch* is an independent clause. However, another kind of clause, a **subordinate clause,** does not express a complete thought and cannot stand by itself as a sentence.

FRAGMENT	When Paris carried off the beautiful Helen of Troy. [What happened when Paris carried off Helen?]
SENTENCE	When Paris carried off the beautiful Helen of Troy, he started the Trojan War.
FRAGMENT	Who was a great hero of the Greeks. [The reader needs to know more—whom does this subordinate clause describe, and what did that person do?]
SENTENCE	Odysseus, who was a great hero of the Greeks, took part in the Trojan War.
FRAGMENT	Because the wooden horse concealed Greek soldiers. [What was the result of the concealment?]
SENTENCE	Because the wooden horse concealed Greek soldiers, the Greeks finally won the Trojan War.
FRAGMENT	Which was Achilles' only vulnerable spot. [What was Achilles' only vulnerable spot?]
SENTENCE	An injury to his heel, which was Achilles' only vulnerable spot, led to that hero's death.

NOTE A subordinate clause telling *why, where, when,* or *how* is called an **adverb clause.** Usually you can place an adverb clause either before or after the independent clause in a sentence.

EXAMPLE **After he started home from the Trojan War,** Odysseus had many more adventures.

or

Odysseus had many more adventures **after he started home from the Trojan War.**

If you put the subordinate clause first, use a comma to separate it from the independent clause. The comma makes the sentence easier for the reader to understand.

Reference Note

For more on **punctuating introductory adverb clauses,** see page 281.

Exercise 2 Revising Subordinate Clause Fragments

The following paragraph contains some subordinate clause fragments. First, find these clause fragments. Next, revise the paragraph, joining the subordinate clauses with independent clauses. (There may be more than one way to join them.) Change the punctuation and capitalization as necessary.

EXAMPLE   When you look at eyeliner. You may not think of ancient Egypt.

When you look at eyeliner, you may not think of ancient Egypt.

People have been using cosmetics for thousands of years. In Africa, the ancient Egyptians used perfumes, hair dyes, and makeup. That they made from plants and minerals. While they often used cosmetics to improve their appearance. They also used them to protect their skin from the hot sun. Today, cosmetics are made from over five thousand different ingredients, including waxes, oils, and dyes. The cosmetics business is a huge industry. Advertisers are extremely successful in selling cosmetics. Because they appeal to our desire to be attractive. Advertisers often hint. That their products will make us beautiful, happy, and successful.

Exercise 3 Using Subordinate Clauses in Sentences

Use each of the following subordinate clause fragments as part of a complete sentence. Add whatever words are necessary to make the meaning of the sentence complete. Add capitalization and punctuation as necessary.

EXAMPLE   1. when our windows started glowing

1. *We were eating dinner when our windows started glowing.*

1. as we watched the spaceship land
2. who approached the house in long leaps
3. which startled the dog
4. so that we could get a better look
5. when they handed me a glowing sphere

6. because they liked us
7. which looked very complex
8. before we could object
9. since we didn't complain
10. even though no one would believe our story

NOTE A **series of items** is another kind of fragment that is easily mistaken for a sentence. Notice that, in the following example, the series of items in dark type is not a complete sentence.

FRAGMENT   I ate several things for lunch. **A sandwich, an apple, four pieces of celery, and some popcorn.**

To correct the fragment, you can

• make it into a complete sentence

or

• link it to the previous sentence with a colon

SENTENCE   I ate several things for lunch. I ate a sandwich, an apple, four pieces of celery, and some popcorn.

or

I ate several things for lunch: a sandwich, an apple, four pieces of celery, and some popcorn.

Review A Identifying and Revising Fragments

Some of the following groups of words are sentence fragments. Identify each fragment, and make it part of a complete sentence, adding commas where necessary. When you find a complete sentence, write *C*.

Reference Note

For more on **punctuating introductory phrases,** see page 281.

EXAMPLE   1. Originally raised to hunt badgers. Dachshunds are now popular as pets.

1. *Originally raised to hunt badgers, dachshunds are now popular as pets.*

1. Humans have kept dogs as pets and helpers. For perhaps ten thousand years.
2. Herding sheep and cattle and guarding property. Many dogs more than earn their keep.
3. Descended from wolves. Some dogs are still somewhat wolflike.
4. There are over one hundred breeds of dogs now.
5. If you have a Saint Bernard. You have one of the largest dogs.

6. Because Yorkshire terriers are very tiny and cute. Many people keep them as pets.
7. Since they are all born blind and unable to take care of themselves. Puppies need their mothers.
8. Most dogs are fully grown by the time they are one year old.
9. Dogs live an average of twelve years. Although many live to be nearly twenty.
10. If you like dogs. Consider having one for a pet.

Run-on Sentences

A *run-on sentence* is two or more complete sentences run together as one. Because they do not show where one idea ends and another one begins, run-on sentences can confuse your reader. There are two kinds of run-ons. In the first kind, called a *fused sentence,* the sentences have no punctuation at all between them.

RUN-ON   Schools in the Middle Ages were different from ours students usually did not have books.

CORRECT   Schools in the Middle Ages were different from ours. Students usually did not have books.

In the other kind of run-on, the writer links together sentences with only a comma to separate them from one another. This kind of run-on is called a *comma splice.*

RUN-ON   Schools today have books for every student, many schools also have televisions and computers.

CORRECT   Schools today have books for every student. Many schools also have televisions and computers.

Revising Run-on Sentences

There are several ways you can revise run-on sentences. As shown in the examples above, you can always make two separate sentences. However, if the two thoughts are equal to one another in importance, you may want to make a *compound sentence.*

RUN-ON   Canada has ten provinces each province has its own government. [fused]

Canada has ten provinces, each province has its own government. [comma splice]

COMPUTER TIP

You can use a grammar-checking program to flag sentences in your writing that are longer than a certain number of words—sentences that have a higher chance of being run-ons. You can then use the information in this chapter to determine whether or not the flagged sentences are run-ons.

TIPS & TRICKS

To spot run-on sentences, read your writing aloud. Each point where you hear yourself making a pause as you read is a point where you should ask, *Do I need to create separate sentences here? Do I need to add a semicolon or period? Do I need a comma and a conjunction instead? Do I need additional punctuation here?*

1. You can make a compound sentence by using a comma and a coordinating conjunction (such as *and, but,* or *or*).

CORRECTED   Canada has ten provinces**, and** each province has its own government.

2. You can make a compound sentence by using a semicolon.

CORRECTED   Canada has ten provinces**;** each province has its own government.

3. You can make a compound sentence by using a semicolon and a word such as *therefore, instead, meanwhile, still, also, nevertheless,* or *however.* These words are called ***conjunctive adverbs.*** Follow a conjunctive adverb with a comma.

CORRECTED   Canada has ten provinces**; also,** each province has its own government.

Reference Note

For more on **compound sentences,** see page 109.

NOTE Before you join two sentences in a compound sentence, make sure that the ideas in the sentences are closely related to one another. If you link unrelated ideas, you may confuse your reader.

UNRELATED   Canada is almost four million square miles in size, and I hope to visit my relatives there someday.

RELATED   Canada is almost four million square miles in size, but most of its people live on a small strip of land along the southern border.

Exercise 4 **Revising Run-on Sentences**

The following items are confusing because they are run-on sentences. Clear up the confusion by revising the run-ons to form clear, complete sentences. To revise, use the method given in parentheses after each sentence.

EXAMPLES   1. Hollywood is still a center of American moviemaking fine films are made in other places, too. (Use a comma and a coordinating conjunction.)

1. *Hollywood is still a center of American moviemaking, but fine films are made in other places, too.*

2. How much do you know about the history of movies how much would you like to know? (Make two sentences.)

2. *How much do you know about the history of movies? How much would you like to know?*

1. Movies entertain millions of people every day the cinema is popular all over the world. (Make two sentences.)
2. Many films take years to make they require the skills of hundreds of workers. (Use a comma and a coordinating conjunction.)
3. The director of a movie has an important job the cast and crew all follow the director's instructions. (Use a semicolon.)

George Eastman and Thomas Edison

4. The director makes many decisions,the producers take care of the business end of moviemaking. (Use a semicolon and a conjunctive adverb.)
5. The first movie theaters opened in the early 1900s they were called nickelodeons. (Make two sentences.)
6. Thomas Edison was a pioneer in early moviemaking he and one of his assistants invented the first commercial motion-picture machine. (Use a semicolon.)
7. The machine was called a Kinetoscope, it was a cabinet that showed moving images through a peephole. (Make two sentences.)
8. Edison worked with George Eastman, another inventor, to make roll film Eastman is now remembered for his contributions to film-making. (Make two sentences.)
9. The first sound films were shown in the late 1920s they marked a milestone in moviemaking history. (Use a semicolon.)
10. Movies are great entertainment they are also an art form. (Use a semicolon and a conjunctive adverb.)

Review B **Revising Fragments and Run-on Sentences**

The following paragraph contains several sentence fragments and run-on sentences. Revise all fragments and run-ons, adding words and changing the punctuation and capitalization as necessary to make each sentence clear and complete.

EXAMPLES
1. I just started researching my paper on American women in the military would you like to know what I've learned so far?

1. *I just started researching my paper on American women in the military. Would you like to know what I've learned so far?*

2. Women served in the Civil War. Not just men.

2. *Women, not just men, served in the Civil War.*

During the Civil War. Women who were
nurses showed remarkable heroism. They
took care of sick and wounded soldiers,
they risked their lives carrying supplies.
To military hospitals. Sally L. Tompkins
one such woman. She ran a military
hospital in the South she was one of two
female captains in the Confederate Army.
Clara Barton was another heroic Civil War
nurse, she worked tirelessly. Caring for
sick and wounded soldiers in the North.
In 1864, Barton superintendent of nurses
for the Union Army. She later founded the
American Red Cross Society. Served as
president of the Red Cross. Until 1904.

Clara Barton

Chapter Review

A. Identifying Sentences, Sentence Fragments, and Run-ons

Identify each of the following word groups as a *sentence,* a *sentence fragment,* or a *run-on sentence.* If a word group is a sentence fragment, rewrite it to make a complete sentence. If a word group is a run-on sentence, rewrite it to make it one or more complete sentences.

1. Whenever the class goes on a field trip.
2. Let's go skating instead, everyone has already seen that movie.
3. The rain had been falling for days, the creeks were full to their banks.
4. The house on our street that was recently painted bright blue.
5. Crouching in the tall grass, the cat watched the birds closely.
6. A young boy, not more than ten years old.
7. When we went to Virginia last summer, we visited several Civil War battlefields.
8. May I borrow your ruler, I think I left mine at home?
9. Meanwhile, in another room of the castle.
10. That restaurant, owned by the same family for thirty years, is very popular.

B. Revising Run-on Sentences

Rewrite each run-on sentence to form clear, complete sentences. For some of the items, the revision method you should use is given in parentheses.

11. On Sunday mornings, my family always makes a big breakfast, everyone especially likes omelets.
12. Making an omelet is not very difficult, you must have all the ingredients ready and take your time. (Use a semicolon, a conjunctive adverb, and a comma.)
13. I like chopped tomatoes, onions, and green peppers in my omelets, my sister likes to add mushrooms, too.
14. Sometimes I grate a little cheddar cheese for the top of the omelet, you don't have to use cheese if you don't like it. (Use a semicolon, a conjunctive adverb, and a comma.)

15. An omelet pan looks much like a frying pan, the bottom of an omelet pan is slightly rounded.

16. These eggs are very fresh, we bought them at the farmers' market yesterday. (Use a semicolon.)

17. Carefully break three eggs into a deep bowl, wash your hands after you break the eggs. (Make two sentences.)

18. Use a whisk to beat the eggs, you can use a fork if you don't have a whisk.

19. Don't stir the eggs while they are cooking, lift the edge of the eggs and let the uncooked part run under the cooked part.

20. Sometimes my omelets look like scrambled eggs, they still taste great. (Use a comma and a coordinating conjunction.)

C. Revising Sentence Fragments and Run-on Sentences

The following paragraphs contain sentence fragments and run-on sentences. Revise the paragraphs, making each sentence clear and complete. You will have to add words and change the punctuation and capitalization in some sentences.

```
    Of all the great apes, the gorilla may
be the most mysterious and misunderstood,
many people think gorillas are aggressive
and ferocious, but researchers have found
that gorillas are actually quite shy.
Unless they are threatened or disturbed.
The leader of a gorilla group will beat his
chest, roar, and rush at an intruder,
rarely does his display lead to a fight.
    Gorillas, the largest of the great apes,
have long, powerful arms and short, thick
legs, adult males, who are sometimes twice
the size of the females, can grow to almost
five and a half feet. Up to six hundred
pounds. Although the hair of the gorilla
is usually black, grown males have an area
of gray or silver hair on their lower
backs, sometimes mature males are called
"silverbacks."
```

Gorillas in the forests of equatorial Africa. You may be surprised to learn that gorillas are vegetarians, they eat leaves and shoots and spend a lot of time looking for food. Gorilla family groups are made up of six to twenty animals, one or two silverbacks lead and defend each group. Each group has a territory, between ten and sixteen square miles, several groups may share the same area. Every night, each gorilla in a group builds a new nest of leaves and branches. Sometimes in a tree and sometimes on the ground.

Like its close relative, the chimpanzee, the gorilla is highly intelligent, gorillas have demonstrated the capacity to remember, to anticipate, and to solve problems. Gorillas have shown that they can learn sign language from humans. Maybe even more readily than chimpanzees.

Gorillas have become more and more endangered in Africa, the destruction of the gorilla's habitat continues, humans clear the forests for farming, grazing, and lumbering. In addition, female gorillas typically give birth only once every four years, most births are single. Baby gorillas weigh less than five pounds and are completely helpless. For several months. The destruction of habitat and the gorilla's slow reproduction rate have made the gorilla vulnerable to extinction, illegal hunting also threatens the animal's survival. One kind of gorilla, the mountain gorilla, is especially rare, only five hundred to one thousand mountain gorillas survive today.

Writing Effective Sentences

Diagnostic Preview

A. Combining Sentences by Inserting Words or Phrases

Combine the sentences in the following items by inserting words or phrases from one sentence into the other sentence.

EXAMPLES
1. The miners trudged up the mine shaft. They were covered with coal dust.
   1. *The miners, covered with coal dust, trudged up the mine shaft.*
2. The baby is sleepy. The baby is ready for his afternoon nap.
   2. *The sleepy baby is ready for his afternoon nap.*

1. I'm tired today because a dog disturbed my sleep last night. The dog was barking.
2. My sister designed the invitation to the wedding. She is a talented artist.
3. Rita won the math contest. She won by answering all the questions correctly.
4. The children ran toward the playground. The children were laughing and shouting with excitement.
5. The team looked great in the new uniforms. The uniforms are gold.

B. Combining Sentences by Using Compound Subjects and Compound Verbs

Combine the sentences in the following items by using compound subjects or compound verbs.

EXAMPLE   **1.** The American history test lasted one hour. The test had fifty questions.

    1. The American history test lasted one hour and had fifty questions.

6. I carefully washed the ripe grapes. I put them in a bowl in the refrigerator.

7. Neil is a good writer. Kate is also a good writer. They have written many articles for the school newspaper.

8. Selma and James ride the bus most of the time. Selma and James decided to walk to school today.

9. We will visit the museum on Saturday morning. We will have lunch at that restaurant afterward.

10. Charles plays the violin in the student orchestra. Charles's sister Anita also plays the violin in the student orchestra.

C. Combining Sentences by Forming Compound and Complex Sentences

Combine the sentences in the following items by forming compound or complex sentences.

EXAMPLE   **1.** Our part of the state rarely gets snow. Last week was certainly an exception!

    1. Our part of the state rarely gets snow, but last week was certainly an exception!

11. The snow started in the morning. By early evening a foot of new snow had fallen.

12. No one could drive or even ride bicycles. The roads were barely visible.

13. We tried to clear a path from the door to the road. Drifting snow covered our work.

14. The cold was bone chilling. Everyone in our neighborhood wanted to go sledding.

15. We are not used to the cold and snow. We couldn't stay out more than an hour.

D. Revising a Paragraph to Improve Sentence Style

Revise the following paragraph to improve the writing style by varying sentence beginnings, correcting nonparallel structures, and revising stringy or wordy sentences.

EXAMPLE
1. The purpose of this essay is to convey my interest in applying for the summer science program and to let you know that I have been fascinated by botany for many years, at least from the time I was five or six years old.

1. *I am applying for the summer science program because I have been fascinated by botany since I was five or six years old.*

When other children were collecting insects and shells, I was looking at leaves and flowers, and whenever my brother and I went fishing, I spent more than a majority of the time studying the vegetation on the riverbanks. Now collecting, drawing, and study of plants take up many of my recreational hours. I never go anywhere without my magnifying glass, and I never leave the house without my notebook, and also, I always remember to bring my watercolors and my colored pencils. I have built a small greenhouse in our backyard. The greenhouse is where I experiment with seeds. I also grow tropical plants in the greenhouse. Outside the greenhouse, plants are grown by me in a large garden. The plants are mostly of the type that can be consumed by humans, but in addition, some are being raised simply because they are considered by many to have beautiful flowers. I keep careful records of the products of my cultivation, including, but not limited to, date of planting and germination for each particular variety of seed, date of appearance of first true leaves, date of harvesting, and how I control pests and diseases. The written records of my efforts in the garden, in the form of my notebooks, including the illustrations, are being included by me as a part of this application.

Combining Sentences

Short sentences are often effective; however, a long, unbroken series of them can sound choppy. For example, notice how dull the following paragraph sounds.

> I have seen a lot of earthling-meets-alien movies. I have seen The Last Starfighter. I have seen all the Star Trek movies. I have noticed something about these movies. I have noticed that there are good humans in these movies. There are bad humans. There are good aliens. There are bad aliens. The humans and aliens are actually not so different from each other.

Notice how much more interesting the paragraph sounds when the short, choppy sentences are combined into longer, smoother sentences.

> I have seen a lot of earthling-meets-alien movies, including The Last Starfighter and all the Star Trek movies. I have noticed that there are good and bad humans in these movies, as well as good and bad aliens. The humans and aliens are actually not so different from each other.

Inserting Words

You can combine short sentences by inserting a key word from one sentence into another. You usually need to eliminate some words in sentences that are combined. You may also need to change the form of the key word.

Using the Same Form	
Original	Edgar Allan Poe led a short life. His life was tragic.
Combined	Edgar Allan Poe led a short, **tragic** life.
Changing the Form	
Original	Edgar Allan Poe wrote strange stories. He wrote horror stories.
Combined	Edgar Allan Poe wrote strange, **horrifying** stories.

NOTE Some verbs can be made into adjectives by adding *–ed* and *–ing*, and some adjectives can be made into adverbs by adding *–ly*.

EXAMPLES   to bore—boring, bored   quick—quickly
                 to tilt—tilting, tilted   modest—modestly

Exercise 1   Combining Sentences by Inserting Words

In the following sets of sentences, some words have been italicized. Combine each set of sentences by inserting the italicized word (or words) into the first sentence. The directions in parentheses will tell you how to change the word form if it is necessary to do so.

EXAMPLE   **1.** Edgar Allan Poe was a writer who wrote stories and poems. Edgar Allan Poe was an *American* writer.

           1. *Edgar Allan Poe was an American writer who wrote stories and poems.*

1. The mother of Edgar Allan Poe died three years after he was born. She was *young*.
2. Poe was taken in by Mrs. John Allan and her husband. Their taking him in was *fortunate*. (Add *–ly* to *fortunate*.)
3. Poe created stories. He created *detective* stories.
4. Poe inspired the author of the Sherlock Holmes stories. The author had *talent*. (Add *–ed* to *talent*.)
5. Poe had theories about the writing of fiction. His theories were *original*.
6. Poe also wrote poems. The poems were *numerous*.
7. Poe wrote the poem "The Raven." It is a *well-known* poem.
8. Poe worked for literary magazines. He worked for *several* of them.
9. Poe wrote literary criticisms about authors. The authors were *comtemporary*.
10. I enjoy Edgar Allan Poe's short stories. His short stories are *terrifying*.

Exercise 2   Combining Sentences by Inserting Words

In Exercise 1, the words you needed to insert were italicized. Now, try using your own judgment to combine sentences. There may be more than one way to combine each set; do what seems best to you. Add commas and change the forms of words when needed.

EXAMPLE   **1.** Luis Valdez is a talented and famous playwright. He is a Mexican American.

        1. Luis Valdez is a talented and famous Mexican American playwright.

1. Valdez was born in Delano. Delano is in California.
2. He grew up in a family of farm workers. They were migrant workers.
3. As a child, Valdez began to work in the fields. He was six years old.
4. He champions the cause of underpaid migrant farm workers. He also champions the cause of migrant farm workers who suffer from overwork.
5. He organized the Farm Workers' Theater, a troupe of actors and musicians. The troupe travels.
6. The Farm Workers' Theater has performed in the United States. It has also performed in Europe and Mexico.
7. Valdez received an award in 1990. It was the Governor's Award.
8. Valdez wrote the play *Zoot Suit.* It was a success.
9. The play was produced on Broadway. The play was popular.
10. Valdez is a member of the California Arts Council. He is a founding member of the council.

Inserting Phrases

You also can combine closely related sentences by taking a phrase from one sentence and inserting it into another sentence.

Prepositional Phrases

A *prepositional phrase,* a preposition with its object and any modifiers of that object, can usually be inserted into another sentence with no changes. Just omit some of the words in one of the sentences.

ORIGINAL   Twelve million immigrants came to the shores of the United States. They came through Ellis Island.

REVISED   Twelve million immigrants came to the shores of the United States **through Ellis Island.**

Participial Phrases

A *participial phrase* contains a verb form that usually ends in *–ing* or *–ed.* The entire phrase acts as an adjective, modifying a noun or a pronoun. Sometimes, you can change the verb from one sentence into a participle by adding *–ing* or *–ed* or by dropping the helping verb if the

COMPUTER TIP

You can use a word-processing program's cut and paste commands to find the best placement for a participial phrase within a sentence.

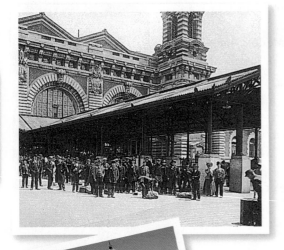

main verb already ends in *–ing* or *–ed.* Then, you can combine the two sentences. To avoid confusing your reader, place the participial phrase close to the noun or pronoun it will modify.

ORIGINAL   Many immigrants faced long months of waiting at Ellis Island. They were weakened by their journeys.

REVISED   Many immigrants, **weakened by their journeys,** faced long months of waiting at Ellis Island.

Appositive Phrases

An ***appositive phrase*** usually follows a noun or pronoun and helps to identify it. Sometimes you can combine sentences that have nouns or pronouns referring to the same thing by changing one of the sentences to an appositive phrase.

ORIGINAL   My grandfather was an immigrant. My grandfather brought with him photographs that are now souvenirs.

REVISED   My grandfather, **an immigrant,** brought with him photographs that are now souvenirs.

Reference Note

For more information on **phrases,** see page 68.

Exercise 3   Combining Sentences by Inserting Phrases

Revise each of the following sets of sentences to create one sentence. There may be more than one way to combine the sentences. In numbers 1 through 5, the words you need to insert are italicized. In numbers 6 through 10, change the forms of words or omit words as indicated in parentheses, and add commas wherever they are needed.

EXAMPLE   **1.** Auguste Piccard was a Swiss physicist who studied the upper atmosphere. He studied it *by going up in balloons.*

      1. *Auguste Piccard was a Swiss physicist who studied the upper atmosphere by going up in balloons.*

1. Auguste Piccard was an inventor, scientist, and explorer. He was *from Switzerland.*

2. Piccard once spent sixteen hours in a balloon. He was *floating across Germany and France.*

3. Piccard attended the Swiss Institute of Technology. The institute is *in Zurich, Switzerland.*
4. Piccard was a young man when he became a professor. He became a professor *at the Swiss Institute.*
5. Piccard created an important invention. He invented *an airtight gondola.*
6. The gondola took Piccard ten miles into the air. The gondola was attached to a balloon. (Omit *The gondola was.*)
7. Piccard then made numerous balloon trips. He studied electricity. (Change *studied* to *studying.*)
8. Piccard turned his interest to the ocean depths. He designed a deep-sea diving ship. (Change *designed* to *designing.*)
9. Piccard and his son Jacques went two miles below the surface of the Adriatic Sea. They went in 1953. (Omit *They went.*)
10. Another deep-sea diving ship went almost ten miles below the surface of the ocean. It set the world's depth record in 1960. (Change *set* to *setting.*)

Using Compound Subjects and Verbs

Another way to combine sentences is to make compound subjects and verbs. First, look for sentences that have the same subject or the same verb. Then, make the subject or verb compound by adding a coordinating conjunction such as *and, but, for, or, nor, so,* or *yet.*

ORIGINAL	The Angles were fierce people. The Saxons were fierce people. [different subjects with same verb]
REVISED	The **Angles and the Saxons** were fierce people. [compound subject with same verb]

ORIGINAL	The Angles and Saxons invaded Britain. The Angles and Saxons conquered Britain. [different verbs with same subject]
REVISED	The Angles and Saxons **invaded and conquered** Britain. [compound verb with same subject]

ORIGINAL	The Angles conquered Britain. The Saxons also conquered Britain. They both pushed back the native Celts. [different subjects and different verbs]
REVISED	The **Angles and the Saxons conquered** Britain and **pushed** back the native Celts. [compound subject and compound verb]

Reference Note

For more information on **agreement of subjects and verbs,** see page 121.

NOTE When you combine sentences by making compound subjects and compound verbs, make sure that your new subjects and verbs agree in number.

ORIGINAL   The Angle dialect is an ancestor of Modern English. The Saxon dialect is also an ancestor of Modern English.

REVISED   The Angle dialect and the Saxon dialect **are** ancestors of Modern English. [The plural compound subject takes the plural verb *are*.]

Oral Practice **Creating Compound Subjects and Compound Verbs**

Here are five sets of short sentences. Read each set aloud. Then, combine each set into one sentence that has a compound subject, a compound verb, or a compound subject and a compound verb.

EXAMPLE   1. Yesterday Tina and I bought a coconut. We cracked it open.

1. *Yesterday Tina and I bought a coconut and cracked it open.*

1. Bananas are a popular tropical fruit. Coconuts are another popular tropical fruit.
2. Brazil produces bananas. India produces bananas. Both countries export bananas.
3. Some bananas are cooked as vegetables are. They are eaten as vegetables are.
4. By A.D. 600, the Egyptians were eating coconuts. Indians and Koreans were also eating coconuts.
5. Coconuts are not a major crop in the United States. Bananas are not a major crop in the United States, either.
6. The United States imports much of the world's banana crop. Likewise, Great Britain imports much of that crop.
7. Christopher makes dried banana chips. Christopher eats dried banana chips, too.
8. Coconut is delicious in fruit smoothies. Banana is delicious in fruit smoothies.
9. My mother has many recipes that use bananas. My uncle also has many recipes that use bananas.
10. Vitamin C is found in bananas. Potassium is also found in bananas.

Creating a Compound Sentence

You can combine two sentences by creating a compound sentence. A *compound sentence* is two or more simple sentences linked by

- a comma and a coordinating conjunction

  or

- a semicolon

  or

- a semicolon, a conjunctive adverb, and a comma

Before linking two thoughts in a compound sentence, make sure that the thoughts are clearly related and equal in importance. Be sure that you do not link two thoughts in a compound sentence when one thought is clearly more important than the other.

ORIGINAL	The cat knocked over a lamp. The dog chewed up my shoe.
REVISED	The cat knocked over a lamp, **and** the dog chewed up my shoe. [comma and coordinating conjunction]
	The cat knocked over a lamp; the dog chewed up my shoe. [semicolon]
	The cat knocked over a lamp; **meanwhile,** the dog chewed up my shoe. [semicolon and conjunctive adverb]

NOTE You can use the coordinating conjunctions *and, but, nor, for, yet, or,* and *so* to form compound sentences. However, you should avoid overusing them. Too many coordinating conjunctions can be a sign that you are writing stringy sentences. When you join two sentences with a coordinating conjunction, remember to use a comma before the conjunction.

Reference Note

For more information on **compound sentences,** see page 109.

TIPS & TRICKS

Using conjunctive adverbs to join sentences allows you to emphasize the relationship between ideas. Some of the frequently used conjunctive adverbs are *also, besides, consequently, however, meanwhile, moreover, otherwise, then,* and *therefore.*

Reference Note

For more about **stringy sentences,** see page 463.

Exercise 4 **Combining Simple Sentences to Create Compound Sentences**

The sentences in the following pairs are closely related in meaning. Using the methods you have learned, combine each pair into a compound sentence. Remember to add commas and semicolons where they are needed in your combined sentences.

EXAMPLE	**1.** My class is studying American Indians. We will use our research to create an encyclopedia.
	1. My class is studying American Indians, and we will use our research to create an encyclopedia.

SENTENCES

1. The Hopi live on a reservation. They have many separate villages.
2. Many Hopi grow crops. Some make jewelry, baskets, pottery, and other crafts.
3. Hopi crops include corn, beans, and pumpkins. The Hopi have farmed these crops successfully for generations.
4. The Hopi live in houses made of stone and plaster. The houses are built by women of the tribe.
5. The Hopi are peaceful people. Their religion is very important to them.
6. The Hopi religion includes a profound respect for nature. One of the most famous Hopi rituals is a rain dance called the Snake Dance.
7. The Hopi are one of several Pueblo peoples. My class is planning to study at least three different Pueblo groups.
8. The various groups of Pueblo peoples traditionally spoke different languages. The cultures of the different villages are closely related.
9. Some Pueblo peoples live in Arizona. Others live in New Mexico.
10. Spanish settlers noted the distinctive villages made of apartment-like stone and adobe structures built by Southwestern Indian tribes. The name *Pueblo* comes from the Spanish word for "village."

Creating a Complex Sentence

A *complex sentence* includes one independent clause—a clause that can stand alone as a sentence. It also has one or more *subordinate clauses*—clauses that cannot stand alone as sentences.

Adjective Clauses

You can make a sentence into an *adjective clause* by inserting *who*, *which*, or *that* in place of the subject. Then you can use the adjective clause to provide information about a preceding noun or pronoun.

ORIGINAL   Many people are afraid of bats. They are usually harmless creatures.

REVISED   Many people are afraid of bats, **which are usually harmless creatures.**

NOTE   When you use adjective clauses to combine sentences, remember that *which* is not used to refer to a person, only to places and things. Use *who, whom, whose,* and *that* to refer to people.

Adverb Clauses

You can turn one sentence into an *adverb clause* and combine it with another sentence. The adverb clause may modify a verb, an adjective, or another adverb in the sentence (the independent clause) to which it is attached.

Adverb clauses begin with subordinating conjunctions like *after, although, because, if, when,* and *where.* You have to choose these conjunctions carefully. They show the relationship between the ideas in the adverb clause and those in the independent clause. For example, *when* shows how the ideas are related in time, *where* shows how the ideas are related in space, and *although* shows under what conditions the ideas occurred. When you use an adverb clause at the beginning of a sentence, you need to be sure to separate it from the independent clause with a comma.

ORIGINAL Many people are afraid of bats. Bats have a bad reputation.

REVISED Many people are afraid of bats **because bats have a bad reputation.**

ORIGINAL Some people think bats are dangerous. Bats rarely attack humans.

REVISED **Although some people think bats are dangerous,** bats rarely attack humans. [Note that a comma follows the adverb clause that begins the sentence.]

Noun Clauses

You can make a sentence into a *noun clause* and insert it into another sentence just as you would an ordinary noun. You create a noun clause by inserting a word like *that, how, what, which,* or *who* at the beginning of the sentence. When you place the noun clause in the other sentence, you may have to change or remove some words.

ORIGINAL Dracula is such a frightening character. This does not help the bat's reputation.

REVISED **That Dracula is such a frightening character** does not help the bat's reputation. [The word *that* introduces the noun clause, which becomes the subject of the verb *does help.*]

REVISED **What does not help the bat's reputation** is that Dracula is such a frightening character. [The word *what* introduces the noun clause, which becomes the subject of the verb *is.*]

Reference Note

This in the original sentence is an unclear (general) pronoun reference. General references can be corrected by creating a noun clause, as in the revised sentence. For more on **clear pronoun references,** see page 193.

Exercise 5 Combining Simple Sentences to Create Complex Sentences

Following are ten sets of short, choppy sentences that need revision. Use subordinate clauses to combine each set of sentences into a single complex sentence. You may see different ways to combine some of the sets; choose the way that seems best to you. You may need to change or delete some words to make smooth combinations.

EXAMPLE
1. My sister is fascinated by sharks. My sister is studying biology.

1. *My sister, who is studying biology, is fascinated by sharks.*

1. My sister first saw a shark on a family vacation. We took the vacation five years ago.
2. The sharks scared me. They intrigued her.
3. My sister took me to a large outdoor aquarium. It had sharks on display.
4. She told me a lot about the sharks. The sharks were swimming in circles in the aquarium.
5. The shark is a member of a fish family. The family includes the largest and fiercest fish.
6. Most sharks have long bodies, wedge-shaped heads, and pointed back fins. The back fins sometimes stick out of the water.
7. Sharks live mostly in warm seas. Some sharks have been found in bodies of cold water.
8. The whale shark is harmless to people. It feeds on plankton.
9. The whale sharks eat plankton. They strain the plankton out of the water.
10. However, many sharks are ruthless killers. They feed on flesh.

Review A Revising a Paragraph by Combining Sentences

Using all of the sentence-combining techniques you have learned, revise and rewrite the following short paragraph. Use your judgment about what sentences to combine and how to combine them. Work for clear, varied sentences that read smoothly; however, do not change the meaning of the original paragraph.

EXAMPLE
Audrey visited England last April. She sent us a postcard.

When Audrey visited England last April, she sent us a postcard.

Stonehenge is in southwestern England.
It is a series of stones. They are huge
stones. They weigh as much as fifty tons
each. Stonehenge was built about five thousand years ago. The stones were moved to
their present site. They were moved by as
many as one thousand people. There are many
theories about the purpose of the stones.
One popular theory is that the stones
served as an observatory. The observatory
was astrological. At one point in the summer, the sun rises over one of the stones.
It rises directly over that stone.

Improving Sentence Style

In the first part of this chapter, you learned some techniques for making smooth sentence combinations. Now you will learn how to style
your sentences by making them clear, balanced, and varied.

Using Parallel Structure

When you combine several related ideas in one sentence, it is important to make sure that your combinations are balanced. You create balance in a sentence by using the same form or part of speech to express
each idea. For example, you balance a noun with a noun, a phrase with
a phrase, and a clause with a clause. This balance is called parallelism,
or *parallel structure.*

NOT PARALLEL   I am not much of an athlete, but I like softball, soccer,
and playing hockey. [two nouns and a phrase]

PARALLEL   I am not much of an athlete, but I like **softball, soccer,**
and **hockey.** [three nouns]

NOT PARALLEL	Dominic does not have enough time to play soccer, join the debating team, and band. [two phrases and a noun]
PARALLEL	Dominic does not have enough time **to play soccer, to join the debating team,** and **to participate in band.** [three phrases]

NOT PARALLEL	He said that he would meet you at the soccer field and not to be late. [clause and phrase]
PARALLEL	He said **that he would meet you at the soccer field** and **that you should not be late.** [two clauses]

Exercise 6 Revising Sentences to Create Parallel Structure

Bring balance to the following sentences by putting the ideas in parallel form. You may need to add or delete some words. If a sentence is already correct, write *C.*

EXAMPLE
1. My favorite subjects are art, taking Spanish, and geography.

1. *My favorite subjects are art, Spanish, and geography.*

1. I find geography most interesting; I like to study faraway locations and learning about famous cities.
2. Do you believe that reading about a beautiful place is almost as good as to visit it?
3. My favorite sources of information are *National Geographic* magazine, encyclopedias, and on the Internet.
4. I'm working on a presentation on European capitals for my social studies class and a report about Parisian culture for my French class.
5. For my report, I included photos of famous Paris monuments such as the Eiffel Tower, the Arc de Triomphe, and showing the Louvre.
6. Paris, the capital of France, is famous for its history, culture, and eating in excellent restaurants.
7. The Seine River runs through the city and supplies water to all Parisians.
8. Visiting the Notre Dame Cathedral, walking through the Louvre Museum, and the Eiffel Tower are all favorite pastimes of tourists.
9. It is interesting that Paris has always attracted artists and refugees have always been welcome.
10. Many famous Americans, including Ernest Hemingway, lived and were writing in Paris during the 1920s.

Revising Stringy Sentences

Linking together related ideas is a good way to bring variety to your writing. If you overdo it, however, you may end up with a *stringy sentence.*

A ***stringy sentence*** just goes on and on. It usually has too many independent clauses strung together with coordinating conjunctions like *and* or *but.* Since all the ideas are treated equally, your reader may have trouble seeing how they are related.

There are three ways you can fix a stringy sentence. You can

- break the sentence into two or more sentences
- turn some of the independent clauses into subordinate clauses or phrases
- use a combination of the above strategies

STRINGY   The fire alarm bell rang, and everyone started to file out of school, but then our principal came down the hall, and he said the bell had been rung by mistake, and we went back to class.

BETTER   The fire alarm bell rang, and everyone started to file out of school. Then our principal came down the hall to say the bell had been rung by mistake. We went back to class.

BETTER   When the fire alarm bell rang, everyone started to file out of school. Then our principal came down the hall. He said the bell had been rung by mistake, and we went back to class.

MEETING THE CHALLENGE

Journalists, especially if they write for newspapers, develop a style that uses mostly short sentences. Cut a short article out of a newspaper, read it, and then rewrite the article, using stringy sentences. Next, revise the sentences once again, using a blend of sentence structures. Compare the three articles now. Which is easiest to read? Which has the most impact? Which version do you prefer?

SENTENCES

Exercise 7   Revising Stringy Sentences

Decide which of the following sentences are stringy and need revision. Then, revise the stringy sentences by (1) breaking each sentence into two or more sentences, (2) turning some independent clauses into subordinate clauses, or (3) turning some independent clauses into phrases. If you find a sentence that is effective and does not need to be improved, write *C.*

EXAMPLE   1. Alexandre Gustave Eiffel was a French engineer, and he designed the Eiffel Tower, and he designed the frame for the Statue of Liberty, but his greatest accomplishment may have been proving that metal was an important building material.

        1. *Alexandre Gustave Eiffel was a French engineer who designed the Eiffel Tower and the frame for the Statue of Liberty. His greatest accomplishment may have been proving that metal was an important building material.*

1. Alexandre Gustave Eiffel was a famous Frenchman, and he was born in 1832, and he died in 1923.
2. Eiffel graduated from the College of Art and Manufacturing, and then he worked with a Belgian company, and then he founded his own company.
3. Eiffel was an engineer, and he designed the Eiffel Tower, and it was built for the World's Fair of 1889.
4. In 1889, the French government planned the World's Fair, and the World's Fair celebrated the hundred-year anniversary of the French Revolution.
5. The Centennial Committee held a contest for the design of an appropriate monument, and over one hundred plans were submitted, but the committee chose Eiffel's plan.
6. After the Eiffel Tower was built, it served as the entryway to the fair.
7. Eiffel specialized in bridges, and he designed an arching bridge, and it was the highest bridge in the world for many years.
8. Eiffel's chief interest was bridges, and the Eiffel Tower displays his bridge-designing skills, and so does another historical monument, and it is a monument that you know.
9. In 1885, Eiffel used his engineering knowledge to design part of a great American symbol, the Statue of Liberty in New York Harbor.

10. Toward the end of his life, Eiffel studied the effects of air on airplanes, and then in 1912, he built a wind tunnel and an aerodynamics laboratory, and later he conducted experiments from the Eiffel Tower, which is now a favorite tourist attraction.

Revising Wordy Sentences

If someone says, "It would please me greatly if you would diminish the volume of your verbalizing during the time I am perusing this reading material," you might wonder what language is being spoken. How much easier and clearer it is to say "Please be quieter while I am reading."

Here are three tips for creating sentences that are not too wordy.

- *Do not use more words than you need.*
- *Do not use fancy words where simple ones will do.*
- *Do not repeat yourself unless it is absolutely necessary.*

WORDY	It is with deepest sorrow and regret that I come to you to beg your forgiveness for my thoughtlessness.
IMPROVED	I am really sorry, and I want to apologize for my thoughtlessness.
WORDY	In the event that we are unable to go to the movie, we can play basketball at Alicia's house.
IMPROVED	If we cannot go to the movie, we can play basketball at Alicia's house.
WORDY	My friend Ken is a talented drummer who plays the drums with great skill.
IMPROVED	My friend Ken is a talented drummer.

Exercise 8 **Revising Wordy Sentences**

The writer of the following letter wants to make a complaint, but the wordiness of the letter gets in the way. Revise the letter, making it clearer and more effective. Replace fancy words with simple ones, and eliminate unnecessary repetition. You may add details if you wish.

EXAMPLE **1.** I was so upset at the horrendous occurrences that occurred on the day in question that was yesterday that I felt it was my only option to write a letter to the child's parents.

 1. I was so upset at the horrendous occurrences yesterday that I had to write a letter to the child's parents.

Dear Mr. and Mrs. Wilson,

  At this point in time, it is my unhappy duty to inform you of the fact that I will no longer be available to baby-sit Charles. On the evening of July 13, I was hired by you to perform the duties of baby sitter for your three-year-old son. These duties were performed by me to the best of my ability. However, I do not feel that any baby sitter should be in a position of having to deal with the threat of harm to the baby sitter's person. I feel that Charles's hurling of objects at my person and his action of locking me in the closet were threats to my safety. The situation being what it is, I feel I cannot safely perform my duties, and I will no longer place myself in danger by sitting with your son.

                Sincerely,

                Miguel Garza

Beyond Sentence Style

Previously in this chapter, you learned how to combine sentences smoothly and how to make sentences clear, balanced, and varied. Now you will learn how sentences work together in the larger structure of the paragraph.

Varying Sentence Beginnings

Basic English sentences begin with a subject followed by a verb. However, beginning every sentence with a subject makes your writing dull. Notice how boring the following paragraph sounds.

  The theater was packed. Jan and I managed to find our seats. The play began thirty minutes late. We were bored. We read the program four times. Jan wanted to find out the reason for the delay. She asked an usher. The usher was amused. The usher said that the star's costume had been damaged by her dog. We laughed because the play was <u>Cats</u>.

Now, notice how much more interesting the same paragraph sounds with varied sentence beginnings. To create the varied beginnings, the writer has combined sentences. Some sentences became words, some became phrases, and others became subordinate clauses.

```
    Although the theater was packed, Jan and
I managed to find our seats. The play began
thirty minutes late. Bored, we read the pro-
gram four times. To find out the reason for
the delay, Jan asked an usher. Amused, the
usher said that the star's costume had been
damaged by her dog. We laughed because the
play was Cats.
```

Varying Sentence Beginnings

Single–Word Modifiers

Excitedly, Marcia opened her presents. [adverb]
Hungry, the family stopped at the restaurant. [adjective]
Swaying, the couple danced to the music. [adjective]

Phrases

With tears of joy, Carla received her prize. [prepositional phrase]
Smiling happily, Tanya told us the good news. [participial phrase]
To make good grades, you must study. [infinitive phrase]
A fine teacher, Mr. Ramos is also a master gardener. [appositive phrase]

Subordinate Clauses

Because the coach was angry, the team had to run ten laps. [adverb clause]

When Tom found the kitten on his doorstep, he decided to keep it. [adverb clause]

TIPS & TRICKS

To check your writing for varied sentence beginnings, put parentheses around the first five words of each of your sentences. If most of your subjects and verbs fall within the parentheses, you need to begin more of your sentences with single-word modifiers, phrases, or subordinate clauses.

NOTE If you use a prepositional phrase telling *when, where,* or *how* to vary your sentence beginnings, you can sometimes put the verb of the sentence before the subject. In the following example sentence, the subject is underlined once, the verb twice.

EXAMPLE   Down the street rumbled an old cart.

Exercise 9 **Varying Sentence Beginnings**

The following sentences are all good, but they would make a boring paragraph. Here is your chance to practice varying sentence beginnings. The notes in parentheses tell you whether to start your revised sentence with a single-word modifier, a phrase, or a clause. In some cases, you may also want to add or delete a word to make the sentence sound better.

EXAMPLE   **1.** We are learning many interesting facts in our biology class. (phrase)

       1. *In our biology class, we are learning many interesting facts.*

1. Animals are in danger of extinction in many different parts of the world. (phrase)
2. The aye-aye is a small animal related to the monkey, and it is one of the less well-known of the endangered animals. (phrase)
3. The aye-aye is endangered because the rain forest on its home island is being destroyed. (subordinate clause)
4. You must travel to the Pyrenees, Portugal, or the former Soviet Union to see the desman, a water-dwelling mammal. (phrase)
5. People are threatening the desman's survival by damming mountain streams. (phrase)
6. The giant otter of South America is protected, but poachers continue to threaten its survival. (subordinate clause)
7. Mountain lions are cautious and generally stay away from humans, who hunt them relentlessly. (single-word modifier)

8. The great peacock moth of Europe is in trouble because its home is being damaged by acid rain. (subordinate clause)
9. Wolves are expert hunters, and they prey on large animals. (phrase)
10. Gray wolves, sadly, are an endangered species. (single-word modifier)

Exercise 10 Revising Sentences to Create Variety

Use what you have learned about varying sentence beginnings to revise the following paragraph. Reword some sentences so that they begin with single-word modifiers, phrases, or clauses. Some sentences may be reworded in several ways; choose the way that seems best to you. (Consult the chart on page 467 for help.)

EXAMPLE 1. Some find it disturbing that land animals aren't the only creatures at risk of extinction.

1. *Disturbingly, land animals aren't the only creatures at risk of extinction.*

Ocean animals unfortunately are often on endangered-species lists. Penguins are at risk in oceans of the Southern Hemisphere. Many penguin species have problems today because of oil pollution and commercial fishing. Turtles are endangered because they are slaughtered for food and for their beautiful, highly prized shells. Lobsters become threatened when people overfish. Mediterranean monk seals also are threatened by increased land development and tourism.

Review B Revising a Paragraph

The following paragraphs have many of the problems you have reviewed in this section. Show your writing style by rewriting and revising the paragraphs (1) to correct nonparallel structures, (2) to correct stringy and wordy sentences, and (3) to vary sentence beginnings. You may add or delete details as necessary.

EXAMPLE 1. My family loves animals, the outdoors, and to go on picnics.

1. *My family loves animals, the outdoors, and picnics.*

One time in the recent past, we went on a picnic in Big Bend National Park in Texas. It had rained heavily all night north of the park. A friend of ours, Mrs. Brown, went with us. She had lived in that part of Texas for a large number of years. She knew all about what to expect if it rained. She told us that there could be a flash flood in the park and about how the park could be dangerous even if it did not rain there because the water could run across the dry desert sand.

Mrs. Brown made us turn our cars around to face in the other direction because she wanted us to be able to leave the low area quickly if a flood came. The sun was shining with great brightness, and everyone thought Mrs. Brown was crazy, and we started to eat our picnic.

A very high wall of water four feet high came toward us suddenly. We jumped into the cars and getting away just in time. We were glad to be alive, and we thanked Mrs. Brown.

Chapter Review

A. Combining Sentences

Combine the following sentences by inserting words or phrases, forming compound subjects or compound verbs, or forming compound or complex sentences.

1. The tall woman over there is Mrs. Randolph. She is the editor of the newspaper.
2. Frank picked up the shovel and the rake. He put them away in the garden shed.
3. We saw the school play last night. We went over to Trisha's house.
4. I think she said the game was at five o'clock. Maybe she said the game was at six.
5. Announcements are made at the end of the day. Announcements are made during the last class period.
6. In one of the offices, a telephone was ringing constantly. No one answered it.
7. Kathy heard the knock at the door. Her brother heard the knock at the door. Kathy and her brother ran downstairs to greet Aunt Marci.
8. The flags flapped wildly in the gusty wind. The flags were French and Canadian.
9. I couldn't watch that program last night. I had to finish my math homework.
10. The crowd rose to its feet when the team scored. The crowd was clapping and stomping.

B. Revising Stringy or Wordy Sentences

Revise the following stringy or wordy sentences. Some of the sentences may be both stringy and wordy.

11. The game, which was the final game of the series, was postponed because of the excessive downpour.
12. We took the subway, and then we got off at our stop, and then we got on a bus, and we went to the museum.

13. Owing to the fact that no one in the class has finished the assignment to completion, we will have a pop quiz at this point in time.

14. The woman who is my great-grandmother is in all probability the person of whom I am the most admiring.

15. The reason they were late to school was because John had set his alarm clock to a time that was an hour later than he was supposed to have set it.

16. The passenger vehicle was proceeding in a westwardly direction.

17. First, Nora borrowed my book, and then Nathan wanted to look at my notes, and then Naomi needed to use my pen, and by the time I got to class, my backpack was almost empty.

18. I knew I would have to study for the test when I got home, so I didn't answer the phone because I didn't want to be disturbed, but my father called because he wanted to let me know that he was going to be late, but I missed the call.

19. The book, which I just finished reading, has many characteristics that could cause me to recommend it to you as a book you should schedule some time to read in the future.

20. The style of the writing of the author of the book is difficult to describe with any degree of accuracy.

C. Revising a Paragraph to Improve Sentence Style

Revise the following paragraph, combining choppy sentences, correcting unparallel structures, improving wordy or stringy sentences, and using a variety of sentence beginnings to improve the style of the writing.

```
    No one in my family enjoys giving our two
dogs baths. Our dogs do not like baths. One
of the dogs really hates baths. His name is
Spike. Spike somehow seems to know when we
want to give him a bath. Spike runs away and
hides under the bed when we fill up the tub.
It's no easy task to get that dog out from
under the bed, put him in the tub, and keep-
ing him there. Ike, our other dog, handles
baths differently. He knocks over the tub.
Water splashes everywhere. Water pools on
```

the floor and drips from the walls. Water thoroughly soaks whoever is giving the dogs a bath. Then Ike leaps away from the tub and tears through the house. He speeds from room to room, and then he jumps onto the couch and shakes off all the water. We always have to clean the utility room after we bathe the dogs. We usually have to clean up the rest of the house, too. We spend hours mopping up the floors, wiping down the walls, and to wash all the towels. The last time we bathed the dogs, we reminded ourselves that using a professional dog-grooming service would be better than to exhaust the whole family.

CHAPTER

20 | Sentence Diagramming

The Sentence Diagram

A *sentence diagram* is a picture of how the parts of a sentence fit together and how the words in a sentence are related.

Reference Note

For more about **subjects** and **verbs,** see page 42.

Subjects and Verbs

The sentence diagram begins with a horizontal line intersected by a short vertical line that divides the complete subject from the complete predicate.

EXAMPLE   Fish swim.

Fish	swim

HELP

Notice that a sentence diagram shows the capitalization but not the punctuation of a sentence.

Understood Subjects

EXAMPLE   Wait!

(you)	Wait

Reference Note

For information about **understood subjects,** see page 51.

Nouns of Direct Address

EXAMPLE   Sit, **Fido.**

```
            Fido
    (you)  |  Sit
```

Reference Note

For information about **nouns of direct address,** see page 284.

Sentences Beginning with *There*

EXAMPLE   **There** is hope.

```
            There
    hope  |  is
```

Reference Note

For information about **sentences beginning with *there*,** see page 50.

Compound Subjects

EXAMPLE   **Carmen** and **Basil** were fishing.

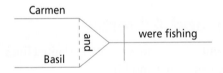

Compound Verbs

EXAMPLE   They **stopped** and **ate.**

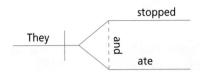

Reference Note

For more about **compound subjects,** see page 52. For more about **compound verbs,** see page 53.

The following diagram shows how a compound verb is diagrammed when the helping verb is not repeated.

EXAMPLE   They are **sitting** and **reading.**

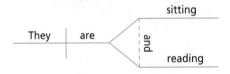

SENTENCES

Compound Subjects and Compound Verbs

EXAMPLE   **Coaches** and **players jumped** and **cheered.**

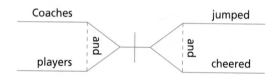

Sometimes the parts of a compound subject or a compound verb are joined by correlative conjunctions. Correlatives are diagrammed like this:

EXAMPLE   **Both** Bob **and** Teri can **not only** draw **but also** paint.

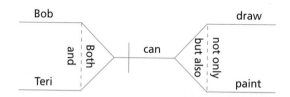

Reference Note

For more about **adjectives,** see page 10. For more about **adverbs,** see page 21.

Adjectives and Adverbs

Both adjectives and adverbs are written on slanted lines connected to the words they modify.

EXAMPLE   **That old** clock has **never** worked.

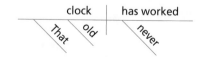

When an adverb modifies an adjective or an adverb, it is placed on a line connected to the word it modifies.

EXAMPLE   This **very** beautiful glass **almost** never breaks.

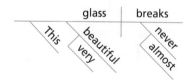

Notice the position of the modifiers in the following example:

EXAMPLE   **Soon** Anne and **her** sister will graduate and will move.

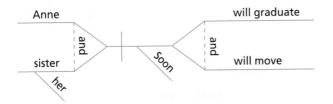

Above, *her* modifies only one part of the compound subject: *sister.* *Soon* modifies both parts of the compound verb: *will graduate* and *will move.*

When a conjunction joins two modifiers, it is diagrammed like this:

EXAMPLE   The **English** and **Australian** athletes worked **long** and **very hard.**

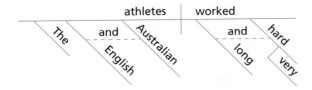

Subject Complements

The subject complement is placed on the horizontal line with the subject and verb. It comes after the verb. A slanted line separates the subject complement from the linking verb.

Predicate Nominatives

EXAMPLE   Cathedrals are large **churches.**

Reference Note

For more about **predicate nominatives,** see page 58.

Reference Note

For more about **predi-cate adjectives,** see page 58.

Predicate Adjectives

EXAMPLE   Cathedrals are **large.**

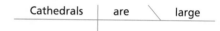

Compound Subject Complements

EXAMPLE   My friend is **small** and **quiet.**

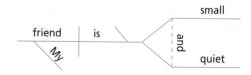

Objects

Direct Objects

Reference Note

For more about **direct objects,** see page 59.

A vertical line separates a direct object from the verb.

EXAMPLE   We like **music.**

Compound Direct Objects

EXAMPLE   We like **plays** and **movies.**

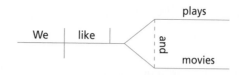

Indirect Objects

Reference Note

For more about **indirect objects,** see page 60.

The indirect object is diagrammed on a horizontal line beneath the verb.

EXAMPLE   Pete bought **Mario** a sandwich.

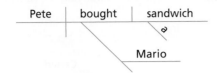

Compound Indirect Objects

EXAMPLE   Latoya gave her **family** and **friends** free tickets.

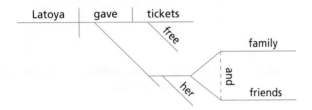

Phrases

Prepositional Phrases

The preposition is placed on a line slanting down from the word the phrase modifies. The object of the preposition is placed on a horizontal line connected to the slanting line.

EXAMPLES   **By chance,** a peasant uncovered a wall **of ancient Pompeii.** [*By chance* is an adverb phrase modifying the verb; *of ancient Pompeii* is an adjective phrase modifying the direct object.]

Reference Note

For more information about **prepositional phrases,** see page 70.

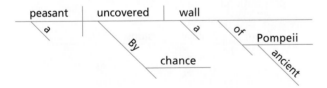

Our team practices late **in the afternoon.** [adverb phrase modifying an adverb]

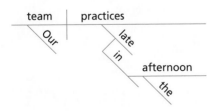

They drove **through the Maine woods** and **into southern Canada.** [two phrases modifying the same word]

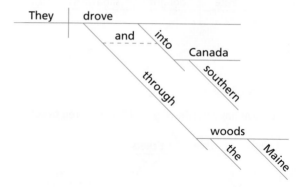

Mom taught the game **to my father, my uncles, and me.** [compound object of preposition]

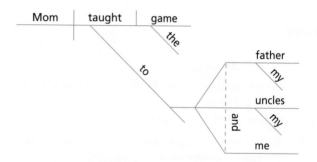

Follow the signs **to Highway 3 in Laconia.** [*In Laconia* is a prepositional phrase modifying the object of another preposition.]

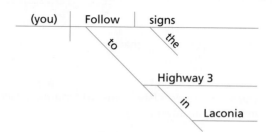

Participles and Participial Phrases

EXAMPLES I found him **crying.**

Wagging its tail, the large dog leaped at me.

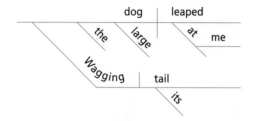

Notice that *tail*, the direct object of the participle *Wagging*, is diagrammed like any other complement.

Gerunds and Gerund Phrases

EXAMPLES **Walking** is healthful exercise. [gerund used as subject]

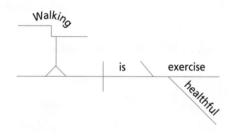

The constant cold is a good reason for **taking a vacation in the winter.** [gerund phrase used as the object of a preposition]

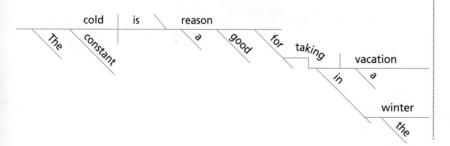

Reference Note

For more information about **participles** and **participial phrases,** see page 77.

Reference Note

For more about **gerunds** and **gerund phrases,** see page 81.

SENTENCES

Reference Note

For more information about **infinitives** and **infinitive phrases,** see page 85.

SENTENCES

Infinitives and Infinitive Phrases

EXAMPLES   **To leave** would be rude. [infinitive used as subject]

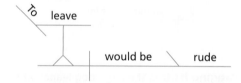

To join the Air Force is her longtime ambition.
[infinitive phrase used as subject]

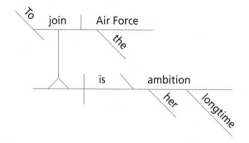

Infinitives and infinitive phrases used as modifiers are diagrammed much as prepositional phrases are.

EXAMPLES   I am happy **to help.** [Infinitive phrase used as adverb]

I am leaving early **to get the tickets.** [infinitive phrase used as adverb]

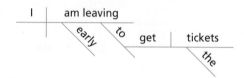

Appositives and Appositive Phrases

Place the appositive in parentheses after the word it identifies or explains.

EXAMPLES   My brother **Josh** is a drummer in the band.

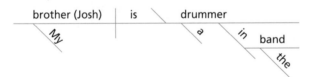

Reference Note

For more information about **appositives** and **appositive phrases,** see page 89.

The next show, **a musical comedy,** was written by Mike Williams, **a talented young playwright.**

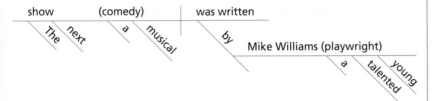

Subordinate Clauses

Adjective Clauses

An adjective clause is joined to the word it modifies by a broken line leading from the relative pronoun to the modified word.

EXAMPLES   The restaurant **that we like best** serves excellent seafood.

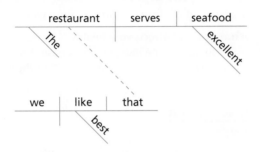

Reference Note

For more about **adjective clauses,** see page 101.

SENTENCES

He is the teacher **from whom I take lessons.**

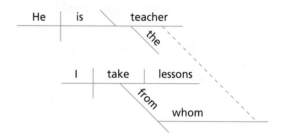

Reference Note

For more about **adverb clauses,** see page 104.

Adverb Clauses

Place the subordinating conjunction that introduces the adverb clause on a broken line leading from the verb in the adverb clause to the word the clause modifies.

EXAMPLE   **If you visit Texas,** you should see the Alamo.

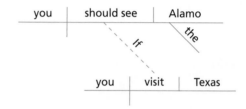

Reference Note

For more about **noun clauses,** see page 106.

Noun Clauses

Noun clauses often begin with introductory words such as *that, what, who,* or *which.* These introductory words may have a function within the subordinate clause, or they may simply connect the clause to the rest of the sentence. How a noun clause is diagrammed depends upon its use in the sentence. It also depends on whether or not the introductory word has a grammatical function in the noun clause.

EXAMPLES   **What you eat** affects your health. [The noun clause is used as the subject of the independent clause. The introductory word *What* functions as a direct object in the noun clause.]

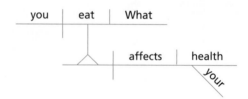

We strongly suspected **that the cat was the thief.** [The noun clause is the direct object of the independent clause. The introductory word *that* does not have a grammatical function within the noun clause.]

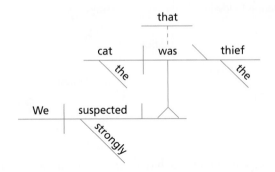

Sometimes the introductory word in a subordinate clause may be omitted. In the example above, the word *that* can be left out: *We strongly suspected the cat was the thief.* To diagram this new sentence, simply omit the word *that* and the solid and broken lines under it from the diagram above. The rest of the diagram stays the same.

Sentences Classified According to Structure

Simple Sentences

EXAMPLES   George Vancouver was exploring the Northwest.

Cities in Washington and British Columbia are named for him.

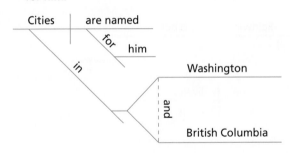

Reference Note

For more about **simple sentences,** see page 109.

SENTENCES

Compound Sentences

EXAMPLE   James Baldwin wrote many essays, but he is probably more famous for his novels.

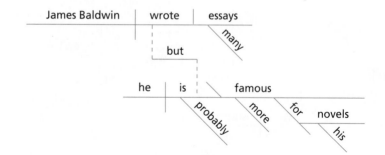

If the compound sentence has a semicolon and no conjunction, place a straight broken line between the two verbs.

EXAMPLE   Baldwin was a distinguished essayist; his nonfiction works include *Notes of a Native Son.*

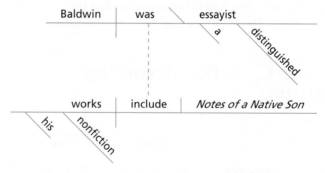

If the clauses of a compound sentence are joined by a semicolon and a conjunctive adverb, place the conjunctive adverb on a slanting line below the verb it modifies.

EXAMPLE   Baldwin was born in New York; however, he lived in France for a while.

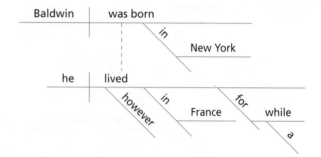

Complex Sentences

EXAMPLE   Jaime Escalante always believed that his students could do well in math.

Reference Note

For more about **complex sentences,** see page 110.

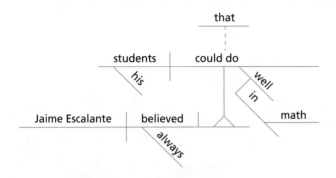

Compound-Complex Sentences

EXAMPLE   Before her plane mysteriously disappeared in 1937, Amelia Earhart had already forged the way for women in aviation, and she was later recognized for her achievements.

Reference Note

For more about **compound-complex sentences,** see page 110.

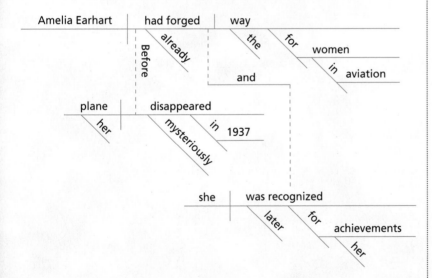

SENTENCES

PART 3

Resources

GO TO: go.hrw.com

- Manuscript Form
- The History of English
- Test Smarts
- Grammar at a Glance

Manuscript Form

Why Is Manuscript Form Important?

What is manuscript form, and why should you care about it? *Manuscript form* refers to the overall appearance of a document. A legible, professional-looking manuscript gives the impression that the writer cares not only about what he or she has to say but also about what the reader thinks. A manuscript that is an illegible jumble, on the other hand, gives the impression that the writer is careless, is not thinking clearly, or does not respect the reader.

Such impressions affect our lives every day. For example, a busy employer faced with the task of evaluating multiple job résumés may simply discard the sloppy ones without ever reading them. If we value what we write and want others to understand and value it too, then we should present our ideas in the best form possible. To help you present your ideas as effectively as possible, this section of the book covers basic guidelines for preparing and presenting manuscripts and provides a sample research paper as a model.

General Guidelines for Preparing Manuscripts

The following guidelines are general style rules to use in formal, nonfiction writing. Such writing includes papers and reports for school, letters of application for jobs or colleges, letters to the editor, and press releases for clubs and other organizations.

Content and Organization

1. Begin the paper with an introductory paragraph that contains a thesis sentence.

2. Develop and support your thesis in body paragraphs.

3. Follow the principles of unity and coherence. That is, develop one and only one big idea (your thesis), and make sure that your paragraphs and sentences flow smoothly without any gaps in the sequence of ideas.

4. Place charts, graphs, tables, and illustrations close to the text they illustrate. Label and number each one.

5. Follow the conventions of standard grammar, usage, capitalization, punctuation, and spelling.

6. Include a conclusion.

Appearance

1. Submit manuscript that is legible. Type or print out your paper using black ink; or when your teacher permits handwriting, write neatly using blue or black ink. (Other colors are harder to read.) If the printer or typewriter you are using is printing words that are faint and hard to read, change the ink cartridge or the ribbon.

2. Keep all pages neat and clean. If you discover errors and if you are working on a word processor, you can easily correct the errors and print out a fresh copy. If you write your paper by hand or on a typewriter, you generally may make a few corrections with correction tape and insert the revisions neatly. To replace a letter, word, or phrase, neatly cross out what you want to replace. Then, insert a caret mark (^) below the line, and write the inserted item above the line.

EXAMPLE

The ~~daily~~ ^weekly^ broadcasts continued all that summer.

Paper and Font

1. Use quality 8½ × 11 inch paper.
2. Use only one side of the paper.
3. When using a word processor, use an easy-to-read font size. Size twelve is standard.
4. Use a standard font, such as Times New Roman, that does not call attention to itself. Flowery, highly stylized fonts are hard to read. They look unprofessional, and they distract the reader from the ideas you are trying to convey.

Plagiarism

Do not plagiarize. Plagiarism is the unacknowledged borrowing of someone else's words or ideas and the submission of those words or ideas as one's own. Honest writers document all borrowings, whether those borrowings are quoted or merely paraphrased.

Back-up files

When you are ready to submit your work, be sure to save a copy—a printout, a photocopy, or an electronic file—for yourself.

Academic Manuscript Style

In school you will write some very formal papers—research reports or term papers, for example. For such assignments, you will need to follow not only general manuscript guidelines but also some very specific guidelines especially for academic manuscripts.

The academic manuscript style summarized on the following pages follows the style recommended by the Modern Language Association in the *MLA Handbook for Writers of Research Papers.* Two other popular manuscript styles are the format recommended by the American Psychological Association, known as APA style, and the one published in *The Chicago Manual of Style.* Style manuals are updated from time to time, so be sure you are using the most current version. When formatting papers for school, be sure to follow your teachers' instructions on which manuscript style to use.

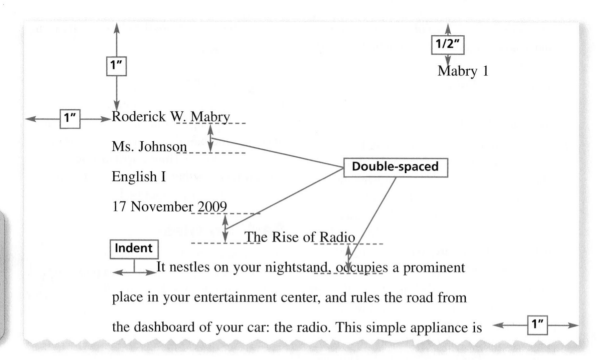

The following labels appear in the illustration:

1/2″

Mabry 1

1″

1″ Roderick W. Mabry

Ms. Johnson

English I

Double-spaced

17 November 2009

The Rise of Radio

Indent

It nestles on your nightstand, occupies a prominent

place in your entertainment center, and rules the road from

the dashboard of your car: the radio. This simple appliance is **1″**

Title Page, Margins, and Spacing

1. Leave one-inch margins on the top, sides, and bottom of each page.
2. Starting with the first page, number all your pages in the upper right-hand corner. Precede each page number with your last name. Computer software can help you create this "header."
3. Place your heading—your name, your teacher's name, your class, and the date—in the upper left-hand corner of the first page. (If your teacher requires a separate cover sheet, follow his or her instructions.)
4. Double-space between the header and the heading. Double-space the lines in the heading. Double-space between the heading and your title. (This rule does not apply if your teacher requires a cover sheet.)
5. Center the title, and capitalize the appropriate letters in it.

6. Double-space between the title and the body of the paper.
7. Do not underline or use quotation marks to enclose your own title at the head of your own paper. If you use someone else's title within your title, use quotation marks or underlining, as appropriate, with the other person's title only.

EXAMPLE

An Analysis of Symbolism in Yeats' "The Second Coming"

8. When typing or word-processing, always double-space the lines. (In a handwritten paper, skip every other ruled line unless your teacher instructs you otherwise.)
9. Do not use more than a double-space, even between paragraphs.
10. Indent the beginning of each paragraph one-half inch (five spaces).

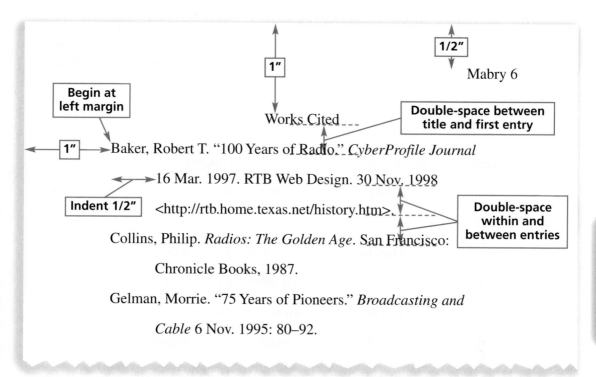

Mabry 6

1/2"

1"

Begin at left margin

1"

Works Cited

Double-space between title and first entry

Baker, Robert T. "100 Years of Radio." *CyberProfile Journal*

16 Mar. 1997. RTB Web Design. 30 Nov. 1998

Indent 1/2"   <http://rtb.home.texas.net/history.htm>.

Double-space within and between entries

Collins, Philip. *Radios: The Golden Age*. San Francisco:

Chronicle Books, 1987.

Gelman, Morrie. "75 Years of Pioneers." *Broadcasting and*

Cable 6 Nov. 1995: 80–92.

Documenting Sources

Works Cited Page

1. In a research paper or any other paper that incorporates information from other sources, add a works cited page at the end.
2. Continue numbering the pages of your paper through the works cited page.
3. The entries on the works cited page should be in alphabetical order, according to the last name of the author. For works with no author, the entry should be alphabetized according to the first main word in the title.
4. Do not number the sources on your works cited page.

Documentation in the Body of the Essay

1. Use parenthetical citations within the body of your paper to acknowledge any paraphrased idea or quotation that you have borrowed from someone else. The parenthetical citation refers to specific source documentation on the works cited page. Place the parenthetical citations at the **end** of the material that you borrowed from some other source.

EXAMPLE

Newspapers worried that radio would drive them out of business (Henderson 90).

2. If the citation appears at the end of a sentence, the citation comes before the closing period, as shown above. If the citation appears at the end of a dependent clause or after the first half of a compound sentence, the citation comes before the sentence comma.

EXAMPLE

Newspapers worried that radio would drive them out of business (Henderson 90), but it did not.

3. For quotations of five or more lines, indent all of the lines one inch (about ten spaces) from the left margin. Do not use quotation marks to enclose indented quotations. Also, place end punctuation at the end of the quoted material, not after the closing parenthesis.

In the following passage, we see how effectively the author sets the mood. With a little imagination, we can almost feel the moist air and hear the murmured conversations.

←—— 1" ——→ The streetlights along Toole Street, which meandered downhill from the Language Academy to the town, were already lit and twinkled mistily through the trees. Standing at the gates were small groups of students, clustered together according to nationality. As Myles passed by, he could not help overhearing intense conversations in Spanish, German, and Japanese; all of his students had momentarily abandoned English in the urgency of deciding where to go for the weekend and how to get there. (Boylan 58)

Model Research Paper

The following final draft of a research paper closely follows the guide-lines for MLA style given on the preceding pages. (Note: The pages of the model paper are smaller than 8½ × 11, and the margins of the paper are less than one inch wide to allow room for annotations.)

Mabry 1

Roderick W. Mabry

Ms. Johnson

English I

17 November 2009

The Rise of Radio

It nestles on nightstands, occupies a prominent place in many home entertainment centers, and rules the road from car dashboards: the radio. This simple appliance is so common that most people take it for granted, yet radio is a relatively new invention. In fact, the first commercial radio station, KDKA in Pittsburgh, did not go on the air until 1920 (Stark 120). Before long, however, the new medium dramatically affected the nation's entertainment, information delivery, and economy.

The invention of radio was made possible by a number of earlier developments. German physicist Heinrich Hertz, drawing on established mathematical principles, discovered the existence of radio waves in 1887. Eight years later, in Italy,

(continued)

HEADING
your name
your teacher's name
your class
date

THESIS SENTENCE: tells focus of the paper

TOPIC SENTENCE: tells focus of the paragraph and is a sub-topic of the thesis

RESOURCES

(continued)

Mabry 2

FIRST REFERENCE: Full name of inventor is used.

SECOND REFERENCE: last name only

This parenthetical citation indicates that paraphrased information in the paragraph comes from Yenne, page 77. *Yenne* refers to *Yenne, Bill* on the works cited page.

Guglielmo Marconi successfully completed the first wireless transmission of Morse code signals. An American invention helped move radio closer to reality: Lee De Forest's 1907 Audion, which made it possible to transmit sounds, not just signals. A full decade before KDKA debuted, De Forest broadcast a live performance by famed Italian tenor Enrico Caruso from New York City's Metropolitan Opera House (Yenne 77).

Few people were equipped to hear that landmark broadcast, however, because radio was still very much a do-it-yourself project; most people built their own receivers. In 1921, one such "tinkerer," twenty-eight-year-old Franklin Malcolm Doolittle of New Haven, Connecticut, even used his homemade transmitter to broadcast the Yale-Princeton football game from his home (Gelman 80). The first commercially produced receivers became available in 1920, when a Pittsburgh department store began offering sets for ten dollars. The response was so enthusiastic that Westinghouse began mass producing the appliances (Baker).

In the Baker citation, no page number is listed because this information comes from an unpaginated online source.

When radio found its way into the majority of American households, it brought the nation together in an unprecedented way. Radio reached into "once dreary homes, reducing the

isolation of the hinterlands and leveling class distinctions"

(Henderson 44). At first radio programming simply duplicated

existing forms of entertainment: singers, musicians, comedians,

lecturers. Coping with technical difficulties left little time for

creating new types of shows. Later, as the technical problems

were resolved, programmers began adapting existing formats

and experimenting with new types of shows, including variety

shows, serials, game shows, and amateur hours ("Radio as a

Medium of Communication"). As programming expanded,

radio truly became, in researcher Amy Henderson's words, "a

theater of the mind" (144).

     The introduction of radio also radically altered the way

people learned about events in the outside world. For the first

time in history, everyone could receive the same information

simultaneously. As sociologists Robert and Helen Lynd, writing

in the 1920s, noted, "With but little equipment one can call the

life of the rest of the world from the air . . ." (qtd. in Monk 173).

Live coverage gave news events an immediacy far greater than

newspapers or newsreels could provide. In fact, most people

When parenthetical documenta-tion follows closing quotation marks at the end of a sentence, the period should be placed after the parentheses.

These parentheses contain only the page number because the author is named in the text.

This citation tells us that the quotation from Robert and Helen Lynd was found in a book edited by Linda R. Monk.

RESOURCES

(continued)

(continued)

Mabry 4

first learned of such historic events as the 1941 Japanese attack on Pearl Harbor from the radio (Stark 120).

> Equally important was radio's impact on the economy. The first, and most noticeable, effect was to add a new consumer product to people's wish lists. Most early sets were strictly functional—"a box, some wire, and headphones" (Baker). Once the initial demand was satisfied, however, manufacturers began stimulating repeat sales by offering new models each year, with the goal of placing a "radio in every room" (Collins 10).

The demand for sets was a boon to manufacturers, but it struck fear into some other segments of the economy. Newspapers worried that radio would drive them out of business (Henderson 90). Similarly, members of the traditional entertainment industry feared that the new technology would cut into the sales of tickets and recordings (Stark 120).

Surprisingly, advertisers were slow to realize the opportunities radio offered. At first, most business people assumed that profits would come solely from the sale of sets and replacement parts. In addition, paid advertising was considered

Note again how strong topic sentences control the content of the paragraph and develop a subtopic of the thesis sentence.

The parenthetical citation for Henderson is placed directly at the end of the paraphrase.

improper for what was initially viewed as a "new, pure instrument of democracy" (Weiner). Instead, early programs were underwritten by "sponsors," with companies receiving only a brief, discreet acknowledgment in return for their support. Eventually, however, this approach gave way to the direct advertising that is familiar today (Weiner).

Reviewing the rise of radio makes clear how instrumental the medium was in shaping the nation's entertainment, information delivery, and economy. Today, with the advent of television and the Internet, radio is no longer the primary source of news and entertainment for most people, nor is its impact on the economy as far-reaching. Still, each day millions of listeners wake, work, and play to the rhythms of radio, and many would be lost without it. The radio may have been muted, but it has not been unplugged.

Mabry ends his paper with a concluding paragraph that is entirely his own statement. First, he restates the thesis in the form of a conclusion. Then, he places the history of the radio in its modern context.

(continued)

RESOURCES

(continued)

Mabry 6

Works Cited

Baker, Robert T. "100 Years of Radio." *CyberProfile Journal* 16

    Mar. 1997. RTB Web Design. 30 Nov. 1998 <http://rtb.

    home.texas.net/history.htm>.

Collins, Philip. *Radios: The Golden Age*. San Francisco:

    Chronicle Books, 1987.

Gelman, Morrie. "75 Years of Pioneers." *Broadcasting and*

    Cable 6 Nov. 1995: 80–92.

Henderson, Amy. *On the Air*. Washington, DC: Smithsonian

    Institution Press, 1988.

Monk, Linda R., ed. *Ordinary Americans*. Alexandria, VA:

    Close Up, 1994.

"Radio as a Medium of Communication." *The Encyclopedia*

    Americana. International ed. 1998.

Stark, Phyllis. "On the Air." *Billboard* 1 Nov. 1994: 120–124.

Weiner, Neil. "Stories from Early Radio." *Background Briefing*.

    14 April 1996. 28 Mar. 1999. <http://www.background

    briefing.com/radio.html>.

Yenne, Bill. *100 Events That Shaped World History*. San

    Francisco: Bluewood, 1993.

Center and capitalize *Works Cited,* but do not put it in quotation marks or underline it.

Entries are alphabetized according to the last name of the author.

Carefully punctuate all entries.

Indent second and subsequent lines of entries five spaces.

If no author is listed, alphabetize according to the first main word in the title.

The online address (URL) is enclosed by these signs: < >.

The History of English

Origins and Uses

The English language was first written about 1,300 years ago, but was spoken long before that. Over the centuries, English has grown and changed to become the rich, expressive language we use today. The history of this development is a story of people, places, and times.

Beginnings of English   Many of the world's languages come from an early language called *Proto-Indo-European.* We have no records of this parent language, but it was probably spoken by Eastern Europeans six or seven thousand years ago. Tribes of these people slowly migrated across Europe and to India. As they wandered in different directions, each tribe developed its own *dialect,* or distinct version of the language. The dialects eventually developed into separate languages. The map on this page shows how the Indo-European root word *mater* (mother) developed in some of these languages. The arrows indicate directions of migration.

Old English   Around A.D. 450, tribes known as the Angles and the Saxons invaded Britain. They took over land that had been settled earlier by the Celts. The separate dialects these tribes spoke eventually blended into one language—*Old English,* sometimes called Anglo-Saxon. Modern English still bears traces of its Anglo-Saxon roots. For example, the words *eat, drink,* and *sleep* come from the Old English words *etan, drincan,* and *slæp.* The Anglo-Saxons used an *−s* to form the plurals of many nouns, just as we do. We also have Old English to thank for irregular verb forms such as *swim, swam,* and *swum.*

Middle English   In 1066, the Normans from France seized control of England. For the next 150 years, French was the official language of government, business, and law. Therefore, many

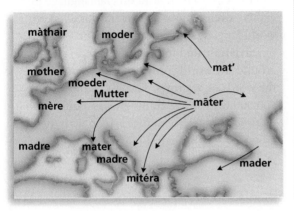

English words that are connected with wealth and power, such as *governor, attorney,* and *fashion,* come from the French. The common people of England, however, still spoke English—a changing form of the language we call **Middle English.** The grammar of English was becoming simpler as many of the complicated word endings disappeared.

The following lines are matching excerpts from the Lord's Prayer (Matthew 6:9–13) in Old English and Middle English. As you can see, Middle English looks much more like the English you know.

Old English: Fæder ure þu þe eart on heofonum, si þin nama gehalgod.

Middle English: Fader oure þat art in hevene, i-halwed bee þi name.

Modern English   Before 1476, speakers and writers in different parts of England used different versions of the language, and therefore they often had trouble understanding each other. When William Caxton set up the first printing press in England around 1476, all of this changed. Early printers standardized spelling, and since London was the center of English trade and culture, they printed all books in London English. London English soon became the standard throughout England. Once standards were set, people wanted to learn the proper way to speak and write their language. Soon, grammar and usage handbooks sprang up, along with the first English dictionaries.

Two other factors influenced Modern English. One factor was its expansion into an international language through the discovery of new lands. From the sixteenth century through the nineteenth century, English merchants, explorers, and settlers spread English to other parts of the globe. They also learned new words from other languages, enriching English with international imports.

EXAMPLES

Japanese: soy   **Dutch:** cruise

Turkish: yogurt   **Spanish:** siesta

The language was also affected by the scientific revolution of this time. Words had to be created to name the new discoveries being made.

EXAMPLES

atmosphere   **pneumonia**   **skeleton**

American English   Immigration to the American colonies brought about a new version of the language—**American English.** Like the United States itself, American English represents a variety of cultures and peoples. Native Americans, Africans, and immigrants from most countries around the world have enriched the language with words from their native tongues. For example, Native Americans gave us *coyote* and *squash; jazz* and *gumbo* came from Africa; and Italian immigrants added *spaghetti* and *ravioli* to the menu.

English in the Twenty-first Century

English has become the most widely used language in the history of the world, with over 750 million users. It is an official language in eighty-seven nations and territories. It is the world language of diplomacy, science, technology, aviation, and international trade. As people around the world contribute to the language, the word count grows. The last count was over 600,000 words. The count grows so quickly that dictionary makers cannot keep up with the growth of English vocabulary.

Varieties of English

English is a rich and flexible language that offers many choices. To speak and write effectively—at home, at school, and on the job—you need to know what the varieties of English are and how to choose among them.

Dialects of American English   Like all languages, American English has many distinct versions, called **dialects.** Everyone uses a dialect, and no dialect is better or worse than another. Each has unique features of grammar, vocabulary, and pronunciation.

■ **Regional dialects**   The United States has four major regional dialects: the *Northern,* the *Midland,* the *Southern,* and the *Western.* Pronunciations of words often vary from one dialect region to another. For example, some Southerners pronounce the words *ten* and *tin* the same way—as "tin." Similarly, regions differ in grammar and vocabulary. For example, you may say "sick *to* my stomach" if you come from New York but "sick *at* my stomach" if you come from Georgia. You may drink *soda, tonic,* or *pop* depending on what part of the country you come from.

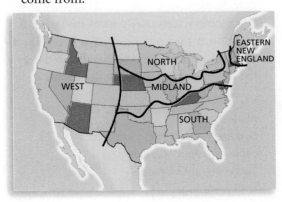

■ **Ethnic dialects**   An ethnic dialect is used by people who share the same cultural heritage. Because Americans come from many different cultures, American English includes many different ethnic dialects. The most widely used ethnic dialects are African American Vernacular English and Hispanic Vernacular English. Many everyday words began as ethnic dialect words but then became part of the general English vocabulary. For example, African Americans introduced the words *banana* and *tote* into English, and Hispanic Americans added words such as *avocado* and *patio.*

Standard American English   Every variety of English has its own set of rules and guidelines. No variety is the best or the most correct. However, **Standard American English** (SAE) is the one variety of English that is more widely used and accepted than others in the United States. Because it is commonly understood, SAE allows people from many different regions and cultures to communicate with one another clearly. It is the variety of English you read and hear most often in books and magazines, on radio and television. It is the kind of English that people are expected to use in most school and business situations. This textbook presents many of the rules and guidelines for using Standard American English. To identify the differences between Standard American English and other varieties of English, this book uses the labels *standard* and *nonstandard.* Nonstandard does not mean wrong language. It means language that is inappropriate in situations where standard English is expected.

Standard English—Formal to Informal

Depending on your audience, purpose, and occasion, the language you use can be formal, informal, or somewhere in between. The following chart shows some of the appropriate uses of very formal and very informal English.

Uses of Formal and Informal English

Formal

Speaking: formal, dignified occasions, such as banquets and dedication ceremonies

Writing: serious papers and reports, tests, business letters

Informal

Speaking: everyday conversation at home, school, work, and recreation

Writing: personal letters, journal entries, and many newspaper and magazine articles

You can say the same thing in many different ways. For example, *chow down* and *dine* both mean "eat," but one is much more formal than the other. The main differences between formal and informal English are in sentence structure, word choice, and tone.

Features of Formal and Informal English

Formal

Sentence Structure: longer and more complex

Word Choice: precise, often technical or scientific

Tone: serious and dignified

Informal

Sentence Structure: shorter and simpler

Word Choice: simple and ordinary; often includes contractions, colloquialisms, and slang

Tone: conversational

Uses of Informal English In informal speaking and writing, people constantly make up new words and give new uses to old ones. This makes informal English flexible. Dictionaries help you to see this flexibility by giving labels to different informal uses of words. The two most commonly listed usage labels are **colloquialisms** and **slang.**

- **Colloquialisms** *Colloquialisms* are the informal words and phrases of conversational language. They bring flavor and color to everyday speech and a friendly, conversational tone to writing. Many are figures of speech that aren't meant to be taken literally.

EXAMPLES

I may have made a mistake, but you don't have to **fly off the handle** about it.

Today, many young couples **foot the bill** for their weddings rather than having their parents pay for them.

My mother told us to quit **making such a racket.**

- **Slang** *Slang* is made up of newly coined words or of old words used in unconventional ways. It is usually clever and colorful. It is often a special language for specific groups of people, such as students and military personnel. Some people use slang to be up-to-date. Sometimes a slang word becomes a lasting and widely used part of the language. More often than not, however, it lives a short and limited life. Slang is generally used only in the most informal speaking situations.

EXAMPLES

beat—tired
bummer—a depressing experience
cool—pleasing, excellent
hassle—to annoy, harass
kooky—strange

Test Smarts

Taking Standardized Tests in Grammar, Usage, and Mechanics

Becoming "Test-Smart"

Standardized achievement tests, like other tests, measure your skills in specific areas. Standardized achievement tests also compare your performance to the performance of other students at your age or grade level. Some language arts standardized tests measure your skill in using correct capitalization, punctuation, sentence structure, and spelling. Such tests sometimes also measure your ability to evaluate sentence style.

The most important part of preparing for any test, including standardized tests, is learning the content on which you will be tested. To do this, you must

- listen in class
- complete homework assignments
- study to master the concepts and skills presented by your teacher

In addition, you also need to use effective strategies for taking a standardized test. The following pages will teach you how to become test-smart.

General Strategies for Taking Tests

1. **Understand how the test is scored.** If no points will be taken off for wrong answers, plan to answer every question. If wrong answers count against you, plan to answer only questions you know the answer to or questions you can answer with an educated guess.

2. **Stay focused.** Expect to be a little nervous, but focus your attention on doing the best job possible. Try not to be distracted with thoughts that aren't about the test questions.

3. **Get an overview.** Quickly skim the entire test to get an idea of how long the test is and what is on it.

4. **Pace yourself.** Based on your overview, figure out how much time to allow for each section of the test. If time limits are stated for each section, decide how much time to allow for each item. Pace yourself, and check every five to ten minutes to see if you need to work faster. Try to leave a few minutes at the end of the testing period to check your work.

5. **Read all instructions.** Read the instructions for each part of the test carefully. Also, answer the sample questions to be sure you understand how to answer the test questions.

6. **Read all answer choices.** Carefully read *all* of the possible answers before you choose an answer. Note how each possible answer differs from the others. You may want to make an *x* next to each answer choice that you rule out.

7. **Make educated guesses.** If you do not know the answer to a question, see if you can rule out one or more answers and make an educated guess. Don't spend too much time on any one item, though. If you want to think longer about a difficult item, make a light pencil mark next to the item number. You can go back to that question later.

8. **Mark your answers.** Mark the answer sheet carefully and completely. If you plan to go back to an item later, be sure to skip that number on the answer sheet.

9. **Check your work.** If you have time at the end of the test, go back to check your answers. This is also the time to try to answer any questions you skipped. Make sure your marks are complete, and erase any stray marks on the answer sheet.

Strategies for Answering Grammar, Usage, and Mechanics Questions

The questions in standardized tests can take different forms, but the most common form is the multiple-choice question. Here are some strategies for answering that kind of test question.

Correcting parts of sentences

One kind of question contains a sentence with an underlined part. The answer choices show several revised versions of that part. Your job is to decide which revised version makes the sentence correct or whether the underlined part is already correct. First, look at each answer carefully. Immediately rule out any answer in which you notice a grammatical error. If you are still unsure of the correct answer, try approaching the question in one of these two ways.

- **Think how you would rewrite the underlined part.** Look at the answer choices for one that matches your revision. Carefully read each possible answer before you make your final choice. Often, only tiny differences exist between the answers, and you want to choose the *best* answer.

- **Look carefully at the underlined part and at each answer choice, looking for one particular type of error, such as an error in capitalization or spelling.** The best way to look for a particular error is to compare the answer choices to see how they differ both from each other and from the underlined part of the question. For example, if there are differences in capitalization, look at each choice for capitalization errors.

After ruling out incorrect answers, choose the answer with no errors. If there are errors in each of the choices but no errors in the underlined part, your answer will be the "no error" or "correct as is" choice.

EXAMPLE

Directions: Choose the answer that is the **best** revision of the underlined words.

1. My neighbor is painting his <u>house and my brother helped him.</u>

   A. house; and my brother is helping him.
   B. house, and my brother had helped him.
   C. house, and my brother is helping him.
   D. Correct as is

Explanation: In the example above, the possible answers contain differences in punctuation and in verb tense. Therefore, you should check each possible answer for errors in punctuation and verb tense.

   A. You can rule out this choice because it has incorrect punctuation.
   B. This choice creates inconsistent verb tenses, so you can rule out this answer.
   C. This choice has correct punctuation and creates consistent verb tenses.
   D. You can rule out this choice because the original sentence lacks correct punctuation between the clauses.

Answer: Choice C is the only one that contains no errors, so the oval for that answer choice is darkened.

Correcting whole sentences
This type of question is similar to the kind of question previously described. However, here you are looking for mistakes in the entire sentence instead of just an underlined part. The strategies for approaching this type of question are the same as for the other kind of sentence-correction questions. If you don't see the correct answer right away, compare the answer choices to see how they differ. When you find differences, check

each choice for errors relating to that difference. Rule out choices with errors. Repeat the process until you find the correct answer.

EXAMPLE

Directions: Choose the answer that is the **best** revision of the following sentences.

1. After Brad mowed the lawn, he swept the sidewalk and driveway, then he took a shower. And washed his hair.

   A. After Brad mowed the lawn, he swept the sidewalk and driveway. Then he took a shower and washed his hair.
   B. After Brad mowed the lawn, he swept the sidewalk and driveway. Then he took a shower, and washed his hair.
   C. After Brad mowed the lawn. He swept the sidewalk and driveway; then he took a shower and washed his hair.
   D. Correct as is

Explanation: The original word groups and answer choices have differences in sentence structure and punctuation, so you should check each answer choice for errors in sentence structure and punctuation.

   A. This choice contains two complete sentences and correct punctuation.
   B. This choice contains two complete sentences and incorrect punctuation.
   C. This choice begins with a sentence fragment, so you can rule it out.
   D. You can rule out this choice because the original version contains a sentence fragment.

Answer: Choice A is the only one that contains no errors, so the oval for that answer choice is darkened.

Identifying kinds of errors
This type of question has at least one under-lined part. Your job is to determine which part, if any,

contains an error. Sometimes, you also may have to decide what type of error (capitalization, punctuation, or spelling) exists. The strategy is the same whether the question has one or several underlined parts. Try to identify an error, and check the answer choices for that type of error. If the original version is correct as written, choose "no error" or "correct as is."

EXAMPLE

Directions: Read the following sentences and decide which type of error, if any, is in the underlined part.

1. Marcia, Jim, and Leroy are participating in <u>Saturday's charity marathon. they</u> are hoping to raise one hundred dollars for the new children's museum.
   A. Spelling error
   B. Capitalization error
   C. Punctuation error
   D. Correct as is

Explanation: If you cannot tell right away what kind of error (if any) is in the original version, go through each answer choice in turn.
   A. All the words are spelled correctly.
   B. The sentences contain a capitalization error. The second sentence incorrectly begins with a lowercase letter.
   C. The sentences are punctuated correctly.
   D. The sentences contain a capitalization error, so you can rule out this choice.

Answer: Because the passage contains a capitalization error, the oval for answer choice B is darkened.

Revising sentence structure Errors
covered by this kind of question include sentence fragments, run-on sentences, repetitive wording,

misplaced modifiers, and awkward construction. If you don't immediately spot the error, examine the question and each answer choice for specific types of errors, one type at a time. If you cannot find an error in the original version and if all of the other answer choices have errors, then choose "no error" or "correct as is."

EXAMPLE

Directions: Read the following word groups. If there is an error in sentence structure, choose the answer that best revises the word groups.

1. Mary Lou arranged the mozzarella cheese and fresh tomatoes. On a platter covered with lettuce leaves.
   A. Mary Lou arranged the mozzarella cheese and fresh tomatoes on a platter covered with lettuce leaves.
   B. Mary Lou arranged the mozzarella cheese and fresh tomatoes, on a platter covered with lettuce leaves.
   C. Mary Lou arranged the mozzarella cheese and fresh tomatoes; on a platter covered with lettuce leaves.
   D. Correct as is

Explanation: The original word groups and answer choices have differences in sentence structure and punctuation.
   A. This choice is correctly punctuated and contains a correct, complete sentence.
   B. This choice contains an incorrect comma, so you can rule it out.
   C. This choice contains an incorrect semicolon, so you can rule it out.
   D. The original word groups contain a sentence fragment, so D cannot be correct.

Answer: Choice A is the only one that contains no errors, so the oval for that answer choice is darkened.

Questions about sentence style

These questions are often not about grammar, usage, or mechanics but about content and organization. They may ask about tone, purpose, topic sentences, supporting sentences, audience, sentence combining, appropriateness of content, or transitions. The questions may ask you which is the *best* way to revise the passage, or they may ask you to identify the *main* purpose of the passage. When you see words such as *best*, *main*, and *most likely* or *least likely*, you are not being asked to correct errors; you are being asked to make a judgment about style or meaning.

If the question asks for a particular kind of revision (for example, "What *transition* is needed between sentence 4 and sentence 5?"), analyze each answer choice to see how well it makes that particular revision. Many questions ask for a general revision (for example, "Which is the *best* way to revise the last sentence?"). In such situations, check each answer choice and rule out any choices that have mistakes in grammar, usage, or mechanics. Then, read each choice and use what you have learned in class to judge whether the revision improves the original sentence. If you are combining sentences, be sure to choose the answer that includes all important information, that demonstrates good style, *and* that is grammatically correct.

EXAMPLE

Directions: Choose the answer that shows the **best** way to combine the following sentences.

1. Jacques Cousteau was a filmmaker and author. Jacques Cousteau explored the ocean as a diver and marine scientist.
   A. Jacques Cousteau was a filmmaker and author; Jacques Cousteau explored the ocean as a marine scientist.
   B. Jacques Cousteau was a filmmaker and author, he explored the ocean as a diver and marine scientist.
   C. Jacques Cousteau was a filmmaker and author who explored the ocean as a diver and marine scientist.
   D. Jacques Cousteau was a filmmaker, author, diver, and scientist.

(A) (B) (C) (D)

Explanation:
   A. Answer choice A is grammatically correct but unnecessarily repeats the subject *Jacques Cousteau* and leaves out some information.
   B. Choice B is a run-on sentence, so it cannot be the correct answer.
   C. Choice C is grammatically correct, and it demonstrates effective sentence combining.
   D. Choice D is grammatically correct but leaves out some information.

Answer: Because answer choice C shows the best way to combine the sentences, the oval for choice C is darkened.

Fill-in-the-blanks

This type of question tests your ability to fill in blanks in sentences, giving answers that are logical and grammatically correct. A question of this kind might ask you to choose a verb in the appropriate tense. A different question might require a combination of adverbs (*first, next*) to show how parts of the sentence relate. Another question might require a vocabulary word to complete the sentence.

To approach a sentence-completion question, first look for clue words in the sentence. *But*, *however*, and *though* indicate a contrast; *therefore* and *as a result* indicate cause and effect. Using sentence clues, rule out obviously incorrect answer choices. Then, try filling in the blanks with the remaining choices to determine which answer choice makes the most sense. Finally, check to be sure your choice is grammatically correct.

Directions: Choose the words that **best** complete the sentence.

1. When Jack _____ the dog, the dog _____ water everywhere.

   A. washes, splashed

   B. washed, will be splashing

   C. will have washed, has splashed

   D. washed, splashed

Explanation:

   A. The verb tenses (present and past) are inconsistent.

   B. The verb tenses (past and future) are inconsistent.

   C. The verb tenses (future perfect and present perfect) are inconsistent.

   D. The verb tenses (past and past) are consistent.

Answer: The oval for choice D is darkened.

Using Your Test Smarts

Remember: Success on standardized tests comes partly from knowing strategies for taking such tests—from being test-smart. Knowing these strategies can help you approach standardized achievement tests more confidently. Do your best to learn your classroom subjects, take practice tests if they are available, and use the strategies outlined in this section. Good luck!

Grammar at a Glance

abbreviation An abbreviation is a shortened form of a word or a phrase.

■ **capitalization of** (See page 249.)

TITLES USED WITH NAMES	**M**r.	**D**r.	**J**r.	**P**h.**D**.
KINDS OF ORGANIZATIONS	**A**ssn.	**I**nc.	**D**ept.	**C**orp.
PARTS OF ADDRESSES	**A**ve.	**S**t.	**B**lvd.	**P.O. B**ox
NAMES OF STATES	[without ZIP Codes]	**K**y.	**T**ex.	
		Tenn.	**N. D**ak.	
	[with ZIP Codes]	**KY**	**TX**	
		TN	**ND**	
TIMES	**A.M.**	**P.M.**	**B.C.**	**A.D.**

■ **punctuation of** (See page 267.)

WITH PERIODS	(See preceding examples.)
WITHOUT PERIODS	VCR ESPN NAACP FCC
	DC [D.C. without ZIP Code]
	kg lb tsp km ft
	[Exception: inch = in.]

action verb An action verb expresses physical or mental activity. (See page 16.)

EXAMPLES Kurt **ran** toward the ledge.

Owen correctly **guessed** the number of jelly beans in the jar.

active voice Active voice is the voice a verb is in when it expresses an action done by its subject. (See page 163. See also **voice.**)

EXAMPLE Napoleon's armies **conquered** most of western Europe.

┌ H E L P ─

Grammar at a Glance is an alphabetical list of special terms and expressions with examples and references to further information. When you encounter a grammar or usage problem in the revising or proofreading stage of your writing, look for help in this section first. You may find all you need to know right here. If you need more information, **Grammar at a Glance** will show you where in the book to turn for a more complete explanation. If you do not find what you are looking for in **Grammar at a Glance,** turn to the index on page 537.

RESOURCES

adjective An adjective modifies a noun or a pronoun. (See page 10.)

EXAMPLE   **The** peninsula has **high** mountains and **winding** roads.

adjective clause An adjective clause is a subordinate clause that modifies a noun or a pronoun. (See page 101.)

EXAMPLE   The man **who disappeared** was soon found again.

adjective phrase A prepositional phrase that modifies a noun or a pronoun is called an adjective phrase. (See page 71.)

EXAMPLE   We approached the highest peak **in the Alps.**

adverb An adverb modifies a verb, an adjective, or another adverb. (See page 21.)

EXAMPLE   Helen **rarely** loses her temper.

adverb clause An adverb clause is a subordinate clause that modifies a verb, an adjective, or an adverb. (See page 104.)

EXAMPLE   We will try to get indoors **before the storm arrives.**

adverb phrase A prepositional phrase that modifies a verb, an adjective, or an adverb is called an adverb phrase. (See page 73.)

EXAMPLE   Terry cleaned his room **in a few minutes.**

agreement Agreement is the correspondence, or match, between grammatical forms. Grammatical forms agree when they have the same number and gender.

■ **of pronouns and antecedents** (See page 135.)

SINGULAR   **Ethan** politely asked for an increase in **his** allowance.
PLURAL   Ethan's **brothers** politely asked for an increase in **their** allowances.

SINGULAR   **Everyone** in the play made **his or her** own costumes.
PLURAL   **All** of the performers made **their** own costumes.

SINGULAR   Is **Matthew or Terence** looking forward to reciting **his** poem in front of **his** classmates?
PLURAL   **Matthew and Terence** are looking forward to reciting **their** poems in front of **their** classmates.

- **of subjects and verbs** (See page 121.)

SINGULAR	The art **teacher has painted** a mural on a wall of the cafeteria.
	The art **teacher,** with the help of her students, **has painted** a mural on a wall of the cafeteria.
PLURAL	The art **students have painted** a mural on a wall of the cafeteria.
PLURAL	The art **students,** with the help of their teacher, **have painted** a mural on the wall of the cafeteria.

| SINGULAR | **Everyone** in this class **is learning** sign language. |
| PLURAL | **All** of the students **are learning** sign language. |

| SINGULAR | **Neither Diego nor I was** ready to compete in the battle of the bands. |
| PLURAL | **Salsa, reggae, and zydeco were** among the kinds of music played at the band competition. |

| SINGULAR | Here **is** your book **bag.** |
| PLURAL | Here **are** your **books.** |

| SINGULAR | **Ten dollars is** the cost of the ticket. |
| PLURAL | In this stack of bills, ten **dollars are** torn. |

| SINGULAR | **Two thirds** of the freshman class **has voted.** |
| PLURAL | **Two thirds** of the freshmen **have voted.** |

| SINGULAR | *Symphonies of Wind Instruments* **was composed** by Igor Stravinsky. |
| PLURAL | Stravinsky's other **symphonies were** also well **received.** |

| SINGULAR | **Is mathematics** your favorite school subject? |
| PLURAL | **Are** my **binoculars** in your locker? |

ambiguous reference Ambiguous reference occurs when a pronoun incorrectly refers to either of two antecedents. (See page 193.)

AMBIGUOUS	Martina is supposed to meet Jada at the library after she practices her cello lesson.
CLEAR	After **Martina** practices **her** cello lesson, **she** is supposed to meet Jada at the library.
CLEAR	After **Jada** practices **her** cello lesson, **she** is supposed to meet Martina at the library.

antecedent An antecedent is the word or words that a pronoun stands for. (See page 6.)

EXAMPLE **Alfred** sent **Julie** and **Dave** the money **he** owed **them.**
[*Alfred* is the antecedent of *he. Julie* and *Dave* are the antecedents of *them.*]

apostrophe

- **to form contractions** (See page 335.)
  EXAMPLES couldn's   let's   o'clock   '99

- **to form plurals of letters, numerals, symbols, and words used as words** (See page 337.)
  EXAMPLES   *p*'s and *q*'s   *A*'s and *I*'s

  10's and *20*'s   *$*'s and *¢*'s

- **to show possession** (See page 327.)
  EXAMPLES   gymnast's routine

  gymnasts' routines

  children's toys

  everyone's opinion

  Whitney Houston's and Denzel Washington's performances

  a year's [*or* twelve months'] leave of absence

appositive An appositive is a noun or a pronoun placed beside another noun or pronoun to identify or describe it. (See page 89.)

EXAMPLE   My great-aunt **Rina** was born in Poland.

appositive phrase An appositive phrase consists of an appositive and its modifiers. (See page 89.)

EXAMPLE   Kublai Khan, **the first emperor of the Yuan dynasty,** united China under his rule.

article The articles, *a, an,* and *the,* are the most frequently used adjectives. (See page 12.)

EXAMPLE   On **an** overpass south of **the** city, **an** incident occurred that convinced John that he needed **a** new car.

bad, badly (See page 203.)

NONSTANDARD   Do you think these leftovers smell badly?

STANDARD   Do you think these leftovers smell **bad**?

base form
The base form, or infinitive, is one of the four principal parts of a verb. (See page 145.)

EXAMPLE   This computer program has helped me [to] **learn** Spanish.

brackets (See page 354.)

EXAMPLE   The history book points out that "the name Hundred Years' War is a misnomer **[**a wrong name**]**, for the name refers to a series of wars that lasted 116 years **[**1337–1453**]**."

capitalization

- **of abbreviations and acronyms** (See **abbreviations.**)

- **of first words** (See page 246.)

    EXAMPLES   **M**y sister writes in her journal every night.

    Omar asked, "**W**ould you like to play on my soccer team?"

    Dear Ms. Reuben:

    Sincerely yours,

- **of proper nouns and proper adjectives** (See page 248.)

Proper Noun	Common Noun
James Lovell, Jr.	astronaut
Alexander the Great	leader
South America	continent
Appalachian Mountains	mountain chain
Minnesota Vikings	team
Democratic Party (*or* party)	political party
French and Indian War	historical event
Jurassic Period	historical period
Mother's Day	holiday
General Motors Corporation	business

■ **of titles** (See page 257.)

EXAMPLES   **G**overnor Pataki [preceding a name]

Pataki, the **g**overnor of New York [following a name]

Thank you, **G**overnor. [direct address]

Aunt Ramona [*but* our **a**unt Ramona]

***D**ust **T**racks **o**n **a** **R**oad* [novel]

***T**he **L**ion **K**ing* [movie or play]

***N**ova* [TV program]

***M**ona **L**isa* [work of art]

"**T**he **S**tar-**S**pangled **B**anner" [song]

"**A**migo **B**rothers" [short story]

"**N**othing **G**old **C**an **S**tay" [poem]

case of pronouns Case is the form a pronoun takes to show how it is used in a sentence. (See page 177.)

NOMINATIVE   **He** and **I** are making vegetable quesadillas.

Two of the class officers are Eric and **she.**

Either player, Cheryl or **she,** can play shortstop.

We volunteers have worked very hard on the recycling campaign.

Is Ernesto Galarza the author **who** wrote *Barrio Boy*?

Do you know **who** they are?

I helped Ms. Wong as much as **he.** [meaning "as much as he helped Ms. Wong"]

OBJECTIVE   This jacket will not fit Yolanda or **her.**

Aunt Calista brought **him** and **me** souvenirs of her trip to the Philippines.

Were you three cheering for **us** or **them**?

The mayor thanked **us** volunteers for our contributions.

Maya Angelou, **whom** many readers admire, is certainly my favorite author.

One of the candidates for **whom** I will vote is Tamisha.

I helped Ms. Wong as much as **him.** [meaning "as much as I helped him"]

POSSESSIVE   **Your** interpretation of **her** poem was different from **mine.**

clause A clause is a group of words that contains a verb and its subject and is used as part of a sentence. (See page 98.)

INDEPENDENT CLAUSE   Theo installed the blinds

SUBORDINATE CLAUSE   while Dorothy worked on the wiring

colon (See page 303.)

▪ before lists

EXAMPLES   The recipe calls for the following herbs: thyme, basil, cilantro, and oregano.

The documentary profiled three women artists of the twentieth century: Audrey Flack, a painter; Louise Nevelson, a sculptor; and Margaret Bourke-White, a photographer.

▪ in conventional situations

EXAMPLES   6:30 A.M.

Ecclesiastes 11:7–10

Computers and You: A Video Guide

Dear Sir or Madam:

comma (See page 271.)

▪ in a series

EXAMPLES   Tony, Julian, and Katie helped me make the fruit salad by cutting up the oranges, bananas, grapes, and papayas.

We rode our bicycles to the park, bought snacks at the juice bar, found a picnic table, and then played chess for an hour.

The silly cat had run through the living room, over the sofa, between my feet, through the door, across the hall, and up the stairs.

▪ in compound sentences

EXAMPLES   I like all kinds of music, but jazz is my favorite.

The students listened to each candidate's speech, and then they left the auditorium to cast their votes.

▪ with nonessential phrases and clauses

EXAMPLES   Didn't Mount Etna, Europe's largest volcano, erupt a few years ago?

In the mid-1900s, the Inuit, whose ancestors had led nomadic lives of hunting and fishing, began settling in urban areas of the Arctic region.

David will be bringing fresh salsa, which his father makes from tomatoes and herbs that they grow in their garden.

■ **with introductory elements**

EXAMPLES   In the first match of the tennis tournament, Pablo competed against the player who was ranked first in the state.

When the exciting game was over, many of the fans raced onto the field to praise and congratulate the winning player.

■ **with interrupters**

EXAMPLES   The most memorable part of our vacation, however, was our visit to the Smithsonian Institution.

You might consider making a mobile, for example, or some other simple present.

The most demanding role, I believe, is that of King Lear in Shakespeare's tragedy of the same name.

■ **in conventional situations**

EXAMPLES   On Monday, June 5, 2000, the Walkers flew from Detroit, Michigan, to San Juan, Puerto Rico, to attend their family reunion.

I mailed the package to 1620 Palmetto Drive, Tampa, FL 33637, on 15 September 2000.

comma splice A comma splice is a run-on sentence in which two sentences have been joined with only a comma between them. (See page 441. See also **fused sentence** and **run-on sentence.**)

COMMA SPLICE   My sister Eileen has a paper route, I help her sometimes, especially when the weather is bad.

REVISED   My sister Eileen has a paper route, **and** I help her sometimes, especially when the weather is bad.

REVISED   My sister Eileen has a paper route; I help her sometimes, especially when the weather is bad.

REVISED   My sister Eileen has a paper route. I help her sometimes, especially when the weather is bad.

comparison of modifiers (See page 205.)

■ comparison of adjectives and adverbs

Positive	Comparative	Superlative
strong	strong**er**	strong**est**
happy	happ**ier**	happ**iest**
ambitious	**more** ambitious	**most** ambitious
quietly	**less** quietly	**least** quietly
well/good	**better**	**best**

■ comparing two

EXAMPLES   Which is **longer,** the Nile River or the Amazon River?

Of the cheetah and the gazelle, which animal can run **more swiftly**?

Mount Everest is **higher** than **any other** mountain peak in the world.

■ comparing more than two

EXAMPLES   Of all of the lakes of the world, the Caspian Sea is the **largest.**

In the school's walkathon, one of the freshmen walked the **farthest.**

complement A complement is a word or word group that completes the meaning of a verb. (See page 55.)

EXAMPLES   I gave **Sally** that **picture.**

This is an old **sofa,** but it's very **comfortable.**

complex sentence A complex sentence has one independent clause and at least one subordinate clause. (See page 110.)

EXAMPLE   Beethoven, who had a hearing impairment most of his adult life, wrote his ninth symphony after he had become deaf.

compound-complex sentence A compound-complex sentence has two or more independent clauses and at least one subordinate clause. (See page 110.)

EXAMPLES   While Arianna was at the shopping mall, she checked both
            bookstores for Barbara Kingsolver's latest novel, but neither
            store had a copy in stock.

            At the cookout on Saturday, we served yakitori; it is a
            Japanese dish of bite-sized pieces of meat and vegetables
            that are placed on skewers and grilled.

compound sentence A compound sentence has two or more
independent clauses and no subordinate clauses. (See page 109.)

EXAMPLES   My family and I recently moved into a new house, and now I
            have a room of my own.

            By area, New York City is the largest city in the world; how-
            ever, by population, Tokyo-Yokohama is the world's largest
            urban area.

conjunction A conjunction joins words or groups of words. (See
page 31.)

EXAMPLES   **Both** Robin **and** Michelle arrived early, **but** all the good
            seats were taken.

            While you were sleeping, I worked out.

contraction A contraction is a shortened form of a word, a numeral,
or a group of words. Apostrophes in contractions show where letters or
numerals have been omitted. (See page 335. See also **apostrophe.**)

EXAMPLES   **you're** [you are]   **there's** [there is *or*
                                                          there has]

            who's [who is *or* who has]   **they're** [they are]

            weren't [were not]   **it's** [it is *or* it has]

            '91–'94 model [1991–1994 model] **o'clock** [of the clock]

dangling modifier A dangling modifier is a modifying word,
phrase, or clause that does not clearly and sensibly modify a word or a
word group in a sentence. (See page 213.)

DANGLING   Riding the Ferris wheel, most of the park's other attractions
            could be seen.

 REVISED   **Riding the Ferris wheel, we** could see most of the park's
            other attractions.

dash (See page 349.)

EXAMPLE   One of the substitute teachers—Ms. Narazaki, I believe—
will accompany us on the field trip.

declarative sentence A declarative sentence makes a statement
and is followed by a period. (See page 63.)

EXAMPLE   People still enjoy going to movies, despite the popularity
of videos.

direct object A direct object is a word or word group that receives
the action of the verb or shows the result of the action. A direct object
answers the question *Whom?* or *What?* after a transitive verb. (See
page 59.)

EXAMPLE   They gave the **oats** to the horse.

double comparison A double comparison is the nonstandard use
of two comparative forms (usually *more* and *–er*) or two superlative
forms (usually *most* and *–est*) to express comparison. In standard
usage, the single comparative form is correct. (See page 210.)

NONSTANDARD   These small boxes are much more heavier than
they appear.

STANDARD   These small boxes are much **heavier** than they appear.

double negative A double negative is the nonstandard use of two
or more negative words to express a single negative idea. (See page
237.)

NONSTANDARD   The annual sports banquet doesn't cost the athletes
nothing.

STANDARD   The annual sports banquet **doesn't** cost the athletes
anything.

STANDARD   The annual sports banquet costs the athletes **nothing.**

NONSTANDARD   Yesterday, my throat was so sore that I couldn't hardly
eat no solid food.

STANDARD   Yesterday, my throat was so sore that I could **hardly** eat
any solid food.

double subject A double subject occurs when an unnecessary
pronoun is used after the subject of a sentence. (See page 231.)

NONSTANDARD	Laura and her sister they have a large aquarium of tropical fish.
STANDARD	**Laura and her sister have** a large aquarium of tropical fish.

end marks (See page 265.)

with sentences

EXAMPLES   Tiger Woods has won the golf tournament. [declarative sentence]

How long has Tiger Woods been playing professional golf? [interrogative sentence]

Oh! [interjection]

What a remarkable golfer Tiger Woods is! [exclamatory sentence]

Imagine how you would feel if you were playing in a tournament with Tiger Woods. [imperative sentence]

Don't talk while someone is hitting the ball! [strong imperative sentence]

with abbreviations (See abbreviations.)

EXAMPLES   We are planning to go to Washington, D.C.

When are you going to Washington, D.C.?

essential clause/essential phrase An essential, or restrictive, clause or phrase is necessary to the meaning of a sentence and is not set off by commas. (See page 277.)

EXAMPLES   The man **whose sudden appearance caused the uproar** rose to identify himself. [essential clause]

Students **going on the field trip** should meet in the gym. [essential phrase]

exclamation point (See end marks.)

exclamatory sentence An exclamatory sentence expresses strong feeling and is followed by an exclamation point. (See page 64.)

EXAMPLE   That's absolutely incredible!

fragment (See sentence fragment.)

fused sentence A fused sentence is a run-on sentence in which sentences have been joined together with no punctuation between them. (See page 441. See also **comma splice** and **run-on sentence.**)

FUSED   According to my research, the Dome of the Rock was built in Jerusalem during the seventh century it is the oldest existing Muslim shrine.

REVISED   According to my research, the Dome of the Rock was built in Jerusalem during the seventh century. It is the oldest existing Muslim shrine.

REVISED   According to my research, the Dome of the Rock was built in Jerusalem during the seventh century; it is the oldest existing Muslim shrine.

general reference A general reference is the incorrect use of a pronoun to refer to a general idea rather than to a specific noun. (See page 193.)

GENERAL   The illusionist escaped from a locked trunk, made various fruits and vegetables dance in the air, and levitated. This thrilled her audience.

REVISED   The illusionist thrilled her audience by escaping from a locked trunk, making various fruits and vegetables dance in the air, and levitating.

REVISED   The illusionist escaped from a locked trunk, made various fruits and vegetables dance in the air, and levitated. These illusions thrilled her audience.

gerund A gerund is a verb form ending in –*ing* that is used as a noun. (See page 81.)

EXAMPLE   **Fishing** for blue crabs is especially popular in the Gulf Coast states.

gerund phrase A gerund phrase consists of a gerund and its modifiers and complements. (See page 83.)

EXAMPLE   **Photographing old stone bridges** is one of Tracy's hobbies.

good, well (See page 203.)

EXAMPLES   Benita is a **good** saxophone player.

Benita played extremely **well** [not *good*] at the tryouts for the school orchestra.

hyphen (See page 344.)

- **to divide words**

  EXAMPLE   In their flower garden, they planted zinnias, mari-
  golds, and dahlias.

- **in compound numbers**

  EXAMPLE   They planted twenty-three varieties of those kinds of
  flowers.

- **with prefixes and suffixes**

  EXAMPLES   All of the flowers were in full bloom by mid-July.

                  Our garden is pesticide-free.

imperative mood The imperative mood is used to express a direct
command or request. (See page 171.)

EXAMPLES   **Sit** down! [command]

             Please **read** the minutes of our last meeting. [request]

imperative sentence An imperative sentence gives a command or
makes a request and is followed by either a period or an exclamation
point. (See page 63.)

EXAMPLES   Please return this to the display case. [request]

             Clean this room now! [command]

incomplete construction An incomplete construction is a clause
or phrase from which words have been omitted. (See page 192.)

EXAMPLE   I like cheddar cheese more **than he [likes cheddar
cheese].**

indefinite reference An indefinite reference is the incorrect use of
the pronoun *you, it,* or *they* to refer to no particular person or thing.
(See page 193.)

INDEFINITE   In the first issue of the school newspaper, it shows a calendar
of the school's major events.

REVISED   The first issue of the school newspaper shows a calendar of
the school's major events.

REVISED   In the first issue of the school newspaper is a calendar of the
school's major events.

independent clause An independent clause (also called a *main clause*) expresses a complete thought and can stand by itself as a sentence. (See page 98.)

EXAMPLE   **Shawna planted the sunflower seeds and tried to imagine** what the flowers would look like.

indicative mood The indicative mood is used to express a fact, an opinion, or a question. (See page 171.)

EXAMPLES   Georgia O'Keeffe **is** famous for her abstract paintings. [fact]

Georgia O'Keeffe, in my opinion, **was** the most talented American artist of the twentieth century. [opinion]

Didn't O'Keeffe **paint** *Cow's Skull: Red, White, and Blue*? [question]

indirect object An indirect object is a noun, pronoun, or word group that often appears in sentences containing direct objects. An indirect object tells *to whom* or *to what* (or *for whom* or *for what*) the action of a transitive verb is done. Indirect objects generally precede direct objects. (See page 60.)

EXAMPLE   Sandy gave **Grandma** the watch.

infinitive An infinitive is a verb form, usually preceded by *to*, used as a noun, an adjective, or an adverb. (See page 85.)

EXAMPLE   Patty tried **to play** the trumpet but decided she preferred **to learn** the clarinet.

infinitive phrase An infinitive phrase consists of an infinitive and its modifiers and complements. (See page 86.)

EXAMPLE   Ms. Snyder tried **to explain the meaning of the phrase,** but we still found it hard to understand.

interjection An interjection expresses emotion and has no grammatical relation to the rest of the sentence. (See page 33.)

EXAMPLE   **Oh no!** I completely forgot!

interrogative sentence An interrogative sentence asks a question and is followed by a question mark. (See page 64.)

EXAMPLE   Did you visit Las Cruces when you were in New Mexico❓

intransitive verb An intransitive verb is a verb that does not take an object. (See page 19.)

EXAMPLE   The queen **waved** good-naturedly.

irregular verb An irregular verb is a verb that forms its past and past participle in some way other than by adding *–d* or *–ed* to the base form. (See page 147. See also **regular verb.**)

Base Form	Present Participle	Past	Past Participle
be	[is] being	was, were	[have] been
drive	[is] driving	drove	[have] driven
fall	[is] falling	fell	[have] fallen
go	[is] going	went	[have] gone
run	[is] running	ran	[have] run
sing	[is] singing	sang	[have] sung
speak	[is] speaking	spoke	[have] spoken
think	[is] thinking	thought	[have] thought
write	[is] writing	wrote	[have] written

italics (See page 311.)

■ **for titles**

EXAMPLES   *Their Eyes Were Watching God* [book]

U.S. News & World Report [periodical]

The Ascent of Ethiopia [work of art]

Mozart Portraits [long musical recording]

■ **for words, letters, and symbols used as such and for foreign words**

EXAMPLES   Notice that the word *Tennessee* has four *e*'s, two *n*'s, and two *s*'s.

A *jeu de mots* is a pun or a play on words.

its, it's (See page 379.)

EXAMPLES   **Its** [The coyote's] howling frightened the young campers.

It's [It is] six o'clock.

It's [It has] been raining all day.

lie, lay (See page 167.)

EXAMPLES   I think I will **lie** down and take a short nap before dinner.

               I think I will **lay** this quilt over me.

linking verb A linking verb connects the subject with a word that identifies or describes the subject. (See page 16.)

EXAMPLE   Renata's grandma **looked** great at the party.

misplaced modifier A misplaced modifier is a word, phrase, or clause that seems to modify the wrong word or words in a sentence. (See page 215.)

MISPLACED   Standing in line behind us, we thought we saw the star of the play.

REVISED   We thought we saw the star of the play **standing in line behind us.**

modifier A modifier is a word, phrase, or clause that makes the meaning of another word more specific. (See page 200.)

EXAMPLE   We **closely** watched him apply the finish **during his demonstration.**

mood Mood is the form a verb takes to indicate the attitude of the person using the verb. (See page 171. See also **imperative mood, indicative mood,** and **subjunctive mood.**)

nonessential clause/nonessential phrase A nonessential, or nonrestrictive, clause or phrase adds information not necessary to the main idea in the sentence and is set off by commas. (See page 276.)

EXAMPLE   Granddad's Hudson convertible, **which he bought new in 1951,** was the next item up for auction.

noun A noun names a person, place, thing, or idea. (See page 3.)

EXAMPLE   Before the **war,** most **people** I know never gave the **Balkans** a **thought.**

noun clause A noun clause is a subordinate clause used as a noun. (See page 106.)

EXAMPLE   **What's really going to amaze you** is how much I paid for it!

number Number is the form a word takes to indicate whether the word is singular or plural. (See page 120.)

SINGULAR   bird   I   foot   woman
PLURAL   birds   we   feet   women

object of a preposition An object of a preposition is the noun or pronoun that completes a prepositional phrase. (See page 28.)

EXAMPLE   Faced with a huge **pile** of **papers** when she arrived, she took a deep breath and plunged in. [*With a huge pile* and *of papers* are prepositional phrases.]

parallel structure Parallel structure is the use of the same grammatical forms or structures to balance related ideas in a sentence. (See page 461.)

NONPARALLEL   My parents promised to buy a video camera and that they would let me take it on my school trip.

PARALLEL   My parents promised **to buy a video camera** and **to let me take it on my school trip.** [two infinitive phrases]

parentheses (See page 348.)

EXAMPLES   Ganymede **(**see the chart on page 322**)** is our solar system's largest satellite.

Ganymede is our solar system's largest satellite. **(**See the chart on page 322.**)**

participial phrase A participial phrase consists of a participle and its complements and modifiers. (See page 79.)

EXAMPLE   At the wildlife park, we were startled by the gibbons **swinging through the trees.**

participle A participle is a verb form that can be used as an adjective. (See page 77.)

EXAMPLE   The **exhausted** hikers headed for home.

passive voice The passive voice is the voice a verb is in when it expresses an action done to its subject. (See page 163. See also **voice.**)

EXAMPLE   The posters on the bulletin board outside the principal's office **were changed** once a week.

period (See **end marks.**)

phrase A phrase is a group of related words that does not contain both a verb and its subject and is used as a single part of speech. (See page 70.)

EXAMPLES   **A man of elegance and style,** Uncle Jesse lives **in Georgia.** [*A man of elegance and style* is an appositive phrase. *Of elegance and style* and *in Georgia* are prepositional phrases.]

Press this lever **to open the cage door.** [*To open the cage door* is an infinitive phrase.]

Smiling at her fans, the actress signed autographs. [*Smiling at her fans* is a participial phrase. *At her fans* is a prepositional phrase.]

Being on time for appointments is courteous. [*Being on time for appointments* is a gerund phrase. *On time* and *for appointments* are prepositional phrases.]

predicate The predicate is the part of a sentence that says something about the subject. (See page 42.)

EXAMPLE   They **had been living in California for twenty years.**

predicate adjective A predicate adjective is an adjective that is in the predicate and that modifies the subject of a sentence or a clause. (See page 57.)

EXAMPLE   Does the garage smell **strange**?

predicate nominative A predicate nominative is a word or word group that is in the predicate and that identifies the subject or refers to it. (See page 57.)

EXAMPLE   Federico Fellini was a famous **filmmaker.**

RESOURCES

prefix A prefix is a word part that is added before a base word or root. (See page 363.)

EXAMPLES   un + known = **un**known   il + legible = **il**legible

                      re + write = **re**write   pre + school = **pre**school

                      self + confidence   trans + Siberian =
                          = **self**-confidence   **trans**-Siberian

                      mid + August =   ex + president =
                          mid-August   **ex**-president

preposition A preposition shows the relationship of a noun or a pronoun to some other word in a sentence. (See page 28.)

EXAMPLE   He came **from** Mexico and settled **near** Houston to find jobs **for** his family.

prepositional phrase A prepositional phrase is a group of words that includes a preposition, the object of the preposition (a noun or a pronoun), and any modifiers of that object. (See page 70.)

EXAMPLE   Having breakfast **on the Bar X Ranch** was a real treat **for all of us.**

pronoun A pronoun is used in place of one or more nouns or pronouns. (See page 6.)

EXAMPLES   Colin thinks **he** might be moving upstate.

                      Did **you** paint **your** room by **yourself**?

                      Some of the puppies look like **their** mother.

question mark (See **end marks.**)

quotation marks (See page 314.)

■ **for direct quotations**

EXAMPLE   **"**Before the secretary of state returns to Washington, D.C.,**"** said the reporter, **"**she will visit Dar es Salaam, Tanzania, and Nairobi, Kenya.**"**

■ **with other marks of punctuation** (See also preceding example.)

EXAMPLES   **"**In which South American country is the Atacama Desert**?"** asked Geraldo.

Which poem by Edgar Allan Poe begins with the line "Once upon a midnight dreary, while I pondered weak and weary"?

Carlotta asked, "Did Langston Hughes write a poem titled 'A Dream Deferred'?"

■ **for titles**

EXAMPLES   "The Rockpile" [short story]

"Muddy Kid Comes Home" [short poem]

"River Deep, Mountain High" [song]

regular verb A regular verb is a verb that forms its past and past participle by adding *–d* or *–ed* to the base form. (See page 146. See also **irregular verb.**)

Base Form	Present Participle	Past	Past Participle
ask	[is] asking	asked	[have] asked
drown	[is] drowning	drowned	[have] drowned
suppose	[is] supposing	supposed	[have] supposed
use	[is] using	used	[have] used

rise, raise (See page 169.)

EXAMPLES   The hot-air balloon is **rising.**

She is **raising** the windows to let in some fresh air.

run-on sentence A run-on sentence is two or more complete sentences run together as one. (See page 441. See also **comma splice** and **fused sentence.**)

RUN-ON   In 1903, Marie Curie and her husband, Pierre, won the Nobel Prize in physics in 1911 she alone won the Nobel Prize in chemistry.

REVISED   In 1903, Marie Curie and her husband, Pierre, won the Nobel Prize in physics. In 1911, she alone won the Nobel Prize in chemistry.

REVISED   In 1903, Marie Curie and her husband, Pierre, won the Nobel Prize in physics; in 1911, she alone won the Nobel Prize in chemistry.

semicolon (See page 296.)

■ **in compound sentences with no conjunction**

EXAMPLE   Salma decided to read Amy Tan's *The Joy Luck Club*; her English teacher recommended it.

■ **in compound sentences with conjunctive adverbs**

EXAMPLE   Elizabeth went to the library to check out Carson McCullers's *The Member of the Wedding*; **however,** another reader had already checked out the library's only copy.

■ **between items in a series when the items contain commas**

EXAMPLE   This summer I read three great books: *The House on Mango Street,* a collection of short stories by Sandra Cisneros; *Pacific Crossing,* a novel by Gary Soto; and *The Piano Lesson,* a play by August Wilson.

sentence A sentence is a group of words that contains a subject and a verb and expresses a complete thought. (See page 41.)

                        S   **V**

EXAMPLE   The leaves scattered on the autumn wind.

sentence fragment A sentence fragment is a group of words that is punctuated as if it were a complete sentence but that does not contain both a subject and a verb or that does not express a complete thought. (See page 434.)

FRAGMENT   The spider monkey, found chiefly in Costa Rica and Nicaragua.

SENTENCE   The spider monkey, found chiefly in Costa Rica and Nicaragua, is an endangered species.

simple sentence A simple sentence has one independent clause and no subordinate clauses. (See page 109.)

EXAMPLES   Dr. Mae C. Jemison is an astronaut.

               Who first walked in space?

sit, set (See page 168.)

EXAMPLES   The music students **sat** quietly, enjoying a sonata by Frédéric Chopin. [past tense of *sit*]

               The music director **set** the sheet music on each student's desk. [past tense of *set*]

slow, slowly (See page 204.)

EXAMPLE   Proceeding **slowly** [not *slow*] through the food court, the mariachi band played festive music to entertain the diners.

stringy sentence A stringy sentence is a sentence that has too many independent clauses. Usually, the clauses are strung together with coordinating conjunctions like *and* or *but.* (See page 463.)

STRINGY   Yesterday afternoon, my friends and I were playing kickball in my backyard, and when Rahm kicked the ball to the fence, we spotted a wren, and it was hobbling on one leg, so I gently picked up the bird and carried it inside to my mother, and she tried hard to make a splint for the injured leg, but she was unsuccessful, so finally she and I decided to take the wren to our veterinarian.

REVISED   Yesterday afternoon, my friends and I were playing kickball in my backyard. When Rahm kicked the ball to the fence, we spotted a wren hobbling on one leg. I gently picked up the bird and carried it inside to my mother. Although she tried hard to make a splint for the injured leg, she was unsuccessful. Finally, she and I decided to take the wren to our veterinarian.

subject The subject tells whom or what a sentence is about. (See page 42.)

EXAMPLE   Isn't the **mayor** going to be there?

subject complement A subject complement is a word or word group that completes the meaning of a linking verb and identifies or modifies the subject. (See page 57.)

EXAMPLE   My grandfather, who is usually **cheerful,** is an **optimist.**

subjunctive mood The subjunctive mood is used to express a suggestion, a necessity, a condition contrary to fact, or a wish. (See page 171.)

EXAMPLES   It is essential that Luisa **attend** the meeting on Monday. [necessity]

If I **were** you, I would apply for the scholarship. [condition contrary to fact]

Ashley wishes she **were** able to go with you to the Juneteenth picnic. [wish]

RESOURCES

subordinate clause A subordinate clause (also called a *dependent clause*) has a subject and a verb but does not express a complete thought and cannot stand alone as a sentence. (See page 99. See also **adjective clause, adverb clause,** and **noun clause.**)

EXAMPLE   **After they had dinner,** they sat on the porch and remembered old times.

suffix A suffix is a word part that is added after a base word or root. (See page 363.)

EXAMPLES   brave + ly = brave**ly**   kind + ness = kind**ness**

happy + ness = happi**ness**   obey + ing = obey**ing**

drop + ed = dropp**ed**   dream + er = dream**er**

tense of verbs The tense of verbs indicates the time of the action or the state of being expressed by a verb. (See page 156.)

Present Tense

I give	we give
you give	you give
he, she, it gives	they give

Past Tense

I gave	we gave
you gave	you gave
he, she, it gave	they gave

Future Tense

I will (shall) give	we will (shall) give
you will (shall) give	you will (shall) give
he, she, it will (shall) give	they will (shall) give

Present Perfect Tense

I have given	we have given
you have given	you have given
he, she, it has given	they have given

(continued)

RESOURCES

T

(continued)

Past Perfect Tense

I had given	we had given
you had given	you had given
he, she, it had given	they had given

Future Perfect Tense

I will (shall) have given	we will (shall) have given
you will (shall) have given	you will (shall) have given
he, she, it will (shall) have given	they will (shall) have given

transitive verb A transitive verb is an action verb that takes an object. (See page 19.)

EXAMPLE   Ms. Southall **excused** me when I **explained** the situation.

underlining (See **italics**.)

verb A verb expresses an action or a state of being. (See page 14.)

EXAMPLES   The waters of the Brahmaputra River **flow** from the Himalayan snows.

He **is** happy.

verbal A verbal is a verb form used as an adjective, a noun, or an adverb. (See page 77.)

EXAMPLES   **Chattering** and **screaming,** the monkeys disappeared into the treetops.

I especially enjoyed the **dancing.**

Is that hard **to see**?

verbal phrase A verbal phrase consists of a verbal and its modifiers and complements. (See page 77. See also **participial phrase, gerund phrase,** and **infinitive phrase.**)

EXAMPLES   **Pleased to see his master,** Alf the dachshund wagged his tail vigorously.

Studying together helps me.

He'd like **to give Ella a gift.**

verb phrase A verb phrase consists of a main verb and at least one helping verb. (See page 14.)

EXAMPLE   Strange as it **may seem,** I **have** never **eaten** an avocado.

voice Voice is the form a transitive verb takes to indicate whether the subject of the verb performs or receives the action. (See pages 163.)

ACTIVE VOICE   Steven Spielberg **directed** the movie.
PASSIVE VOICE   The movie **was directed** by Steven Spielberg.

weak reference A weak reference is the incorrect use of a pronoun to refer to an antecedent that has not been expressed. (See page 193.)

WEAK   I was surprised to learn that my aunt Frances, who is a programmer for a computer company, does not have one in her home.

REVISED   I was surprised to learn that my aunt Frances, who is a programmer for a computer company, does not have a computer in her home.

well (See *good, well.*)

who, whom (See page 187.)

EXAMPLES   Enrique, **who** had applied for a part-time job at the animal clinic, asked me to write a letter of recommendation.

Enrique, **whom** I had recommended for a part-time job at the animal clinic, learned today that he will start working this weekend.

wordiness Wordiness is the use of more words than necessary or the use of fancy words where simple ones will do. (See page 465.)

WORDY   In spite of the fact that my friend Akira, who is my best friend, is moving to another state, we think that, in our opinion, we will continue to remain good friends due to the fact that we have so much in common.

REVISED   Although Akira, my best friend, is moving to another state, we think we will remain good friends because we have so much in common.

Complex sentences
> combining sentences into, 458–59
> definition of, 110, 458, 519
> description of, 458–59
> diagramming sentences, 487
> example of, 53

Compound-complex sentences, 110
> definition of, 110, 519–20
> diagramming sentences and, 487
> example of, 53

Compound direct object, diagramming sentences and, 478

Compound indirect objects, diagramming sentences and, 479

Compound nouns
> commas and, 273
> definition of, 4
> plurals of, 370
> proper adjectives and, 12

Compound numbers (numerals), hyphen with, 345

Compound prepositions, 29, 122

Compound sentences
> combining sentences and, 457
> conjunctive adverbs and, 442
> coordinating conjunctions and, 442, 457
> definition of, 457, 520
> description of, 109–10, 441–42
> diagramming sentences and, 486
> example of, 53
> punctuation of, 275, 442, 517
> related ideas in, 441, 442, 457

Compound subjects
> agreement and, 126–27
> combining sentences with, 455–56
> definition of, 52
> diagramming sentences and, 475, 476

Compound verbs
> combining sentences with, 455–56
> definition of, 53
> diagramming sentences and, 475, 476

Compound words
> hyphens and, 345–46
> possessive form of, 333

Computers
> cut and paste commands for revision, 453
> grammar-checking programs, 441
> spellchecker programs, 225, 361
> style-checking software uses, 41, 85
> thesaurus software programs, 13
> varying sentence structure and, 110

Conjugation
> in active voice, 157
> in passive voice, 164

Conjunction(s)
> with compound subjects, 52
> with compound verbs, 53
> coordinating conjunctions, 31–32, 442

> correlative conjunctions, 32
> definition of, 31, 520
> diagramming sentences and, 477
> subordinating conjunctions, 105, 459

Conjunctive adverbs
> compound sentences and, 442, 457
> definition of, 24
> examples of, 442
> independent clauses and, 98
> punctuation of, 442

Connections between ideas. *See* **Direct references**

Consul, council, councilor, counsel, counselor, 377–78

Content and organization
> of research paper, 490–91

Context, definition of, 34

Contractions
> agreement and, 128–29, 131
> apostrophes and, 335–36
> definition of, 520
> possessive pronouns confused with, 330, 336

Coordinating conjunctions. *See also* **Conjunction**(s)
> combining sentences with, 455
> compound sentences and, 442, 457
> definition of, 31
> list of, 32
> run-on sentences and, 442
> semicolons and, 298–99

Correlative conjunctions, 32, 476

Cost, **principal parts of,** 148

Could of, 228

Council, councilor, consul, counsel, counselor, 377–78

Course, coarse, 376

Cut, **principal parts of,** 148

Dangling modifiers, 213–14, 520

Dashes, 349, 521

"Death of a Tree, The," (Teale), 435

Declarative sentences
> definition of, 63, 521
> punctuation of, 265

Dependent clauses. *See* **Subordinate clauses**

Desert, dessert, 378

Diagramming sentences, 474–87

Dialects
> definition of, 501, 503
> ethnic, 503
> regional, 503

Dialogue
> ellipsis points and, 354
> quotation marks and, 317
> writing dialogue, 325

Diction. *See* **Formal English; Informal English**

Get, **principal parts of,** 148
Give
    conjugation in passive voice, 164
    principal parts of, 148
Glossary, definition of, 223
Go, **principal parts of,** 148
Good, well, 203, 228–29, 523
Greek, loan words, 371
Grow, **principal parts of,** 148

Had ought, hadn't ought, 231
Hardly, scarcely, 237
Have, **principal parts of,** 149
Hear, **principal parts of,** 149
Hear, here, 379
Helping verbs, 14–15, 45, 53
He, she, they, **as double subjects,** 231
Hide, **principal parts of,** 149
His or her, 136, 239
History of English, 501–502
Hit, **principal parts of,** 149
Hold, **principal parts of,** 149
Hyphens
    compound adjectives with, 346
    compound numbers with, 345, 524
    compound words with, 345–46
    fractions and, 345
    prefixes and suffixes with, 345, 524
    prefix *half-* with, 345
    word division and, 344–45, 524

Imperative mood, 171, 524
Imperative sentences, 63, 266, 524
Incomplete construction
    definition of, 524
    pronouns in, 192
Indefinite articles, 12, 224
Indefinite pronouns
    as adjectives, 125
    examples of, 9
    possessive case, 331
    subject-verb agreement and, 124–25
Indefinite reference, definition of, 193, 524
Independent clauses
    commas and, 275
    complex sentences and, 458–59
    definition of, 438, 525

    punctuation of, 98
    semicolons and, 296–300
Indicative mood, 171, 525
Indirect objects, 60–61, 182
    definition of, 525
    diagramming sentences and, 478–79
Indirect questions, 265
Indirect quotations, 314–15
Infinitive(s)
    definition of, 85, 525
    diagramming sentences and, 482
    prepositional phrases distinguished from, 30, 85
    split infinitives, 85
    with *to* omitted, 86
Infinitive clauses, 86
Infinitive phrases, 86, 482, 525
Informal English, 223, 504
Inside, 232
Intensive pronouns, example of, 8
Interjections, 33–34, 525
Internet. *See* Computers
Interrogative pronouns, examples of, 8
Interrogative sentences
    definition of, 64, 525
    parts in, 49–50
    punctuation of, 265–66
    subject complement in, 57
Interrupters, commas punctuating, 282–86, 518
In-text citation, manuscript form and, 493–94
Intransitive verbs, 14, 19–20, 526
Introductory elements, commas and, 280–81, 518
Invent, discover, 228
Irregular comparison of modifiers, 206
Irregular verbs
    definition of, 147, 526
    list of, 148–50, 526
Italics (underlining)
    for foreign words, 313
    for titles of manuscripts and works of art, 312, 526
    for transportation vehicles, 313
    uses of, 311–13
    for words, letters, symbols, and numerals, 313, 526
Items in a series
    commas and, 272–73, 517
    semicolons and, 300
Its, it's, 379, 526

Keep, **principal parts of,** 149
Kind, sort, type, 231
Know, **principal parts of,** 149

reflexive pronouns, 8
relative pronouns, 8, 101–02
usage of, 176–93
who, whom, 187–88
Pronoun-antecedent agreement. *See* **Agreement** (pronoun-antecedent)
Proper adjective, 11, 248, 515
Proper nouns
    capitalization of, 248, 515
    definition of, 3
***Proto-Indo-European* language,** 501
Punctuation
    abbreviations, 267–70, 511
    apostrophes, 327–37
    brackets, 354
    colons, 303–304
    commas, 271–88
    of compound sentences, 442, 457
    dashes, 349
    ellipsis points, 352–54
    end marks, 265–66
    exclamation point, 266
    hyphens, 344–46
    of independent clauses, 98
    italics, 311–13
    parentheses, 348
    period, 265, 266
    possessive case and, 327–34
    question marks, 265–66
    quotation marks, 314–20
    semicolons, 296–300
    of titles, 304
    underlining (italics), 311–13
***Put,* principal parts of,** 149

Question marks, 265–66, 316
Questions. *See also* **Interrogative sentences**
    abbreviations, 267
    sentence parts in, 49–50
    test-taking skills and, 506–10
Quiet, quite, 381
Quotation marks
    dialogue and, 317
    direct quotations and, 314–18, 530
    in long passages, 318
    manuscript form and, 494
    in multiple paragraphs, 318
    with other marks of punctuation, 316
    paragraphs and, 317–18
    quotation within quotation, 318
    single quotation marks, 318

titles and, 531
    for titles of articles, short stories, etc., 320
    uses of, 314–20, 530–31
Quotations. *See also* **Dialogue; Direct quotations**
    brackets within, 354
    manuscript form and, 494
Quoted sentences
    capitalization for, 315
    punctuation of, 314–16

Raise, rise, 169, 531
***Read,* principal parts of,** 149
***Real, really,* as modifiers,** 204
Reason, because, 233
Reflexive pronouns, examples of, 8
Regional dialects, 503
Regular comparison of modifiers, 205–06
Regular verbs, definition of, 146, 531
Relative adverbs, 24, 102
Relative pronouns, 8, 101–02
Research paper. *See* **Manuscript form**
Restrictive clauses or phrases. *See* **Essential clauses or phrases**
***Ride,* principal parts of,** 149
***Ring,* principal parts of,** 149
Rise, raise, 169, 531
***Run,* principal parts of,** 149
Run-on sentences
    comma splices and, 441
    definition of, 441, 531
    fused sentences, 441
    revision of, 441–42

***Say,* principal parts of,** 149
Second person pronouns, 178
***-sede, -cede, -ceed,* spelling rule for,** 362
***See,* principal parts of,** 149
***Seek,* principal parts of,** 149
Semicolons
    compound sentences and, 442, 457, 532
    with conjunctive adverbs, 298, 442, 532
    coordinating conjunctions and, 298–99
    independent clauses and, 98, 296–99
    between independent clauses not joined by *and,* etc., 299
    items in a series and, 300, 532
    quotation marks and, 316

formal usage, 223\
informal usage, 223\
Used to, use to, 234

ACKNOWLEDGMENTS

For permission to reprint copyrighted material, grateful acknowledgement is made to the following sources:

From "El Mago" by Ronald Arias from *El Grito: A Journal of Contemporary Mexican-American Thought*, Spring 1970. Copyright © 1970 by **Ronald Arias.** Reproduced by permission of the author.

From "The Death of a Tree" from *Dune Boy* by Edwin Way Teale. Copyright 1943, © 1971 by Edwin Way Teale. Reproduced by permission of **University of Connecticut as Executor of the Estate of Edwin Way Teale.**

Abbreviation used: (tl) top left, (tc) top center, (tr) top right, (l) left, (lc) left center, (c) center, (rc) right center, (r) right, (bl) bottom left, (bc) bottom center, (br) bottom right.

COVER: Kim Taylor/Bruce Coleman, Inc.

TABLE OF CONTENTS: Page iv, Scala/Art Resource, NY; v, Pat Street; vi, Jerez/Viesti Collection, Inc.; vii, Image Copyright © 2003 Photodisc, Inc.; viii, Image Copyright © 2003 PhotoDisc, Inc./HRW, ix, Shaker Village of Pleasant Hill; x, Pete Saloutos/Corbis Stock Market; xi, The Granger Collection, New York; xii, Louis Psihoyos/Matrix International; xiii, Jerome Wexker/Photo Researchers, Inc.; xiv, Image Copyright © 2003 PhotoDisc, Inc./HRW; xv, Peter Steiner/Corbis Stock Market; xviii, Sam Dudgeon/HRW; xix, Sam Dudgeon/HRW; xx, Sam Dudgeon/HRW.

CHAPTER 1: Page 6, Walter Choroszewski; 9, Culver Pictures Inc./SuperStock; 23, John Lemker/Earth Scenes; 25, © 1984 by Sidney Harris-Punch; 27, SuperStock.

CHAPTER 2: Page 43, Fairfield Processing Corp.; 56, Image Copyright © 2001 Photodisc, Inc.; 60, Image Copyright © 2001 Photodisc, Inc.; 64, Image Copyright © 2003 Photodisc, Inc.

CHAPTER 3: Page 73, (tr) (rc), John Harrison; 76, (rc) (br), Archive Photos; 84, Cartooning Fundamentals, Al Ross, Stravon; 88, HRW Photo Research Library; 89, HRW Photo; 91, Culver Pictures, Inc.

CHAPTER 4: Page 100, Robert E. Daemmrich/Tony Stone Images; 106, Archive Photos; 108, Eadweard Muybridge/Culver Pictures, Inc.; 111, International Museum of Children's Art, Oslo, Norway; 112, Jerome Wexler/Photo Researchers, Inc.; 114, (bl) (br),Courtesy of Ursula Gibson.

CHAPTER 5: Page 120, Torquay Natural History Society; 122, (lc) (l) (bl) (bc), Kodansha International Ltd.; 126, Copyright 1905 Fred Harvey; 132, Eric Beggs/HRW Photo; 138, Image Copyright © 2003 Photodisc, Inc.

CHAPTER 6: Page 152, Jacques Pavlovsky/CORBIS; 155, Marian Anderson/Culver Pictures, Inc.; 162, Image Copyright © 2001 Photodisc, Inc.; 166, Image Copyright © 2001 Photodisc, Inc.; 170, The Granger Collection, New York; 172, From Prairie Fires and Paper Moons: The American Photographic Postcard:1900-1920, Hal Morgan and Andreas Brown, David R. Godine (Publisher), Boston, 1981.

CHAPTER 7: Page 179, Brown Brothers; 185, David R. Frazier Photolibrary; 191, (cr), Scala/Art Resource, NY; 191, (br), National Portrait Gallery, London/SuperStock; 194, Image Copyright © 2001 Photodisc, Inc.; 184, David R. Frazier Photolibrary.

CHAPTER 8: Page 203, Image Copyright © 2003 Photodisc, Inc.; 212, (lc), Gary Griffen/Animals Animals/Earth Scenes; 212, (bc), Pete Saloutos/The Stock Market; 217, Cosmo Condina/Tony Stone Images; 208, Jerez/Viesti Collection.

CHAPTER 9: Page 227, Louis Psihoyos/Matrix International; 230, Andrew Eccles/Alvin Ailey American Dance Theater; 233, Corbis images; 236, Eric Brissaud/Gamma Liaison.

CHAPTER 10: Page 255, Random House, Inc.

CHAPTER 11: Page 279, Topham/The Image Works; 282, The Newark Museum/Art Resource, NY; 286, Image Copyright © 2001 Photodisc, Inc.

CHAPTER 12: Page 297, (rc), CORBIS/Philip Gould; 297, (br), Library of Congress/HRW; 299, Image Copyright © 2003 Photodisc, Inc.; 301, Doug Perrine/Innerspace Visions Photography; 303, Photo courtesy of TEXAS HIGHWAYS magazine.

CHAPTER 13: Page 317, Greenwich Suit of Armour, c. 1 Christie's Images, London, UK/Bridgeman Art Library; 322, Image Copyright © 2003 Photodisc, Inc.

CHAPTER 14: Page 330, The Stock Market; 332, Shaker Village of Pleasant Hill, KY; 333, Shaker Village of Pleasant Hill; 337, Joe Viesti/Viesti Associates, Inc.

CHAPTER 15: Page 351, One Mile Up, Inc.; 352, HRW Photo Library/courtesy Gibbs Memorial Library, Mexia, Texas

CHAPTER 16: Page 363, Pat Street; 367, Gutzon Borglum/FPG International; 377, Image Copyright © 2003 Photodisc, Inc.

CHAPTER 17: Page 397, Image Copyright © 2003 Photodisc, Inc.; 401 Image Copyright © 2003 Photodisc, Inc.; 404, Image Copyright © 2003 Photodisc, Inc.; 405, HRW Photo/Mary Miller; 417, Image Copyright © 2003 Photodisc, Inc.; 420, Image Copyright © 2003 Photodisc, Inc.

CHAPTER 18: Page 434, Culver Pictures, Inc.; 437, Archive Photos; 443, HRW Photo Research Library; 444, Bettmann/CORBIS.

CHAPTER 19: Page 453, Fotos International/Archive Photos; 454, (lc), Ted Horowitz/The Stock Market; 454, (tl) Seidman/HRW Photo Library; 455, Bettmann/CORBIS; 461, SuperStock; 464, Doug Armand/Tony Stone Images; 468, K.G. Vock/Okapia, 1989/Photo Researchers, Inc.; 470, David Muench/CORBIS; 460, James D. Watt/Mo Yung Productions/ © 2000 Norbert Wu.